SIXTIES RIN

Manchester Airport 1960 – 1969

Part of the 'RINGWAY THROUGH THE DECADES' series

Written and researched by Mark Williams

Published by. RINGWAY PUBLICATIONS

www.ringwaypublications.com

RINGWAY PUBLICATIONS

First published in Great Britain 2014

A catalogue record of this book is available from the British Library

ISBN No: 978-0-9570826-5-6

Printed and bound in Great Britain by:
Crossprint Ltd
21 Barry Way
Newport Business Park
Newport
Isle of Wight
PO30 5GY
www.crossprint.co.uk

CONTENTS

PHOTOGRAPH CREDITS

Front Cover:
1967 – This summer afternoon line up features a BEA Trident, Channel Airways Viscount and a BEA Viscount.
(Bob Thorpe)

Back Cover:
1969 – BOAC VC-10 G-ARVB is seen taxiing for departure.
(Geoff Ball)

ACKNOWLEDGEMENTS

I would like to thank everyone who has contributed by supplying photographs, data, documents, information and encouragement.

I would also like to thank everyone who has visited our historic website, www.ringwaypublications.com from the UK and the rest of the world. Particular thanks go to those who have participated by sharing their memories, stories and photographs.

My eternal gratitude also goes out to:

MANCHESTER AIRPORT ARCHIVE

Michael Hancock, Business Records Officer, for his ongoing helpfulness since 2007, Patsy McClements and the late Paul Isherwood for allowing access to their records since 1994, which included relevant documents, movement sheets, ATC Watch Logs and photographs.

MANCHESTER CENTRAL LIBRARY

The Local Studies Department for arranging ongoing access to their archives since 1992.

PHOTOGRAPH CREDITS

My thanks go to Geoff Ball for his superb collection and to (in alphabetical order): Avro Heritage Centre, Graham Davies, Ken Fielding, S.L. Hall, Ian Hawkridge, Dave Jones, Dave Lawrence, Manchester Airport Archive, Hubert Parrish, Dave Peel Collection, Lloyd Robinson, Malcolm Taylor and Bob Thorpe for use of their wonderful photographs.

PROOF READER

Martin Dennett

CONTRIBUTORS/RESEARCH/MOVEMENTS

Geoff Ball, Ian Barrie, Martin Dennett, David Esther, Peter Hampson, Peter Hardy, David McCartney, Lloyd Robinson, Air-Britain, and former aviation societies such as Centreline/Manchester Aviation Society.

Mark Williams

RINGWAY PUBLICATIONS

BOOKS:

SEVENTIES RINGWAY 1970 – 1979
EIGHTIES RINGWAY 1980 – 1984
EIGHTIES RINGWAY 1985 - 1989
WOODFORD IN PICTURES
MANCHESTER AIRPORT 75th ANNIVERSARY 1938 - 2013

Coming next:
SIXTIES & SEVENTIES DIVERSION DAYS

Forthcoming:
NINETIES FOOTBALL - AIRCRAFT ARRIVALS MANCHESTER AIRPORT
EIGHTIES DIVERSION DAYS
NINETIES DIVERSION DAYS
NOUGHTIES FOOTBALL – AIRCRAFT ARRIVALS MANCHESTER AIRPORT
FIFTIES RINGWAY
NINETIES RINGWAY
CLASSIC JETS
CLASSIC PROPS
WOODFORD IN PICTURES 2
MILITARY MANCHESTER

MANCHESTER MOVEMENT DATA CDs/DOWNLOADS:

50 YEARS OF DIVERSIONS MANCHESTER AIRPORT 1960 - 2010
SIXTIES MOVEMENTS
SEVENTIES MOVEMENTS
EIGHTIES MOVEMENTS
NINETIES MOVEMENTS
NOUGHTIES MOVEMENTS

Our books can be purchased from our online shop, through our stockists or any good bookshop.

Visit our historic website coverings all aspects of Manchester Airport from 1938 to the present day:

www.ringwaypublications.com

We can be contacted via our website or by email:
info@ringwaypublications.com

3

INTRODUCTION
by MARK WILLIAMS

In order to put this publication into context, we have to take a look at how things were at the end of 1959, and going into 1960.

The following airlines were operating international services from Manchester:
AER LINGUS - Amsterdam (3 x weekly), Brussels (2 x weekly), Copenhagen (2 x weekly), Frankfurt (2 x weekly) & Zurich (1 x weekly), all operated by Viscounts. Mail and Freight flights were operated by Douglas DC-3s.
BEA - Amsterdam/Dublin/Dusseldorf/Paris & Zurich.
BOAC - Boston (2 x weekly), Montreal (2 x weekly), New York (6 x weekly) & Toronto (2 x weekly), with the majority of flights operated by Britannias, although some DC-7 flights were also used.
KLM - Amsterdam (2 x weekly) with Viscounts.
SABENA - New York (2 x weekly outbound only) with Douglas DC-7s, plus an inbound cargo flight operated on Fridays by a Douglas DC-6.
SWISSAIR - Basle & Zurich both operated 2 x weekly with Convair CV-440s as well as a 2 x weekly cargo service to New York with Douglas DC-6s.

The airport was operating three runways:
06/24 - 5,900ft   This was the main active runway.
10/28 - 3,480ft   Used for light aircraft.
02/20 - 3,600ft   The least used runway. Utilised for aircraft from/to Fairey's hangar, occasional light aircraft and when crosswinds were an issue for larger aircraft using 06/24. It was generally not used by larger aircraft due to the restricted length.

FAIREY AVIATION
From April 1952 to March 1956, Fairey Aviation had produced 97 Vampires and 37 Venoms for the RAF and Fleet Air Arm. This was due to the three De Havilland factories at Chester, Hatfield & Christchurch having difficulties meeting the Ministry's requirements in the allotted timeframe. During this time, Fairey were also building and servicing Fireflies and Gannets. They also converted various Firefly AS.5s & AS.6s into U.9 target drones, which were painted in eye-catching red and yellow colours. If all that didn't keep them busy, they were also involved in servicing a considerable number of German-based B-26 Invaders prior to their return to the USA, although 12 of these were delivered to the French Air Force. Several aircraft were based for varying periods in connection with the Fairey Fireflash missile tests. These included a Supermarine Swift, a Gloster Meteor F.4 and two Meteor NF.11 night fighters. By 1960 however, due to a restructure of the whole Fairey group, their aviation activity had wound down considerably and by the end of the year had virtually ceased. But in 1961, Fairey received a Ministry contract to assemble 49 Australian-built and designed Jindivik aircraft, which would be destined for use on the Aberporth and Llanbedr ranges.

SOUTH SIDE HANGARS
The closure of British Eagle's maintenance facility in 1959 (Hangars 521/522/523) would present the airport with an opportunity for these hangars to be made available for the housing of Ringway's resident light aircraft, which in 1955 only totalled six aircraft. Although it was a mere five aircraft that were residents at the beginning of 1960, this was to expand rapidly through the decade:
G-AGYP   Auster J5   Based until June 1961. (Operated by Airviews).
G-AKEI   Miles M.65 Gemini   "   "   October 1960.
G-APMV   DH.114 Heron   "   "   February 1972. (Owned and operated by Ferranti).
G-APMY   PA-23 Apache   "   "   April 1968.
G-APVA   PA-22 Tri-Pacer   "   "   May 1965.

AIRPORT DIARY 1960

JANUARY 1960

4th Gannet XA350, the second aircraft to be delivered to the Indonesian Navy, performed its first test flight of the year today, before departing for White Waltham on 10th January as LA-18.

6th Gannet AS-3, formerly Royal Navy XA397, departed on delivery to the Indonesian Navy. It had arrived at Ringway on 15th October 1959 in a very poor state on the back of a truck, but was completely rebuilt within three months.

10th RAF Burtonwood located two miles NW of Warrington was opened in 1940. It was transferred to the USAF in June 1942, when it became a servicing centre for several squadrons. Although it was transferred back to the RAF in June 1946, it eventually became a base again for the United States Air Force. A number of WB-50D Superfortresses were transferred to Burtonwood for the collection of weather data for the US weather bureau and MATS (Military Air Transport Service). It was also used by MATS as a cargo and passenger transport facility, where it saw frequent transatlantic flights, operated by Douglas C-54, C-118, C-124, C-133 and Lockheed C-130 Hercules aircraft. The facility also serviced European-based aircraft such as F-84 Thunderjets, F-84F Thunderstreaks and F-86 Sabres. However, all this came to an end when the USAF withdrew from Burtonwood in April 1959, although some use of the runway was made by gliders of the RAF Air Training Corps. As a result of this, many of these USAF military transport flights were operated from Manchester instead, which included visits by C-47, C-54, C-119, C-124 and C-130 aircraft. Today saw the first of these flights this year, with the arrival of C-47 Skytrain 0-15996 at 1709 (Janet 21) from RAF Bovingdon. A further C-47, 0-348675, also visited on the 27th from RAF Scampton as FAN58.

13th Dove G-AJLV (f/t Stansted) made the first of many visits throughout the decade by the various aircraft operated by the Ministry of Aviation. Their fleet consisted of Doves G-AJLV, G-ALFT, G-ALFU, G-ALVS, G-ANAP, G-ANOV (until 1966), G-ANUT, G-ANUU & G-ANUW; Percival Princes G-AMKW, G-AMKX, G-AMKY and President G-APMO. Amongst their many and varied roles were the calibration of airfield and navigational aids.

24th January 1960 - In November 1958, Swissair began operating a twice-weekly cargo service between Zurich & New York, via Manchester. The first was operated by DC-6B HB-IBB, as seen above. These flights lasted until December 1960 with HB-IBB operating the last one on 1st December 1960. (Hubert Parrish)

5

19th Executive travel was in its infancy during the 1960s. The scene would be initially dominated by older types such as Dragon Rapides and Austers, but things were soon to change. Very much the shape of things to come was the production of aircraft by the American company, Piper. One of the earliest examples of a foreign-registered Piper was the first of two visits this month (with the other being on the 27th) by German-registered PA-23 Apache D-GARY from its temporary base at Southend.

FEBRUARY 1960

ILS visitors noted were RAF Hastings WD478 (12th) en route Syerston-Silloth, and Argosy G-APVH (24th).

1st The month began on a mild, wet and windy note. In the region more than an inch of rain was recorded in the following 24 hour period, with wind gusts recorded as high as 64kts. USAF Douglas C-47 0-24095 made the first of two visits during the month today, from/to Wiesbaden. On its second visit on the 9th, it remained parked up until the 11th.

3rd The Vickers Valetta is basically the military version of the Vickers Viking but with uprated engines, a side cargo door and a substantially strengthened floor. It was not a common type at Manchester, which made it all the more remarkable that two (VW825 & VW197) arrived today and operated a round-trip from RAF Manby the following day. These two C.1s would be used for carrying troops and paratroops, supplying/dropping, freighting and also as an ambulance. Withdrawals of the type had already begun by 1960 and all had disappeared from service by the mid-1960s.

7th Over at Fairey Aviation, the following aircraft were scrapped today: Firefly AS.7 WJ157, Meteor NF.11s WD743 & WD745 and Meteor Mk.7 WA738. The latter was used as a photographic chase aircraft as part of the Fairey Fireflash missile programme, with trials being carried out at RAF Valley. The project initially named 'Pink Sky' began in 1949 and eventually became the UKs first air-to-air guided missile programme to see service with the RAF. It was briefly deployed during the 1950s and utilised radar beam-riding guidance. About 300 missiles had been produced by 1955, but the Royal Air Force soon decided not to retain it in their inventory.

9th Dan-Air Avro York G-ANTJ made its first visit of the year, operating BEA's Glasgow-Heathrow freight flight, which is regularly operated by Dan-Air Yorks. This aircraft had been in storage for nearly four years at Lasham, but was prompted to be reactivated in late 1958 due to the loss of G-AMUV in May 1958.

18th During the early 1960s, some RAF units were using unusual callsigns, such as Lilac, Football, Firestone and Angry to name but a few. RAF Anson C.19 VM324 made two visits during the day with the callsign 'Kidnap Alpha'. Another Anson C.19, VM340 (27th), arrived from Ternhill as 'Lilac AA'. The C.19, one of several variants operated by the RAF, are utilised as Communication and Support aircraft.

20th Cessna 180 SE-CNU arrived at 1207 from White Waltham in day-glo colours. In between local flights each day, it remained inside Fairey's flight shed until its departure back to White Waltham (25th).

21st Flying Tiger L-1049H N6921C, operating LH040 FRA-MAN-IDL, was noted in full Lufthansa colours.

24th Armstrong-Whitworth Argosy G-APVH beat up the airfield, en route to Woodford for work with Avro.

MARCH 1960

BEA began promoting cheap off-peak fares between Manchester and London. Available during April and May, prices started at £5.10s (equivalent to £97 today) for a fifteen day excursion return.

The latest extension of the main runway 06/24 at the north eastern end is half finished; and the run up for piston-engined aircraft (also at the north eastern end), is due for its finishing touches. Meanwhile the new control tower is rapidly nearing completion and is expected to be ready within the next few months.

Fairey Aviation were busy this month test-flying various aircraft that had been present for various modifications and conversion: Firefly's VT413 (10th/11th/21st), VX416 (24th) & WB391 (21st).

1st Unusually mild weather prevailing in towards the end of February continued into early March, when afternoon temperatures of 16°C were recorded. There were several Constellation freight flights during the month, mostly operating Lufthansa's weekly New York cargo service, until the German airline had converted enough of their own. Aircraft seen were Seaboard & Western N1006C (1st), N1009C (23rd), N6501C (22nd), N6502C (2nd) and Flying Tiger N6921C (6th/13th).

4th Curtiss C-46 LN-FOS positioned in from Southend at 1607, and departed to Stavanger two days later with competitors for a ski-jumping contest. Built for the U.S.A.F. in 1944, it was one of three surplus aircraft bought by Fred Olsen in 1957, which all continued in service with the Norwegian carrier until 1971 when they were sold in Laos.

6

6th The second of two Ringway converted Fairey Gannets for the Indonesian Naval Air Arm, AS.3 (ex-XA397), departed on delivery at 1515. The colour scheme worn by this, and the previous Gannet was similar to the Royal Navy scheme, but with the national insignia on the nose.

8th Four USAF C-130As arriving today were 60515 (arr.1644 Evereux/Torrejon), 60527 (arr.1437 Evereux/Torrejon), 60537 (arr.2107 Evereux/Casablanca) & 60546 (arr.2024 Evereux/Torrejon). They were involved in airlifting relief supplies after a massive earthquake struck the Moroccan city of Agadir, killing 15,000 people and leaving a further 35,000 homeless. Another USAF visitor today was C-119 Flying Boxcar 38138, making two visits routing Dreux/Mildenhall and return before night-stopping.

10th Although the type had visited before, Piaggio P.166 HB-LAY (f/t Zurich) was the first foreign registered aircraft of its type to make an appearance. This unique twin-engined pusher-type aircraft would become a familiar sight at airports all over the UK in the 1960s. In fact three different examples based at Manchester at various times were G-APWY (March-April 1962), G-APXK (July 1960-March 1968) & G-APYP (February 1961-December 1962).

11th It was an exciting day for movements, with some interesting diversity. Apart from the test-flight of Fairey Firefly VT413, also noted was RAF Anson C.19 VM324 arriving from Wyton to operate a round-trip to Leeming; PA-23 Apaches EI-AKI & G-APVK, Silver City Bristol 170 G-AIFV on a freight flight to Ronaldsway and a pair of East Anglian AS aircraft, Bristol 170 G-AIFO & Viking G-AGRU. They both positioned in from Southend and departed in the early hours of the 13th carrying newspapers to Dublin. Some of the more regular traffic included Sabena DC-7 OO-CFJ (New York-Brussels) & DC-6F OO-CTO (Halifax-Brussels) and BOAC Britannias G-AOVL (BA646: Toronto-Montreal-Prestwick-MAN-Heathrow), G-AOVR (BA560:New York-Prestwick-MAN-Heathrow) & G-AOVI (BA557-Heathrow-MAN-Prestwick-New York).

15th Another example of the crazy RAF callsigns was Anson C.19 TX182 arriving as 'Jacknife 02'. Other Anson C.19 visits this month were TX219 (22nd: Jacknife 04), VM312 (31st: Clockwork AA) & W982 (25th: Porter 44). The latter Avro Anson visitor was a T.21 variant, used as a navigational trainer and based at RAF Woodvale.

15th Queen's Flight Heron XM296 arrived as Kitty 1 at 1114 from Liverpool. It returned three days later from RAF Benson to collect a member of the royal family on a tour of the North West. In 1968 it was transferred to the RAF Germany Communications Squadron following the introduction of HS.748 aircraft.

16th USAF Douglas C-47 38986 arrived from Chateauroux at 1034, departing later for RAF Bovingdon.

23rd March 1960 - Seaboard & Western L-1049H N1009C is seen here, having recently arrived on a flight from Frankfurt. The airline, which was renamed Seaboard World in April 1961, was a frequent visitor to Manchester, operating family flights for US-based personnel at RAF Burtonwood. (Hubert Parrish)

17th Civilian Avro Anson G-AMBE, operated by Federated Fruits and based at Liverpool, made an outbound newspaper flight to Dublin. It positioned in again the next morning and made a repeat performance. Another Federated Fruits operated Anson was G-ALXC, which appeared on Dublin flights (24th/29th/31st). These flights continued on a fairly regular basis throughout the year and into early 1961 utilising both aircraft, but by 1961 the company's days were drawing to a close. New requirements were to be implemented whereby all commercial operators would require an Air Operator's Certificate (AOC) with effect from 1st April 1961, rather than just a customary visit by a Ministry Inspector. Although the company decided it wasn't cost effective, they operated right up to the deadline date of 31st March 1961.

27th RAF Chipmunk WD375 arrived at 0915 for a 20 minute stay on a round-trip from RAF Woodvale as 'Lilac 05'. The Royal Air Force received 735 British-manufactured Chipmunks, mainly as flight trainers. By 1960 the numbers had dwindled and this was the last RAF Chipmunk to visit Manchester. Earlier in the month (1st) a former RAF Chipmunk, now registered G-AOSY, made a visit from its Coventry base.

APRIL 1960

The Cunard Steamship Company has bought British Eagle, which now operates as Cunard Eagle Airways.

4th Fairey Aviation flight-tested one aircraft this month, Firefly VX416, which undertook three flights today.

4th April 1960 - This was the penultimate year of DC-7 passenger operations with BOAC. Apart from two, all had been sold by the end of 1961. The two retained, G-AOII & G-AOIJ, were converted into cargo configuration. This shot is of Douglas DC-7C G-AOIH about to depart back to Heathrow as BA538. As far as security is concerned, it demonstrates how different the 1960s were compared to today! (Hubert Parrish)

9th Cunard Eagle Vikings G-AIVL & G-AIHA both positioned up from Heathrow to operate out to Paris-Le Bourget, before returning the following evening. Both had been withdrawn by January 1961 and August 1960 respectively. Another interesting arrival today was night-stopping German PA-22 Tri-Pacer D-EHAS.

10th Lufthansa continued their once-weekly cargo flight with L-1049 Constellations, routing Frankfurt-Manchester-Gander-New York. Due to aircraft shortages, they are still using Flying Tigers aircraft. L-1049H N6921C was utilised today and again on the 17th/24th/29th.

11th Cessna 310 HB-LBD, arriving at 1324 from Zurich, was a first visit of type. Other foreign light aircraft visitors during the month included PA-24 Comanche D-EMIN (14th) & PA-22 Tri-Pacer D-EHAS (26th).

12th Sabena Boeing 707 OO-SJD arrived at 1017 to operate a crew-training detail prior to the type entering service on the Manchester-New York route later in the month. This was also a first visit of type.

12th Fred Olsen C-46 LN-FOS, which arrived at 1320 from Oslo, was returning the ski-jumpers that flew out last month. It was supplemented by Fred Olsen Viscount LN-FOK on a return trip to Oslo.

13th Vickers Viking OO-EEN, operated by Aviameer Airlines, arrived from Southend on its only visit to operate an outbound pilgrimage flight to Lourdes. The airline began operations from Antwerp in April 1958

with this sole aircraft nicknamed 'Sinjoor', which wore an attractive red and white livery with a metallic underside. They flew charter flights all over Europe including the UK, but by July 1960 the airline had folded and OO-EEN was withdrawn at Southend, before eventually being scrapped there two years later.
15th BEA Viscount G-AMOA suffered a brake failure during an engine run, and collided with the tail of another BEA aircraft, DC-3 G-AGHS. Both aircraft sustained damage and several days later G-AGHS was noted in a hangar tail out, with the BEA tail logo painted over, but it eventually returned to service.
19th RAF Vulcan B.2 XH557 performed a beat up of the airfield on a test flight out of Woodford.
20th Sabena Boeing 707 OO-SJD made its second visit today, operating the first Sabena B.707 transatlantic flight via Manchester (SN546 New York-Brussels). On the 27th, B.707 OO-SJB, made its first visit also operating SN546. Flights are currently twice-weekly, Fridays as SN545 BRU-MAN-IDL and Wednesdays as SN546 IDL-MAN-BRU.
21st TX219 was the first of two Avro Ansons during April. Arriving from Andover as 'Trigger 02', it visited again the next day. The second Anson was TX226 (23rd) on a round-trip from Ronaldsway as 'Uplift 07'.
22nd The only appearance by the United States military this month was represented by Army L-20 Beaver 51-6568, making two visits (also 26th) as 'Covet 12' from/to Sculthorpe.

23rd April 1960 - LTU Bristol 170 D-BODO arrived at 1541 from Hamburg to operate a cargo flight to Amsterdam. Registered to LTU in 1957, this was the aircraft's third and final visit to Manchester. It eventually made its way to Fairey Aviation (Gosselies) as OO-ABC and later as OO-FAG, making several visits between 1962 and 1965. (Dave Lawrence)

28th Another first visit of type this month was today's arrival of BEA Vanguard G-APED (arr.1753 from Hanover) on a crew training flight.
29th PA-23 Apache N6735P, arriving at 1332, was on its delivery flight routing Shannon-Rotterdam.
MAY 1960
Last month's figures showed a big reduction in transatlantic passengers from the United States during the period April 1959-March 1960, compared to the previous twelve months However, the stats revealed that the 11,000 fewer passengers were due to a reduction in MATS family flights over the past year.
The following operators could be seen during the summer months operating ITs to various destinations: Air Links (Treviso), British Eagle (Bergen/Ostend), Continental AS (Palma), Dan-Air (Basle/Ostend) and Overseas Aviation (Palma/Perpignan/Pisa).
4th For the second month running, the only US Forces flights were operated by an Army L-20 Beaver. This time it was 52-6132 making its first visit, operating as 'Pete 21" from/to Sculthorpe.

4th The Miles Marathon was a civil twenty passenger propliner that first flew in 1946. Three were purchased by Derby Airways in 1955 and today one of these, G-AMGW, arrived at 1128 to operate a flight to/from Dublin, which would operate most Wednesdays throughout the summer. Their other two aircraft, G-AMEW & G-AMHR, were also used but by early 1961 all three Marathons had been withdrawn and were parked up at their base at Burnaston.

4th Today was the first visit by Hong Kong based Cathay Pacific, with the arrival of Douglas C-54 Skymaster VR-HFF at 1903 from Nice. On a flight originating in Hong Kong operating a seamen's charter, it was one of initially two operating for the airline, with the other being VR-HEU which crashed in 1954.

8th PA-23 Apache OY-ABW (Amsterdam/Leeds) was the first of four foreign registered aircraft this month. The second Cessna 210, N7307E (25th), was a first visit of type on a demo flight from/to Birmingham. This aircraft would eventually become UK-registered as G-ARDC up until 1982, when it was sold in Greece. Also during May was PA-23 Apache D-GABA and PA-22 Tri-Pacer D-EHAS (both 31st).

8th Flying Tigers continued operating the Lufthansa New York cargo service with L-1049s. Used this month were N6914C (8th) & N6921C (22nd/29th), but the flight was cancelled on all other dates.

10th May 1960 - British Eagle Vickers Viking G-AJPH. The Viking was the dominant type during 1960, with over 45 different aircraft visiting during 1960 alone. By the following year the number of different Vikings visiting had been reduced by almost half, with most being withdrawn from service. (Dave Lawrence)

10th The regular visits by RAF Avro Anson's continued. Two different examples arriving today were TX219 as 'Weasel 04' & VM324 as 'Retire A'. Also during the month were Anson C.19s TX166 (16th) as 'Nasty 28' routing Waddington-Finningley and TX196 (26th) as 'Backslide A'.

11th The third Sabena B.707 to Ringway was OO-SJA, on its first visit as SN546 (New York/Brussels).

13th Silver City Hermes' G-ALDG & G-ALDP and Starways DC-4s G-APEZ & G-APYK were used to fly England fans out to Madrid for an England v Spain friendly match taking place two days later. England was convincingly beaten 3-0 and the fans returned to Manchester on the 16th on the same aircraft.

18th French Navy ND.312 Flamant No.198 arrived at 1718 from Villacoublay, bringing in a number of French Naval officers. They were collected the following day by another Flamant, No.204, which arrived at 1018 from RAF Leconfield before departing at 1053 for Villacoublay.

20th French Navy ND.312 Flamant No.204 visited again, clearing customs en route t/f RAF Leconfield.

25th RAF Valetta VW825 made the first of two visits today on consecutive days. Both flights operated from/to RAF Manby using callsign 'Fusspot BY'.

23rd May 1960 - RAF Comet C.2 XK716 took a party of school teachers to Germany, returning the next afternoon. It was the first visit of a military Comet to Ringway. It was operated by RAF Transport Command at Lyneham, but shamefully it only saw ten years active service. It had been withdrawn at RAF Halton by June 1967, and succumbed to the military scrapman during 1973. (MA Archive via Ringway Publications)

25th More than a month after Sabena first appeared with one of their brand-new Boeing 707s, not to be outdone the first BOAC Boeing 707-436, G-APFD, arrived at 1432 on a crew training flight from/to Heathrow. Two days later the same aircraft operated the very first B.707 revenue earning service from London to New York.

29th An interesting end to the month, was the arrival from Frankfurt of Seaboard & Western Douglas DC-4 N1220V, which departed stateside via Shannon in the early hours the following morning.

30th Fairey Firefly WB350 undertook a 23 minute test flight late morning as 'Rafon 1'.

JUNE 1960

In a generally warm, sunny month, there was some unusual weather. Dust devils about 100yds wide developed on the sands at Weymouth on the 20th and a whirlwind caused slight damage to buildings at Walton-on-Naze on the 28th.

Auster 5 G-AOFJ was planned to be operated in the colours of the newly formed Manchester Flying Club. They were hoping to operate from Ringway, but were defeated by Manchester Corporation. It was based between Barton and Liverpool during the month. Another aircraft due to operate for the club was Luton Major G-AOVX, which was being built by a gentleman called Jack Cowap. It was due for completion by the end of May, but subsequently abandoned half complete by the club. It was later sold to the R.A.F. Waddington Group and incorporated into another new build, the Luton Major as G-ARAF. The following month, the flying club moved their Auster 5, G-AOFJ, to the wartime Calveley airfield approximately six miles east of Crewe, and in consequence they were renamed as the Cheshire Flying Club!

Sabena revised their transatlantic operations with SN545 New York outbound now operating Wed/Fri and SN546 New York inbound operating Thu/Fri/Sun.

1st PA-23 Apache D-GABA, arriving at 2218 from Denham, began this month's light aircraft contingent. Others during June were PA-23 Aztec D-IBAD (16th), CP.301 Emeraude F-BTFH (22nd) & PA-24 Comanche D-EGYG (28th).

1st Although the popularity of Piper and Cessna aircraft was still to be realised, the venerable Dragon Rapide was still common in numbers. Seen at Ringway during the month were G-AGYO (11th), G-AHLM (9th/10th/11th), G-AIDL (1st), G-AJKW (13th/25th), G-AKRS (6th/28th), G-ALBC (29th/30th) & G-ALBI (2nd).

4th June 1960 - Dan-Air had been operating a freight/mail flight from Glasgow to Heathrow via Manchester for several years on behalf of BEA, with their Avro Yorks. These flights operated late evening on weeknights, as well as Saturday afternoons. G-ANTI is seen here having just arrived from Glasgow on a warm afternoon. (Hubert Parrish)

4th   Another Dakota visit was Martin's Air Charter PH-MAB, operating an outbound flight to Ostend today on behalf of Overseas Aviation.

4th   USAF Douglas C-47 44-76656 arriving at 1537 from Toulon, cleared customs en route to RAF Wethersfield. It returned the following evening, again from RAF Wethersfield to clear customs before leaving for Toulon. Another example, 0-48065, made a return trip to RAF Wethersfield on the 9th. This particular air base had been reopened in 1952, and became part of the 3rd Air Force under the United States Air Force in Europe (USAFE). It was assigned the mission of providing support for NATO forces. In 1955 it was upgraded to Wing status as the 20th Tactical Fighter Wing, equipped with the F-100 Super Sabre, which replaced the F-84 Sabre in 1957.

5th   Flying Tigers continued to operate the Lufthansa New York cargo service. L-1049s used this month were N6917C (5th) & N6921C (12th/19th/26th).

5th   Aviaco CV-440 EC-APU operated their first IT from Manchester, with a weekly flight from/to Palma. They operated until 1st October with EC-APU and two other CV-440s which were EC-APT & EC-APV.

13th   RAE Devon C.1 VP975 (Nugget 06) operating from/to Northolt today, would only make two more visits during the decade (17th Aug 1964 & 17th Nov 1967). Initially delivered to the RAF in 1949, it was transferred to the R.A.E. at Farnborough, with whom it served continuously until its retirement in 1985, having clocked up 12,685 hours.

13th   Swedish Air Force Douglas C-47 79005 arrived at 1745 from Amsterdam, and stayed for two days. This was one of only two visits by the Swedish Air Force this decade. Ironically the second was by the same aircraft four years later.

14th   Overseas National Douglas DC-6 N650NA arrived at 1601 operating a New York charter via Shannon. It would be another six years before this US charter airline would visit Ringway again.

14th   RAF Anson C.19 TX256 made its second of three visits during 1960. Operating from/to Andover, it undertook a round-trip to Hawarden in between. Another C.19 visit was VP509 (20th), routing Ternhill/Wyton as 'Mothball B'.

16th   An unusual arrival today from its home base at Barton, was Chrislea CH3 Super Ace G-AKVF. This was a British-manufactured high-wing four seat monoplane, with a tricycle undercarriage and two fins. There were plans to build thirty-two aircraft, but eleven of these were either scrapped or not completed. This aircraft would not visit Manchester again, despite the fact that it is still flying today!

16th   Fairey Firefly WB374 undertook a 30 minute test flight late-morning as 'Rafon 1'.

19th June 1960 - Air Links occasionally used Handley-Page Hermes G-ALDA on its fortnightly IT flight to Treviso during the summer. It was also used the following summer, flying holidaymakers to various destinations. Its final visit was its only one in 1962, operating a trooping flight from/to Dusseldorf on the 21st December. (MA Archive via Ringway Publications)

17th OO-SJC is the fourth and latest Sabena B.707 to visit Ringway, operating SN546 New York-Brussels. The next one, OO-SJE, made its first visit two days later (19th) also operating SN546.

20th Aviaco CV-440 EC-APU arrived 24 hours late with engine trouble, on its weekly IT flight from Palma.

21st French Air Force B-26 Invader 44-34763 arrived at 1043 from Bretigny to clear customs, before proceeding on to Warton. It returned in the opposite direction at 1646, again clearing customs before leaving again for Bretigny.

22nd German-based USAF Douglas C-47A 42-24299 arrived at 1746 from/to Bitburg.

22nd Another new light aircraft type to visit Manchester was CP.301 Emeraude F-BFTH, which stayed for two days from/to Lympne. It was a wooden construction, low-wing cantilever monoplane, with a fixed undercarriage. Although this was a type that made its way onto the UK register, they were also manufactured in the UK by Fairtravel and designated the 'Linnet'. The first British Emeraude to visit Ringway was G-ARDD on 15th August 1960.

23rd British Eagle Britannia G-APYY made its only visit to Ringway today. It was operating a transatlantic charter originating at Heathrow, before later departing for Prestwick. Delivered to Cubana in 1958, it was leased to British Eagle during 1960/1961, before returning to Cubana in September 1961.

24th Balair began a late-evening IT flight f/t Basle with Vickers Vikings. HB-AAR operated the first flight and was regularly used throughout the summer, along with HB-AAN.

29th RAF Vulcan B.2 XH559 performed an ILS approach and overshoot.

JULY 1960

The weather for July was generally cool and wet with below average temperatures and sunshine hours. Frequent thunderstorms were recorded and a small whirlwind observed on the 20th caused structural damage at Taversham, near Northwich.

KLM added a third weekly Amsterdam flight, operating as KL149/150 on Fridays.

1st Flying Enterprise Douglas C-4 OY-AAH arrived from Copenhagen at 0207, before departing for Keflavik, on the first of several visits during the month. It also appeared on the same routing on the 16th & 29th and in the reverse direction on the 17th & 30th. It was one of five Argonauts bought from BOAC in 1960, but when this Danish airline folded four years later, OY-AAH would find its way back to the UK with Air Links, restored to its original registration of G-ALHT.

13

3rd Flying Tigers operated the Lufthansa New York freight flight for the final time today, with L-1049 N6921C. The following week it reverted to Lufthansa aircraft L-1649 D-ALUB, which also operated the remaining dates during the month.

6th SAS Douglas DC-7 SE-CCB (SK915 from Copenhagen) at 0400 was a weather diversion from Prestwick.

7th Beech 18 PH-LPS operated by Philips Electronics, night-stopped from Hamburg before departing back to the company's base at Eindhoven at 1534. It was a regular visitor to Manchester up until 1967, when it was replaced by a Falcon 20 with the same registration.

10th July 1960 - Air Condor Bristol 170 G-AHJD is seen here prior to its departure back to Ostend. It had been leased by the airline in April 1960 to cover for the loss of G-AGPV, which had been involved in an accident at Southend the same month. However, the writing was on the wall for this aircraft and the airline, as by December 1960 Air Condor had gone into receivership. The aircraft had a limited stay of execution, when it was leased to BKS and then Leeds-based North South Airlines, but by September 1962 it had been withdrawn and was broken up in August 1964. (Dave Lawrence)

11th Making its first visit as an airline, was Canadian Pacific Airlines DC-6B CF-CZS arriving at 1912 (CP011 from Prestwick). It was a further seamen's charter, which departed two hours later for Goose Bay.

12th Another first visit by a Canadian Pacific aircraft and the second in six hours, was Britannia CF-CZC *'Empress of Madrid'* arriving at 0043 (CP351 from Amsterdam), which was also a seamen's charter.

14th Another German-based USAF Douglas C-47 was 42-24178, arriving at 1256 from/to Bitburg.

14th The month was half way through before a foreign light aircraft was recorded. Commander 500 D-IBUC made a first visit of type today and others during the month were exclusively German, with PA-24 Comanche D-EGYG (15th) and PA-23s D-IBAD (21st) & D-GABA (29th).

15th USAF Douglas C-47 0-293181 made an emergency landing at 1404, en route from Prestwick to Fairford with an oil leak. This led to another USAF C-47, 0-49713, arriving at 1449 to collect the passengers from the stricken C-47 for onward transportation to Fairford.

15th BOAC had problems with its late-evening BA557 Heathrow-MAN-Prestwick New York flight. It was cancelled due to technical problems, so one of BOAC's rarely seen Britannia 102s, G-ANBH, was sent up to collect the Manchester passengers. Arriving at 2306, it took them to Prestwick to catch another flight. Meanwhile the actual BA557 eventually arrived at Manchester ten hours late, appearing at 0919 on the 16th under the command of Douglas DC-7 G-AOIE, rather than the usual Britannia 312.

16th Board of Trade Pembroke G-AMKW was the only aircraft noted carrying out ILS approaches during the month. It overshot at 1007 en route from Blackpool to Stansted.

20th Recently acquired by Capitol Airways, L-1049G N4903C arrived at 1345 on an inbound charter from New York, via Shannon. It served with the airline for another eight years, before being withdrawn and eventually scrapped.

20th USAF C-47s 43-15732 & 43-48675 both visited today, from/to RAF Wethersfield & RAF Bovingdon respectively.

21st KLM L-1049G Constellation PH-LKI arrived at 0413 (KL061 from Amsterdam) on a tech-stop, before continuing onwards on its transatlantic flight.

21st USAF Douglas C-47 76304 arrived at 1029 from RAF Bovingdon to clear customs, before proceeding on to RAF Dishforth. It returned in the opposite direction at 1521, clearing customs before leaving again for Bovingdon.

22nd In a month proving to be a good one for USAF C-47 visits, and a week after C-47 0-293181 made an emergency landing, another one arrived at 1215 today with problems. This time it was 0-76304 en route Fairford-Aberdeen with engine trouble, which brought in yet another C-47, 0-49409, up from RAF Bovingdon with the screwdriver!

22nd Royal Navy Sea Prince WP311 arrived at 1125 (Rochester 719) with a flight crew to deliver Fairey Firefly U.9 WB374 to Rochester.

24th Douglas DC-3 LN-PAS, which formerly served with the Royal Air Force as FZ625 until its sale to Braathens in 1947, arrived at 1715 today on a flight from Amsterdam, later departing to Southend.

26th Helicopter movements were still quite scarce during 1960, but today Westland Widgeon demonstrator G-APTW arrived at 1636 from a private site in Wolverhampton.

29th USAF C-124 Globemaster 30044 made an emergency landing at 1358 on a flight from Evereux. It eventually departed with freight bound for the Congo. Also known as 'Old Shakey', the C-124 could carry more than 200 troops. It had clamshell-type loading doors, built-in double hydraulic ramps and an elevator under the aft fuselage. It could load tanks, field guns, bulldozers and trucks. Deliveries of the C-124A Globemaster II began in May 1950, and before production ended in 1955 the USAF had bought 448 aircraft. Globemaster IIs provided airlift support in the Far East and Southeast Asia, and went on resupply missions to Antarctica. The aircraft also evacuated refugees from the Congo, and made mercy flights to Morocco, Chile and elsewhere throughout the world following floods and other natural disasters.

AUGUST 1960

1st August 1960 - Argonaut G-ALHY was one BOAC's entire fleet of 19 aircraft sold during 1959/60. It was acquired by Derby Airways in 1961, following the collapse of Overseas Aviation. (Dave Lawrence)

It was another disappointing month weather-wise, with an extensive low pressure dominating the UK until the 19th, producing generally cool, thundery and wet conditions. Another tornado was recorded on the 27th, this time affecting parts of Wiltshire and the Cotswolds.

Possibly a little known fact was that BOAC had passenger rights from/to Heathrow on the transatlantic services it operated through Manchester. Businessmen had the choice of flying with BEA, or travelling by train on the Pullman services operated by British Railways. For £12, the cost of a first-class return ticket between London and Manchester, passengers got the Bristol Britannia luxury of reclining armchairs, canapés and a regular supply of drinks and cigarettes. As a keepsake they were also given a BOAC writing pad complete with a folder, and a foreign travel handbook.

Lufthansa's cargo operation was a sporadic this month. The first was actually eastbound (D-ALUB as LH041-11th), thereafter operating on 14th/18th/27th with D-ALUB. Interestingly on the 8th a passenger flight (LH808 Frankfurt-New York) called in at Manchester on a tech stop, operated by L-1649 Starliner D-ALER.

6th After the various USAF C-47s visits last month, August only produced one, which was 42-51133 arriving at 1004 for a brief visit from/to RAF Northolt.

9th Icelandair Douglas C-54 TF-IST arrived at 0551 on a round-trip from Reykjavik with a consignment of fish bound for Grimsby (also on 19th/20th). It was leased to the Danish government in 1961, but two years later it was destroyed by fire in Greenland.

10th A possible precursor for the future, was the arrival of KLM Cargo Dakota PH-DAW (KL009 from Amsterdam), leaving later for Heathrow. The airline would eventually begin freight flights from Manchester on 1st March 1962.

12th Mooney G-APVV was a first visit of type today. This aircraft became a resident during the 1970s.

12th PA-23 Apache D-GABA made another visit today, operating from Denham to Cologne. The only foreign light aircraft visits this month were both operated by Philips Electronics, with Beech 18 PH-LPS (17th) & Dove PH-FST (18th).

12th Canadian Pacific Britannia CF-CZX *'Empress of Santa Maria'* arrived at 2157 (CP014 from Montreal/Prestwick). It made the first of several more flights over the next few days (also 13th/14th/15th/16th/21st & 27th), due to a continuing shipping strike. The aircraft returned to Montreal each time, stopping off at Prestwick to pick up oceanic weather forecasts. The flight on this occasion departed at 2346 with 111 passengers and 8 crew, operating at maximum weight.

15th Fairey Firefly VT430 flew two test flights, before departing for Yeovilton on the 22nd as 'Transit 702'.

15th Firefly WB331 also made two test flights today, leaving for Yeovilton on the 22nd as 'Transit 710'.

16th Also operating a seamen's charter in the early hours on behalf of Canadian Pacific Airlines, was Transair Douglas DC-6 SE-BDF, routing Malmo-Keflavik.

17th Making a pleasant change from the C-47s, was the arrival of USAF Douglas C-54 0-49046 at 1511 from Evereux. Delivered brand new in 1945, this aircraft went on to become the last USAF C-54 (actually VC-54) based in Europe. It made its final flight in February 1970, when it flew from RAF Northolt to Tucson, Arizona (Davis-Monthan AFB) for disposal and salvage. It had plush commercial airline seats, a full galley for the flight steward to prepare gourmet meals and serve fine wines and liquors from the extensive inventory. The rear lockable compartment had a desk with flight instruments and a bed. At one time 49046 was used as General MacArthur's personal aircraft when he was "Emperor" of Japan.

18th Westland S.55 helicopter G-AOCZ called in at 1042 on a demonstration flight en route from Newcastle to the Westland's factory at Yeovil.

19th Capitol L-1049H Constellation N1927H made its last visit today, arriving at 1223 on an outbound New York charter via Shannon. It was withdrawn in 1968, but sold on in 1969 to Canairelief as CF-AEN.

20th Don Everall Viking G-AMNK made its last visit today, arriving on a holiday flight from Basle at 1843, before positioning to Birmingham. Four days later it crashed into the sea after takeoff from Heraklion.

22nd Royal Navy Sea Prince WP311turned up again this month, with two flight crews this time, delivering Fairey Firefly U.9s VT430 & WB331 to Yeovilton.

23rd Armstrong-Whitworth Argosy G-APRN was a first visit of type, arriving at 1022 for demonstration purposes from/to Bitteswell. It was the second of three aircraft delivered to BEA in late-1961.

23rd Seven Seas Douglas DC-4 N90521 called in at 0540 from Shannon, en route to Zurich. This was the first of four visits by the US-charter airline set up in 1957. The carrier had contracts to fly passengers, military cargo and relief aid supplies. They also undertook holiday charters around Europe and transferred ships crews throughout the world.

28th Having positioned in from Gatwick to operate a newspaper flight to Belfast, Falcon Airways Hermes G-ALDA had an engine fire on start up. It couldn't depart until the 6th September, when it flew to Bournemouth for further work.

29th RAF Vickers Valetta VW197 made a short round-trip from RAF Manby as 'Football BY'.

SEPTEMBER 1960

A changeable month, with frequent thunderstorms and below average temperatures and sunshine hours.

Lufthansa's cargo operation appeared to be random again. Westbound flights (LH040) were D-ALAN (2nd/10th/17th/30th) & D-ALUB (11th/15th/24th), and the eastbound flights (LH041) were D-ALAN (18th) & D-ALUB (27th).

1st Firefly U.9s WB391 & WB392 performed test flights during the afternoon, with callsign 'Rafon 1'.

4th Canadian Pacific Douglas DC-6 CF-CZT, *'Empress of Lisbon'*, operated the first of four further seamen's charters over the following week. CF-CZT arrived at 0431 today (CP550 from Montreal/Gander) before departing for Lisbon, and again on the 7th/9th & 11th. These were the only visits to Ringway by this aircraft, which incredibly soldiered on with the airline until 1969, although by this time it was only operating domestic flights. These flights were supplemented by another Canadian DC-6 on the 7th, when CF-CZF, *'Empress of Hong Kong'*, arrived at 1056 (CP550 from Montreal).

5th September 1960 - Aer Lingus DC-3s were common visitors to Ringway and other major UK airports until their complete withdrawal in 1964. They operated scheduled passenger services from Ringway to Dublin until September 1962 and cargo/mail flights until April 1964. (MA Archive via Ringway Publications)

7th This month's foreign light contingent consisted of two different aircraft, both Ringway regulars. PA-23 Aztec D-IBAD visited today and D-GABA on the 12th & 28th.

7th The first visit to Manchester of a RAF Valiant B1 took place late evening, when WP206 arrived as 'Avro 6' from Woodford. It cleared customs and night-stopped, before departing at 1248 the following day. This aircraft was the first production B1 delivered to No.138 Sqn at RAF Gaydon on 8th February 1955 in the standard RAF lightweight matt aluminium 'high speed silver' finish. It moved to No.49 Sqn in June 1956 and later on it was one of five Valiant's that went to Marshalls of Cambridge for Blue Steel missile development work.

12th In a repeat performance of five days earlier, RAF Valiant B1 WP206 arrived at 2131 from Woodford as 'Avro 6' to clear customs and night-stop. Its appearance marked the second of only two visits of the type to Ringway. On 12th October 1961 it departed the UK for Blue Steel trials at Edinburgh Field, South Australia, returning to the UK on 27th May 1963. It was eventually sold for scrap in February 1964.

15th Seven Seas Douglas DC-4 N5519V arrived on a ship's charter at 1650 from La Guardia, departing for Keflavik. It was the first of two appearances, with the second and final visit being made on 15th November, before it crashed in India four months later.

16th Finnair Douglas DC-3 OH-LCC arrived at 0911, on a cargo flight from Amsterdam. This aircraft also came to grief the following year, when it crashed on landing in northern Finland on 1st March, killing all twenty-five onboard. The Accident Report subsequently concluded that both pilots were drunk.

18th Another lean month for RAF visitors, with a single representation in the form of Valetta VW198 arriving at 1339 from Sylt, northern Germany to night-stop, departing to Coventry the next afternoon. It was last based at Singapore-Seletar and continued operating for the RAF until 1966, when it was struck off charge.

23rd Morton Air Services' Doves and Herons were fairly common to Ringway, but much rarer was Dragon Rapide G-AGUG, which was also operated by Morton's. Operating from/to Gatwick, it was one of three still being utilised at the time and it was also the last one to be sold by the airline in December 1962.

24th Swissair DC-8 HB-IDB was a first visit of type, arriving at 1140 (SR851 from Heathrow) to collect passengers from CV-440 HB-IMC which had gone tech.

26th BOAC Britannia 102 G-ANBK (BA628 from Prestwick), made its first visit to Ringway on a cool but sunny day. Others were Dragon Rapide G-AFFB from recently formed Trans European and Liverpool-based Fox Moth G-AOJH at 1257, before departing for Coventry. This aircraft was frequently seen on Southport sands, offering pleasure flights. Finally, Auster G-APTU arrived at 1748 from Rearsby to operate a series of banner towing flights until the 10th October.

27th After many test flights during the year, Firefly WB391 left for Yeovilton today as 'Transit 710'. It had arrived at Ringway on 17th May 1956, before leaving for Llanbedr on 26th July 1957. It returned on 12th June 1958 and remained at Ringway until its departure today. The second Firefly leaving today was WB392, departing to Yeovilton as 'Transit 706'. Previously it had arrived on 12th September 1956, before departing for Llanbedr on 12th February 1958 and returning on 20th January 1959.

27th Also on a test flight and a very rare outing was Meteor VT340, which was in the air for around 50 minutes. It also flew a test flight the following day and two more on the 29th.

27th BOAC Comet 4 G-APDE (BA512 from Prestwick) became the third of the type to visit Ringway.

28th Meteor VT340 carried out three test flights.

28th Westland Widgeon G-APPS arrived at 1501 from Battersea, departing later for Belle Vue. This helicopter was the company's demonstrator from 1949-1961, when it was eventually sold to Bristows and registered in the West Indies.

29th A new Swedish airline to Ringway, which was formed in 1951, was today's visit of Transair Douglas DC-6 SE-BDO, night-stopping on a round-trip from Copenhagen. It was bought earlier this year in March and served the airline until 1967. This aircraft and several others were formerly operated by SAS.

OCTOBER 1960

October was cool, wet, and dominated by low pressure systems again, with flooding in the South West.

This month's Lufthansa cargo operations were Westbound flights (LH040) D-ALAN (9th/15th) & D-ALUB (16th) and eastbound flights (LH041), D-ALAN (16th) & D-ALUB (2nd/9th).

Sabena now operate twice-weekly to New York both ways, with SN545 outbound on Tue/Sat & SN546 inbound on Wed/Sun. Meanwhile Swissair have reduced their Basle/Zurich flight to once-weekly.

Although it didn't produce any interesting aircraft into Ringway, King Mahendra and Queen Ratna of Nepal arrived as part of their State Visit to Britain. They were taken for a tour of Taylor Brothers, the manufacturers of railway wheels on the massive Trafford Park Industrial Estate.

BOAC began Boeing 707 operations from Manchester (BA539/40) on the 16th, with first time visitor G-APFG. Other first visits during the month were G-APFB (17th - BA608 Heathrow diversion), G-APFC (18th), G-APFF (3rd - training flight), G-APFH (13th - training flight), G-APFI (23rd) & G-APFK (25th).

1st The latest German light aircraft visit was PA-24 Comanche D-EDYN from Southend. Other visits during October were PA-23 Apaches D-GABA (27th/28th), D-GARY (24th) & PA-23 Aztec D-IBED (7th/13th).

2nd BOAC Britannia 102 G-ANBB made its first visit to Manchester, arriving at 0129 today from Heathrow (BA627), leaving later for Shannon/Montreal.

2nd By September 1960, the days of UK carrier Continental Air Services were numbered. In early October, one of their Vikings was impounded at Southend due to non-payment of fees, and the writing was on the wall. The airline flew its last service from Manchester on 2nd October, when DC-4 G-APID operated a charter flight to Palma. Their final passenger service followed five days later, when Viking G-AJCE flew a charter from Malta to Birmingham.

3rd Meteor VT340 had an active month test flying, with a 40 minute flight today and more on the 11th/12th/13th. The latter date proved to be its last visit, as it was slowly dismantled thereafter and scrapped completely by 1962.

5th Firefly U.9 VX416 flew its final test flight prior to its departure to Yeovilton as 'Rochester 702' (12th).

7th KLM L-1049G Constellation PH-LKL arrived at 0414 from Amsterdam as a Prestwick diversion. It was leased to World Airways in July 1962 as N45516 and sold to Flying Tigers twelve months later.

10th USAF Douglas C-47 0-50943 arrived at 1103 from Brussels, later departing for Bovingdon.

12th Firefly AS.5 VT413 was another aircraft splitting its time between Manchester and Llanbedr. It had arrived at Ringway in October 1956, but from June 1958 it was a permanent fixture on the Fairey ramp. It made frequent local flights since then, after being converted to U.9, and it finally departed today for Yeovilton as 'Rochester 706'. The crew transport for this, and the second Firefly, VX416, was again provided by Sea Price WF131 f/t Rochester as 'Rochester 719'.

15th Flying Tiger L-1049H N6912C made the first of two visits during the decade today, operating a military charter, en route from Mildenhall to Gander. Its second and final visit was 3rd March 1962.

16th Following the lead by a foreign operator, which proved too often to be the case throughout Ringway's history, BOAC matched Sabena this month by introducing their Rolls-Royce powered Boeing 707-436 onto their LHR-MAN-Prestwick-New York service (BA539/540). However, the limitations of the main 06/24 runway still prevented consistent BOAC jet operations. After today's first flight by G-APFG, the service was extremely patchy right through until January 1961. This date also coincided with the final transatlantic service (New York-Heathrow), operated by a BOAC Comet 4.

17th Widespread fog lasting most of the day only produced two diversions, both first visits from Heathrow, BOAC B.707 G-APFB at 1017 (BA608 from Montreal) & Comet G-APDK at 1154 (BA116 from Rome).

17th An interesting equipment change was KLM CV-340 PH-CGG (KL151/2), instead the usual Vickers Viscount.

23rd The first Sud-Aviation Caravelle to visit was F-BHHI on a demonstration flight on 30th July 1958. The second was Alitalia SE.210 I-DAXE, diverting in today at 0001 from Heathrow (AZ288 from Milan).

25th Aero Commander 680 N590 arriving at 1850 today from Newcastle, was a first visit of type. The aircraft, which stayed for two days before departing for Glasgow, was operated by electronics-giant IBM from April 1960 until late-1961.

26th Douglas DC-4F D-ANEK & Braathens Douglas DC-4F LN-SUP both positioned up from Gatwick and night-stopped. They left the following day for Hamburg, with Rolls-Royce engines for Lufthansa.

28th RAF Avro Anson C.19 VL351 operated from/to Woodford as 'Rolling 05'.

29th Westland Widgeon G-APPS made another visit today, on a short stay round-trip from Liverpool.

NOVEMBER 1960

November was mild with frequent rain, heavy at times. Apart from an anti-cyclone around the 6th/7th, the month saw vigorous low pressure systems crossing the country every few days. A tornado some 200ft wide did considerable structural damage locally, in its passage from Crewe to the Manchester area on the 1st.

Overseas Air Transport, who operated two leased Herons during the year, G-AOZN & G-ANCI, have now set up a base at Manchester in the original terminal hangar.

British (Cunard) Eagle made plans to break BOAC's British monopoly on transatlantic routes. They had applied to operate a daily Britannia service from London, Manchester, or Prestwick to Philadelphia, Baltimore or Washington. These applications were on condition they were approved by the UK & US governments, and would include technical stops at Keflavik, Shannon or Gander if required, meaning that Manchester had links with three new US cities. Cunard Eagle had come about in March 1960, when they purchased a controlling majority of 60% in the Eagle group of companies. During April 1960 their first Britannia, G-APYY, was delivered on a seven month lease from Cubana. It then operated between London, Bermuda, Miami & New York throughout 1960 and into 1961, supplemented by regular ad hoc flights to the USA. During late-1961, Cunard Eagle had been granted rights to operate London-New York services, and as a result two Boeing 707s had been ordered for delivery in 1962. However, due to objections by BOAC the licence was revoked before the flights started. The airline was now facing financial difficulties. Many routes were withdrawn and a number of aircraft were put up for sale. Their new B.707s delivered in 1962 were put up for sale initially, but in the end they went into service, although hopelessly under-utilised. In June 1962 after the Cunard Steamship Company got 'cold feet' with its airline associate, Cunard formed a new company, BOAC-Cunard. Finally in September 1962, Cunard Eagle became an all-European based airline once again.

This month's Lufthansa cargo operations were westbound flights (LH040) D-ALAN (6th) & D-ALUB (18th/26th) and eastbound flights (LH041), D-ALUB (27th).

The winter schedules were now in force and the airlines amended their international services to:

AER LINGUS - Amsterdam (3 x weekly), Brussels (2 x weekly), Copenhagen (2 x weekly), Dusseldorf (2 x weekly), Frankfurt (2 x weekly) & Zurich (1 x weekly), all operated by Viscounts.

BEA - Amsterdam/Dublin/Dusseldorf/Paris & Zurich, no change.

BOAC - Introduced B.707s on a number of New York flights. BA539 operates Tue/Fri/Sat/Sun, returning as BA540 on Mon/Wed/Sat/Sun. Bristol Britannias still operated some passenger flights, Boston (1 x weekly), Montreal (3 x weekly), New York (1 x weekly) and Toronto (2 x weekly). From December they also added a weekly night-time cargo flight to Montreal/New York with DC-7s. Two Boeing 707s making their first visits were G-APFJ (2nd) & G-APFM (15th).

KLM - Operated to Amsterdam twice-weekly, with one of these flights operating onwards to Dublin.

SABENA - Operating twice-weekly: New York outbound operated as SN545 - Mon/Wed & SN546 eastbound - Mon/Fri. A direct night-stopping Brussels service also operated twice-weekly with CV-440s.

SWISSAIR - Maintained a weekly Basle/Zurich flight until 16th December, when the Zurich operation (SR116/7) was increased to twice-weekly and Basle got its own direct flight (SR718/9) from 23rd December. The twice-weekly cargo flight to New York was terminated on 11th December.

2nd   German light visitors were PA-23 Apache D-GABA (2nd/21st) & D-GARY (4th/8th/12th/16th).

2nd   Canadian Air Force Douglas C-54 VC-BCA at 0308 from Gutersloh was a weather diversion.

5th   RAF Vulcan B.2 XH563 was one of two aircraft noted on the ILS this month. The second was the remarkable sight of Peruvian Air Force Canberra 208 (23rd), which was delivered later in the year.

7th   Another KLM L-1049G Constellation visitor was PH-LKN, arriving at 0055 (KL062 from New York) for fuel en route to Amsterdam.

15th November 1960 - Although this photo was not taken at Ringway, today's appearance of this unique and interesting aircraft deserves a mention. Arriving from Orly at 1015 and departing for Prestwick at 1312, in between it performed a 30 minute photographic detail in the area with callsign TW5551. Of all the 224 Fairchild C-82 Packets, this is probably the most famous, the most photographed, hardest-working and most commercially successful of them all. Initially registered as N2047A, it was TWA that made the type famous with N9701F performing the role of a Flying Repair Station around Europe throughout the 1960s. The airline invested in major modification work to the C-82, by updating all of its systems, and later the engines. It was capable of carrying engines, work stands, tools, and all other parts needed for an engine change. On call 24 hours a day from its Paris-Orly base, the crew could perform an engine change within 10 hours on any B.707 within a 1,000 mile radius of Paris. (MA Archive via Ringway Publications)

11th Ex-Continental Air Services Douglas DC-4 G-APCW arrived at 2146 from Gatwick for storage. It finally left on the 17th December, when it departed to Frankfurt. In 1962 it became 9Q-PCW, serving with the Congolese Air Force.

15th UTA Douglas DC-6 F-BGSN arrived with Reims fans for the first of a two-legged UEFA Cup match with Burnley FC, which the Lancashire side won 2-0.

16th The only USAF visit this month was C-47 0-48686, routing RAF Lyneham-Evereux.

16th Seven Seas Douglas DC-4 N30048 was operating another ship's charter. It day stopped after arriving in the early hours from Luxembourg, before departing for Santa Maria at 2115. This aircraft was the eighteenth to be converted from a C-54 to a DC-4 after the war. It was also notable for having square windows to make it look like a DC-6!

21st Boeing 720 EI-ALA, which was newly acquired by Aer Lingus, arrived from Prestwick at 1713 on a proving flight. The airline was due to start transatlantic flights between Dublin and Boston and New York on 14th December, and Manchester was being assessed as a diversionary airport.

21st A couple of Birmingham weather diversions during the evening were Transocean Douglas DC-4F LX-IAL arriving at 1600 from Belfast, and Martin's Air Charter DC-3 PH-MAA at 1622 from Rotterdam.

22nd Transair Sweden Curtiss C-46 SE-CFC arrived at 1903 on a freight charter from Stockholm. The following month it was leased to the UN for use in the Belgian Congo until 1963.

22nd November 1960 - Taken from the newly-constructed tower block, this view shows the airport's fuel farm, complete with period vehicles. In the background are some of the former-RAF buildings that sprang up during the Second World War. In the foreground, work is taking place extending what would eventually become stand 22, forming part of the new domestic pier. The entire site which was redeveloped in 1988, became a multi-storey car-park for the new domestic pier, as by this time the fuel services had moved to the west side of the airport. (MA Archive via Ringway Publications)

23rd Unfortunately, the second DC8 to visit Ringway today was the same aircraft as the first one! HB-IDB called in 1535 (SR832 from Zurich) and after a short stop it left for Shannon.

24th A nine hour power cut caused by a modification to an electrical substation, put Ringway back into a 'time-gone-by'! The airport took on an 'olde-worlde' appearance, when storm lanterns were used to light enclosed corridors. As the public address system was silent, staff sought out passengers individually to assist them to their aircraft or the customs hall.

26th Irish Beech 35 EI-ALI made the first of many visits on a round-trip from Liverpool. It was registered in the UK as G-ASHR in April 1963.

DECEMBER 1960

December was changeable and cold, with low pressure dominating at the start and at the end of the month. From the 8th & 17th, the country was stuck between two anticyclonic systems, bringing in cold weather and widespread snow on the 18th-19th.

In reply to local criticism that BOAC's transatlantic 707 services from London had been over-flying Manchester Airport, BOAC issued the following statement:

'The runway is short and its surface is comparatively smooth by present day international airport standards. Water remains on the surface after rain in greater quantity and for a longer time than is usual. The level of the runway rises along its length from the south-west to a point towards the north-east end. This point is about the normal touch-down position for a 707 landing towards the south-west into the prevailing wind, such a landing is therefore performed downhill. The wind direction is frequently across the runway. There is no ILS installation for approaches towards the south-west. One, or even more, of these factors would not necessarily present any appreciable problems, but in total they have been considered by our operations department to be sufficient reason for setting BOAC's landing limits rather higher than at other airports. We are in touch with Manchester Corporation with a view to the improvement of the runway conditions. The lengthening of the runway by 500ft would greatly ease the present position: improvement of the runway surface and drainage would help considerably'.

Since B.707 operations began on 16th October, 20 of the 49 flights scheduled to land at Ringway were unable to. Because of this, the airport authorities provided chartered aircraft to take passengers to London for a direct service, or to Prestwick to join their flights there. Also when required, cars would be laid on for passengers to get to Prestwick.

Iberia took the first step to introducing a direct service between the North West and Spain, by opening a sales office in Barton Square, Manchester, opposite the Royal Exchange Air Terminus. However, these links were a little way off yet, as a direct service between Manchester and Barcelona/Palma was not introduced until June 1965.

This month's Lufthansa westbound cargo flights were (LH040): D-ALAN (3rd/11th/27th) & D-ALUB (4th).

3rd BOAC commenced an all-cargo service across the North Atlantic using DC-7F aircraft. Services from Manchester began five days later.

5th The US Air Force once-monthly flight was made by C-47 0-50943, from Bovingdon to Dublin.

6th Flying Tigers Constellation N6913C arrived at 2038 on a freight flight from Benghazi via Brindisi. Another freight charter today was Fred Olsen Douglas DC-3 LN-IAA, from/to Oslo.

8th BOAC introduced a DC-7F freight service operating Heathrow-Manchester-Gander-Montreal-New York, with the first flight (BA573) being operated by G-AOIJ. The airline flew both G-AOII (8th September) & G-AOIJ (26th September 1960) to Santa Monica for conversion into a pure-freight configuration. Installed were large cargo doors, heavy duty flooring and other refinements, before returning to Heathrow on 5th December and 22nd November respectively.

8th The UK was affected by fog and although two Birmingham diversions arrived late evening, Ringway missed out on plenty of 'Heathrow heavy metal', diverting to airports as diverse as Prestwick & Gatwick.

11th Swissair's twice-weekly cargo flight to New York operated for the final time. DC-6B HB-IBB, which made the inaugural flight in November 1958, also operated the last one (SR792). This DC-6B continued to operate as a cargo aircraft until the following April, when it was sold to World Airways as N45501.

13th RAF Communications Squadron Pembroke C.1 WV729, which served with the RAF until 1977, arrived at 1213 from Northolt, departing later for Paris-Orly.

13th Another ex-Continental Air Services Douglas DC-4, G-APID, arrived for storage and left on 25th January 1961 for Southend. Although it remained British registered, it then spent the next seven years out on lease to a variety of carriers, including Starways, Lloyd International, Transmeridian, Dan-Air, Invicta and Spantax! The Spanish airline did not use it for long and it was withdrawn in August 1967, before eventually becoming a snack-bar in Seville!

13th Bad weather at Heathrow produced the first visit of SAS SE.210 OY-KRC at 1257 today (SAS501 from Copenhagen). Also of note was BOAC Comet 4 G-APDB at 1303 (BA116 from Rome).

17th The first BEA scheduled passenger service with a Vickers Vanguard took place today, but it would be another twelve months before the type became commonplace on Manchester-Heathrow services. The airline denied there was anything sinister about the introduction, or lack of it, onto Manchester flights. They simply had other plans for the aircraft delivered so far, which were running nine months late due to engine problems.

18th The region was experiencing a cold spell, with sleet showers turning to snow. By late evening the snow had reached as far as Heathrow, and it wasn't long before the diversions started to arrive. Of the six arrivals, the following three were all first visits: BOAC Comet 4s G-APDO at 2156 (BA662 from Madrid) & G-APDT at 2316 (BA933 from Zurich) and Britannia 102 G-ANBN at 2246 (BA211 from Rome).

19th December 1960 - BOAC Comet G-APDO was one of several snow diversions from Heathrow last night. It served with BOAC until 1966, when it was sold to Dan-Air. (MA Archive via Ringway Publications)

23rd Swissair's Zurich flight SR118/9 was upgraded this evening, and operated by Douglas DC-7 HB-IBK due to pre-Christmas loads.

23rd PH-MAB was the second Martin's Air Charter to appear at Manchester. It made two visits this month, today and the 30th, operating an early morning freight charter, both times from/to Brussels.

29th This year's last movement of interest was Braathens Douglas DC-4F LN-SUP on a cargo flight from Kristiansand.

FIRST/LAST ARRIVALS & DEPARTURES 1960

First arrival: Dan-Air Avro York G-ANXN from Prestwick at 0551
First departure: Dan-Air Avro York G-ANXN to Heathrow at 0654
Last arrival: BEA Viscount G-AMOF from Glasgow at 2118
Last departure: BEA Viscount G-AMOB to Zurich at 2218

Airport Stats 1960 (+/- % on Previous Year)		
Scheduled Passengers	644,000	+ 24.9%
Inclusive & Charter Passengers	24,000	+100%
Freight & Mail (Tonnes)	14,900	+ 34.2%
Movements	34,000	+ 3.9%

23

AIRPORT DIARY 1961

JANUARY 1961

The month's weather was changeable, cold and mainly cyclonic, with troughs or depressions moving eastwards over or near the British Isles, except between the 17th to 25th, when an anticyclone centred over northern Europe, bringing in more settled weather. It was sunny by day, but cold with fog at night.

In light of last month's criticism by BOAC regarding the state of Manchester's runway, it was decided to go ahead with the 500ft extension of the main runway to 7,500ft. Of this, 5,000ft would be grooved to increase the breaking power of aircraft and to clear lying water in wet weather. Although it would cost around £60,000, Boeing 707s would still be precluded from taking off with a full fuel load. Also during the month the airport committee recommended the city council accepts a proposal to extend the main runway by 3,500ft at the south-westerly end, to give a total of 10,500ft.

BKS operated a Saturday evening newspaper flight to the Isle of Man until the middle of May. A Bristol 170 would usually position in from Belfast or Dublin, but Ambassadors were also used on occasion.

Air France said they would resume Manchester-Paris passenger services after a six year break, serving Paris-Orly with brand new Caravelles, which were 15 minutes quicker than the current BEA Viscounts serving Le Bourget.

Lufthansa's cargo operation was light again this month, with just two westbound flights (LH040): D-ALAN (22nd & 29th).

4th   KLM Constellation PH-LKI arrived from Damascus at 1632, operating a charter flight originating in Hong Kong.

5th   Seaboard & Western L-1049H Constellation arrived at 0238 (SB02C from Heathrow) on an outbound cargo flight for Gander/New York. Seaboard was also phasing out their fleet of Constellations, and this aircraft ended up with Capitol Airways the following year.

6th   A good day for US military visitors with two rare types, beginning with US Navy Beech C-45 Expeditor (military version of the Beech 18) 51105 from West Malling, going tech on arrival at 1225. Another US Navy aircraft, Douglas R-4D8 12437, arrived an hour later from Liverpool with spares for the C-45, before leaving for West Malling. The R-4D8 (later designated the C-117D), was an updated and upgraded Douglas Dakota, recognisable by a squarer tail than the standard DC-3. It also visited (7th/9th) f/t West Malling with more spares and expertise for the C-45, which finally left on the 9th.

6th   Swissair again used a Douglas DC-6, HB-IBO, on its Zurich flight SR116/7 due to increased inbound loads. Another Swissair DC-6 this month was cargo-configured HB-IBB (27th), as SR1822 to Goose Bay.

7th   US Navy R.4 12437 arrived from West Malling with spares for US Navy C.45 51105.

11th   1947-built RAF Anson VL351 arrived at 1514 today from Hawarden, before departing to its base at RAF Andover. It saw service until 1968, when it was struck off charge. Further Ansons this month were TX177 (23rd) & TX256 (24th).

13th   The first UK-registered Commander 500, G-ARGW, made its debut today from/to Boxted. This aircraft soldiered on until 1978, when it was sold in the USA.

14th   A very bleak day due to thick fog, saw just one departure and no arrivals, as temperatures didn't get above freezing.

15th   PA-22 Tri-Pacer G-AREV arrived at 1337 on a short round-trip from Cambridge, or at least that was the intention! It departed 40 minutes later, only to return with radio failure. It finally left at 1204 the following day, but due to poor weather at Cambridge it made a forced landing at Polebrook, a village in East Northamptonshire.

16th   The latest BOAC B.707 to make its first visit was G-APFL (BA540 from New York/Prestwick). However, the airline would operate only three outbounds (BA539) and four inbounds (BA540) this month, with the last being G-APFK (BA540 from New York/Prestwick-30th), before flights were stopped due to the runway extension work. From 7th February until 7th May, the airline began operating a Douglas DC-7 'shuttle-service' from/to Prestwick, transferring passengers to/from their transatlantic flights.

17th   Further flights from/to Hamburg transporting aero engines on behalf of Lufthansa were operated today by Braathens DC-4F LN-SUP & Transair Sweden DC-6 OO-SDD. Both aircraft brought engines in for servicing at Rolls-Royce, Derby and flew more out two days later.

25th RAF Valetta VW197 (callsign MABRC) arrived at 1529 for an 8 minute visit from/to RAF Manby.

25th Percival President G-ARCN, operated by the Bristol Aircraft Company and later the British Aircraft Corporation, made its first visit of the year on a round-trip from Bristol-Filton. This was the civil version of the Pembroke, which would make regular visits to Manchester until its last on 4th January 1967.

29th The only foreign light visitors showed up at the end of the month. Today saw 'regular' PA-23 Aztec D-IBED and the following day another common visitor, Philips Dove PH-FST, operating from/to Twenthe.

31st An FA Cup 4th Round replay at Burnley was the reason for the appearance of two Air Safari Vikings, G-AHPC & G-AJFT. They were bringing in the Brighton & Hove Albion team and a small number of fans for the game, which the south coast side lost 2-0.

FEBRUARY 1961

England recorded its mildest February since 1901, and it was the eighth successive month with above average rainfall, except for mid-month which was relatively dry. There were also gales. A gust of 101kt was recorded at Tiree on the 26th and the day prior, a tornado accompanied by heavy rain caused damage to buildings in Buckinghamshire.

The airport's plan to extend the main runway was approved by the city council without discussion. As it entailed extending into the Bollin Valley and diverting the main A538 Altrincham-Wilmslow road, the Ministry of Aviation will be asked to pay half the costs.

BEA served a writ on Manchester Corporation, following a difference of opinion on the airlines' right to load its own aircraft at Ringway. BEA wanted a court ruling by April in time for the summer season, but the case was not resolved and there were further loading problems later in the year.

Lufthansa Cargo operated the following westbound flights: (LH040): D-ALAN (25th) & D-ALUB (17th).

1st Two Philips aircraft on the ground at the same time today were Dove PH-FST from/to Twenthe and Heron PH-ILO (also 2nd) from/to Eindhoven. The latter was a regular until December 1966, when it was sold soon afterwards.

3rd February 1961 - An increasingly popular type in 1961 was the unique Piaggio P.166. Several different aircraft were based at Ringway at various times during the early 1960s. G-APVE seen here, was operated by the Earl of Derby and made regular visits up until April 1963, when it was sold in Australia later that year as VH-SMF. (MA Archive via Ringway Publications)

6th A new German visitor to Ringway was Twin Bonanza D-IGUS, arriving at 1956 today from/to Cologne. It made regular visits all month, but its last appearance was in December 1961. Unfortunately, this aircraft was written off at Heathrow on 4th March 1963 in a landing accident.

11th Braathens Douglas DC-3 LN-PAS operated a charter from/to Kristiansand.

12th Today OH-LCI became the third Finnair DC-3 to visit Manchester (also 19th/22nd), operating freight flights from Amsterdam, all departing for Glasgow as AY021. On a further visit (23rd), it was operating in the opposite direction.

15th USAF Douglas C-47 0-48913 arrived at 1032 from Northolt, diverting in from RAF Sculthorpe due to fog. Several other diversions arrived late-evening from Heathrow, including Swissair SE.210 HB-ICX at 2259 (SR700 from Zurich) on its first visit and BEA Viscount G-AOHG at 2333 (TP762 from Lisbon).

15th Today saw the welcome return of a Sabena Douglas DC-7. By now all their aircraft were operating as freighters. DC-7C OO-SFC called in whilst operating a Brussels-New York early hours cargo flight.

17th Skyways L-749 Constellation G-ANUR was another Heathrow weather diversion, arriving at 0928 from Beirut. The next time it would visit Ringway in June 1962, it would be part of the Euravia fleet.

18th USAF C-124 Globemaster 20954 arrived at 1225 from Frankfurt, departing at 1701 to Evereux.

19th The weather produced another four Heathrow diversions. Amazingly three of these were first visits, with BOAC Britannia 102 G-ANBM at 0805 (WT926 from Barcelona), BEA Comet 4 G-APMD at 0901 from Basle & BOAC Comet 4 G-APDM at 0950 (BA973 from Dusseldorf).

19th Cunard Eagle Viscount VR-BBJ arrived at 2326 (EG500 from Keflavik), on a short fuel stop prior to continuing its journey to Heathrow. It had been operating in the Caribbean with Eagle Airways (Bermuda) and was returning to the UK to be leased to the parent operator, Cunard Eagle, as G-ARKH.

22nd USAF Douglas C-47 0-77218 made a short-stop at 1108 from Upper Heyford, before continuing on to Prestwick.

25th Making its first visit today, was BOAC Britannia 102 G-ANBH at 0847 (BA052 from Heathrow), on an outbound charter to Rome. A further flight to Rome operated by Britannia 102 G-ANBB took place on 1st March and a return flight from Rome (BA071) was operated on 17th March by G-ANBD.

26th Flying Tiger L-1049H Constellation N6911C arrived at 1605 from Tripoli for fuel, before leaving at 1938 for Toronto via Keflavik. Just over twelve months later it was damaged beyond repair in a landing accident at the Adak Naval Air Station, Aleutian Islands, Alaska.

27th RAF Pembroke WV736 arriving at 1053 (callsign MOPYB) routing RAF Northolt-Filton, would make two further visits in 1969. It was struck off charge in 1977, after a twenty-three history with the RAF.

MARCH 1961

The month was generally mild, registering the driest March since 1944. High pressure dominated over the British Isles until the middle of the month, bringing a high of 22°C at Goldington on the 16th. The end of the month saw cooler weather, but relatively near normal temperatures.

Lufthansa's cargo flights were confined to just one eastbound flight with D-ALAN (LH041-20th).

1st USAF C-47 visitors began today with 0-50943 (Brussels-Bovingdon) & 0-15996 (16th) routing Chateauroux-Mildenhall.

3rd Fred Olsen Curtiss C-46 LN-FOS arrived at 0202 on a tech-stop, routing Oslo-Le Bourget.

5th L-1049H N1007C arriving from Prestwick at 0955, was the final Seaboard Western Constellation to visit. All their Connie's were soon to be sold, which seems to be in line with their rebranding into Seaboard World in April 1961.

7th USAF VIP Douglas C-54 0-49046 made the first of two visits during March (also 13th). It stayed overnight from RAF Greenham Common, before departing the following afternoon to RAF Northolt.

9th This month's RAF visitors began today with Devon C.1 VP965 (callsign MONYY) routing Andover-Northolt & Avro Anson C.19 VM338 at 1748 (callsign Redhot AA) from Little Rissington. It stayed 20 minutes, before leaving for its base at Church Fenton. On the 24th another Avro Anson C.19, TX256, arrived at 1558 from Hawarden (callsign 'Angry 05'), before departing back to its RAF Andover base.

12th A first visit of both airline and aircraft was made today by EL AL Britannia 4X-AGC at 1705 (LY421 from Tel Aviv). The Israeli airline operated five Britannias between 1957 and 1966, and this aircraft was leased to BUA as G-ARWZ from February 1962 until March 1965 before returning to EL AL.

14th Beech 65 Queen Air G-ARFF was a first visit of type, arriving on demonstration from Liverpool today. It appeared again on the 1st August, this time to take up residency at Ringway. It was owned and operated by Davy-Ashmore, a major player in the steel industry.

17th Douglas DC-4F D-ANEK arrived from Hamburg at 1836 with another consignment of aero engines bound for Rolls-Royce, Derby.

22ⁿᵈ March 1961 - A fine close up of the Board of Trade's Percival Prince G-AMKY. Registered in August 1951, it was one of three (with the others being G-AMKW & G-AMKX), that were used for the flight inspection of navigational aids throughout the UK. Many visits were made to Ringway, until its last on 4ᵗʰ November 1969. The livery of all three aircraft changed around 1962 to the familiar colours of red, white and black. It was withdrawn at Stansted in October 1970 and used by the fire school, but was still present and in use by the late 1970s. (MA Archive via Ringway Publications)

23ʳᵈ Finnair Douglas DC-3 OH-LCI, operating a flight from Copenhagen, was making the last of its six visits to Ringway during the year. In January 1962 it was transferred to the Finnish Air Force as D-06.

29ᵗʰ The previous year saw four visits of the new US transport plane, the Lockheed C-130, which all occurred on the same day, the 8ᵗʰ March 1960. This year's one and only visit was today's appearance of USAF C-130 60527, one of the batch from last year. Arriving at Ringway 1344 from RAF Scampton for customs clearance, it departed for Chateauroux.

APRIL 1961

April was mild, wet and mainly dull. Rain on the 4ᵗʰ was preceded by snow in the North West. On the 25ᵗʰ a particularly vigorous low pressure brought gales and heavy rain over the UK.

The switch over to the new Airport Control Tower took place on the 19ᵗʰ, after several days of delays caused by faults in the standby electrical generating equipment and air conditioning. It had all mod-cons, including luxurious rest rooms and an electric kitchen, unheard of in the last building. Most of the 130ft building, the first phase of the £1.8m terminal scheme, had been taken over by traffic, comms and admin staff by the end of the month. The air traffic control section started work in the glass viewing tower, where controllers had direct views of the whole airfield. In the same area at a slightly lower level, were the radar controllers. Traffic control staff will work directly with the radar staff when handling aircraft movements. The old control tower would be demolished to expand the apron to facilitate loading and unloading of the new domestic pier, currently under construction beneath the tower building. The telecommunications and GPO section took over parts of the ground and first two floors and the meteorological section and aeronautical information service would move into the 3ʳᵈ floor by the end of the month. British European Airways would be the first airline to be allocated space in the new tower, moving its flight control, apron and load control sections into the 4ᵗʰ, 5ᵗʰ & 6ᵗʰ floors. Other airlines would soon follow suit.

Work has been completed extending Runway 06-24 by 500ft at the north-east end, with much of its length grooved to for better drainage to improve aircraft braking.

British Eagle began a new three-weekly service to Hamburg/Copenhagen. Operated by Vickers Viscount, it complemented their once-weekly Bergen service which resumed this month. Both services were summer-only, terminating in October. Unfortunately, Hamburg/Copenhagen did not to return in 1962.

There was a significant increase in Lufthansa freight flights during the month, all westbound (LH040/2) with D-ALAN (1st/5th) & D-ALUB (9th/15th/22nd/29th).

International flights were operated during the summer as follows:

AER LINGUS - Amsterdam (3 x weekly), Brussels (2 x weekly), Copenhagen (2 x weekly), Dusseldorf (2 x weekly), Frankfurt (2 x weekly) & Zurich (1 x weekly), all operated by Viscounts.

BEA - Amsterdam/Dublin/Dusseldorf/Paris & Zurich & summer routes to Basle/Barcelona/Milan & Palma.

BOAC - Introduced a daily B.707 New York service (BA537/8) from 9th June-17th September, thereafter reverting to 3 outbound and 4 inbound flights. Bristol Britannias operated Boston (3 x weekly), Montreal (5 x weekly), New York (2 x weekly) & Toronto (5 x weekly). The DC-7 cargo operation was twice-weekly to Montreal/New York and the following Boeing 707s made their first visits: G-APFF (16th June), G-APFI (14th May), G-APFN (8th May, G-APFO (20th May) & G-APFP (11th June).

KLM - Operated to Amsterdam three-times-weekly, which increased to five-weekly from June-September (KL149/150), with one of these flights operating onwards to Dublin (KL151/2).

SABENA - Twice-weekly to/from New York, then thrice-weekly from July, but cut back to once-weekly from October. Brussels was operated twice-weekly with CV-440s and Ostend June-September with a mix of CV-440s/DC-4s & DC-6s.

SWISSAIR - Operated twice-weekly from/to Basle/Zurich (SR118/9 & SR718/9), scheduled to operate with CV-440s but frequent equipment changes occurred.

1st Swissair Douglas DC-4F HB-IBB arrived at 1927 (SR1789) on a cargo flight originating from Sydney, Australia. Five days later it made a further visit as SR2006, routing Zurich-New York.

5th Royal Navy Sea Prince WM786 arrived at 1129 (Navair 756) and night-stopped from/to Exeter. This aircraft had a relatively short career and had been withdrawn by 1966.

6th RAF Shackleton MR.3 WR966 (Avro 8) overshot on a test flight from Woodford.

6th April 1961 - Auster Autocrat G-AGYP is seen here just over a week before its fatal accident. It departed at 1041 on the 14th for another banner towing sortie, but unfortunately it crashed near Wythenshawe Hospital. This practice was vulnerable to engine failure and banned shortly afterwards. (Dave Lawrence)

7th   RAF Vulcan XJ823 also overshot today on a test flight from Woodford.

9th   KLM Cargo Dakota PH-DAB, the second example to visit, operated as KL003E/4E f/t Amsterdam.

11th RAE Devon C.2 XG496 (callsign MPDXS) arrived at 0950 from its base at Farnborough. It served the military well into the 1980s, but now currently resides in Australia in private hands. Another UK military visitor today was Anson C.19 TX219 (callsign Scabbard 02) from/to RAF Andover.

13th British Eagle Viking G-AJPH & Viscount G-ARKH made crew training flights from/to Heathrow.

14th Ringway was treated to several different USAF C-47 arrivals this month, starting today with 43-48675 (formerly ex-RAF KJ905) f/t its base as RAF Bovingdon. The second, 0-49025 (20th), routed Chateauroux-Wiesbaden. It returned to the USA in 1968 and went on to serve with the Guatemalan AF between 1969 and 1980. The others were 0-49409 (21st) operating f/t RAF Bovingdon with a round-trip to West Freugh in between and finally another European-based C-47 was 00746 (27th) routing Chateauroux-Leconfield.

15th April 1961 - Beech 65 Queen Air N936B was an occasional visitor until February 1963. It was beaten by G-ARFF to be the first Queen Air to appear at Manchester by a little over a month. It is seen here receiving some attention before departing to Brussels. (Dave Lawrence)

22nd Percival P.40 Prentice G-AOLR was one of a considerable number finding their way onto the UK register in 1956, once pensioned off by the RAF. It arrived into a cloudy Manchester on a day trip from its home at Biggin Hill. It was one of the few making it to flying condition, once discarded by the RAF. Most of the others never flew and were scrapped at Southend or Stansted. However, the days of flying for G-AOLR were numbered, as it crashed at Kilsyth, North Lanarkshire on 30th July 1961.

MAY 1961

The weather was notable this month for the dry conditions persisting after the first week of unsettled conditions. Temperatures reached as high as 24°C on the 13th and although the end of the month remained dry, the wind direction changed to northerlies, bringing in some hard frosts.

Overseas Air Transport changed their name to Mercury Airlines, to avoid confusion with Overseas Aviation. A new service between Manchester and Sandown, Isle of Wight was inaugurated on the 20th May with Heron G-AOZN. During the summer the airline will also operate to Sandown from Leeds and Birmingham, in addition to flights to Ostend from Derby (Burnaston) and Birmingham.

Lufthansa freight flights were operated by (LH042 westbound), D-ALAN (6th/20th) & D-ALUB (13[th]28th).

The following could be seen during the summer months, operating ITs to various destinations: <u>Air Safari</u> (Barcelona/Klagenfurt/Malaga/Rimini/Valencia), <u>Aviaco</u> (Palma), Balair (Basle), <u>British Eagle</u> (Bergen/Ostend/Pisa/Bergen), <u>Channel Airways</u> (Ostend), <u>Dan-Air</u> (Ostend), <u>Overseas Aviation</u> (Malaga/Naples/ Nice/Palma/Perpignan/Rimini/Tangier/Valencia/Venice), <u>SAM</u> (Rimini), Silver City (Luxembourg) & <u>Starways</u> (Dinard/Newquay).

1st   The arrival of Globe Air Ambassador HB-IEK was a nice start to the month, operating from/to Basle, it stayed until the 4th. It had been sold to the Swiss airline in November 1960, operating with two others, HB-IEL & HB-IEM. In late 1963 the Ambassadors were being phased out in favour of Heralds, and HB-IEK was purchased by Autair as G-ALZS. In September 1967 it was withdrawn and scrapped several months later.

3rd   Dove PH-MAD operated by Martin's Air Charter made its first visit today (also 5th) from/to Amsterdam. It was an occasional visitor until September 1965 and was sold in Cameroon the following year.

5th May 1961 - Meteor F4 VT340 had been semi-based since 1955 for missile trials/radar development, in conjunction with Fairey Aviation & Ferranti. After its final flight on 13th October 1960, it was then parked on the Fairey complex, slowly being dismantled until it was totally scrapped in 1962. (Dave Lawrence)

7th   The last scheduled BOAC passenger DC-7 took place today, operated by G-AOID (BA538/9 f/t Prestwick), although they would still make occasional visits on charters or as aircraft substitutions until 12th November 1962. The final visit would take place with G-AOIH, on a crew training flight f/t Heathrow. The cargo DC-7s, G-AOII & G-AOIJ, would continue to operate through Ringway until January 1964.

9th   KLM operated fifteen Douglas DC-7s into the decade, and at this point they were all in passenger configuration. In June 1960 the first of these, PH-DSE, was converted into a freighter, closely followed by PH-DSF. Two more converted in 1962 were PH-DSG & PH-DSI. These four aircraft, along with their fleet of DC-3s, operated freight services across Europe. Having introduced services from Manchester in April 1962 with Dakotas, DC-7s were introduced onto the route on a regular basis from November 1964. Today, the first of these converted DC-7s, PH-DSE, arrived at 0139 from Amsterdam, before departing for Heathrow.

11th   Two ILS visitors from Woodford were RAF Vulcans B.2 XH539 & B.1 XA903. Rather more mundane on the ILS was Dove G-AMDD (16th), but this improved considerably when USAF Douglas C-118A 51-3823 appeared (21st). Finally RAF Shackleton MR.2 XG555 (29th) operated by 210 Sqn and coded 'U', rounded off an excellent month!

12th   Dragon Rapide G-AIYR, operated by Hunting Surveys, arrived at 1104 from Elstree. It was based until the 18th operating each day on a local photographic detail.

13th   PA-24 Comanche ZS-CNL was based at Fairoaks, having first arrived in the UK in June 1960. It made its only visit as such, before becoming G-ARIE in June.

14ᵗʰ Aviaco began their summer IT programme (ending 1ˢᵗ October), with CV-440 EC-APU operating the first of their weekly flights from/to Palma. Three further aircraft also used were EC-APT, EC-APV & EC-AQK.

15ᵗʰ RAF Comet C.2 XK697 was the second to visit Ringway (callsign MOTAZ from Lyneham). Again it was taking school teachers out to RAF Wildenrath, Germany, before returning the following afternoon.

17ᵗʰ JAT Convair CV-440 YU-ADK arrived at 1454 on an ad hoc charter flight from Zagreb. Although the airline operated seven CV-440s from 1957 to 1973, this was their only CV-440 visit to Ringway.

25ᵗʰ Grumman Mallard N2990 *'Jemima Puddleduck'*, made its only visit to Ringway at 1349 today from Southampton, before departing for Luton. Owned by American horse-breeder Daniel G.Van Clief, it was based in the UK from May-September, and seen at various airports during this time. It returned to the USA via Gatwick on 21ˢᵗ September 1961.

27ᵗʰ Balair began a late-evening IT flight f/t Basle with Vickers Vikings. HB-AAR operated the first flight, and was regularly used throughout the summer, along with HB-AAN.

29ᵗʰ European based Beech 18 N34L, which was owned and operated by Life Magazine, arrived at 1114 today routing Brussels-Paris Le Bourget.

31ˢᵗ Transatlantic Douglas DC-4 N6531D arrived at 2157 from Gatwick to night-stop, before departing the following morning to Frankfurt. It was the first of seven visits during the year, with the last being 9ᵗʰ October, when it arrived on a flight from Palma. It had been withdrawn at Delhi by 1965.

JUNE 1961

1ˢᵗ June 1961 - Air France introduced the first jet service to a European destination from Manchester today, when SE.210 Caravelle F-BHRD (only the tenth built) touched down on Runway 06 at 1122. It was operating the inaugural Manchester-Paris service (AF960/1). (Hubert Parrish)

Apart from a period from the 7ᵗʰ - 12ᵗʰ, the month's weather was dominated by high pressure. It was dry, mainly sunny and very warm towards the end. On the 30ᵗʰ, a high of 31°C was recorded, but during the unsettled period there were air and ground frosts in various places.

Lufthansa freight flights operating during the month were (LH041 eastbound) D-ALUB (10ᵗʰ) and (LH042 westbound) D-ALAN (4ᵗʰ/10ᵗʰ/17ᵗʰ/24ᵗʰ).

The month saw a number of equipment changes on European scheduled services: KLM (KL149): L-1049C PH-LKX (12ᵗʰ) & CV-340 PH-CGC (16ᵗʰ) and Swissair (SR116): DC-6 HB-IBE (5ᵗʰ/12ᵗʰ), DC-7 HB-IBP (26ᵗʰ) & first visit SE.210 SE-DAC (19ᵗʰ). With the start of operations by Air France there were many

SE.210 first visits: F-BHRA (4th), F-BHRB (26th), F-BHRC (29th), F-BHRD (1st), F-BHRE (7th), F-BHRF (10th), F-BHRG (24th), F-BHRH (23rd), F-BHRI (17th), F-BHRJ (3rd), F-BHRL (2nd), F-BHRM(14th), F-BHRQ (13th), F-BHRR (6th), F-BHRS (5th), F-BHRT (21st), F-BHRU (16th), F-BHRX (22nd), F-BHRY (15th), F-BHRZ (19th), F-BJTA (12th) & F-BJTB (11th). Other first visits were made by BEA Vanguards G-APEB (3rd) & G-APEC (10th) and BOAC B.707s G-APFE (16th) & G-APFP (11th).

1st   RAF Shackleton MR.2 WG555 from 210 Sqn made another low pass and overshoot today.

3rd   Seven Seas Douglas DC-4 N30048 made the first of five visits during 1961. It positioned from Luxembourg today to operate a round-trip to Malaga, on behalf of Overseas Aviation.

3rd   Overseas Aviation had become one of the major charter operators within Europe. For 1961 they had an extensive summer IT programme from Belfast, Birmingham, Gatwick, Prestwick and Ringway; in addition to a comprehensive network of holiday routes radiating from West Germany. In the face of this expansion, it was inevitable they would have to add more aircraft to their fleet of Vikings and Argonauts, so on the 1st June they purchased eight Canadair DC-4M North Stars and two Canadair C.4 Argonauts from Trans Canada Airlines. The first of these to be delivered was CF-TFO, which made its first visit today, positioning up from Gatwick at 0756 to operate a flight to Venice. Of these ten new aircraft, only four would visit Ringway prior to the airline's collapse this August. These were North Stars CF-TFK (f/v-28th July), CF-TFL (f/v-8th July), CF-TFM (f/v-10th June), & CF-TFT (f/v-10th June).

7th   Martin's Air Charter Dakota PH-DAI was a first time visitor, operating an inbound charter from Basle.

8th   A new USAF Douglas C-47 to visit was 42-93066, arriving from RAF Greenham Common at 1215.

10th   Manchester based Auster 5 G-AMPV, owned and operated by Bruce Martin for pleasure flights and banner towing, had the indignity of its undercarriage collapsing whilst taxiing for departure. This interesting aircraft, designated as an Auster 5 J/5, had a J/1 Autocraft tail and a J/1N Alpha nose.

12th   Aviaco introduced a second weekly Palma flight, with Douglas DC-4s until the 16th October. Today's first flight was operated by EC-AEO, and others used were EC-ACD, EC-ACE, EC-ACF, EC-AEK & EC-AEP.

12th   RAF Pembroke WV703 (callsign MDPYE) arrived from Northolt at 1847 and night-stopped. It left the following afternoon for the short flight over to Woodford.

13th June 1961 - L-1049G D-ALIN (LH809 New York-Frankfurt), which arrived at 1809 today for fuel, was making the penultimate visit of a Lufthansa passenger Connie. Seen in the background flanked by its towering chimney, is Jacksons Brickworks. (Hubert Parrish)

14th   Sabena Boeing 707 OO-SJD (SN545) departed at 1415 on the first non-stop flight from Manchester to New York. This was only possible due to a lighter than usual load. By the end of the year this became a more common occurrence due to the colder weather, when loads of up 120 passengers were carried.

15th Cessna 210 OY-AET made its only visit arriving at 1704 from Liverpool and staying for two days. It was sold as D-EBQE in 1965, but crashed in August 1969.

16th BOAC Britannia 102 G-ANBF was making its first visit today, operating a charter to Venice (BA112). It also operated the return flight (BA113) two days later.

17th Beech Bonanza EI-ALL was another first time visitor (f/t Liverpool), becoming a regular until October 1961, when it took up residency still as EI-ALL. It finally took up British marks in March 1966 as G-ATSR.

18th Italian charter airline SAM (Societa Aria Mediterranea) began a weekly DC-6 flight f/t Rimini, with I-DIMA operating the inaugural flight. Other aircraft used were I-DIME (f/v - 2nd July) & I-DIMD (f/v - 23rd July) until the 17th September when the flights ended.

18th Jersey Airlines Herald G-APWA was a first visit of type, arriving at 0954 operating from/to Jersey.

24th Widgeon G-APTW, operated by the Westland Company (callsign Judwin 1), arrived for fuel at 1600 from a private location in nearby Alderley Edge. It had been specially chartered for a honeymoon couple, to transport them to Yeovil. The clue to the newlyweds' was probably in the callsign!

29th Two Vulcan B.2s (XH555 & XL317) from Woodford performed practice ILS and overshoots today.

JULY 1961

The weather followed a similar pattern to June, apart from six days mid-month when it was dominated by high pressure. Apart from a high of 34°C recorded on the 1st, it was cooler and cloudier, but a dry month.

Overseas Aviation introduced a short lived Prestwick-Gatwick via Manchester service from the 31st, intended to meet the requests of businessmen wanting earlier departure times to London and to help with transatlantic flights. However, these flights ceased less than two weeks later, when the airline slipped further into financial oblivion!

Lufthansa freight flights operated as follows: (LH041 eastbound), D-ALAN (19th), (LH042 westbound), D-ALAN (1st) & D-ALUB (15th/22nd/29th).

Equipment changes on the European scheduled services were KLM (KL151): L-1049E PH-LKD (29th) and Swissair (SR116): DC-7s HB-IBK (3rd/17th), HB-IBP (26th); plus first visit SE.210 HB-ICY (31st). After last month's glut of Air France SE.210s first visits, the only two this month were F-BHRK (4th) & F-BHRV (25th).

2nd July 1961 - Douglas DC-6B N90772 arrived at 1616 from Gander, before departing to Keflavik later. This aircraft had been purchased from American Airlines in November 1960, but sold to Japan Air Lines in 1964. In 1963 Saturn began operating ex-BOAC DC-7s in the UK on transatlantic flights, when in turn they were replaced by Douglas DC-8s in 1968. (Dave Lawrence)

3rd Flying Tiger L-1049H N6923C arrived at 2015 from Turin to night-stop, before leaving the following afternoon for Shannon. This Constellation made another visit on 5th February 1962 (Frankfurt-Goose Bay). Tragically seven months later it was on a military troop flight from Gander to Frankfurt, when it ditched 500 miles off the coast of Ireland due to double engine failure and pilot error, killing 28 of the 76 onboard. This was one of four fatal crashes that year involving Flying Tiger Constellations. There was much speculation that the pressure of moving so many troops around the world so quickly may have resulted in a significant reduction in the maintenance of these aircraft and others.

6th TMA Douglas DC-6F OD-ADV (LH930/1) arrived at 0049 today on a freight charter from/to Frankfurt for Lufthansa.

11th RAF Vulcan XH535 arrived at 1115 from Goose Bay to clear customs. It had been in the USA on Skybolt trials and after clearing customs it continued onwards to Woodford.

11th Douglas DC-6B CF-CZQ arrived at 0944 on a seamen's charter from Goose Bay to night-stop, before departing for Montreal the following morning. This was the last time a Canadian Pacific DC-6 would visit Ringway. All future transatlantic flights during the next few years would be operated initially by Bristol Britannias and Douglas DC-8s.

12th RAF Vulcan B.2 XJ825 was noted around lunchtime performing an ILS approach and overshoot.

13th SAS Convair CV-440 SE-BSS made its first visit today, at 0258 on a charter from Copenhagen. The passengers were picked up three days later by CV-440 OY-KPC, which was also a first visit.

13th BOAC's inbound New York flight (BA538) was terminated at Prestwick until the 21st, but ironically the outbound (BA537) was unaffected. This meant that the airline had to bring the Manchester passengers down from Prestwick during this period. Aircraft used were Seven Seas Aviation DC-4 N30048 (14th/19th) & L-1049G N4903C (16th).

15th The second Flying Tiger L-1049H visit this month was N6922C at 2133, routing Gatwick-Shannon.

19th Air France SE.210 Caravelle F-BJTB (AF960/1) went tech on arrival with hydraulic problems, before eventually leaving the following evening.

19th Having been part of the 'furniture' for several years, Firefly U.9 WB416 was finally broken up today.

19th Today was the final visit of Seven Seas Aviation, when DC-4 N30048 operated a charter on behalf of BOAC. The US charter airline was declared bankrupt in November 1961.

19th Today was fairly typical of the varied collection of propliners visiting Ringway during the early 1960s. Seen were USAF Douglas C-54 44-9046 (Amsterdam-RAF Greenham Common), Seven Seas DC-4 N30048 (mentioned above), Lufthansa L-1649 D-ALAN, Sabena DC-7 OO-SFC (New York-Brussels), Dan-Air Bristol 170 G-AINL, Avro York G-ANTJ & Ambassador G-ALZX and Tradair Viking G-AIXR.

21st Although the aircraft did not land, Heron G-APKU was crew-training at Ringway today prior to entering service with Leeds-based North-South Airlines.

22nd Queen's Flight Heron XH375 (Kitty 3 from RAF Benson) arrived at 1124 on a royal flight. It became the first Heron operated by the Royal Flight, and unofficially it ended up as the Duke of Edinburgh's aircraft.

22nd Cunard Eagle Douglas DC-6B VR-BBQ made the first of two visits on consecutive days from/to Heathrow. It had been leased from Canadian Pacific (ex-CF-CUQ) earlier in the year and was registered as G-ARWJ in March 1962. It returned to Canadian Pacific at the end of 1962, but in July 1965 it crashed and was destroyed following a bomb explosion north of Vancouver.

22nd Fairways Douglas DC-3 PH-SSM made the first of several visits over the next few years. The aircraft, which was ex-BEA G-AJDE, was purchased by the Rotterdam-based airline in June 1961. They operated two Dakotas (the other being PH-SCC) and for a short time ran a scheduled service between Rotterdam and Southampton. In 1964 they became part of Martin's Air Charter.

23rd L-1049G D-ALIN (LH807 New York-Hamburg), which arrived at 1134 for fuel, was making the final visit of a Lufthansa passenger Connie.

28th RAF Devon C.2 VP965 (callsign MONYY) day-stopped on a round-trip from RAF Northolt. It operated with 207 Sqn for thirty-five years, until it was disbanded in June 1984.

31st Falck Air DH.114 Heron OY-ADV arrived at 1809 today from Copenhagen. This aircraft started life in 1954 as LN-NPI, but was written off in January 1957. It was rebuilt with parts from another Heron, LN-SUR, which had crashed in 1956. OY-ADV operated for Falck Air until 1970, when it was sold to short-lived Norwich-based outfit, Progressive Airways.

12th July 1961 - BEA Viscount G-AOYN arrived on a specially chartered flight from Heathrow with a very unusual passenger, Russian cosmonaut Yuri Gagarin, the first man in space. The visit had been arranged at the request of the Amalgamated Union of Foundry Workers, one of the world's largest unions. It took everyone by surprise when the Soviets accepted the invitation. Today's visit of Major Yuri Gagarin took place exactly three months after his historic space flight. It should be remembered that this was only the second stop outside the Soviet Bloc, on what became a very long world-tour. Gagarin had just visited Finland and he went on to visit many other countries. In contrast to some of his later visits, concentrating on meeting royalty and presidents, his Manchester stop was deliberately organised to create a sense of solidarity between English and Soviet workers. The flight was Gagarin's first in a British plane, and for a short time he took over the controls on the way to Manchester. Thousands turned out in the pouring rain to welcome him and huge crowds had pushed though the airport gates and onto the tarmac. As Gagarin stepped from the plane, a surge from the crowd carried him away from the party of officials waiting to greet him. The police eventually managed to force a path for Gagarin to make his way back to the jostled city representatives. They included the Mayor of Stretford, who was introduced to Gagarin, but he didn't get chance to say anything, because of the noise from the cheering and applauding crowds. Gagarin then tried to make his way to a waiting car, but was swept up by the crowds again, this time sending him into a sea of backslapping fans at the end of a hangar, far away from his car. Throughout, Gagarin never lost his composure, smiling and waving before finally reaching his transport. Airport officials stated it was the biggest and most enthusiastic welcome given to anyone visiting the airport. From the airport, he was driven to the union's Moss Side headquarters, through streets lined with cheering and waving crowds, despite the pouring rain. His next stop was the giant AEI works at Trafford Park, known as 'Metros', where thousands of workers mobbed him, after the police had stopped the traffic and forced back the crowds to allow his vehicle through the gates. His welcome was tumultuous, but he maintained his smiling composure throughout. His final engagement in the region was a civic banquet at Manchester Town Hall. Huge crowds lined his route again, which passed by the Manchester United football ground. The United players all came out to cheer him and a train driver sounded his whistle in salute, to which Gagarin responded with a wave and a grin. Although the Town Hall had only been given 24 hours notice of Gagarin's visit, a crowd of over 6,000 were waiting to see him, the largest the police could remember. The Russian National Anthem was played, and the red flag was raised over the Town

Hall. As Gagarin saluted, a small boy broke through the police cordon. He shook the Mayor's hand, took a quick photo of Gagarin, and then stood still, staring at the cosmonaut. When Gagarin was introduced to Sir Bernard Lovell at the luncheon, he thanked Sir Bernard for all the assistance Jodrell Bank had given to the Soviet space programme, in tracking their early launches. Sir Bernard had hoped Gagarin would have time to visit Jodrell Bank, but the day's schedule was too tight. While Gagarin was in Manchester, the Russian trade minister was busily visiting factories and boosting orders for the Soviet Union. Russian fashion designers and machinists from Moscow had been handing out Sputnik badges and small hammer-and-sickle pins as souvenirs, but the badges were by far the most popular. Having undertaken a whistle-stop round of engagements, he returned to Ringway for the return flight to London aboard Viscount G-AOYN. Thousands were still waiting for him, and as he reached the top of the steps leading onto the aeroplane, he turned, grinned, and blew a kiss at the crowds. Worn out, he used the flight as an opportunity to get some sleep before arriving in London, where he attended a press conference, which was broadcast live on the BBC and ITV. After this he was presented with a gold medal by the President of the British Interplanetary Society. His next day was spent meeting with officials and the monarchy.

Tragically, on 27th March 1968 whilst on a routine training flight from Chkalovsky Air Base, Gagarin and flight instructor Vladimir Seryogin died in a MiG-15 crash near the town of Kirzhach.
(MA Archive via Ringway Publications)

AUGUST 1961

The first couple of weeks were generally cool and changeable, but from the 12th a large high pressure dominated, although occasional weather fronts passed through bringing rain. From around the 27th, the winds changed to a southerly direction, bringing in warmer conditions. On the 29th several places throughout the UK reached a high of 32°C.

An impending crisis was brewing in Berlin, with an ultimatum being demanded by the Russians that Western forces should withdraw from West Berlin. This eventually culminated in the erection of a partition within the East German section, which became known as the Berlin Wall. In light of this, Ringway would become a major air-trooping centre, with plans being made for a weekday service to the following four German airfields, Dusseldorf, Hanover, Gutersloh & Wildenrath with effect from 2nd October. These would be operated by British United with Viscounts under contract from the Air Ministry, who decided that all further troop movements will be by air. Until now forces and their families have travelled to and from Germany by land and sea from Harwich to the Hook of Holland. Initially these flights would be introduced as a peace-time efficiency measure, but if the situation in Berlin was to deteriorate, the operation would be extended to move troops to Germany in large numbers.

BOAC announced they would extend their New York flights to Baltimore four-times-weekly from October.

1st USAF C-47 0-76650 was the latest to make its first visit to Manchester. It was a remarkable aircraft, designated as a Douglas TS-62, but due to a shortage of engines after the war, it was fitted with Russian-made engines.

8th This month's British military visitors began today with Avro Anson C.19 TX219. Other Anson C.19s were VL351 (9th) & TX172 (18th). Finally, Vickers Valetta VW825 visited on the 30th.

14th After three years serving many IT routes from Manchester, North Star CF-TFO made the last visit of Overseas Aviation. The day prior, British Petroleum had announced that they would no longer supply fuel to the airline, and they intended to present a petition for the company's involuntary liquidation to the High Court. Eventually the entire fleet would be grounded, leaving more than 5,000 passengers stranded overseas, and the airline's creditors would be owed over half a million pounds. At the time of the collapse, Overseas Aviation operated the second largest fleet of any British independent airline, second only to British United.

15th Whirlwind G-AOCZ arrived from Jodrell Bank after lifting a radio transmitter into place. Dragon Rapide G-AKRS and resident Auster G-AMPV had both been hired by the 'Daily Mail' to operate photographic sorties over the site.

16th TAI Douglas DC-6B F-BGOC was operating an outbound flight to Quebec, Canada.

17th Flying Tiger L-1049H N6917C was operating on behalf of Lufthansa.

19th Despite the collapse earlier this month of Overseas Aviation, their programme still had to be fulfilled. TAI Douglas DC-6B F-BHMR operated a flight to/from Nice today and another of their DC-6s, F-BHVA, operated the flight the following week (26th).

22nd Beech 95 D-IBAF & BEA Vanguard G-APEI were present today, making their first visits to Ringway.

26th August 1961 - TAI Douglas DC-6B F-BHVA is seen here on short-finals, positioning from Paris-Orly to operate a former Overseas Aviation charter flight to Nice. In 1962 it was registered to Iran Air as EP-AES, and during the following year TAI merged with Union Aéromaritime de Transport to form UTA French Airlines. (Dave Lawrence)

SEPTEMBER 1961

The month provided a wide variety of weather types over the UK, ranging from warm anticyclonic through to thunderstorms and vigorous depressions. The 16th was particularly stormy, and on the 2nd the month's highest temperature of 32°C was recorded at Gatwick.

BEA made plans to operate Vanguards four-times-daily from next April. This would also increase capacity, as the Viscounts currently flying the route have a maximum capacity of 65 seats, compared with the Vanguard's 113. In the meantime from November the Vanguard will be introduced on a weekday evening service (BE4050/9 1815/2010).

The move of Ringway's based light aircraft over to the south side (Hangars 521/522/523) has been completed.

Lufthansa freight flights were numerous this month, with (LH041 eastbound), D-ALAN (3rd/7th) & D-ALUB (11th), (LH042 westbound), D-ALAN (9th/16th/23rd) & D-ALUB (1st/8th).

2nd The Nice flight, which was part of Overseas Aviation's summer programme, continued to be sub-chartered by other airlines. Transair Sweden DC-6 SE-BDO (today), SE-BDF (9th) the following week, TAI DC-6 F-BHVA (16th) & Trans World Douglas DC-4 G-ARIC (23rd), which was the final flight of the series.

2nd The fine and very warm weather at the end of August, persisted into the first few days of this month, bringing in widespread overnight fog. Ringway handled fourteen diversions during the morning. They were mainly BEA flights, but some of the others were Lufthansa Viking D-BORA at 0508, Cunard Eagle DC-6As G-ARMY & VR-BBQ and BOAC B.707 G-APFO at 1029 (BA512 from Philadelphia).

2nd A new UK airline to Ringway was Lloyd International, with the arrival of Douglas DC-4 G-ARLF operating a flight from Southend to Cambridge (also 18th/25th/29th/30th). The airline was set up in January 1961 with a single DC-4, which spent most of the year operating IT flights for other airlines or flying in the Far East. On the 18th October 1961 it was written off at Malaga. It was completely burnt out when a fuel bowser exploded and caught fire during refuelling. It was on a charter flight from Tangier to Manchester with 34 passengers onboard, when it stopped at Malaga for fuel and to pick up an additional 32 passengers.

4th There were plenty of US military visitors in September, starting with US Army L-20 Beaver 26137 at 1203 today from RAF Wethersfield. US Army Dakotas were represented by two examples, 0-15207 (5th/7th) & 0-48959 (21st/28th).

6th Dove G-ALFU was based until the 18th, operating daily except at weekends on PAR training flights.

6th There were two ILS visitors today. Dove G-ARDE at 1215 from Tatenhill and the more noteworthy Israeli Air Force Nord 2501 Noratlas 4X-CAU. Although this didn't land, it was the first appearance of the type at Ringway.

7th Two Danish light aircraft making their first visits this month began with Commander 560 OY-ADS today, on a flight from Amsterdam before departing to Gatwick. Registered in 1958, it remained on the Danish register until 1988. The second, PA-23 Apache OY-AIU (23rd) was also from Amsterdam, clearing customs, before departing for Hawarden the following afternoon. This aircraft would make one more visit to Ringway in June 1962, but was written off in February 1963.

10th What must have been a remarkable scene for anyone witnessing it, was the sight of two USAF C-97 Stratofortresses landing within 5 minutes of each other today. C-97s 1224 (Shiny 1 from Stephenville) & 92589 (Shiny 2 from Stephenville) touched down at 0614 & 0619 respectively on Runway 24. Both aircraft were from the Oklahoma Air Guard, but the reason they diverted into Manchester is unknown.

13th Aviation history was being made at Manchester today by a Texan pilot, Captain Walter Moody, who flew in Mooney M20B G-ARTB on a 20 hour flight from Boston, Massachusetts. It was the first non-stop transatlantic flight by a light plane into Ringway. The aircraft was being delivered to Mercury Airlines, who are also the North of England agents for the type. The rear seats had been removed from the single-engined plane, to make room for the long-range fuel tanks.

15th The arrival of Flying Tigers CL-44 N447T at 1844 from Ingolstadt was a first visit of type. At 2320 it departed for an hour-long local flight, before leaving at 0244 bound for Newark.

17th Trans Atlantic Airlines DC-4 N6531D arrived from Birmingham to operate a return IT flight to Palma. PA-23 Apache N3146P, (also operated by the airline), brought in a fresh crew for the outbound flight.

17th The final Balair flight for the summer was operated by Viking HB-AAN on its penultimate visit to Ringway. Both of the airlines Vikings, HB-AAN & HB-AAR (last visit 10th Sept), were sold in February 1963 as G-AIVF & G-AIVD respectively. For their 1962 summer programme, the Vikings were replaced with ex-Swissair DC-4s.

21st Four very early morning fog diversions from Heathrow produced two first visits, with Swissair SE.210 HB-ICZ at 0222 (SR700 from Zurich) & Alitalia Douglas DC-6B I-DIMB at 0314 (AZ302 from Milan). Another first visit today but not a diversion, was Beech Bonanza D-INAS (Birmingham/Gatwick).

23rd USAF C-124 30049 arrived at 1521 from Dublin, departing the following afternoon for Woodford. It was possibly carrying US-built Skybolt missiles, the UK's new nuclear deterrent replacing the Blue Steel missile project which was cancelled in December 1959. The penultimate C-124 Globemaster to visit took place three days later, but it remained unidentified having arrived at 0032 from Mildenhall (callsign Haiti 33), departing for Chateauroux at 1047.

24th The Douglas R5D-5 was the US Navy version of the C-54 Skymaster. The only example to visit Ringway was 50887, which arrived at 2052 from Chateauroux. It stayed for an hour, before departing for RAF Bovingdon.

29th RAF Anson C.19 VM316 (callsign Parole 22) made two visits today from/to RAF Andover.

OCTOBER 1961

A dominant high pressure over European Russia during the first week, led to Atlantic frontal systems becoming slow moving over the UK. The middle of the month became more settled, but the rest was cyclonic and stormy. Minor tornadoes caused considerable damage in parts of Bournemouth on the 6th.

Cunard Eagle cancelled all plans, at extremely short notice, to operate from Ringway during the winter. It was hoped that the recently introduced service to Hamburg and Copenhagen would continue, maybe at a reduced frequency, but it was terminated due to lack of passengers. Also, they were due to take space in the new terminal building when it came into operation next year, but they decided to leave their flight handling to BEA.

The Saturday evening newspaper flight which last operated in May restarted during the month, this time with Silver City Bristol 170s.

Lufthansa freight flights were numerous during the month, with (LH040/2 westbound), D-ALAN (11th/24th) & D-ALUB (7th/15th/21st/25th/28th), and just one eastbound, D-ALAN (LH041R-26th).

2nd Two Birmingham weather diversions today were Balair Viking HB-AAN at 1032 on its last visit, and Trans Atlantic Douglas DC-4 N90443 at 0312.

5th USAF Douglas C-54G Skymaster 45-0481 arrived at 1552 from RAF Greenham Common and departed to Hahn the following afternoon. It served the US military until its retirement at Davis-Monthan in July 1973.

6th The first of two Avro Anson C.19s making their only visits this year was VL306 (callsign 'Engross 02') today. The second was TX196 on the 12th.

8th Swissair DC-8 HB-IDB, which made a tech stop en route New York-Zurich (SR861), had visited before. However, Heathrow Diversion DC-8 HB-IDC arriving at 1403 on the 15th (SR100 from Zurich), was a first visit.

9th KLM Electra PH-LLL arrived at 1629 operating a passenger charter from/to Amsterdam. This was the first Electra from the Dutch airline to visit Ringway.

9th Sabena B.707 OO-SJF was their sixth aircraft to visit Ringway (SN547 Brussels-New York), whilst on the 27th, Douglas DC-7 OO-SFJ was used on the evening Brussels service (SN623), in place of the regular Convair CV-440.

11th In addition to the larger executive aircraft operated by Dutch-electronics firm, Philips, they also owned a smaller type, Cessna 172A PH-MAF, which made a round-trip from Southend today. It was sold to a private individual in 1962, and remained on the Dutch register until 1969. Other foreign lights this month were Beech Bonanza HB-GAW (13th/16th) & Cessna 310 HB-LBL (16th - f/t Munster).

11th The only Alitalia Viscount to visit Ringway was today's arrival of I-LIZO (AZ2884/5 f/t Milan). This aircraft operated for the Italian airline for ten years until 1968, when it was sold to Aerolineas TAO as HK-1058.

12th A couple of Douglas DC-6 aircraft making their first visits on consecutive days began today with Transair Sweden SE-BDN (TB209 from Aarhus). The second, UAT Douglas DC-6B F-BGSN, night-stopped on the 13th f/t Le Bourget.

14th Braathens Fokker F.27 LN-SUG, arriving at 1453 from Torp today, was a first visit of type. Braathens would go on to operate ten different F.27 aircraft, a type which became very popular worldwide.

15th The UK was affected by widespread dense fog, persisting all day in parts of the Midlands and the southeast, which led to eighteen diversions descending on Ringway. Foreign airlines included first visit SAS SE.210 OY-KRD at 1540 (SK501 from Copenhagen) & KLM L-1049G PH-LKB (KL129 from Amsterdam). British Eagle produced DC-6 G-ARMY (from Benina) & Viscount G-ARKI (from Palma), along with eight Comets! BOAC Comet 4s were G-APDK at 1424 (BA122 from Rome), first visit G-APDL at 1528 (BA662 from Madrid) & G-APDS at 1436 (BA797 from Dusseldorf). Also five BEA Comet 4Bs were G-APMB/APMC (first visit)/ARCP (first visit) & ARJK.

15th USAF Douglas VC-47D 43-48186 arrived from Blackpool at 1722 to clear customs, before departing back to its Ramstein base.

24th Flying Tigers L-1049H N6913C arrived at 0023 from Frankfurt, before departing for Gander. This Constellation was another one of the four that crashed the following year. The probable cause of the accident, whilst on approach to Burbank in foggy conditions, was put down to the incapacitation of the pilot. This was possibly due to coronary artery disease, sufficient enough in severity to have caused partial/complete incapacitation or even death.

30th Another three weather diversions this morning were British United Britannia G-APNA at 0820 (BR102 from Entebbe) and BOAC B.707s G-APFI at 0720 (BA592 from Montreal) & B.707 G-APFP at 1147 (BA500 from New York). The latter diversion was piloted by Gilbert Alcock and Edward Brown; 42 years after the original 'Alcock & Brown' made the first Atlantic crossing in their Vickers Vimy. Both Captains had been asked many times previously if they were the original aviation pioneers, but Captain Alcock replied that he was a distant relative.

31ˢᵗ A new type, ultimately destined to sell in massive numbers around the world, made its first visit to Ringway today. Piper PA-28 Cherokee G-ARRP had the honour of being the first; arriving at 1522 from Wolverhampton, before making the short hop over to Barton. Incredibly in 2014 it survives as a flying aircraft, now registered as G-LIZI.

31ˢᵗ Dan-Air Avro Yorks were used for the final time on BEA's Glasgow freight service, with the honour going to G-ANTK. Arriving from Glasgow at 2011, it departed at 2200 for Heathrow. The type made further visits to Manchester going into 1962.

NOVEMBER 1961

The weather for November was mostly dry and sunny, although the first half was mainly dominated by low pressure. The 26ᵗʰ saw some areas suffering from persistent freezing fog.

In an effort to improve links between Manchester and the West Country, Mercury Airlines applied for licences to operate between Manchester and Swansea; with an optional stop at Sandown and a separate service to Swansea with optional stops at Exeter and Newquay. However, these were opposed by Starways and Cambrian Airways.

BEA announced they would introduce their new Argosy freighters onto their Heathrow-Manchester-Glasgow route from 8ᵗʰ January. Although this was put back to the 26ᵗʰ January, they did operate the Argosy on various non-scheduled freight flights between Glasgow and Heathrow. The first, G-APRN, was delivered on the 6ᵗʰ November. The type, capable of carrying 12 tonnes of freight, made its operational debut on the 26ᵗʰ November on its four-times-weekly service to Milan. The only Lufthansa freight flight this month was (LH041 eastbound): D-ALAN (16ᵗʰ).

International flights were operated during the winter as follows:

AIR FRANCE - Twice-weekly (Wed/Fri).

AER LINGUS - Amsterdam (2 x weekly), Brussels (2 x weekly), Copenhagen (2 x weekly), Dusseldorf (2 x weekly), Frankfurt (2 x weekly) & Zurich (1 x weekly), all operated by Viscounts.

BEA - Amsterdam/Dublin/Dusseldorf/Paris & Zurich.

BOAC - B.707s to New York were (BA537: 4 x weekly outbound & BA538: 3 x-weekly inbound) and from this month it extended to serve Baltimore. Bristol Britannias serve Boston (2 x weekly), Montreal (4 x weekly), New York (3 x weekly) & Toronto (4 x weekly). The DC-7 cargo operation remained unchanged at twice-weekly to Montreal/New York.

KLM - Operated to Amsterdam twice-weekly (KL149/150), with one flight operating onwards to Dublin (KL151/2).

SABENA - Twice-weekly to/from New York with B.707s (SN545/6) & DC-7s (SN549/550). The evening Brussels service remains twice-weekly with CV-440s.

SWISSAIR - Operated once-weekly from/to Basle/Zurich (SR116/7) with CV-440s. From 23ʳᵈ December a second flight was added (SR718/9).

1ˢᵗ BEA introduced the Vanguard onto their Manchester-Heathrow service, with G-APEF making today's inaugural flight (BE4050/9). Although this aircraft had visited previously, there were also some first visits with G-APEH (24ᵗʰ), G-APEJ (3ʳᵈ), G-APEK (7ᵗʰ) & G-APEL (6ᵗʰ).

2ⁿᵈ Avro Anson C.19 TX256 (callsign 'Facer 05') made its third visit this year, arriving from RAF Andover. It was on the ground for a mere five minutes, before leaving for Bicester. The following day Devon C.2 VP971 (callsign 'Facer 03') also made a brief appearance f/t RAF Andover, which was also a first visit.

2ⁿᵈ Three further USAF Douglas C-47s making first visits this month were 93701 (today) & 15661 (6ᵗʰ), staying briefly f/t Evereux. The third, 48715, stayed overnight on the 29ᵗʰ f/t Chateauroux.

8ᵗʰ British United Widgeon G-APPR recently acquired by Bristows, arrived at 1251 from Coventry for a brief-stop before departing for Grizedale in the Lake District. In May 1962 it was transferred to Bristows (Nigeria) as 5N-ABV.

10ᵗʰ A couple of Liverpool diversions this morning were Dan-Air DC-3 G-AMSU from Cardiff, and the second visit of Braathens Fokker F.27, with LN-SUG arriving at 1124 from Kristiansand.

11ᵗʰ Sabena operated several DC-3 cargo flights this month, with OO-AUY (today), OO-AWZ (15ᵗʰ/27ᵗʰ) & OO-AWG (18ᵗʰ). These extra flights were due to a strike by the Ministry of Aviation's loaders' over pay which started on the 6th and declared official on the 9th. BEA domestic and European flights were affected, with just one piece of hand luggage per passenger being allowed. No freight moved, but long-haul flights were unaffected and normal operations resumed on the 17th. Due to the huge backlog at various airports, it took several weeks to return to normal after the strike which cost BEA more than £300,000.

12th KLM CV-340 PH-CGC, arriving at 0850, was operating a charter flight from Amsterdam on behalf of BEA. Another CV-340, PH-CGE (18th) and DC-7 PH-DSE (20th), were both uploading freight due to the loaders' strike.

13th BOAC B.707 G-APFM was crew training during the afternoon, as was G-APFH (15th).

13th German Air Force Pembroke C.54 SC-302 arrived at 1124 from Kiel as a diversion from RAF Marham. They were operated as light transport/liaison aircraft, and used well into the 1970s.

17th BEA Argosy G-APRN arrived from Heathrow at 1134, departing on a proving flight to Le Bourget. A second aircraft, G-AOZZ, made its first visit on the 27th December en route Heathrow-Glasgow.

19th The only light visitor of note was Commander 680 F-BJUP f/t Clermont, which was also a first visit.

DECEMBER 1961

The first half of the month was cyclonic and changeable. Between the 16th and 22nd an area of high pressure extending from northern Russia across Scandinavia dominated, bringing in very cold and foggy conditions. A freshening easterly thereafter cleared away all the fog, but an exceptionally cold spell followed, producing one of the coldest Christmas periods recorded this century almost everywhere. On the 30th/31st, heavy snow fell with snowdrifts of 3ft in places.

Cunard Eagle put both of their European-based Viscounts up for sale. They announced they will have a limited presence at Ringway next summer, having already cancelled services to Hamburg and Copenhagen. They said their policy over the last eight years had been to develop services from Manchester, and although they had made repeated applications for sufficient scheduled services to provide adequate utilisation of their aircraft, they had been unsuccessful. They cited the example of the London-Manchester route, for which they had made three separate applications to operate in competition with BEA. On the second occasion they demonstrated the public's need for extra services, but the Ministry of Aviation directed BEA to provide the additional services instead of them, and their application was rejected. Similar difficulties were faced on other routes, such as Manchester-Nice.

Air France SE.210 F-BHRO (6th) was the latest making its first visit to Ringway during the month. Further first visits were made by two more BEA Vanguards (BE4050/9), G-APEN (7th) & G-APEP (22nd).

Lufthansa terminated their New York freight flight this month. The final flights were (LH041 eastbound), D-ALUB (2nd), (LH042 eastbound) & D-ALAN (2nd/9th/30th). Note that two aircraft operated on the 2nd.

1st Lufthansa B.720 D-ABOK (LH120 from Frankfurt) arrived at 0932 today as a Heathrow diversion due to snow, with a mere nineteen passengers onboard! It was the second Boeing 720 to visit, and the only Lufthansa example to appear at Ringway.

2nd A good day for Connies! Apart from the two Lufthansa Starliners today, Flying Tiger L-1049E N6914C (also 9th/15th) arrived at 0243 from Frankfurt, before departing for Gander. This was yet another Flying Tiger aircraft that was lost. It crashed on 15th December 1965 flying from Los Angeles to Chicago at night. The crew were possibility disoriented, flying inadvertently below terrain, resulting in the aircraft ploughing into California Peak.

6th RAF Vulcan B.2 XL321 diverted in from Gander as 'Avro 2' due to snow at Woodford. On landing the brake chute got tangled in the wing, but it still managed to taxi to its remote stand and park up. It subsequently froze, with embedded ice in the wing. With this and the continuing weather conditions at Woodford, the aircraft was precluded from leaving until two days later.

6th 1947-vintage Miles Gemini G-AKKB arrived at 1440 from Barton for storage. It was hidden away from view in the south side hangars, until its departure to East Midlands on 5th August 1965.

8th RAF Devon VP965 (callsign MONYY) was making its third visit of the year, night-stopping from RAF Wethersfield. The only other RAF visitor this month was Anson C.19 VS565 (13th) from/to White Waltham as 'IBK 22'.

14th Probably the first Italian light visitor to Ringway to date was Milan-based Beech 65 Queen Air I-OGGI, arriving at 1422 on a round-trip from Gatwick.

15th The first of two significant diversion days this month saw twelve flights arriving from Heathrow, due to dense fog lasting most of the day. Included were first timers SAS Douglas DC-7 SE-CCB at 1558 (SK521 from Gothenburg), BUA Britannia G-ANCE at 1020 (BR812 from Tripoli), WDL Fokker F.27 at 1548 (LH032R from Dusseldorf and EL AL B.707 4X-ATB at 1610 (LY229 from Rome). The latter departed direct to New York, once the passengers for this flight had arrived from London.

20th Just one movement all day was Viscount G-AMOL from Prestwick, arriving at 0025 due to fog.

21st Today went one better with one arrival and six departures, again due to fog.

22nd Due to pre-Christmas loads, Swissair's Zurich flight SR118/9 was upgraded this evening, and operated by Douglas DC-6 HB-IBU. Other extra flights were also operated by DC-6 HB-IBO (SR2664/5) today and CV-440 HB-IMM (23rd) as SR2666/7 both f/t Zurich.

30th L-1649 Starliner D-ALAN operated the final LH042 Frankfurt-MAN-New York cargo flight. It would be another nine years before the airline would operate from Manchester again, although they began a cargo service to Dusseldorf/Frankfurt in November 1966. Aircraft used were from German carriers Transportflug and All-Air until January 1970, when Lufthansa's new B.737QCs were utilised. L-1649 D-ALAN was sold as N179AV in February 1966, but in 1962 it was leased to World Airways for two years. Their other regular, D-ALUB, was also leased to World Airways from 1962 until 1964. It was finally withdrawn and preserved as a restaurant in Hartenholm, Nr Hamburg in 1966. Tragically this graceful machine was destroyed by fire in July 1975.

30th Operated by Granada Television and a regular visitor since October 1961, Dove G-ARSI made its last visit as such today. In January 1962 it was re-registered (for some reason!) as G-ARFZ and due to the frequency of its visits, it could now be considered a semi-resident until they sold it in October 1968.

31st Aer Lingus' second B.720 EI-ALB, made its first visit today operating an extra flight f/t Dublin.

31st Heavy snow affecting the UK brought in fifteen diversions, mainly from Heathrow, arriving at various times during the day. Two were first visits with BEA Comet G-ARCO at 1742 (SK513 from Geneva) and another SAS DC-7, OY-KND at 1417 (SK513 from Stavanger). Others included SAS SE.210 SE-DAC at 1147 (SK501 from Copenhagen), Swissair's DC-6 HB-IBU at 1958 (SR110 from Zurich) & CV-440 HB-IMF at 2015 (SR102 from Paris). Finally was East Anglian Dakota G-ANEG, an uncommon visitor to Manchester, arriving from Dinard at 1334 after fleeing a snowy Birmingham!

31st As if the weather diversions arriving at Ringway weren't enough to arise local spotters from their Christmas slumber, the sight of the first HS.748 for Aerolineas Argentinas, LV-PIZ, performing an ILS and overshoot from Woodford certainly was!

FIRST/LAST ARRIVALS & DEPARTURES 1961

First arrival: BEA Viscount G-AMOB from Heathrow at 0757
First departure: Silver City Bristol 170 G-AHJD to Jurby at 0755
Last arrival: BEA Viscount G-AMOF from Glasgow at 2118
Last departure: BEA Viscount G-AMOB to Zurich at 2218

Airport Stats 1961 (+/- % on Previous Year)		
Scheduled Passengers	822,000	+27.6%
Inclusive & Charter Passengers	37,000	+54.1%
Freight & Mail (Tonnes)	13,200	-11.5%
Movements	39,400	+15.8%

AIRPORT DIARY 1962

JANUARY 1962

The weather for January was dominated by low pressure, apart from the beginning and the end of the month. A minor tornado hitting Egremont, Cumberland, caused substantial damage to houses on the evening of the 16th/17th.

British European Airways lost a high court legal battle, over being able to perform their own baggage handling at Ringway, currently carried out by Manchester Corporation who disputed the claim. Problems arose after the Corporation raised their charges year on year, to the point where BEA said they were too high. The airline claimed they could save £32,000 per year by carrying out their own handling, but under the scrutiny of the judge BEA admitted a miscalculation of £21,000, so it was ruled there was no substance in the argument advanced by BEA.

Spectators will be charged one shilling for admittance to the terraces, when the new terminal building opens. It was also announced that because of the possible risks arising from the closeness to the aircraft and the passengers on the apron below, use of the two piers should be restricted to adults only. However, because the terraces were unmanned, the rule could not be enforced. The airport claimed that the new charges would bring in an additional £59,000 per year.

The Saturday evening newspaper flight operated by Silver City Bristol 170s continued until May 1962 with G-AGVC/AIFM/AIME.

Several more BEA Vanguard first visits this month were G-APEM (7th), G-APEO (5th) & G-APER (22nd).

1st The first day of the New Year was ushered in by very low temperatures. Many parts in England started at -12°C and remained below freezing all day. Ringway was also shrouded in dense fog, and only saw four arrivals.

3rd Another fog-affected day, yet it saw eight arrivals! The only movement of note however, was another ILS approach by Aerolineas Argentinas HS.748 LV-PIZ.

5th Cessna 310 G-ARNU diverted to Manchester due to the state of the runway at Hawarden.

5th Another KLM Constellation visitor to Ringway was L-1049G PH-LKE, which departed on a passenger charter to Rome. Their entire fleet of Constellations had been sold or withdrawn by late 1962.

8th There were plenty of KLM CV-340 visits this month, all operating freight flights, with PH-CGD (18th/30th), PH-CGF (today/12th) & PH-CGG (17th). They continued to be occasional visitors, mainly as substitutions on the KLM freight service which commenced in March. By early 1964 most had left the fleet, with PH-CGI being the final one to leave before becoming N4408 in June 1964.

8th USAF C-47 0-50943 (also 19th Feb) arrived at 1243 f/t Brussels on the first of three visits during 1962. The only other during the month was 0-52548 (31st), routing Wiesbaden-Northolt.

12th Former BOAC L-049 G-AHEL, now operated by Trans European, positioned in at 1129 from Biggin Hill to operate a freight flight to Brindisi. This airline was an uncommon visitor to Ringway.

15th The first of two RAF visitors this month was Avro Anson C.19 VM380 (JPP23 f/t White Waltham). The second, Valetta VW197, operated from/to Manby on consecutive days (23rd/24th).

27th The dense fog earlier in the month returned with a vengeance, affecting the UK over the next two days. Ringway was badly affected again today, with just seven arrivals.

FEBRUARY 1962

February was dry but colder towards the end, with low pressures passing through, bringing in stormy weather mid-month. On the 11th a gust of 106kts was recorded in Lanarkshire and over four inches of rain fell in Kinlochewe.

CSA-Czech Airlines selected Manchester and Prestwick as fuel-stops, should the need arise for their proposed new service. They were planning to operate between Prague and Havana, but ministry officials turned the application down as there could be no Customs inspection of the aircraft unless the passengers attempted to leave the transit lounge.

The Airport Committee gave the go-ahead for night-time departures by jet aircraft this summer, despite numerous protests by the Hale Barns Ratepayers Association. From the 18th May, Swissair will operate a twice-weekly SE.210 service to Basle/Zurich (SR718/9) at 0245/0335. Officials claimed that the French-built Caravelle made less noise than Boeing 707s and even Constellations.

A further two BEA Vanguards making their first visits to Ringway were G-APES (19th) & G-APET (28th). In a month almost totally devoid of anything of interest, Woodford did their best by sending over several aircraft for ILS training, which included Aerolineas Argentinas HS.748 LV-PJA (26th/28th) & RAF Victor XL161 (2nd).

11th An exceptionally stormy front produced two Heathrow diversions, BOAC B.707 G-APFP at 1102 (BA538 from Manchester) and Comet 4 G-APDC at 1111 (CE892 from Rome), operating on behalf of Central African Airways.

23rd KLM Douglas DC-7 PH-DSF arrived at 0248 on a cargo flight from Gander, later departing for Amsterdam.

23rd Adria Airways Douglas DC-6B YU-AFC made the airline's only visit this year. Arriving at 1554 on a freight charter from Zagreb, it returned there following morning. However, in 1963 the airline would begin operating summer IT flights to Yugoslavia for the next few years.

26th BOAC operated two crew training flights, with B.707 G-APFI today & Britannia G-AOVC on the 27th.

26th February 1962 - Balair Douglas DC-4 HB-ILU operated a further freight charter f/t Basle. As well as operating summer charters throughout the decade, Balair DC-4s were used when Swissair began freight services to Zurich in April 1967. This aircraft operated for the airline until 1969, when it was sold to Aer Turas as EI-ARS. In 1989 it was preserved and placed on display as 44-9063 at the United States Air Force Museum in Frankfurt. (Avro Heritage Centre)

MARCH 1962

The month was unusually cold, with high pressure dominating until the end, when it became milder but unsettled. Extreme temperatures saw 15°C at Hoddesdon, Hertfordshire (29th) and a low of -15°C at Alwen, North Wales (6th).

Following a decision taking more than twelve months to reach, the government rejected Ringway's plan to extend the main runway by 3,500ft. The airport said it was needed to enable current and future transatlantic flights to reach their destinations with full fuel and passenger loads; but the government said they could not justify the expense when the national economy was facing a reduction in public sector expenditure. The airport expressed their disappointment, and said they would make a direct protest to the Aviation Minister, once their report giving all the facts on the airport's development and urgent requirement for the runway extension was complete. Manchester Corporation wanted to carry the extension over the River Bollin, but the ministry's alternative scheme was to extend to 9,500ft only, mainly at the eastern end, bringing the runway much nearer to the housing estates and houses located at Wythenshawe and Styal.

Last month's passenger traffic increased by 21%, compared with the same period last year. Passengers handled were 48,340, and cargo handled totalled 1,035 tonnes.

1st   The first and only Iberia Bristol 170 to visit Ringway was EC-AHJ at 1451 from Barcelona, heavily laden with Spanish textiles. Unfortunately, this aircraft was damaged beyond repair the following month in a wheels-up landing at Valencia.

1st   KLM began a scheduled freight service between Manchester and Amsterdam, due to operate four-times-weekly by Douglas DC-3s, but CV-340s CGD (1st) & CGC (2nd) were used for the first two days. Amongst the cargo on today's first inbound flight was a consignment of budgerigars, aircraft parts and Canadian clothing for a Yorkshire firm. In preparation for the commencement of this service, Ringway had opened a new cargo centre (formerly Hangar 6), costing £68,000. It was capable of handling 70,000 tonnes annually, more than four times the amount passing through last year.

1st   As they were no longer operating cargo flights on behalf of BEA, Avro York movements became very rare. However, Dan-Air G-ANTJ arrived at 1725 from Heathrow to operate a cargo flight to Amsterdam.

2nd   BEA Argosy G-APRM arrived at 2123 from Milan, carrying an unregistered Lockheed Santa Maria. On the 4th it was loaded aboard BOAC DC-7F G-AOII bound for New York.

3rd   Flying Tigers L-1049F N6912C arrived from Chateauroux to be loaded with a cargo of machine tools. It departed two days later, bound for Newark and San Diego.

3rd   The month had started well with the arrival of freight charters, but today saw the first visit of an Alitalia Douglas DC-7, when I-DUVA (AZ3970/1) appeared from Milan at 2158 carrying car parts. A second flight was operated on the 7th, with DC-7F I-DUVE (AZ3970/1), also from/to Milan.

5th   BEA's three Argosies, G-APRM/APRN & AOZZ, were all on the ground throughout the day. They had been operating to a variety of European points for several days, but had nothing to do today!

6th   RAF Devon C.2 VP971 made two visits this year, operating from/to its base at RAF Andover today and from/to Shawbury on the 12th. Surprisingly this aircraft would make no further appearances this decade, even though it continued in service until 1984. Another Devon C.2, VP956 (9th), operated from/to RAF Northolt on its first and only visit to Ringway this year.

7th   Another freight movement was Air France L-1049F F-BHBA at 1656 from Heathrow to Paris-Orly.

8th   Queen's Flight Heron XR391 (Kittyhawk - f/t Heathrow) was carrying Princess Margaret.

9th   USAF Douglas C-54 45-0608 arrived at 1815 from Chateauroux on a full emergency with engine failure, before finally departing on the 16th.

10th   USAF L-20 Beaver 26137 (f.Wethersfield) & Douglas C-54 42-72696 (f.Prestwick) both arrived to collect passengers from yesterday's emergency arrival.

14th   Inbound New York flight BA552 operated by Britannia 102 G-ANBL, was the last BOAC Britannia to visit Ringway.

15th   Westland Widgeons G-APTW & G-APVD from/to Liverpool were trial runs in anticipation for the future visit to the region by the Prime Minister, Harold Macmillan.

16th   The U.S. Air Force produced another aircraft in connection with 'broken' C-54 45-0608, with the arrival of 0-15287 at 1227 from Prestwick. This was the only visit of a HU-16 Albatross to Ringway, possibly with a flight crew for C-54 45-0608.

18th   On its first and only visit to Ringway, was PA-23 Apache SE-CBM, the sole light aircraft of note during March. It was sold in Denmark during October 1962 as OY-EAH.

25th   USAF Douglas C-118 51-17644 was noted making several ILS approaches during the day and on the 27th, C-54 45-0481 arrived at 1456 operating from/to Chateauroux.

27th   Army Air Corps Auster AOP.9 XR246 was a rare visitor to Ringway, operating f/t Middle Wallop as 'KQA96'. Built in 1961, it still flies today as XR246 in military colours, although it's in private hands.

APRIL 1962

The stormy weather of late March continued well into April, bringing widespread and occasionally heavy rain, but mid-month was calmer and more settled. Thereafter, weak troughs maintained cyclonic conditions but high pressure had returned by the end. Extreme temperatures saw 23°C at Southampton (26th) and a low of -8°C at Alwen, North Wales (14th).

The Manchester Evening News printed the following small, but fascinating piece, titled:
'The Eagle Eye at Ringway - Plane Spotters from 17 to 60':

"It might have been a skylark rising over the end of the runway, and you had to look twice to be sure that there was, in fact, anything there at all". The grocer's assistant from Stockport knew better. "Dakota" – he informed the rest of us laconically. "It's come from Glasgow. There's a Viscount should've come in before it from Dusseldorf. Its ten minutes late". The speck became a definite line, and then identifiably an aircraft. It swooped over the perimeter of Manchester Airport and whooshed past the crowds in the spectators' enclosure. Indisputably it was a Dakota; probably from Glasgow. A dozen small boys scribbled in notebooks; as many more looked at it disinterestedly; a number of adults regarded the grocer's assistant with admiration. He affected modesty. It wasn't, he explained so very difficult to identify that particular plane at that time of the afternoon. It was a scheduled daily flight and you'd be a bit of a chump if you didn't know what was coming in when you had been plane-spotting regularly for the best part of ten years. He was 17. He'd been cycling out to Ringway on an average of once a week since 1953 just to watch the planes go by.

Plane-spotting seems to be taking over from train-spotting as 'the hobby of the day'. Where the class of '48 would congregate at Crewe or Patricroft and solemnly note the passage of a "Mickey" or a "Jub", their younger brothers line the runways at Ringway to keep meticulous count of the incoming Viscounts and Britannias. Not that it is entirely a juvenile pastime. Thirteen-hundred cars were packed into the spectators' enclosure at Ringway on Easter Monday paying a toll of 1s for a twelve hour spotting levy made only on motorists; small kids on bikes are allowed in free. A gentleman of sixty regularly turns up at the weekend from Preston, and is becoming such a part of the airport scene that he is unofficially permitted to carry out his spotting from the greater convenience of the main buildings. There is also a Society of Northern Aviation Enthusiasts, with thirty-five paid up members whose ages range from fifteen to forty. Their activities tend to be a bit more serious than the mere ticking off of aircraft. One man is writing a history of the Handley Page Herald, there are regular film shows on various aspects of aviation, and the majority of members (even up to the age of forty) have ambitions to "get into the aircraft business", somehow, some day.

But in the spectators' enclosure small boys predominate. For them it is a gripping pastime which, in most cases seems to have developed from an earlier obsession with train-spotting. As one boy put it, "Train-spotting's a bit dull compared with planes. You never see any foreign trains in this country". But the devotion of the grocer's assistant dates from the occasion nine years ago when, with his parents, he watched the first apprehensive plane load of civic dignitaries set off to fly the Atlantic non-stop from Manchester in a Douglas DC-6B. "It's a right laugh sometimes", he remarked irrelevantly. "You get hares running across the runway between the legs of passengers when they're getting out". Then he recollected himself. "That BUA from Dusseldorf is nearly three-quarters of an hour late now".

Some of them travel amazing distances for an eyeful of a really important plane. The Comet, because of its rarity value is the most sought after aircraft at Ringway, followed by the Boeing 707 and the Caravelle. Right at the bottom of the scale comes the Dakota, known among aficionados as the "Flying Coffin". A cycle ride from Stockport is nothing; two boys recently travelled from Bradford. An appearance once a week (Saturday is the busiest day, with the holiday traffic) indicates no more than tepid enthusiasm. One lad turns up every day during the holidays and two or three evenings a week during term-time, when the light holds out. The best time to be around is when London Airport is fogbound. Then you get some really rare diversions, according to one lad. Occasionally a plane bursts a tyre on landing, to liven things up, but this is not a thing that the really keen spotter hopes to see. He appreciates the smooth, uneventful flight as much as any air traffic controller. And he is almost as well equipped, with a pair of binoculars or a telescope and a book which lists every identification number in civil aviation.

The spotters at Ringway have only one complaint when they compare their status with the spotters at London Airport. At London, they say, you can watch the planes go by from a balcony among the terminal buildings, and there is a loud-speaker commentary to keep the doubtful informed of events. The balcony will, in fact, be available at Ringway when the terminal extensions are completed later this year. No one yet knows whether a commentary will be provided.

First visits on scheduled flights were Air France (AF960): SE.210 F-BJTE (22nd) & F-BKGZ (2nd) and Vanguard G-APEU (1st). Equipment changes were KLM (KL019): CV-340s PH-CGG (6th) & PH-CGI (14th). ILS Traffic included Aerolineas Argentinas HS.748s LV-PRJ (9th/12th/18th) & LV-PUC (27th).

International flights were operated during the summer as follows:

AIR FRANCE - Four-weekly to Paris with SE.210s, increasing to six-weekly between July and September. A thrice-weekly cargo flight to Paris was introduced from 5th May with Douglas DC-4Fs.

AER LINGUS - Amsterdam (4 x weekly), Brussels (3 x weekly), Copenhagen (2 x weekly), Dusseldorf (3 x weekly), Frankfurt (4 x weekly) & Zurich (1 x weekly), all operated by Viscounts.

BEA - Amsterdam/Dublin/Dusseldorf/Paris & Zurich. Summer routes to Basle/Barcelona/Palma & Milan.

BOAC - B.707s operate outbound to New York and onwards to Baltimore as BA537 (four-weekly) & inbound as BA538 (five-weekly inbound). Bristol Britannias serve Boston (3 x weekly), Montreal (6 x weekly), New York (3 x weekly) and Toronto (4 x weekly). The cargo DC-7 operation remained unchanged at twice-weekly to Montreal/New York.

KLM - Operated to Amsterdam thrice-weekly (KL149/150), with one of these flights operating onwards to Dublin (KL151/2). Also operated was a four-weekly cargo flight to Amsterdam (KL019/020).

SABENA - Thrice-weekly to/from New York with B.707s (SN545/6) & DC-7s (SN549/550). The evening Brussels service remains twice-weekly with CV-440s and Ostend operated June-September thrice-weekly with a mix of CV-440s/DC-4s & DC-6s.

SWISSAIR - Operated twice-weekly from/to Basle/Zurich (SR118/9 with CV-440s). From 18th May a twice-weekly night service to Zurich was introduced, operated by SE.210s until 25th September.

4th   With the exception of the diverted Valetta, the only RAF movements this month were by Avro Ansons. Starting today was the first of three visits with C.19 TX256 as 'JES 06' f/t Pershore (also 6th/9th), VM340 (12th) as 'AKG 41' f/t Carlisle and VM363 (11th) as 'NOZ 04' f/t Andover.

10th   Royal Navy Sea Devon XK895 (Navair 746) was en route from Lee-on-Solent to Stretton, when it diverted in as a full emergency at 1134, landing on one engine. Subsequent visitors with personnel and spares for the stricken aircraft were Sea Devon XJ324 (10th/13th/16th), XJ350 (12th), XK895 (16th) and Sea Herons XR441 (11th) & XR442 (17th).

13th April 1962 - The Bristol Britannia 312 was the backbone of BOAC's transatlantic operations out of Manchester during the early 1960s. Running in conjunction with, and eventually replaced by, the newly-introduced Boeing 707s. In the background, a short stub of a taxiway can be seen, which formed part of the old eastern dispersal during the Second World War. (Hubert Parrish)

13th   MEA Comet OD-ADT (ME206 from Heathrow) arrived at 1312 to take the Lord Mayor of Manchester and his entourage out to Beirut. The same aircraft made the return visit on the 26th (ME205 from Beirut). A second MEA Comet, OD-ADR, made its first visit on the 24th May, night-stopping from/to Frankfurt.

16th   RAF Valetta VW826 arrived at 1715 (Rafair 5414) en route Benbecula-Northolt as a fuel diversion!

24th A new light aircraft type was the US-built Champion 7EC Traveller, a single-engine, two-seater with fixed landing gear, designed for flight training and personal use. In a colourful red and white livery, N9837Y arrived at 2033 from Prestwick, before departing the following afternoon to its base at USAF Chevelston. In 1967 it was re-registered as G-AVDU, but sold on in Eire twelve years later as EI-BHV.

25th USAF Douglas C-47 48673 made its first visit today from RAF Alconbury, departing later for Wisley.

26th BEA had used the Douglas DC-3 (Pionair) since its inception in 1946 from various UK points, including Manchester. The last year of BEA Pionair operations at Ringway was 1960, but today saw the final visit of one of these long-serving aircraft, with the arrival of Dakota G-AHCU at 1639 from Heathrow, departing to Glasgow at 1831. On the 19th May 1962, G-ALTT operated the type's final service on BEA's Scottish internal network between Islay, Campbeltown and Glasgow (Renfrew).

28th Avro Anson D-IDEK was operated by Aero Exploration, but on charter to the British company Meridian Air Maps. The aircraft, which made the first of two round-trips from Coventry today (also 30th), was used for Ordinance Survey work to conduct a photographic road survey. It was sold later in the year and restored to its original registration of G-AGWA, but never certified. It was cancelled as 'withdrawn from use' in June 1964. Its nose and tail sections were utilised for instructional use later on, but it was scrapped by 1979.

MAY 1962

May's weather was cyclonic for the first and third week, but otherwise high pressure was in control, although thunderstorms with heavy rain were widespread on the 3rd/27th. Extreme temperatures saw 21°C at Herne Bay (7th) and a low of -6°C at Glenmore Lodge, Northern Ireland (19th).

A letter sent in to an aviation magazine gives an insight, although not typical, of what travelling transatlantic from the USA to the UK was like in 1962: *'Having just completed a 13,000 mile journey to California and back, just over half of these were by bus within the United States. The most uncomfortable part of the journey was not, as I feared, the nine nights spent on buses, but the flight back from New York in a BOAC Britannia. Flight BA560 takes thirteen hours from New York to London, with stops at Boston, Prestwick and Manchester. At each of these places, some fifty minutes were spent on the ground and I looked forward to the chance of stretching my legs and making phone calls to my friends in Boston and Manchester. To my amazement, neither at Boston nor Manchester were passengers allowed to leave their seats. The buses had offered a rest stop every two to three hours, and passengers were able to leave their more comfortable seats to walk around the town and/or take refreshments. To keep passengers in their seat for fifty minutes each stop, having already sat there for many hours, borders on cruelty. When I complained, I was told by a BOAC stewardess that it was something to do with the American authorities, which I doubted since there had been no Customs at New York and I could see no reason why we should not mix with the public again at Boston. Exactly the same thing happened on reaching Manchester. We had not yet cleared British Customs, but at Prestwick we had been allowed to walk around, under the supervision of the stewardess. What is possible in Scotland is surely possible in England. The Britannia cannot compete with the buses or with sea travel, but surely these annoying regulations can be removed.'* Responding, a BOAC spokesperson brushed the criticism aside saying "It was the first complaint they had received, and most passengers wanted to reach their final destination as quickly as possible".

The following were seen during the summer months operating ITs to various destinations: Aeromaritime (Nice/Perpignan), Aviaco (Palma), Balair (Zurich), Caledonian (Malaga/Palma), Channel Airways (Ostend), Cunard Eagle Bergen), Dan-Air (Basle/Ostend), Derby Airways (Perpignan), Lloyd Intl (Naples/Nice/Rimini/Venice), SAM (Milan/Rimini), Silver City (Basle/Palma/Stavanger), Starways (Malaga/Newquay/Nice/Pisa/Rimini/Valencia/Venice), T.A.I. (Nice), Tradair (Maastricht) and Transair Sweden (Malaga/Palma/Valencia).

First visits on scheduled flights during the month were Air France (AF960): SE.210s F-BJTF (25th), F-BJTG (11th) & F-BJTI (28th), BOAC (BA538): B.707 G-ARRA (27th), Swissair (SR718): SE.210s HB-ICU (18th) & HB-ICW (25th) and Jersey Airlines Herald G-APWE (25th). Equipment changes were Sabena (SN623): DC-6s OO-CTH (18th) & OO-CTK (25th).

1st Another new airline to Ringway in 1962 was American carrier Riddle Airlines. Douglas DC-7C N8215H (also 3rd/23rd August) arrived at 1857 from Palma, departing later that evening with a cargo of machine tools bound for Buffalo via Shannon. They made further flights with DC-7s N8216H (20th/30th August), N8219H (11th May/27th July), N310G (12th August) & N4059K (2nd August/9th September).

2nd Morane-Saulnier MS.760 Paris D-INGE had the honour of being the first executive jet to land at Manchester. Arriving at 1639 from Hanover, it departed to Frankfurt two days later. A second, D-INGA, also turned up on the 28th.

2nd Cunard Eagle B.707 VR-BBW (Heathrow/Prestwick) arrived on a demonstration flight at 1144. In the light of the Cunard-BOAC tie up, it was re-registered later in the year as G-ARWD and repainted into BOAC colours.

5th Douglas DC-4 F-BELF inaugurated Air France's new Manchester-Paris freight service, marking this particular aircraft's only visit. The flights, which were offering around 7,500-kilos capacity per flight, operated three-times-weekly. Other aircraft used during the month were F-BBDD (10th/17th/23rd/24th/ 26th/30th), F-BBDJ (12th/16th), & F-BHEH (9th/19th).

5th The UK's newest airline, Euravia, made its first appearance today when L-049 G-ARVP (formerly with EL AL) positioned up from Luton to operate their first IT flight from Manchester to Perpignan. Two further Constellation first visits from the airline were L-049 G-AHEN (11th - also ex-EL AL) & L-049 G-ANUR (30th June), which were all regular visitors throughout May and June. G-AHEN had an interesting career to date. On the 8th January 1951, it overshot the runway at Filton on a crew training flight, and was declared a write off. However, it was dismantled and ultimately shipped to New York where it was completely rebuilt with parts salvaged from two other Connies. It was delivered to California-Hawaii Airways in April 1952 as N74192, and served with the airline until October 1953 when it was sold to EL AL.

6th A couple of interesting visitors today were French Air Force Douglas C-47 F-RAFF at 1158 (f/t Villacoublay), and EL AL Boeing 707 at 1556 (LY411/2 - f/t Tel Aviv via Heathrow), which had made its first visit to Manchester in December 1961.

8th Northolt-based US Navy Douglas R4D Skytrain 17151 arrived at 1230 on a round-trip from Paris-Orly. Also two USAF C-47s making their first visits today were 51133 at 0953 (f/t Northolt) & 49560 at 1410 (also f/t Orly). Finally, rounding off a good day for military visitors was the appearance of RAF Pembroke WV704 (Rafair 5485 - Northolt/Biggin Hill).

11th Possibly the best military visitor of the month was German Air Force Dakota CA+015, arriving at 2050 to night-stop, departing the following morning for Southend.

11th May 1962 - Transair Sweden began their first summer IT programme from Ringway today, with Palma as their first destination. The four DC-6s used on the flights operating until the 14th October were SE-BDH (as seen above), SE-BDI, SE-BDM & SE-BDZ. (Hubert Parrish)

12th Aviaco began their summer IT programme, with Douglas DC-4 EC-AEK operating the first of their weekly flights f/t Palma (AO1062/3). A second (AO1068/9) was added on the 10th June, and both flights operated until the 28th & 29th September respectively. Other DC-4s used during the summer were EC-ACD/ACE/ACF/AEK/AEO & AEP.

14th Finnair Douglas DC-3 OH-LCK night-stopped, after arriving from Gothenburg at 1502. It departed the following morning to Copenhagen with a cargo of machine tools.

19th Flying Tiger CL-44 N449T (also 1st July) was the second of its type to visit, operating Chateauroux-Gander. In November their CL-44s temporarily operated transatlantic cargo flights on behalf of BOAC.

19th Dan-Air also began summer IT programmes from Manchester, with today's first flight operated by G-AMAH. They went on to base an Airspeed AS.65 Ambassador, operating to Ostend (Wed/Sat/Sun) & Basle (Sun).

20th Cunard Eagle's programme is much reduced, compared to recent years. They restarted their summer weekly flight to Bergen, but this year it routes via Newcastle. Today's first flight was operated by Douglas DC-6 G-APON.

24th Two Heathrow-based Ambassadors operated by Shell Petroleum for VIP communication flights, were G-AMAA (f/v 5th February 1964) & G-AMAG which arrived today at 1248 from Heathrow. Both aircraft were acquired early 1959. In April 1966, Dan Air lost G-ALZX in a landing accident at Beauvais, so G-AMAG was purchased as a replacement. Dan Air also acquired Shell's other Ambassador, G-AMAA, but it never entered service and was used for spares.

24th The only ILS visitor noted in May was another new Aerolineas Argentinas HS.748, with LV-PUF.

25th Mercury Airlines took delivery of Heron G-ANCI after an overhaul by Hants & Sussex Aviation.

25th Wassmer Super IV F-BKJK from Lindholme, which was a first visit of type, night-stopped inside Mercury Airlines hangar. This was a French-built single engined low-winged monoplane, with a retractable nosewheel. The first British example, G-ATSY, did not appear on the register until 1966 and first visited on the 13th September that year.

26th Yet another airline, this time French operator T.A.I., began a summer programme from Ringway when Douglas DC-6 F-BHEE arrived at 2253 today on a flight to Nice. Apart from F-BHEE, the following DC-6s were also used during the summer: F-BGTY/BGW/BHEF/BHMS/BIAM & BIAO.

26th The third of Aer Lingus' three Boeing 720 aircraft, EI-ALC, made its first visit today. Positioning in from Dublin, it departed on a transatlantic charter via Shannon (IN023).

29th L-40 Meta-Sokol G-APWV was a first visit of type, arriving from Dublin today, before its departure to Biggin Hill. It was also its only appearance at Manchester. Built in Czechoslovakia, it was a sports and touring four-seat single-engine low-wing aeroplane. In July 1965, it was damaged beyond repair in a landing accident at Stapleford Tawney.

30th BKS Ambassador G-ALZW diverted in at 1814 with engine trouble, en route from Newcastle to Belfast.

31st Helicopters were still uncommon visitors to Ringway, so the first appearance of BEA Helicopters Westland S-55, en route Chester-Gatwick, was only the third of the type to visit. It was sold to Bristows in 1969, and withdrawn by 1977.

JUNE 1962

June started and ended with anticyclonic weather, but from the 9th-25th weak frontal systems moved through the UK. The month's temperatures extremes saw 27°C at Wakefield (8th) and a low of -6°C at Santon Downham, Suffolk (1st/3rd). A minor tornado caused structural damage at South Croydon on the 9th.

Questions were being asked in parliament about a Silver City service currently operating from Ringway on behalf of the Atomic Authority. Seen as a covert attempt at more protectionism on behalf of BEA, a Highlands MP complained that BEA were providing a good enough service to Glasgow and Wick, so there was no need for Silver City to fly the route as well. He argued that if the Atomic Authority based at Risley was unable to obtain the service required from BEA, the answer was not necessarily to bring in a private operator. Silver City was operating a Tues/Wed evening departure from Ringway to Dounreay, with return the following morning.

Aircraft making first visits on scheduled flights were <u>Air France (AF960):</u> SE.210s F-BHRN (8th) & F-BJTH (17th), <u>Swissair (SR718):</u> SE.210s HB-ICN (22nd), HB-ICS (8th), & HB-ICT (29th) and <u>Jersey Airlines</u> Heralds G-APWB (1st), G-APWF (9th), G-APWG (16th), G-APWH (17th) & G-APWI (9th). Equipment changes were <u>Air France (AF898):</u> Dan-Air Avro Yorks G-ANTJ (16th/27th/28th/30th) and Bristol 170s G-AMLL

(21st/23rd) & G-APLH (20th), <u>KLM (KL151)</u>: Constellation PH-LKB (16th) & Electra PH-LLF (30th), and <u>Sabena</u> <u>(SN623)</u>: DC-6s OO-CTK (1st/8th).

ILS Traffic noted this month included Aerolineas Argentinas HS.748s LV-PVA (2nd) & LV-PUM (13th).

1st USAF Douglas C-47 47981 (also 6th July) was another first time visitor today, making the first of its two appearances this year. Its stop was very brief, before returning to Pau, northern Pyrenees.

2nd June 1962 - Italian charter airline SAM (Societa Aria Mediterranea) began their IT summer programme today, again with a weekly DC-6 flight (MQ392/3 f/t Rimini). The following week, a weekly Milan flight (MQ312/3) was introduced. Douglas DC-6B I-DIME as seen above was used on today's flight and others used during the summer were I-DIMA, DIMD, DIME, DIMI, & DIMP (f/v - 14th July). (Hubert Parrish)

2nd Aero 145 G-AROE (f/t Birmingham) was one of only three different examples that visited during the decade, with the other two being G-APRR (f/v 28th September 1963) & G-ASYY (f/v 21st May 1967). This unusual looking twin piston-engined aircraft was the first product of Czechoslovakia's post-war aviation industry. It proved a great success, with many of the 590 produced being exported.

3rd British United Douglas C-54 G-AOFW positioned in from Gatwick to operate an IT flight to/from Basle on behalf of Silver City. In December 1955, Freddie Laker's company, Air Charter, acquired the C-54A for transport work in Germany and troop flights from Stansted to Cyprus. In 1959 it was moved from trooping flights onto the Southend-Calais route, flying day-trippers without passports until July 1960, when Air Charter merged with B.U. In April 1963, Aviation Traders began its conversion into an ATL.98 Carvair, with the first flight as such taking place on 11th February 1964.

4th The month saw a number of foreign light aircraft making first visits. PA-23 Apache OY-AIU (today), Jodel OE-AMW (17th), PA-23 Apache OY-DAI (20th) & Twin Bonanza HB-GAY (23rd).

7th KLM operated the first of two New York charters with Douglas DC-7 PH-DSK and PH-DSO (20th).

9th Caledonian began operations from Ringway today, with Saturday flights during the summer to Malaga & Palma with Douglas DC-7C G-ARYE. The airline was formed in April 1961, but the first scheduled flight did not take place until 29th November 1961, when Douglas DC-7C G-ARUD (ex-OO-SFD leased from Sabena) operated Gatwick to Barbados. A major setback occurred on 4th March 1962, when their only aircraft crashed shortly after takeoff at Douala. It was heavily laden, on a charter flight from Lourenco Marques, Mozambique to Luxembourg. One hundred and eleven people were killed, making it the worst accident in British airline history at the time. This left the airline with no aircraft, so a replacement was sought and they turned to Sabena again, leasing Douglas DC-7C OO-SFG as G-ARYE. During the month it achieved a remarkable utilisation of 357 hours, equating to an average of almost 13 hours a day.

9th   Finnair CV-440 OH-LRG arrived at 1838 on a passenger charter (AY3876 from Copenhagen). It had been purchased from Alitalia the previous year, and served with the airline until its final flight on 1st December 1979.

15th   In amongst the growing number of airliners at Ringway was Hornet Moth G-AELO, operated by the Surrey & Kent Flying Club. It arrived at 2022 from Biggin Hill for a weekend stay, on what must have been a very enjoyable VFR flight on a pleasant summer's evening!

15th   Only three weeks into their summer programme, French operator UAT were forced to use Air Afrique DC-6 TU-TBD for two round-trips to Perpignan. It initially arrived from Le Bourget at 0844 and operated further flights to Perpignan and Nice the following day, before positioning out to Gatwick.

16th   US Navy Douglas C-118 51-17640 arrived at 1248 from Shannon, departing over an hour later for RAF Kinloss. This aircraft saw continuous service until 1976, when it was, and still is, preserved at Lackland AFB, Texas.

18th   Today was the last visit by UK airline Trans European, a rare visitor to Ringway, when L-049 G-AMUP arrived at 1939 with a group of nuns from Lourdes. Unfortunately, the receivers were called in the following month due to mounting financial losses, and operations ceased in August when three of their aircraft were impounded at various airports. L-049 G-AMUP was purchased by Euravia, and became a common visitor over the next two years.

21st   The first visit of a US Army U1-A Otter occurred when 55-3303 arrived at 1255 from Frankfurt, later departing to Prestwick. It made further visits on the 7th/17th July, both times routing Frankfurt-Benbecula.

26th   Dornier Do.28 D-IBAQ was a first visit of type, arriving from Gatwick today, before departing to Glasgow on a demonstration flight.

27th   Beech 95 EI-AMC arrived at 1843 from Dublin to become a Ringway resident. In March 1966 it departed to Cranfield and returned as G-ATRC.

30th   Nothing to do with Ringway, but the trials and tribulations of Silver City's Operations Manager at Blackpool were too good to ignore! The story began when Bristol 170 G-AGVC landed at Ronaldsway at 0925 today, one hour late. Whilst taxiing off the runway, its undercarriage collapsed leaving it deposited on the taxiway. The aircraft suffered damage to the wing, tailplane and other parts of the fuselage and was subsequently declared a write off. The only other Bristol 170s at Blackpool were G-AIFM & G-AIME, which were both unserviceable and as a consequence the IOM service was without an aircraft. To remedy this, a BEA Viscount was chartered, but it soon went u/s at Ronaldsway, so there was no aircraft again. A Starways Douglas DC-4 was then chartered, but this too went u/s at Newquay, before arriving at Blackpool. Eventually, two Silver City southern-based aircraft (Bristol 170 G-AIMH & Douglas DC-3 G-AMYV), a Tyne-Tees DC-3 G-AMNV and a Derby Airways Argonaut G-ALHY took over the day's operations, with flights running up to eight hours late.

JULY 1962

The month was mainly dry, but cool, with the exception of the 10th, when heavy rain led to flooding in central and southern England. In Worcestershire, nearly an inch of rain fell in 25 minutes. The month's temperature extremes saw 27°C at Cannington (25th) and a low of -1°C at Alwen, North Wales (6th).

The chairman of BEA revealed the corporation's six busiest routes. Fourth was Heathrow-Manchester, carrying 266,000 passengers to the year ending 30th June 1962, which had doubled over the last two years. BEA passed a notable landmark, by carrying more than 600,000 for the first time in a single month.

Ringway handled 444,823 passengers during the first six months, an increase of 15% over the same time last year.

The only aircraft making first visits on scheduled flights were Aer Lingus: Viscount EI-AMA (12th) & Air France (AF960): SE.210 F-BJTJ (31st). Equipment changes were Air France (AF898): Dan-Air Bristol 170s G-AINL (4th/5th/6th) & G-AMLL (7th) and KLM (KL151): Constellation PH-LKE (28th).

ILS traffic noted included Aerolineas Argentina HS.748s LV-PUP (2nd/17th), LV-PVF (23rd/25th), LV-PVH (19th/20th) and Jodel G-ARRD (31st) carrying out three ILS approaches during the evening.

1st   Viking G-AHOZ was noted today wearing Channel Airways' new colour scheme.

3rd   Three RAF Devons making first visits this month began with Devon C.1 VP976 operated by RAF Transport Command, on its only appearance at Ringway during the 1960s. Arriving at 1128 today from RAF Wyton, and leaving for RAF Woodvale, it returned later in the day from Jurby before departing back to

Wyton. Another Devon C.2 VP955 (7th), made its first visit at 1000 from Northolt, departing to Little Rissington. Finally C.1 VP968 (23rd) arrived from/to Leavesden as callsign 'Samson'.

3rd   This month's foreign light contingent began with the arrival of Cessna 175 D-EHUF at 1834 from Calais, clearing customs before departing to Barton the following morning. Others were Dove PH-VLC (16th/20th) & Beech 65 LN-IKB (22nd).

6th   KLM Douglas DC-8 PH-DCD was the only aircraft of its type to make a first visit this year. It arrived at 1016 today from Amsterdam, operating a passenger charter to New York via Shannon.

7th   Finnair CV-440 OH-LRB (AY4012/3 f/t Copenhagen) was the second to visit in as many months.

7th   Bristows Whirlwind G-AODO arrived at 1808 from Blackpool and stayed for two days, before returning to its Redhill base. In 1963 it was re-registered in Bermuda for their Caribbean operations.

8th July 1962 - A great way to spend a sunny Sunday afternoon! Hermes G-ALDG 'City of Chester' is seen on short finals, with the Airport Hotel in the background. This would be its final year of operation, as it was withdrawn in October and used as a cabin trainer at Gatwick. (MA Archive via Ringway Publications)

11th   There were no USAF C-47s of note this month, but there were two Douglas C-54s, which both made first visits. The first, 44-9045 of the 322 Air Division, arrived at 1215 today from Dreux, departing to Brize Norton. The second, 45-0491 (24th), stayed overnight en route from Wiesbaden to Lajes, in the Azores.

14th   Queen's Flight Heron XM295 (Kittyhawk - f/t Oxford) was carrying Princess Margaret for a local engagement.

14th   Flying Tiger L-1049H N6922C arrived on a tech-stop en route from Goose Bay to Seville. A second, L-1049H N6917C (Gander/Helsinki) on the 19th, became the final Flying Tiger Constellation to visit Ringway on 18th July 1964.

17th   The only Avro Anson this month, which was also a first visit, was C.19 VM367 (Norwich/Leconfield as MAS91). It operated for the No.12 Group Communications Flight at Norwich until February 1963, when it was struck off charge.

22nd Ex-Seaboard L-1049H N1009C, now operated by Intercontinental, arrived at 1500 from Gatwick on the airline's only visit to Ringway. Operating for the airline until 1964, it was eventually sold in Venezuela as YC-C-LBP. For the next six years it was used by several South American airlines, before being withdrawn at Miami in 1970.

30th An interesting aircraft change occurred today, when Iberia L-1049G EC-AQM (AO1068 from Palma) arrived at 0504, due to an unserviceable Douglas DC-4 running nearly twelve hours late.

AUGUST 1962

August was disappointing, with low pressure dominating, bringing generally cool and wet weather. Bank Holiday Monday (27th) was the coldest since 1888. On the 5th, Langdale, Cumbria recorded over five inches of rain over a 24 hour period. The month's temperature extremes saw 27°C at Gillingham (19th) and a low of -1°C at various places (13th/14th).

It was reported that Ringway's new terminal buildings would be completed by 30th September. Only finishing touches would be required to the £2.8million structures, before Prince Philip arrives to open them officially on 22nd October. However, the administrative staff would take until the 1st December before the buildings were fully operational. In the meantime the public had to 'make do' with a jumble of prefabricated buildings acting as the terminal. A number of 'dry-runs' would take place to provide working experience of the baggage conveyors, TV announcing systems and the general communications within the building before Prince Philip's arrival. With electricity supplied from its own substation, the terminal will have sick bays, VIP lounges, a restaurant and customs search rooms, as well as a TV room for Press interviews.

All Air France flights between London, Manchester and Paris were cancelled on the 6th-8th this month, due to a 48 hour strike by Air France navigators over pension rights.

Just one scheduled first visit this month was BOAC (BA537): B.707 G-ARWE (14th). Equipment changes were also in short supply, with KLM (KL151): DC-7 PH-DSD (11th).

ILS Traffic noted during the month included a RAF Comet, overshooting at 1702 as 'MOFFM' en route Prestwick-Lyneham (21st) & RAF Vulcan B.2 XL426 (24th).

1st After many months of flight testing, the first HS.748 finally touched down at Ringway today. Hawker Siddeley demonstrator HS.748 arrived at 1549 from Woodford to clear customs, before departing to Seville on a short sales tour. It returned on the 4th via Exeter, and left for Woodford the following morning.

2nd Avions Fairey Bristol 170 OO-FAG (ex-LTU D-BODO), made the first of several visits as such today, on a round-trip from the Fairey facility at Gosselies. Its arrival was in connection with the GAF Jindivik target drone programme. It is also used for the transportation of F-104 fuselages from Turin for assembly at the company's Belgian factory for the Air Force. Further visits during the year took place on 6th/7th/8th August.

5th KLM Douglas DC-8 PH-DCD made its second visit today, arriving at 0640 from New York.

7th Canadian Pacific Airlines produced two transatlantic charters. Britannia CF-CZC arrived at 1226 today as CP370 from Toronto/Goose Bay and first visit CF-CZA arrived at 1107 (15th) as CP370 from Toronto/Sondre Stromfjord.

7th Saturn Airways also operated two charters during August. Today, DC-6 N90772 operated from Prestwick to Keflavik and N90770 (28th) from Gander to Prestwick. Both of these ex-American Airlines aircraft were sold by 1964.

8th Apart from the visit of Dove PH-VLC today and PH-FST (14th), the only other light aircraft of note was Beech 65 N1401M (17th) operated by IBM.

12th Flying Tiger L-1049H N6919C made its only visit to Ringway today, arriving from Torrejon AFB at 2133. It stayed overnight, before departing to the States via Shannon the following morning.

12th Breguet BR.763 F-BASU, known as the Deux-Ponts (Double-Decker which was not an official name), arrived at 2208 from Paris-Orly with an engine for SE.210 F-BHRC which had gone u/s. Air France ordered twelve aircraft, with the first entering service in 1953. It was capable of carrying 107 passengers on two floors, linked by an elevator. However, it was deemed redundant by 1958, when the Caravelle entered service, which was faster and more comfortable, with a greater range. Six aircraft were transferred to the Armée de l'Air.

22nd A slightly different Avro Anson visit was T.21 WD402. Operated by the Aeroplane and Armament Experimental Establishment at Boscombe Down, it arrived at 1001 today from Andover (callsign KMJ 01).

12th August 1962 - Derby Airways, later British Midland, purchased three Canadair C-4 Argonauts last year, following the demise of Overseas Aviation. G-ALHS is seen taxiing out on an afternoon departure to Klagenfurt, but the Stockport air disaster in 1967 brought the operation of these aircraft to a swift conclusion. (MA Archive via Ringway Publications)

18th August 1962 - Another shot from the footpath that led from Ringway Road to Moss Lane - undoubtedly an excellent location to watch aircraft! Sabena Douglas DC-7F OO-SFC seen here (SN550 from New York), operated for the airline until its withdrawal in May 1968. A year later it was sold to Spantax as EC-BSQ, with whom it ended its flying days in October 1973. It was used as a fire trainer at Las Palmas as late as 2008. (MA Archive via Ringway Publications)

SEPTEMBER 1962

Last month's fine weather continued into the first week of September, but apart from some high pressure from the 18th-24th, it was cool, cloudy and wet. Gales were widespread on the 29th/30th with a gust of 72kt recorded at Lizard Point. The temperature extremes saw 28°C at Writtle, Essex (3rd) and a low of -2°C at Santon Downham, Suffolk (18th).

A record-breaking 130,000 passengers were handled by BEA at Ringway last month, an increase of 4% on the same month last year. More than 35,400 of these were on the Manchester-Heathrow route.

Cunard Eagle has been refused permission by the Air Transport Licensing Board to compete on the Manchester-Heathrow route, meaning the monopoly enjoyed by BEA would continue. The following routes however were granted - Derby Airways could operate a Manchester-Birmingham-Palma scheduled service, alternating with a Manchester-Birmingham-Barcelona service, a Manchester-Ostend service and a weekly service instead of a fortnightly service to Perpignan.

Two scheduled first visits were <u>Air France (AF960)</u>: SE.210 F-BHRP (3rd) and <u>Swissair (SR718)</u>: CV-990 HB-ICE (25th). Equipment changes were <u>KLM (KL151)</u>: Constellation PH-LKE (29th) and <u>Sabena (SN623)</u>: DC-6 EC-ASR (14th/21st/28th).

The only ILS traffic noted during the month was Brazilian Air Force HS.748 C91-2500 (19th).

3rd This month's light aircraft arrivals began with Bonanza D-ENAR. Others were Doves PH-MAD (4th/6th) & PH-FST (17th), Twin Bonanza D-IEHE (5th), Philips Heron PH-ILA (11th) and Beech 65 D-IKOW (17th).

4th KLM Douglas DC-7C PH-DSR, arriving at 0839 today, was operating an inbound charter from New York. This aircraft, which was the last DC-7 built, was sold the following month as N904ME.

10th Canadian Pacific Britannia CF-CZD was another first time visitor, the fourth to Ringway. Arriving from Heathrow at 2306 (CP391), it left for Montreal via Sondre Stromfjord.

10th The latest aircraft used by the Dutch electronics firm Philips, made its first visit today. Fokker F-27 PH-LIP arrived at 2150 from Eindhoven, and stayed until the 13th. It had made its first flight earlier in the year on the 26th March, prior to delivery on the 4th April. It was operated until April 1975, when it was sold to German operator WDL as D-BAKA.

13th Southend-based Avro Anson G-ALIH, operated by Ekco Electronics, arrived at 1136 on a round-trip from Coventry. It was airworthy until September 1967, when its Certificate of Airworthiness expired. In November 1970 it was donated to Newark Air Museum, but it was destroyed by fire the following year.

15th Possibly the best military movement of the year, was the arrival of Danish Air Force Douglas C-54 N-242 at 0942 to night-stop f/t RAF Cottesmore. Formerly with the US Air Force, it served with the Danish military until 1978 and is currently preserved at Rand, Johannesburg with the South African Historic Flight.

16th Over the next couple of days a mass exodus of troops was organised to Brussels and Dusseldorf, with several flights originating from Ringway. The aircraft used operating several times over the two days were Skyways L-749 Constellations G-ALAL & G-ANUR and Dan-Air Bristol 170s G-AINL, G-ALZX, G-AMAE & G-APLH.

19th Bristow's Whirlwind G-AOHE and Widgeon G-APPS operated from/to Belle Vue until the 28th.

21st Canadian Aero Service Douglas DC-3 CF-IMA, which originated from Lagos, arrived at 1616 from Gatwick. Equipped for survey work, it sported a magnetometer boom from its rear fuselage. It was in the UK to carry out a geophysical and photographic survey of parts of Britain on behalf of the Canadian government and private concerns in Canada, and was based at Ringway until the 2nd December.

21st First time visitor Avro Anson VM330 (ESM22 f/t White Waltham) stayed until the 23rd. Another Anson, VM371, arriving the following day, was also a first visit (ESM21 Cambridge/Shawbury).

22nd RAF Pembroke C.1 WV733 (callsign MPTJF), operated by the Flying Training Command, arrived at 1239 today on a sortie from Shawbury.

22nd Beaver AL.1 XP816 (Army 384 f/t Middle Wallop) was the first of the Army Air Corps type to visit. Deliveries began in 1961, with most of the initial batch being based with 656 Sqn at Middle Wallop.

24th Possibly the only visit by a Lockheed 10A Electra occurred today, when F-BERT arrived at 1245 from Gatwick, staying for four hours before returning there. The Lockheed Model 10 Electra was a twin-engine, all metal monoplane airliner, developed by the Lockheed Aircraft Corporation in the 1930s to compete with the Boeing 247 and Douglas DC-2. The type was best known for being flown by Amelia Earhart on her ill fated around-the-world expedition in 1937.

25th Swissair CV-990 Coronado HB-ICE was a first visit of type, ironically operating the last SR718/9 of the season. Eventually eight aircraft would be operated by Swissair, with all becoming regular visitors to Ringway throughout the 1960s.

27th Schiebe Motorspatz D-KEBU was air-freighted into Manchester by Air France DC-4 F-BBDD. It then left by road two days later, inside a glider trailer bound for Newcastle. This unusual type is derived from a Spatz glider, and a two or four-cylinder, two-stroke engine fitted to the nose. It was moved to Leeming eventually, to be near its new owner in Northallerton, North Yorkshire where it became G-ASPY.

29th UK airline Tradair had been operating frequent IT flights from/to Maastricht during the summer, but the arrival of G-AIXR at 1604 proved to their final movement at Ringway. In November 1961, they appointed a receiver at the request of Barclays Bank, who gave them one year to return to profitability. Sadly by November 1962 when the company's debt was almost £200,000, Channel Airways began negotiations for a takeover. On 31st December 1962 Tradair became a wholly owned subsidiary of Channel Airways.

29th One of only two Grumman Mallards to grace the UK register, was G-ASCS making its first visit from Ronaldsway. This ten-seat passenger aircraft was used as the personal transport of Sebastian de Ferranti. Registered to Ferranti from August 1962 to January 1969, its time was divided between Manchester and the electronic czar's country estate at Beaumaris, Anglesey, due to its amphibious capabilities. It was replaced later by Jet Ranger G-AVSN in 1969. On 24th May 1968 it landed at Ringway from Lisbon via Jersey after six months of inactivity when a proposed sale fell through. It spent two days parked at Fairey Aviation, before departing for the final time to Northolt. During June 1968 it was used briefly by Grosvenor Estates Ltd (the Duke of Westminster's main property company) as a temporary replacement for their Grumman Goose amphibian G-ASXG, whilst undergoing modifications to turboprop power in Cambridge. On the 2nd June after two weeks of operations on the Scottish lochs, G-ASCS departed on a business trip to Central Africa. The Mallard cleared Customs at Luton, bound ultimately for Libreville, Gabon; but the outward flight was complicated by a strike in France. Due to this, it took a devious route via Brussels, Geneva, Barcelona, Madrid & Lisbon. Political considerations on the West African coastal route caused minor delays, but the Mallard proceeded via Agadir, Las Palmas, Dakar, Freetown, Abidjan & Cotonou, before arriving at Libreville on the 7th June after a mechanically trouble free journey of 5,280 miles. The return flight of 4,580 miles to Paris Le Bourget, was made in 29+ hours flying time over three days, routing via Abidjan, Freetown, Wakar, El Aoiun (Spanish Sahara), Casablanca & Biarritz.

29th SAS operated two Copenhagen passenger charters on consecutive days, with CV-440s SE-BSX today and OY-KPF on the 30th, which were both first visits to Manchester.

OCTOBER 1962

October was generally dry, with anticyclonic weather lasting until the 24th. From the 15th to the 20th, widespread overnight fog was often dense and slow to clear in some places. The last week saw low pressures passing through the UK. The month's temperature extremes saw 23°C at Gillingham (2nd) and a low of -6°C at Lincoln (29th).

Cheap walk-on fares for unreserved seats on BEA aircraft would be advertised on the Heathrow to Manchester flights, if trials on their Belfast-Edinburgh-Glasgow routes proved successful. Manchester was not included in the trials, due to the large numbers of interline passengers. The Ministry of Aviation faced a dilemma on whether to allow private airlines to compete with BEA, who recently posted a £1.4 million loss. The airline also went on to say, "It would be folly to provide unnecessary and unwanted capacity by allowing private airlines to duplicate services".

There were no scheduled first visits this month, and the only equipment changes were KLM (KL019): CV-340 PH-CGI (13th/20th).

Due to an overbooking, British & Commonwealth Chief Scout Sir Charles Maclean and comedian Tommy Cooper were turned away from their London flight, as they were the last two to check in. BEA provided a private plane at their expense for Sir Charles, to attend an engagement at Dulwich College. Tommy Cooper however, who was flying to London for his wife's birthday, had to wait 3½ hours for the next flight, before returning the following day for his Blackpool show. To prove there were no hard feelings, he offered to buy the twelve BEA staff a drink, but as the regulations would not allow it, they bought him lunch instead. He was served smoked salmon, roast chicken and half a bottle of champagne, costing £2 6s. A BEA official said they would investigate why 60 passengers had been booked onto a 58-seat plane.

22nd October 1962 – Although desperately needed for several years, the terminal still wasn't ready for operation and the Airport Committee had to wait until the 3rd December before it was brought into full passenger use. No longer would the Manchester air traveller pass through a series of ramshackle and spartan buildings, intended as an interim arrangement. Incorporated within the new spacious concourse were four magnificent Venetian chandeliers, which brought much criticism from irate taxpayers and attracted much comment from the Prince during his opening tour. Also of note was the 28,000sq ft of Pirelli rubber flooring, which, for those who remember, had its own unique sound when using anything with wheels! The giant electronic departures board, which would eventually adorn the back wall, was another twelve years in the future. (MA Archive via Ringway Publications)

22ⁿᵈ October 1962 - The Duke of Edinburgh arrived aboard Heron XH375 to officially open the new terminal. The new facilities included domestic and international piers, which kept passengers under cover right up to boarding their aircraft, a first for any European airport. The domestic pier was 720ft long, capable of handling nine aircraft, the international pier was 960ft long and could handle eleven aircraft. The aircraft apron was now 200,000 square yards, compared to 30,000 square yards on the old apron, which would become the freight apron. The increased use of the motor car meant that 1,300 spaces were made available in front of the new terminal, as part of the £2.7m project. A major innovation was a new hydrant aircraft refuelling system that pumped fuel from underground pipes direct to the aircraft stands. A hydrafueller vehicle then passed the fuel through filters into the aircraft's tanks at controlled rates and pressures. This meant that fewer vehicles used the apron itself. Unfortunately due to bad weather during construction, the underground pipe network became contaminated by water and sand seepage. It would take until 1965 to fully clear the system to the exacting standards required to meet aircraft safety requirements. Whilst addressing the gathered VIPs and civil dignitaries, he was 'heckled' by six little sparrows. He commented "This is the only airport I know where flying goes on inside the buildings as well as on the outside". Later he wanted to know more about the birds that became imprisoned ten days earlier when the last sheets of glass were put into the main building. (MA Archive via Ringway Publications)

1ˢᵗ Hunting Surveys' Dragon Rapide G-AHED arrived at 1647 from Glasgow. It was based until the 8ᵗʰ, operating aerial surveys of the local area (also 12ᵗʰ-17ᵗʰ November).

2ⁿᵈ Ringway's latest resident arrived in the shape of DH.114 Heron G-ASCX, operated by Ferranti. It was their second Heron, joining G-APMV which was Edinburgh-based, but made regular visits to Ringway.

2ⁿᵈ Canadian Air Force Beech C-45 Expeditor 1527, arriving from Northolt at 1112, became the only Canadian military version of the Beech 18 to visit Ringway.

3ʳᵈ Gulfstream 1 N1234X, arriving at 0934 on demonstration f/t Heathrow, was also a first visit of type.

4ᵗʰ Today's appearance of Beech Marquis D-ILFI was a first visit of type. Other light visitors during the month were Cessna 310s OY-TRA (16ᵗʰ) & OY-AEV (24ᵗʰ) and Dove PH-FST (22ⁿᵈ/25ᵗʰ).

12ᵗʰ Douglas DC-3 CF-IMA performed local surveys today and on 23ʳᵈ/24ᵗʰ/25ᵗʰ/26ᵗʰ/27ᵗʰ/30ᵗʰ/31ˢᵗ.

16ᵗʰ Fog had affected Heathrow on six occasions during the month, resulting in numerous diversions into Ringway, but today saw the most interesting arrivals. Apart from a couple of BEA flights, BOAC flights diverting in were B.707s G-APFL at 1206 (BA512 from New York) & G-ARWD at 0939 (BA692 from New York) and Britannias G-ANBK at 1029 (BA132 from Cairo) & G-AOVB at 1211 (BA674 from Bermuda). However, the undoubted highlight was Ghana Airways Britannia 9G-AAG arriving at 1006 (GH804 from Accra) on its only visit to Manchester.

16ᵗʰ The diversion of BOAC Britannia 102 G-ANBK into Ringway deserves an extra mention, as the final BOAC Britannia series 102 to visit. All but one of their entire fleet (G-ANBE continued on lease to Malayan Airways) had been withdrawn during November. G-ANBF had the honour of operating the final B.102 service on 22ⁿᵈ November 1962, when it touched down at Heathrow on a flight originating in Hong Kong. By January 1963, all of these aircraft were parked up at Cambridge awaiting their fates. Fortunately they were snapped by other airlines, mostly going to Britannia Airways (formerly Euravia), replacing their Constellations to fuel their expansion plans. By the start of the 1965 summer season, they were operating G-ANBA/ANBB/ANBF/ANBJ/ANBL & ANBO, with G-ANBE & ANBI added in 1966.

22ⁿᵈ Beagle Airedale G-ARXD made its first visit to Manchester today, in connection with the new terminal opening. Arriving from Fairoaks, it looked very attractive in a blue and white colour scheme.

27ᵗʰ Liverpool-based Fairey Aviation Dragon Rapide G-AKJS, formerly operated by Federated Fruits, arrived from Liverpool. It was parked up until the 15ᵗʰ November, when it departed for Liverpool again. It would make no further visits to Ringway. In late 1965, it was sold in France to provide its engines and other spares for the Fokker D.VIIIs being used in the 'Blue Max' film.

30ᵗʰ Avro Anson G-AHKX, which was present until the 2ⁿᵈ November, also operated local aerial surveys.

30ᵗʰ In a year proving to be a good one for cargo traffic, Spantax Douglas DC-3 EC-AQB made its first visit from Barcelona via Dinard (also 2ⁿᵈ November) with a load of textiles for local mills. It returned to Barcelona after a three hour turnaround. Further flights were operated on the 31ˢᵗ October and the 1ˢᵗ/3ʳᵈ/5ᵗʰ November with Spantax DC-3 EC-AQF.

NOVEMBER 1962

The weather was predominantly cyclonic in character until the 24ᵗʰ, apart from a period from the 10ᵗʰ-13ᵗʰ, when a high pressure extended westwards from Scandinavia over the British Isles. It brought cold northerly winds and some snow. High pressure was again in charge during the last week of the month. Widespread dense fog lasting all day in places occurred on the 25ᵗʰ/26ᵗʰ, with patchy fog on most other days. The month's temperature extremes saw 16°C at Moreton Morrell, Warwickshire (5ᵗʰ) and a low of -11°C at Moorhouse (21ˢᵗ).

Mercury Airlines applied to operate a Manchester-Newcastle-Glasgow service, which if granted could start in April 1963. Fares would be set at £6 18s return to Newcastle and £11 return to Glasgow. Meanwhile Cambrian Airways will commence a new service linking Manchester with Liverpool, the Isle of Man and Belfast, also starting in April 1963.

Pan American announced that once Manchester becomes fully operational again after its £2.5 million building programme, it will use Ringway rather than Prestwick as its alternate airport in the event of bad weather at Heathrow.

The only ILS traffic noted during the month was Skyways HS.748 G-ARMX (2ⁿᵈ). Equipment changes were Air France (AF898): L-1049s F-BGNC (29ᵗʰ) & F-BGNI (22ⁿᵈ/28ᵗʰ) both first visits; KLM (KL019): CV-340s PH-CGB (29ᵗʰ/30ᵗʰ) & PH-CGI (10ᵗʰ/17ᵗʰ) and Martin's Air Charter DC-4 PH-MAE (23ʳᵈ).

International flights were operated during the winter as follows:

AIR FRANCE - SE.210s twice-weekly (Wed/Fri), cargo flights thrice-weekly (Wed/Thu/Sat) with DC-4s.

AER LINGUS - Amsterdam (2 x weekly), Brussels (2 x weekly), Copenhagen (2 x weekly), Dusseldorf (2 x weekly), Frankfurt (2 x weekly) & Zurich (1 x weekly), all operated by Viscounts.

BEA - Amsterdam/Dublin/Dusseldorf/Paris & Zurich.

BOAC - B.707s operate three-weekly to New York (BA538/7). Bristol Britannias serve Boston (3 x weekly), Montreal (2 x weekly), New York (2 x weekly) and Toronto (2 x weekly). The DC-7 cargo operation remained unchanged at twice-weekly to Montreal/New York, but now extended to serve Philadelphia.

KLM - Viscounts operated twice-weekly (KL149/150), with one of these flights operating onwards to Dublin (KL151/2). Cargo flights operated five-weekly with Douglas DC-3s.

SABENA - Twice-weekly to/from New York with B.707s (SN545/6); the DC-7 flights have ceased. The evening Brussels service remains twice-weekly with CV-440s.

SWISSAIR - Operated once-weekly from/to Basle/Zurich (SR118/9) with CV-440s. From 22nd December, a second flight was added (SR718/9).

4th   Brantly B-2 G-ARVY was a first visit of type, arriving at 1241 from Shifnal, Derby. It stayed for two days, before departing to Woodford. The Brantly B-2, which first flew on 21st February 1953, was an American two-seat light helicopter. Produced by the Brantly Helicopter Corporation, it had a single main rotor and an anti-torque tail rotor, and first flew on 21 February 1953. G-ARVY didn't last long on the UK register, as it was damaged beyond repair in a landing accident near Kidlington, Oxfordshire. This was one of six British-registered Brantlys that were written off during the decade. A second example, Brantly B-2B G-ARYX (19th), made its first visit on a flight from Ferranti's Oldham factory, departing two days later to a private site in Leicester.

23rd November 1962 – An exterior photograph of the completed new terminal, tower block and spectator terraces, which can be seen to the left of the picture. (MA Archive via Ringway Publications)

61

7th Douglas DC-3 N702S, operated by Standard Telephone & Cables Ltd based at Stansted, arrived at 1034 today for a day-stop. During the month it was re-registered as G-AJRY.

8th Dove PH-VLC, (also 20th), was the only light aircraft visitor this month.

10th Canadian Air Force Douglas DC-3 KJ994 was on delivery to the Indian Air Force, when it diverted in at 1206 with technical trouble, en route Prestwick-Merville. Another Canadian Air Force aircraft, C-4 Argonaut 17502, arrived at 1541 from Prestwick (callsign 'Dollar 06') with spares for the Dakota.

12th G-AOIH was the last visit by a passenger configured BOAC Douglas DC-7. It was operating a crew training detail from/to Heathrow. For the record their final visits to Ringway and subsequent fates are detailed below:

G-AOIA	14th July 1961 - BA808 from Toronto	Sold August 1964 to Saturn as N90803
G-AOIB	2nd October 1961 - BA646A from Prestwick	Sold March 1964 to Saturn as N90802
G-AOIC	3rd April 1961 - BA019B from Heathrow	Sold February 1964 to Saturn as N90801
G-AOID	27th June 1961 - BA851 from Gatwick	Sold May 1963 to Saturn as N90778
G-AOIE	24th December 1961 - BA646A from Prestwick	Sold May 1964 to Caledonian
G-AOIF	20th July 1962 - BA573 from Heathrow	Sold June 1963 to Saturn as N90804
G-AOIG	15th August 1962 - BA5493 from New York	Sold April 1963 to Saturn as N90773
G-AOIH	12th November 1962 - BA'IH from Heathrow	Sold May 1963 to Saturn as N90774

Their two cargo DC-7s, G-AOII & G-AOIJ, remained in service for a further twelve months.

19th Devon C.1 XG496, operated by the Royal Aircraft Establishment, made its first visit today arriving at 1331 (callsign 'Nugget 06') for a night-stop from/to Farnborough. It would only make two further visits during the decade (19th November 1962 & 12th July 1967). Also today, an unidentified RAF Whirlwind made the briefest of stops, (of two minutes (Tarnish Delta), on a round-trip from its Warton base.

26th USAF Douglas C-47 50943, arriving at 1127 from Brussels to clear customs before continuing onwards to Belfast, was the first of two USAF visitors this month. The second, Douglas DC-6 51-3825 (28th) at 0925 from Prestwick, was on a crew training detail, before departing at 1024 for RAF Mildenhall.

DECEMBER 1962

The first week of anticyclonic conditions saw lots of dry, but foggy weather, some of it persisting all day in places, accompanied by sub-freezing temperatures. This was replaced by two weeks of mainly cyclonic weather, with regular troughs moving eastwards across the country. However, the patterns would change significantly, ushering in the second worst winter of the century. The 22nd was a quiet foggy day, with rising pressure giving way to a sunny, but very cold couple of days. Overnight on Christmas Eve, a trough of low pressure then moved south, turning from rain to snow, bringing in significant snowfalls. On the 27th, much of southern England lay under a foot of snow and even the Channel Islands had two inches of the stuff! This was far from the end, as a depression moved north from the Bay of Biscay on the 29th towards the South West. This brought heavy snowfalls, with drifting in the gale force winds. Many towns and villages were cut off by snowdrifts, 15-20ft deep in some places. The month's temperature extremes saw 15°C at Mackworth, Derbyshire (15th) and a low of -16°C at Loggerheads, Staffordshire (29th).

Mercury Airlines have been granted a licence to operate a Manchester-Newcastle service, but the extended sector to Glasgow was turned down due to objections by BEA. Flights will start in April 1963, with a flight time of 55 minutes, operated by DH.114 Herons.

Equipment changes were Air France (AF898): L-1049s F-BGNC (18th), F-BGNI (1st/29th) & Deux-Ponts F-BASY (6th), the second of its type to visit and KLM (KL019): CV-340s PH-CGB (7th) & PH-CGI (1st/19th).

1st BEA Comet G-ARJL spent three hours on a quiet Saturday afternoon doing endless training!

2nd Canadian Aero Service DC-3 CF-IMA arrived from Edinburgh at 1441, on its final flight from Manchester, before returning to Gatwick.

3rd The airport's long overdue terminal building was finally open for business today. This coincided with the closure of the City Air Terminal at the Royal Exchange in central Manchester.

4th Dense fog, which also affected Heathrow all day, prevented any arrivals at Ringway with only eight departures.

6th Overnight dense fog in the South East remained all day in places, particularly at Heathrow and the Thames Valley area. This was the third consecutive day of fog in the south and the worst since the 'great smog' of December 1952. However, there were few diversions, possibly because nothing was managing to leave Heathrow. Two diversions that did make it into Ringway today were both SE.210 Caravelles. First was the first visit of Portuguese airline TAP, who sent in CS-TCC at 1347 (TP450 from Lisbon) and second was Swissair HB-ICX arriving at 1757 (SR102 from Geneva).

6th A Breguet Deux Ponts (F-BASY) was used on Air France's cargo flight for the first time today. It was capable of a max cargo weight of 12,000kg; double that of the regular DC-4.

6th British United made the first of several visits during the month, operating trooping flights from/to Western Germany. Their Douglas DC-6s were used, with G-APNO today (also 13th/14th/18th/19th/20th) & G-APNP (13th/17th/29th).

8th Martin's Air Charter DC-4 PH-MAE (also 16th/17th), which made its first visit last month, came in again today on a freight charter from Brussels.

10th The Austrian government's Twin Pioneer OE-BHV arrived from Amsterdam at 1406, en route to Prestwick for maintenance with Scottish Aviation. In November 1965 it was sold as LN-BFO and ten years later it was UK-registered as G-BDLX, but it never flew again. The end came in 1980, when it was broken up at Staverton.

12th KLM Douglas DC-7F PH-DSE operated an additional cargo flight (KL014 Heathrow/Amsterdam).

14th A new helicopter making its first visit today, was Hiller UH-12C G-ARUF. Several more examples were to appear over the next few years, but this was the only visit to Manchester of this particular example. Having only been built in 1958, it was withdrawn in 1963 and observed in bits at Ludham, Norfolk the following year.

19th Dove 2A G-AMXY arrived from Luton at 1340 to take up residency with its new owners, The Nuclear Power Group. It was formerly operated as XJ323 with the Royal Navy, before being restored to the UK Register late last year.

21st Hermes G-ALDA, now operated by Transglobe, arrived at 1604 from/to Dusseldorf and stayed until the 27th.

22nd Another fog affected day, with just two arrivals and eight departures.

28th Snow affecting much of the country hit the Midlands the worst. Ringway received five diversions from both Birmingham and Liverpool, but there was nothing out of the ordinary amongst them.

28th A silver rose bowl presented to 69 year old Dubliner Mrs Eileen Knee, marked the occasion of her being the one-millionth passenger handled by the airport. This was the first time the figure had been achieved in a single calendar year.

30th Although the southwest of the country bore the brunt of the recent snow, the southeast was also badly hit, resulting in another seven diversions from Heathrow. Included were SAS SE.210s OY-KRC at 1237 (SK513 from Stavanger) & LN-KLR at 1313 (SK501 from Copenhagen); Cunard Eagle B.707 G-APFB at 1135 (EG200 from Bermuda) and BOAC B.707 G-APFP at 1051 (BA610 from Montreal). Much more snow and further freezing conditions would be seen at the start of 1963!

FIRST/LAST ARRIVALS & DEPARTURES 1962

First arrival: Silver City DC-3 G-ALPN @ 0422 Prestwick
First departure: Silver City DC-3 G-ANAE @ 0127 Belfast
Last arrival: BEA Argosy G-APRN @ 2009 from Glasgow
Last departure: Aer Lingus F.27 EI-AKA @ 2252 to Dublin

Airport Stats 1962 (+/- % on Previous Year)		
Scheduled Passengers	917,000	+11.5%
Inclusive & Charter Passengers	88,000	+137.8%
Freight & Mail (Tonnes)	14,900	+12.8%
Movements	40,200	+2.0%

AIRPORT DIARY 1963

JANUARY 1963

The weather was dominated by anti-cyclones, mainly to the north and northwest of Britain, but around the 12th-15th and from the 23rd, high pressure extended southwards covering much of the country, bringing in much colder weather. Low pressure was present for the first ten days, the 19th and the 30th. The cold easterly winds from December continued into January, and lasted for most of the month throughout the UK. There were heavy snowfalls again in the south and southwest on the evening of the 3rd, which produced snowdrifts 15ft deep in places, blocking roads, cutting off rail traffic, and isolating towns and villages. Freezing fog was widespread from the 11th-14th and the 23rd-25th, with some of the coldest temperatures of the month. The last couple of days had widespread snow again, especially in southern England. The month's temperature extremes saw 9°C at Urswick, Cumbria (26th) and a low of -21°C at Stansted (23rd).

Despite the extreme winter weather experienced by Manchester Airport and the rest of the country, the month still saw 2,422 movements, carrying 54,980 passengers.

Aircraft were being asked not to use a 'short cut' between the two piers, and to adhere to the official taxiways, as the asphalt covered island was only designed to carry airport vehicles. However, BEA's flight manager commented that the area would eventually have to be concreted over so that aircraft could use it.

Equipment changes were Air France (AF898): L-1049 F-BGNC (2nd) and KLM (KL019): CV-340s PH-CGB (6th/11th), PH-CGG (18th) & PH-CGI (17th/22nd/25th/30th/31st). Other news featured BOAC increasing their DC-7 cargo flights, by adding a Monday departure to Montreal/New York via Prestwick.

2nd Diversions due to the extreme winter weather brought several first time visitors to Ringway. There were three diversions today, one each from Heathrow, Birmingham & Gatwick. British United Britannia G-ARWZ which made its first visit arriving at 1140 (BR663 from Ankara), was also handicapped with radio failure!

4th Of today's seven diversions from Heathrow, Stansted and Birmingham, the only two of note were BOAC Comet G-APDL at 0709 (BA941 from Beirut) and British United (ex-BOAC) Britannia G-AOVE at 0811 (BR663 from Istanbul).

4th British United made further trooping flights from/to Western Germany during the month. Aircraft used were Douglas DC-6s' G-AOFW (7th/9th/10th) & G-APNO (4th/5th).

8th There were two USAF Douglas C-54 visitors this month, both from RAF Upper Heyford. The first, C-54 44-9045 at 1306 today (callsign SAM49045), departed for Toulouse. The second, C-54 45-0560 at 1306 (11th), had an extended stay due to fog at Ringway, and was unable to depart until the 13th.

9th Just two light aircraft visitors for January were Heron PH-ILA today and Dove PH-FST on the 31st.

10th Although the first example had visited way back on 9th July 1955 (G-ANOC), the Hiller UH-12 helicopter was a rare type to Ringway. G-ASAZ, which was a new example and a first time visitor today, night-stopped from Sale prior to its departure for Southport the following morning before the fog closed in.

12th Today was the start of stubborn and dense fog lasting 48 hours. Ironically the only two arrivals all day were fog diversions from Liverpool!

13th Fog again! Just two arrivals again and no departures.

16th Wideroe's Nord 260 Broussard LN-LMB was a first visit of type, arriving at 1347 from Stavanger. This aircraft would make several further visits during 1963, but due to continual technical problems with this and their other two; the Norwegian airline sold all three during 1964.

18th Another C-54 visitor, but much more exciting, was Brazilian Air Force Douglas C54-2400 at 1254 from Heathrow. This was the first of four visits this year, with three different aircraft, probably in connection with their recent HS.748 order.

20th Thickening fog in the south during the afternoon resulted in nine more diversions. A few were BEA flights, but the following were all from BOAC: Comets G-APDD on its first visit at 1818 (BA211 from Rome) & G-APDS at 1701 (BA662 from Madrid); B.707s G-APFJ at 2242 (BA510 from New York), G-APFK at 1719 (BA592 from Los Angeles) & DC-7F G-AOII at 1808 (BA578 from Montreal) and first visit Swissair SE.210 HB-ICV at 1859 (SR102 from Geneva).

24th The number of Vickers Vikings visiting Ringway were considerably down on several years ago. Although they were being withdrawn at a fast pace, they were regularly seen during the summer. The first to appear this year was Autair G-AGRW today, on a brief stop in the early hours from/to Luton.

24th Amongst the seven Heathrow fog diversions this morning, was the first visit of East African Airways Comet VP-KRL at 1101 (EC716 from Rome). In April 1964 it was re-registered 5Y-AAA, and served with the airline until its withdrawal in January 1971. It was purchased by Dan-Air and flown to Lasham, but it never entered service and was eventually scrapped in February 1973. Other 'heavy-metal' diversions were BOAC B.707s G-APFE at 0821 (BA512 from Boston), G-APFI at 0909 (BA688 from New York) & G-ARRA at 0906 (BA288 from Rome).

25th Pan American made good their promise of making Ringway their main diversion alternate. More fog at Heathrow produced B.707s N758PA at 0751 (PA058 from Chicago) & N714PA at 0811 (PA002 from New York), both first visits. BEA organised trains for the most of the 150 passengers choosing to continue onwards to London by surface transport.

26th British United Carvair G-ANYB (also 27th/ 2nd Feb) was a first visit of type, picking up Ferranti Orion computers for transport to Gothenburg. Although these computers pioneered at the time, they were an economical disaster, and put Ferranti under such financial strain, they withdrew from the computer market.

26th The origins of the Aviation Trader ATL98 Carvair dates back to 1960 when the demand for car ferries was at its height. With the aging Bristol 170 Freighter still in service, it was slow and limited in what it could carry, so a number of British independent airlines started looking for a replacement. Due to the time and the financial undertaking a whole new airframe would cost to develop, it was decided to convert one of the readily available current aircraft. All eyes fell on the Douglas C-54 military transporter, which was chosen by ATEL. It was favoured for the project because it could be bought cheaply from 'surplus to requirements' and 'retired military stock'. It was known to have a robust and reliable performance, with plentiful support and spares available from the DC4. Once the aircraft had been chosen, Aviation Traders started to design a new car ferry. Once the primary conversion design work was completed, ATEL approached the Douglas Aircraft Corporation, for permission to carry out the major changes required. They also needed the technical details of the aircraft's handling and structure. Douglas forced ATEL into signing a contract, promising that the information given would only be used on the one project. It was also written that the Douglas Aircraft Corporation would not be held liable for any problems or liabilities that may arise as a result of the project. The company took DC4 G-ANYB, an aircraft destined for the scrapheap, which was eventually rolled out on 13th May 1961. The name 'Carvair' is a contraction of 'car - via - air', the role the type was originally built for. The first fight of the Carvair was on the 21st June 1961, and the first passenger carrying flights began on 16th February 1962 with Yankee Bravo, which had been named "Golden Gate Bridge". It was put into service along side Channel's Bristol Freighters, with the inaugural passenger flight from Southend to Ostend taking just 45 minutes.

30th Visits by Flying Tiger Constellations were scarce by early 1963, but N6915C made its first visit today (also 17th November), arriving from Rome at 1146 on a tech-stop en route to Gander.

30th Dan-Air Avro York G-ANXN arriving at 2328 from Gatwick, stayed overnight before departing the following morning on a freight flight to Algiers.

FEBRUARY 1963

The cold winter weather continued, and apart from brief interludes the month saw almost continuous frost, so severe at night it ensured that central England was at its coldest since 1740. Winds increased to gale force on the 5th, as rain turned to snow from the southwest. Snowfall was heavy and prolonged, with considerable drifting. Exmoor had 36 hours of continuous snow, with accumulations of up to 2ft and drifts up to 20ft in places. Understandably, transport was badly affected with many farms and villages cut off. In some areas it was the worst blizzard of the winter. The second week saw a brief respite, with good periods of sunshine and temperatures above freezing almost everywhere. By the 14th however, it was downhill again, with another vigorous low pressure bringing in gale force winds and rain, which soon turned to snow. Snowfall was considerable in the Pennines and Scotland over the next few days. The last week of the month was mainly fine and sunny with scattered snow showers, with daytime temperatures just above freezing and severe night frosts. The month's temperature extremes saw 13°C at Aber, South Wales (27th) and a low of -18°c at Corbridge (25th).

A revised plan to extend the main runway finally received approval by the Ministry of Aviation. The original plan was to extend to 10,500ft across the Bollin Valley, but the new plan for a 9,000ft runway would involve extending by 1,000ft at the Bollin end and by 400ft at the Styal end.

Equipment changes this month were <u>Air France (AF898)</u>: L-1049s F-BGNC (16th) & first visit F-BGNG (27th) and <u>KLM (KL019)</u>: CV-340s PH-CGB (1st) & PH-CGI (2nd).

This month's ILS Traffic consisted of Brazilian Air Force HS.748s C91-2501 (22nd) & C91-2502 (18th/25th/28th), Icelandair Douglas C-54 TF-IST (27th) and an unidentified Avro Anson at 1344 (KTX from Scampton - 21st).

1st Austrian government Twin Pioneer OE-BHV made a fuel stop at 1305 from Prestwick, departing for Amsterdam and Vienna. It had visited before on the 10th December, en route to Prestwick for maintenance.

4th BKS HS.748 G-ARMW made the first of three visits this month, due to bad weather at Leeds (also 7th/27th).

4th For the second month running, there were just two light aircraft visitors, Heron PH-ILA today and Beech 65 N936B on the 18th.

8th Fourteen weather diversions from various airports today were ordinary, apart from two first visits from Heathrow with BOAC Comet G-APDN at 1910 (BA231 from Rome) and KLM Electra PH-LLB at 1924 (KL137 from Amsterdam).

10th Further diversions produced two more first visits. The second KLM Electra in three days, was PH-LLA at 2335 (KL145 from Amsterdam) and British United Britannia G-APNB at 2154 (BR452 from Las Palmas). Also appearing was BOAC G-APDD at 2327 (QF745 from Istanbul), operating on behalf of Qantas.

13th BOAC Boeing 707 G-APFO was operating a crew training flight during the morning, f/t Heathrow.

17th DC-8 PH-DCI made its first visit today, arriving at 0800 from Amsterdam, departing to New York via Shannon.

17th Finnair CV-340 OH-LRB made its second visit to Manchester, arriving from Copenhagen at 2024 today to night-stop, before leaving in the morning for Heathrow. It would continue to serve with Finnair until its retirement in 1980.

18th Beech 23 G-ASCL, operated by Short & Harland as their demonstrator, made a first visit of type arriving from Gatwick today. It would make one further visit (16th July), but in June 1966 it crashed on takeoff at Kirkbymoorside. Its parts were used in the rebuild of another Beech 23, PH-MUS, which was re-registered in 1968 as G-AWIK.

21st Avions Fairey Bristol 170 OO-FAG arrived at 1627 from the Fairey facility, Gosselies, in connection with the GAF Jindivik target-drone programme. It would make one further visit this year on the 1st April.

25th The first USAF Douglas C-47 of the year so far, 50943, had visited Manchester previously. It arrived at 1007 from Brussels, before departing for Northolt.

25th Today saw another visit by a Untied States Air Force C-124 Globemaster, when 15208 arrived as an emergency at 1726 en route from Mildenhall to the USA. By 1970, most C-124s were transferred to the Air Force Reserve & Air National Guard. Although only in production for five years, C-124 aircraft had long and useful service lives, before the last was phased out in 1974.

MARCH 1963

Apart from the first three days of the month, which saw near normal temperatures, but severe night frosts and a short anti-cyclonic spell on the 21st-24th, low pressure was firmly in charge. Frequent depressions passing over the British Isles brought occasional very wet and windy weather. The month's temperature extremes saw 17°C at Letchworth (6th) and a low of -15°C at Kielder Castle, Northumberland Corbridge (1st/3rd/4th).

Approval was given by the city's Airport Committee to extend the main runway to 9,000ft, at a cost of nearly £2 million. The main part of the plan, to be carried out at the southwest end of the runway, meant re-routing the main Wilmslow-Altrincham road by creating a tunnel underneath the runway.

It was reported that from 8th April, Air France would operate a one-off direct flight to Nice, operated by a SE.210 Caravelle. The present traffic between the North West and Nice did not warrant a regular direct service, but the airline hinted it could be the shape of things to come. In the end, the flight was cancelled, but from the 1st April, the airline did increase their cargo flights to four-weekly.

The Manchester Zone Airways Radar unit was moved during the month from Antrobus, near Stretton, to the new airport tower block.

Equipment changes were <u>Air France (AF898)</u>: L-1049s F-BGNC (2nd) & first visit F-BGND (16th/20th/21st) and <u>KLM (KL019)</u>: CV-340s PH-CGB (8th) & PH-CGI (7th/14th/16th/20th/28th/29th).

ILS Traffic noted was Brazilian Air Force HS.748 C91-2503 (22nd) & RAF Vulcan B.2 XM573 (both 20th). Training flights were operated by Cunard Eagle DC-6 G-ARMY (12th) & BEA Comet G-APMG (23rd).

6th An unidentified Argosy C.1 arrived at 1027 (Evergreen 70) from/to Boscombe Down. Flown by the Aeroplane & Armament Experimental Establishment (A&AEE), this was first military Argosy to visit Ringway.

12th In a generally poor month for light aircraft visitors, Commander 680 F-BJUP arriving today and Twin Bonanza HB-GAE on the 29th were the only foreign offerings.

12th Cunard Eagle DC-6 G-ARMY was present for several hours on a crew training detail, but after bursting two tyres on an attempted landing, it had to set course for an emergency landing at Manston.

13th Pan American produced another two first visits, both Heathrow weather diversions. The first, DC-8 N811PA arriving at 0953 (PA106 from Boston) was the first of ten Pan Am DC-8s visiting between 1963 and 1968. The second was B.707 N716PA at 1008 (PA120 from Los Angeles/Gander).

20th There were a number of RAF visitors during the month, but unfortunately most were unidentified. Positive identification however was made on today's arrival of Avro Anson TX256 (also 21st).

20th Marking the second visit of Yugoslavian national airline JAT, Convair CV-340 YU-ADB arrived at 1410 from Belgrade via Frankfurt. It was bringing the Red Star Belgrade team in for a friendly with Manchester United, before departing back to Belgrade two days later.

1963 – Manchester Corporation had ten "1½-deck" buses specifically for transporting airline passengers between the city terminal in St. Ann's Square and the airport. Allocated to Parrs Wood garage in Didsbury (now Tesco), their normal route to the airport would have been via Cambridge Street/Lloyd Street, Princess Road, Altrincham Road, Brownley Road, Portway and Cornishway. Very occasionally they may have been seen working some of the other Parrs Wood duties, such as the 31 or 42 services along Wilmslow Road. The fleet numbers were 30 to 39, and their registration numbers were NNB130 to NNB139. 30 to 35 built in 1953 were Leyland PSU1/13 Royal Tigers, and 36 to 39 built in 1956 were Leyland PSUC1/1 Tiger Cubs. Their livery was in two shades of blue, with a silver band at windscreen level. The ten all looked very similar; but detail differences in the 1956 batch included low-level destination display panels on the near side, in addition to the front destination displays. (MA Archive via Ringway Publications)

25ᵗʰ Today saw the first visit of an Aer Lingus Carvair, when EI-AMP operated a one-off freight flight from/to Dublin. Amongst its consignment were a number of pianos and cattle carcasses! Aer Lingus would operate three Carvairs (the others were EI-AMR/ANJ) between 1963 and 1966.

29ᵗʰ German Air Force Dakota CA+016 became the second and final example to visit Ringway. Staying for just under three hours, it was operating from/to Cologne.

APRIL 1963

It was a changeable, cloudy month, with a short-lived spell of westerly winds in the first week. The month's temperature extremes saw 21°C at Mickleham, Surrey (27ᵗʰ) and a low of -6°C at Great Dun Fell (8ᵗʰ).

The local press reported that businessmen were becoming 'plane spotters', by memorising the registrations of BEA Vanguards with thirty first-class seats. The more regular travellers soon realised they could obtain first-class seats between Manchester and London at no extra charge. This was due the Vanguards spending most of their time operating first-class and tourist class combined flights between London and the continent, but as the Manchester service was one-class, priced at £4 12s for a single fare, the first-class seats were available on the flight. Operating on such a tight turn around, there was no time to replace the wider, more comfortable first-class seats with tourist seats. A BEA spokesman commented that some passengers were astute to this, but there was still no demand for first-class on the Manchester route.

Two scheduled first visits this month were <u>BOAC (BA538)</u>: B.707s G-ARRB (26ᵗʰ) & G-ARRC (5ᵗʰ). Equipment changes were <u>KLM (KL019)</u>: CV-340s PH-CGG (12ᵗʰ/13ᵗʰ/25ᵗʰ) & PH-CGI (6ᵗʰ), <u>KLM (KL149)</u>: DC-7 PH-DSP (11ᵗʰ).

Plenty of ILS traffic noted included Brazilian Air Force HS.748 C91-2503 (3ʳᵈ), RAF Vulcan B.2s XM574 (4ᵗʰ) & XM575 (19ᵗʰ) and BKS HS.748 G-ARRW (18ᵗʰ). Training flights were operated by BEA Comet G-APMC (7ᵗʰ), BEA Argosies G-AOZZ (7ᵗʰ) & G-APRN (15ᵗʰ) and BOAC B.707 G-APFN (9ᵗʰ).

International flights operating during the summer were:

AIR FRANCE - Thrice-weekly to Paris with SE.210s, increasing to six-weekly between July and September. Cargo flights increased to four-weekly flights with Douglas DC-4Fs.

AER LINGUS - Amsterdam (4 x weekly), Brussels (3 x weekly), Copenhagen (2 x weekly), Dusseldorf (3 x weekly), Frankfurt (3 x weekly) & Zurich (1 x weekly), all operated by Viscounts.

BEA - Amsterdam/Dublin/Dusseldorf/Paris & Zurich, summer routes to Basle/Barcelona/Palma/& Milan.

BOAC - B.707s operate thrice-weekly from/to New York (BA538/7) and originate/terminate at Ringway daily from 9ᵗʰ June-30ᵗʰ September. Bristol Britannias serve Montreal (up to 6 x weekly), New York (3 x weekly until 6ᵗʰ June) & Toronto (up to 6 x weekly), Boston is no longer served. DC-7 cargo flight operates thrice-weekly to Montreal/New York.

KLM - Operated to Amsterdam four-times-weekly (KL149/150), one of these flights operates onwards to Dublin (KL151/2). Also a five-weekly cargo flight to Amsterdam (KL019/020).

SABENA - Twice-weekly to/from New York with B.707s (SN545/6), increasing to three-weekly between May and September. The evening Brussels service remained twice-weekly with CV-440s and Ostend operated June-September thrice-weekly with a mix of CV-440s & DC-6s.

SWISSAIR - SR118/9 operated once-weekly from/to Zurich until 29ᵗʰ June (Sat). SR718/9 also operated once-weekly June-July (Sun), SR728/9 operated twice-weekly between 21ˢᵗ May-1ˢᵗ October (Tue/Fri), all with SE.210 Caravelles.

1ˢᵗ Mercury Airlines began a three-weekly Manchester-Newcastle service, increasing to five-weekly from July.

3ʳᵈ Sabena introduced a twice-weekly cargo service to Brussels (SN191/2), with Douglas DC-3 OO-AWZ operating the first flight. Others used were OO-AUX (10ᵗʰ), OO-AWG (17ᵗʰ) & OO-AWN (5ᵗʰ).

5ᵗʰ Beech 58 N9605Y, operated by Christensen Diamond Corp, was one of the earliest Barons to the UK. Arriving at 1137 from Bremen on its first visit, it appeared occasionally until 1966 and made a solitary visit on 8ᵗʰ September 1969!

10ᵗʰ Fred Olsen Curtiss C-46 LN-FOS arrived at 1317 from Gothenburg, carrying a cargo of mink pelts.

22ⁿᵈ Another month when light visitors were thin on the ground, especially the overseas types. Regular Dove PH-FST, which night-stopped from/to Twenthe, was one of only two examples.

26ᵗʰ US Army L-20 Beaver 53277, arriving at 1227 today from Verdun, NE France, made a brief visit before departing to Gatwick.

14th April 1963 – BEA Vanguard G-APED 'Defiance' saw continuous service with BEA, before its withdrawal in January 1973, and being scrapped at Heathrow the same year. Note that the BEA tail logo is off-centre. In the background, are the steps leading to the infamous "glass house", the place where many spotters congregated during any kind of weather, rain or shine. Noted for its brown-tinted windows, it was where lots of info and rumours were exchanged in pre-internet days, in addition to several air band radios, all tuned to different frequencies, covering the airport and surrounding airways. (Ken Fielding)

27th Ryan Navion Rangemaster G-1 HB-ESN, which made the first of three visits during 1963, was another first visit of type. This single-engine, four-seat aircraft originally designed and built by North American Aviation, was later built by the Ryan Aeronautical Company. No Ryan Navions ever made it to the UK register and this particular aircraft was sold in 1968.

27th For the third time this year, Pan American diverted a couple of flights into Manchester. Early morning fog at Heathrow produced two more first visits with B.707s N726PA at 0919 (PA058 from Chicago) and N727PA at 0939 (PA727 from Winnipeg).

28th The second visit of a Brazilian Air Force Douglas C-54 took place today, with the arrival of C54-2407 at 1227 from Toulouse, to pick up military ordinance before departing for Lisbon on the 30th.

MAY 1963

The first two weeks were dominated by cyclonic weather, with troughs or depressions moving eastwards across the country. There was a transitional period during the third and the final week, when high pressure took firm charge, making it warmer by the end of the month. The month's temperature extremes saw 27°C at Southampton (31st) and a low of -4°C at Santon Downham (4th).

During the early part of the 1960s, transatlantic charters were comparatively rare at Manchester. Flights to the USA & Canada were mainly for the independent wealthy, or the business/diplomatic elite. Prices were fixed by IATA at a level comfortable to the scheduled airlines, with no regard for the needs or aspirations of the average citizen. The only loop-hole available, which proved both popular and successful, was the 'affinity-group charter' section of the UK/USA bi-lateral agreement. This section allowed a suitably-equipped charter operator to offer cheap transatlantic flights to so-called 'affinity groups', such as clubs, societies etc, but many groups formed for the sole purpose of obtaining cheaper air travel. An important sub-clause stated that the intending passengers must have been members of the chartering organisation for more than six months prior to the departure date. The consequence was a marked increase in flights to the USA from Manchester, which gained further momentum over the next few years.

The Airport Committee showed great concern over the number of people dodging the entrance fee to the piers, which had become unnecessarily high. Some sort of control was needed, as the turnstiles guarding the piers were so big, enterprising young 'spotters' could crawl through without paying their shilling admission fee. The airport eventually introduced wardens onto the terraces, mainly to give change for the turnstiles and maintain control.

With the airport's striking new terminal in operation for barely six months, Ringway handled a total of 101,619 passengers during May, an increase of 19% on the previous year. Movements recorded were 3,667 (8% increase) and freight figures revealed a 9% increase. Scheduled services were dominated by services to London-Heathrow. Of the 85,393 scheduled terminal passengers, just under half travelled on the London route.

The following could be seen during the summer operating ITs to various destinations: Adria Airways (Zagreb), Aviaco (Palma), Balair (Basle), Braathens (Bergen), British United (Wick), Caledonian (Barcelona/Palma/Valencia), Channel Airways (Ostend), Dan-Air (Basle/Ostend/Tarbes), Derby Airways (Barcelona/Ostend/Palma) Euravia (Genoa/Naples/Palma/Perpignan/Rimini/Valencia/Venice), Itavia (Rimini), SAM (Rimini), Spantax (Malaga/Palma/Valencia), Starways (Newquay/Nice/Palma/Perpignan /Pisa/Rimini/Valencia) and UTA (Nice/Perpignan).

Scheduled first visits this month were Air France (AF960): SE.210s F-BJTL (4th) & F-BJTM (11th) and Sabena (SN191): DC-3 OO-AUZ (22nd). Equipment changes were Aer Lingus (EI826): Carvair EI-AMR (6th - first visit) and KLM (KL149): DC-7 PH-DSK (30th).

No ILS traffic was noted during the month, but there were a few training flights, with BKS HS.748 G-ARRW (4th - first visit) and BOAC B.707s G-APFJ (30th) & G-APFL (29th).

2nd BEA introduced Vanguards on their twice-weekly flights to Palma (BE830/1), which also operates via Glasgow. G-APEO operated tonight's first service, which increased to four-weekly from June-September.

2nd Trans-Canada (eventually becoming Air Canada on 1st January 1965) DC-8 CF-TJC made the first of several visits by the airline during the year, operating charters from/to Toronto. All visiting DC-8s were first time visitors and aircraft used were CF-TJE (10th September), CF-TJF (31st May), CF-TJK (23rd July), CF-TJL (28th August) & CF-TJM (6th June/26th August/7th October).

7th By this time Pipers and Cessnas had not taken over the light aircraft scene fully, and there were still plenty of vintage types to be seen at Manchester. One such aircraft was the Denham based 1947 Ercoupe 415, G-AKFC, which night-stopped before departing to Leeds. Another 'vintage' visitor was Auster 4 G-ANHS (18th) from Little Snoring, departing to RAF Coltishall. In 2014 this aircraft is painted and flying in its former military markings of MT197.

11th Caledonian began their summer operations from Ringway today, with 'new' Douglas DC-7 G-ASHL (ex-Sabena OO-SFK) in charge of CA301 to Palma. Another two DC-7s also added to their fleet were DC-7 G-ASID (ex-Sabena OO-CFE) & G-ASIV (ex-Sabena OO-CFJ), which made their first visits on the 23rd June & 14th June respectively. These three DC-7s all supplemented their other aircraft, G-ARYE.

12th Balair had another equipment upgrade, and are now operating with Douglas DC-6s HB-IBU & HB-IBZ (f/v 2nd June) on their weekly Basle charter, with flights operating until the 22nd September. From the 16th June they also began a DC-4 flight from/to Zurich until the 15th September, routing via Dublin with two aircraft, HB-ILB & HB-ILU.

12th The Spanish airline, Spantax, also began summer flights today, operating at weekends to Malaga, Palma & Valencia. Douglas DC-7 EC-ATR (ex- Sabena OO-CFH) was used for their entire programme.

13th PA-23 Aztec OY-ACR (also 15th) made the first of two visits during the month today. This aircraft was sold as D-IBOK in 1965, but restored to the Danish register as OY-ACR eight years later.

17th US Army U-6A Beaver (formerly designated the L-20) 56385, arrived for a weekend stopover. It returned to its base at Sembach, West Germany on the 20th.

17th New resident Let L-200 Morava arriving at 1825 G-ASFD from Oxford, became one of only three of these twin-engine light aircraft making it onto the British register. Built in Czechoslovakia, it first appeared in the UK on the 27th March, temporarily based at Oxford. Although it was a Ringway resident until January 1982, it spent little time in the air.

17th Euravia began an extensive summer charter from Ringway today, when L-749 Constellation G-ANUR operated the airline's first flight to Perpignan. Constellations G-AHEL, G-AHEN, G-ALAK, G-ALAL, G-ARVP & G-ARXE (wearing Skyways colours during 1963), would form the backbone of Euravia's operations until 1965, when their Bristol Britannias took over.

18th In their final years, Starways would operate two Viscounts (G-APZB & G-ARIR), two Douglas C-54s (G-ARIY & G-ASEN) and a sole Douglas DC-4 (G-APEZ), which would kick-off their summer programme with a flight to Palma today.

24th Channel Airways Douglas DC-4 G-ARYY positioned in from Southend at 1003 to operate an outbound IT flight to Ostend, and many other flights throughout the summer. Apart from being a first visit and the only DC-4 to operate for the airline, it was also notable its 88-seat layout, which compares with only 40/44 seats in the DC-4s visiting in 1950!

26th Norwegian airline Braathens started a weekly charter, operated by Fokker F.27s until the 30th August. Apart from today's visit of LN-SUO (f/v), the F.27s used were LN-SUA (f/v 1st June), LN-SUG & LN-SUN (f/v 8th June).

18th May 1963 - Wing Commander Maurice A. Newnham, OBE, DFC, former Commanding Officer of No.1 Parachute Training School, unveiled this memorial today in honour of the 60,000 paratroopers who trained at the airport during World War Two. The artwork was to commemorate the spirit of co-operation between the Parachute Training School, Royal Air Force, Allied Airborne Forces and the City of Manchester. Designed and made by Margaret Traherne, it conveys the suspense and excitement felt by the parachutists about to jump from their aircraft, epitomizing the spirit of parachuting. The main element in the design was the free interpretation of the winged symbol of the airborne forces. It also incorporates the blue of the Royal Air Force and the red and khaki of the Airborne Forces, along with the colours of the earth and sky. (MA Archive via Ringway Publications)

18th May 1963 - The first visit to Ringway of a RAF Bristol Beverley, was XB283 ('MOPXG' f/t RAF Abingdon), arriving in connection with the unveiling of a memorial commemorating the No.1 Parachute School. Also appearing with various military dignitaries, were two DHC-2 Beavers (Army 384 f/t Aldershot & Army 386 f/t Blackbushe) and a Devon (Rafair 1216 f/t Northolt), but these aircraft escaped identification! (Dave Lawrence)

26th May 1963 - The age of discovery for the Mancunian traveller was further enhanced today, when Adria Airways DC-6B YU-AFE positioned in from Zagreb to collect its first load of tourists bound for the Adriatic Riviera. The airline was formed in 1961 by the Slovenian government, with four ex-KLM aircraft

bought the same year. They first operated into the UK in 1962, with weekly flights on behalf of Yugotours, the state owned package holiday company. Adria continued operations with their DC-6Bs until early 1968. Their last full summer programme from Manchester was in 1966. After failing to notice that jets were more commonplace with tour operators, they were unable to compete with the newer BAC 1-11s and Boeing 737s. In February 1969 the airline ceased all operations, pending a decision on its future with Yugotours, who awarded the contract that year to national carrier, JAT. However later that year the airline was reborn as Inex-Adria after purchasing a DC-9 and continuing operations with three DC-6Bs which soldiered on until 1971. (Ken Fielding)

26th Adria Airways made the first flight of their summer programme from Ringway. Operating until the 29th September, the following DC-6s were used: YU-AFC, YU-AFD (f/v-16th June), YU-AFE (f/v-today) & YU-AFF (2nd June).

31st Apart from the visits so far this year by Fairey's Bristol 170 OO-FAG, there had been no other appearances by this once common type. However, BKS Bristol 170 G-AMLJ arrived at 1547 today from Dublin, before departing for Gatwick. This aircraft would make one further visit as such on the 6th June prior to its sale to Aer Turas as EI-APC.

JUNE 1963

The first twelve days were warm, thundery and mainly anticyclonic. Many places in central England had fifteen hours of sunshine daily for the first ten days, but by the 6th/7th thunderstorms were widespread and heavy, with nearly two inches of rain recorded at Bristol (6th) and Kensington Palace (7th). Troughs and depressions from the Atlantic maintained cool and changeable weather for the rest of June. The month's temperature extremes saw 28°C at St. James' Park (10th) and a low of -1°C at Glenmore Lodge (3rd).

Scheduled first visits this month were BEA Comet G-APME (19th) & British United Herald G-APWJ (16th). Equipment changes were Aer Lingus (EI904): Carvair EI-AMP (5th), KLM (KL019): DC-7 PH-DSI (29th).

The only ILS traffic noted during the month was Brazilian Air Force HS.748 C91-2503 (3rd) & C91-2504 (12th). Training flights were BOAC B.707s G-APFN (5th) & G-ARWE (3rd).

1st Italian charter airline SAM (Societa Aria Mediterranea), began their IT summer programme today, with a weekly DC-6 flight (MQ572/3) f/t Rimini. Flights operated until the 21st September, with the same DC-6s as last year, I-DIMA, DIMD, DIME, DIMI, DIMP and DIMU which operated today.

2nd June 1963 - Aviaco began a weekly flight to Palma (AO1118/9), operated by Iberia L-1049G Constellations. EC-AQN is seen above taxiing out for departure on a glorious Sunday afternoon. (MA Archive via Ringway Publications)

1st UTA, formerly T.A.I. & UAT, began weekend flights today to Nice & Perpignan with Douglas DC-6 F-BGSL. Flights operated until the 30th September, with DC-6s F-BGSN (f/v - 26th August) /BGTY/BGVV/BHEE/BHMR (f/v - 7th June) & BHMS. Two from last year that didn't make it were F-BIAM, which was sold to Air Afrique during 1963, and F-BIAO which crashed May 1963.

1st Wideroe's second Nord 260 Broussard, LN-LME, made its only visit, arriving at 1536 today from Stavanger. This aircraft, along with the airline's other two, were sold during 1964 due to technical issues.

2nd Yet another new airline to Manchester was Italian operator Itavia, beginning a weekly late night flight f/t Rimini (IH420/1). They operate two Handley Page Heralds, I-TIVA & I-TIVE, with the latter being used on the first flight. Both were first time visitors, regularly used on the service, running until the 15th September.

2nd As well as a weekly Constellation flight, Aviaco also operated a late night service to Palma until the 6th October (AO1132/3), exclusively with Douglas DC-6 EC-ASS.

7th South African Airways operated their first flight from Ringway today, when B.707 ZS-CKD arrived from Heathrow (SA223) for an outbound flight to Johannesburg via Rome.

8th Newly purchased by Ferranti, Brantly G-ASEW made its first visit to Ringway. The helicopter, which became a regular visitor, was housed in a specially built hangar at the property of Mr Sebastian Ferranti, complete with its own private refuelling facilities. In September 1966 it was sold British Executive Air Services at Oxford.

11th Danish operators Flying Enterprise were a new airline formed in 1959. They operated as the Danish subsidiary of Overseas Aviation, who ceased trading in 1961. C-4 Argonaut OY-AFC, which arrived at 1215 today, was operating the first of two charters from/to Gothenburg. The second was operated by C-4 Argonaut OY-AAH (13th).

12th Twin Pioneer G-ASHN was the second of its type to visit, arriving at 1838 from Thruxton, before departing to Prestwick the following afternoon. On the 20th June, it departed Prestwick for Ecuador, having been sold as HC-AHT.

14th Fokker F.27 PH-IOP, operated by the National Iran Oil Corp, made its first visit today at 2124 from Stansted for a weekend stay. It was only operated until February 1964, when it was sold to Balair as HB-AAI. Unfortunately, this aircraft was written off the following month in a landing accident at Malaga.

15th KLM Douglas DC-7 PH-DSO (also 3rd July), arrived at 2322 from Amsterdam, on a late night charter to New York. Further flights operated with PH-DSH (3rd July), PH-DSL (13th July), PH-DSO (3rd July) & PH-DSP (3rd August).

23rd American operator Saturn Airways had visited Manchester before, but under new the 'rules' regarding transatlantic charters, they became a fairly regular over the next few months. Having recently purchased seven DC-7Cs from BOAC, the first of their flights took place today, when Douglas DC-7 N90774 departed at 0409 for New York. Each summer until 1967, the airline could be seen at Manchester operating flights to Boston and New York. The last visit of one of their DC-7 aircraft was the 16th August 1967, when N90773 arrived from New York, before positioning out to Le Bourget.

26th US Army Sikorsky CH-34 Choctaw 71705 (also 29th), which was basically a military version of a Sikorsky S-58 or Westland Wessex, was first visit of type. The reason for its visit was unclear, but it could have something to do with President Kennedy's UK visit.

27th SAS Douglas DC-7 LN-MOE was another first time visitor to Manchester, operating a passenger charter from/to Copenhagen (DK1193/4). Apart from a short lease period in 1968, it spent its entire life with SAS until its withdrawal in April 1969.

27th Operated by the Queen's Flight, RAF Whirlwind HCC.12 XR486 arrived at 1007 today from RAF Benson as 'Hover 2', departing forty minutes later to RAF Odiham.

28th New Spanish operator TASSA began the first of a series of fortnightly flights f/t Barcelona. They were formed in 1960, to compete with Spantax in the African oil charter market, before expanding into IT flights. Today's inaugural flight was operated by Douglas DC-6B EC-AUC. DC-6 EC-AVA was also used on the summer programme, which ended with the final flight being operated on the 21st September.

30th Another American charter carrier, Capitol, also operated the first of a short series of flights, when L-1049H Constellation N5401V departed to New York via Gander. Two further departures were N5402V (13th July & 28th July), with return flights operated by L-1049s N9720V (30th July), N9718C (11th August) and N4903C (3rd September).

29ᵗʰ June 1963 - Douglas DC-4 VP-MAA, the first aircraft onto the Maltese register, appeared on its first visit today, on a round-trip to Shannon on behalf of Caledonian Airways. It was an occasional visitor during the summer, mainly on sub-charters and its last appearance was the 6ᵗʰ October 1963, arriving at 2117 from Tarbes. The airline ceased operations in February 1964, and VP-MAA was put up for sale. It was sold in January 1965 to Autair as G-ASZT. (S.L Hall)

JULY 1963

This month's weather was generally disappointing, with average or slightly below temperatures. Rain was occasionally heavy and thundery for the first week. Snow and sleet showers were also recorded over high ground in Scotland on three separate occasions, with not much improvement until the 20ᵗʰ. The month's temperature extremes saw 29°C at Wisley (30ᵗʰ) and a low of -1°C at Santon Downham Lodge (21ˢᵗ).

Scheduled first visits this month were <u>Air France (AF960)</u>: SE.210s F-BJTN (8ᵗʰ) & F-BJTP (25ᵗʰ), KLM (KL151): DC-8 PH-DCE (17ᵗʰ) and <u>Swissair (SR718/728)</u>: CV-990s HB-ICA (20ᵗʰ), HB-ICB (13ᵗʰ) & HB-ICH (26ᵗʰ). Equipment changes were <u>KLM (KL019)</u>: CV-340 PH-CGI (2ⁿᵈ), <u>KLM (KL149/151)</u>: CV-340 PH-CGE (17ᵗʰ) & Electra PH-LLG (1ˢᵗ).

No ILS traffic was noted, and the only training flight was BOAC B.707 G-APFI (24ᵗʰ).

5ᵗʰ In 1961, de Havilland began working on a revolutionary small business jet, the DH.125 Jet Dragon. It was intended to replace the piston engined de Havilland Dove as a business and light transport aircraft. The DH.125 design was for a low-winged monoplane, with a pressurised fuselage accommodating two pilots and six passengers. It was powered by two Bristol Siddeley Viper turbojets, mounted on the rear fuselage. The slightly swept wing employed large slotted flaps and airbrakes to allow operation from small airfields. The first of two prototypes (G-ARYA) flew on the 13ᵗʰ August 1962, with the second (G-ARYB) on the 12ᵗʰ December the same year. The first production aircraft (G-ASEC), which was longer with a greater wingspan than the two prototypes, flew on the 12ᵗʰ February 1963. Today, G-ASEC made a first visit of type to Ringway, arriving from Hatfield. It departed to Heathrow operating a flight for Granada Television instead of G-ARFZ.

6ᵗʰ Fairways Douglas DC-3 PH-SSM arrived at 1330 from Rotterdam, en route to Edinburgh.

8ᵗʰ Registered in 1934 and owned by Derby Airways, Leopard Moth G-ACLL made a late afternoon visit from its base at Castle Donington.

10ᵗʰ Riley 65 Super Rocket N656R (actually a Cessna 310), operated by Keegan Aviation, arrived from Panshangar at 1206 today for demonstration flights in an attractive red, gold and white colour scheme.

10th July 1963 - Not the best quality shot, but definitely worth including, is privately owned A-26B Invader N4000K (also 27th). Operated by Aero Services Corporation, Philadelphia, it made its first visit today at 1433 on a round-trip from Amsterdam. It's a photographic and geophysical survey aircraft, complete with a magnometer boom to the rear, used for surveying in the North Sea area. It made its second and final visit on the 18th October 1963, arriving at 1229 from Edinburgh as a Leeds diversion. On the 4th July 1972, while still operating as a survey aircraft, it sustained considerable damage in a wheels-up incident at Manila. (MA Archive via Ringway Publications)

10th Saturn Airways operated further Douglas DC-7 transatlantic charters from/to New York with N90773 (11th/24th/10th August), N90774 (11th August) and first visit N90778 (10th/27th).

12th Capitol also operated a number of summer transatlantic charters, starting today with L-1049H Constellation N5402V (also 28th) which night-stopped, departing the following afternoon for Gander. L-1049G N9720C arrived at 1706 (30th) on an inbound transatlantic charter via Shannon, later positioning to Tel Aviv. L-1049C N9718C arrived from Shannon at 0954 (11th August), later departing for Gander and finally, L-1049G N4903C arrived at 1504 (3rd September) from Shannon, departing to Frankfurt.

15th Swissair DC-8 HB-IDB (SR851) arrived at 1114 on a fuel stop, routing New York-Zurich.

15th D-IHAK routing f/t Gatwick was the first foreign registered Piaggio P.166 to visit. This aircraft, which was actually designated as a P.166 Albatross, was written off in February 1967.

19th South African Airways operated a further charter from Ringway today, when B.707 ZS-CKC made its first visit arriving from Heathrow at 1919 (SA223), departing to Johannesburg via Rome. A third flight took place on 20th September, with B.707 ZS-CKE which was also a first visit.

20th Cessna 210 N3676Y had been doing the rounds at various UK airfields during the month. Today it was Ringway's turn, when it appeared at 1923 on a round-trip from Blackpool.

22nd Widgeon G-APVD had made several visits previously as a Westland aircraft, but following its purchase by Ferranti in June 1963, it made its first visit today under its new ownership. Its time was spent ferrying personnel from/to the company's various UK factories. Amongst other things, the company was involved in flight director guidance, flight management systems and a stability augmentation system. These systems were developed by Ferranti's aircraft equipment divisions at Failsworth, North Manchester and Bracknell, Berkshire. It would become a regular visitor to Ringway, but despite being operated by Ferranti until 1971, it made no further visits after 1967.

25th Brazilian Air Force C54-2407 made its second visit today, arriving at 1444 from Lisbon. It was collecting more HS.748 spares and stayed for two days.

26th Aero Commander OE-FAG arrived from Munich at 1006 en route to Shannon, before returning from there the following day. It would make no further visits to Ringway, and was written off in August 1971.

30th Beech Musketeer N2327J arriving at 1928 from Blackpool, became a temporary resident until October, looked after by Mercury Airlines. This aircraft would make one more visit on 28th July 1964, on a flight from Liverpool to Gatwick.

31st BOAC Comet G-APDF made its first visit to Manchester today, arriving at 1225 as BA4115/6, operating a scout charter to Athens.

AUGUST 1963

The warm sunny weather at the end of July only lasted into the first day of August. It then settled into a pattern of unsettled cyclonic weather, which brought cool, cloudy and very wet conditions at times. The month's temperature extremes saw 26°C at Oaken, Staffs (1st) and a low of -2°C at Balmoral (29th).

Scheduled first visits were Air France (AF960): SE.210s F-BJTO (20th) & F-BLKF (3rd) and Swissair (SR718): CV-990 HB-ICC (10th). Equipment changes were Air France (AF898): L-1049s F-BGND (10th) & F-BGNI (3rd/7th/24th), KLM (KL151): DC-7s PH-DSL (10th/17th), PH-DSM (24th) and Electras PH-LLB (3rd) & first visit PH-LLK (31st).

The only ILS traffic noted during the month was Aerolineas Argentinas HS.748 LV-PXD (7th).

2nd Bellenca Viking EI-AKR was a first visit of type, arriving at 2147 from Dublin. It was based at Ringway until the 9th November, when it left for Oxford. It eventually became UK-registered as G-ASRD in March 1964. Another Irish visitor during the month, PA-28 Cherokee EI-AME (23rd), also became British registered in April 1965 as G-ATDA.

5th An airline that became a regular at Ringway throughout the 1970s and 1980s made its debut today, with the arrival of Wardair Douglas DC-6 CF-PCI (WD243) at 1928 from Sondre Stromfjord, departing for Gatwick. During the 1960s, the airline only operated occasional charters initially with CF-PCI, but later they would add a Boeing 727, CF-FUN.

6th Flying Enterprise Argonaut OY-AFC (also 13th) made the first of two visits today, operating very early morning return flights to Copenhagen.

9th KLM operated inbound transatlantic charters from New York with DC-7 PH-DSL (today/12th), PH-DSM (7th September) and first visit DC-8 PH-DCK (11th).

10th Beech 65 D-ILDO arrived at 0912 f/t Gatwick. It was notable for its curved windows on the sides, normally associated with maritime patrol aircraft, as it was possibly used for some kind of surveillance.

12th USAF visitors had been thin on the ground for the last few months, and this month only produced another visit of C-47 50943 from Dublin to Brussels today.

12th Bell 47 G-ARIA was another first visit of type, night-stopping after landing from a private site in Littleborough, Lancs. It was operated by Worldwide Helicopters, based at Biggin Hill. The Bell 47 was a two-bladed, single engine, light helicopter, manufactured by Bell. It became the first helicopter certified for civilian use on 8th March 1946. More than 5,600 Bell 47 aircraft were produced, including those under license by Agusta in Italy, Kawasaki Heavy Industries in Japan, and Westland Aircraft in the United Kingdom.

13th Will the next first visit of type sign in please! Bölkow Bo.207 D-EBLO, which arrived at 1142 today from Cologne to night-stop, was a four-seat light aircraft that first flew in October 1960.

17th BOAC Comet G-APDL (BA4121/2) arrived at 1346, operating the return flight of a scout party from Athens.

21st Cunard Eagle Britannia G-ARKA (EG427) was a first time visitor, arriving at 2018 today from Heathrow, on an outbound trooping flight to Istanbul. A second Eagle Britannia, G-ARKB, made its first visit on 1st September, also to Istanbul.

22nd British United Britannia G-ANCD (BR851) was another first visit, on a further troop charter to Istanbul.

23rd BEA Helicopters Whirlwind G-ANFH made regular shuttles to Penistone in the Peak District throughout the day. It was in connection with a missing body, which tragically turned out to be the first "Moors murders" victim.

24th Although Finnair CV-440s had visited before, today's arrival at 0245 (AY5824 from Helsinki) of OH-LRC was a first visit. Unlike the previous ones, this aircraft didn't make it to the end of the 1970s, as it was sold as N999TZ in February 1972.

31st August 1963 - KLM Electra PH-LLK was the fourth to visit Ringway. The airline operated Manchester-Amsterdam services from 1963, until the final aircraft PH-LLB visited on 28th June 1968. (Hubert Parrish)

SEPTEMBER 1963

Low pressure was generally in charge for the first twelve days, superseded by nearly two weeks of anticyclonic weather, to be replaced again in the final week by unsettled weather. The month's temperature extremes saw 26°C at Wrexham (14th) and a low of -3°C at Cannich, Highlands (19th).

Scheduled first visits were <u>KLM (KL149)</u>: Electra PH-LLC (22nd) and <u>Swissair (SR718/728)</u>: CV-990 HB-ICD (14th) & SAS SE.210 LN-KLP (16th). Equipment changes were <u>KLM (KL149)</u>: DC-7 PH-DSD (25th).

ILS traffic noted: Brazilian Air Force HS.748 C91-2505 (2nd) & Aerolineas Argentinas LV-PXH (24th).

8th Malta Metropolitan Douglas DC-4 VP-MAA operated a round-trip from Ostend for Derby Airways.

16th Although September was another busy summer month, it was mainly devoid of any interesting aircraft, so attention was drawn to two new Brantly B-2As making their first visits, G-ASEW today & G-ARZJ (30th).

16th Widespread fog affecting the south over the next two mornings sent in nine diversions today. They were all from Heathrow, apart from Dan-Air Douglas DC-3 G-AMPP at 0945 from Cardiff, which was intended for Liverpool. Three first visits were Pan American B.707 N730PA at 1002 (PA002 from Montreal) & DC-8 N801PA at 1016 (PA102 from New York), and the first appearance of the Australian airline Qantas, with B.707 VH-EBC at 0942 (QF175 from Rome).

17th Another nine diversions today, all from Heathrow, gave the incredible sight of four Pan American aircraft occupying Ringway's tarmac at the same time! First visits were made by B.707s N720PA at 0631 (PA0258 from Chicago), N725PA at 0808 (PA002 from New York) & DC-8 N810PA at 0838 (PA056 from Chicago). The fourth Pan Am aircraft, DC-8 N811PA at 0821 (PA102 from New York), had visited Manchester previously.

18th The only two foreign light visitors this month were Commander 500 D-IBEF at 1528 today as a Leeds diversion, and a week later Beech 65 D-IDIN which night-stopped from Essen (25th).

23rd KLM Douglas DC-7 PH-DSC operated an outbound charter to Hanover and the return three days later.

24th Martin's Air Charter Douglas DC-4 PH-MAE day-stopped on a flight from/to Amsterdam.

29th Aviaco's Constellation flight AO1118/9 f/t Palma operated for the final time today. Iberia's Connies, which had all visited Ringway, were EC-AIN/AIO/AQM/AQN/AMP/AMQ & ARN.

15th September 1963 - Douglas DC-6B F-BGSN is making the last of its three visits to Ringway, all this year. It had been leased to Air Afrique since April 1963, but today it was operating a UTA flight from/to Perpignan. In November 1963 it was re-registered as TU-TCG, and served with the African airline until 1968. (MA Archive via Ringway Publications)

OCTOBER 1963

High pressures dominated the weather, except for the first week which saw rain, occasionally heavy for the last few days of the month. The month's temperature extremes saw 23°C at Letchworth (12th) and a low of -4°C at Huntly (28th).

Sabena have been instructed to reduce their transatlantic winter flights from Ringway. The Ministry of Aviation stated that the amount of traffic to be uplifted was in excess of what had been envisaged. Sabena had intended to operate two flights per week, but had to revise it down to once-weekly.

The only scheduled first visit this month was British United Herald G-ASBP (25th). Equipment changes were Air France (AF898): L-1049 F-BGNG (5th), KLM (KL019): Martin's Air Charter DC-3 PH-MAA (31st), KLM (KL149): CV-340 PH-CGH (17th) & Douglas DC-7 PH-DSM (16th) and Sabena (SN623): DC-6 OO-CTK (28th).

ILS traffic this month had another good selection, with Ghana Airways Viscount 9G-AAW (16th) operating an air test, RAF Vulcan B.2 XM604 (22nd) and Aerolineas Argentinas LV-PXP (28th).

1st French Navy Dakota 100.825 (callsign F-YFGN) arrived at 1222 from Lorient. This aircraft was a former USAF example (42-100825), that served with the French military until 1984.

2nd The second Brantly operated by Ferranti, G-ASLO, made the first of many visits to Ringway up until 1969. In May 1971 it was sold in Eire as EI-AVK.

2nd BOAC replaced their cargo DC-7s, and from today they are operating swing-tail CL-44 N228SW, leased from Seaboard World. Flight number BA065 operates three-times-weekly, routing to New York via Prestwick & Montreal. This aircraft permits palletised cargo for the first time, rather than undergoing the time-consuming bulk-loading system, mandatory for DC-7s. The CL-44 allows BOAC to keep to a minimum turnaround time and transport 30% more freight across the North Atlantic than was previously achieved. The displaced Douglas DC-7s, G-AOII & G-AOIJ, were now on borrowed time. G-AOIJ (last visit 25th Sept) had already been withdrawn, but G-AOII made a couple of visits up until its final one on 14th January 1964.

3rd Queen's Flight Whirlwind XR486 ('Hover 2') had been on local duties in Manchester city centre, when it arrived at 1656 for fuel, prior to its departure to RAF Benson.

8th Aircraft operated by McVitie-Price are frequent visitors to Ringway, due to their factory in Heaton Chapel. Their latest hack is PA-23 G-APVK, which made its first visit today, replacing PA-23 Aztec G-ASEV.

13th October 1963 - Douglas DC-4 G-ASEN is seen operating the final Starways flight from Manchester. On 31st December 1963 the airline ceased operations, and the following day British Eagle took over all routes. After a short period with Icelandair, G-ASEN was leased to Ace Freighters until 1966, when it was purchased by Invicta Airways. (MA Archive via Ringway Publications)

14th The visit of Dutch-side Willem II for a European cup-winners cup match, brought a number of flights into Manchester. The team arrived today on Dakota PH-SSM, which left on the 16th. The fans arrived the following day aboard Martin's Air Charter Dakotas PH-MAC & PH-SCC. Manchester United convincingly thrashed the visitors 6-1, which took them through to the next round to play Tottenham Hotspur.

17th This month's foreign lights consisted of Twin Bonanzas D-INES today & D-IEHE (19th) and PA-23 Apaches F-F-BHEA (19th- first visit) & OY-FAV (21st/23rd).

24th The visit of two Dragon Rapides, G-ALBC & G-AHKV, was pleasing enough, but even more remarkable was their arrival and departure from/to Coventry in military-style formation!

NOVEMBER 1963

Cyclonic weather was firmly in charge, with many gales recorded and an above average rainfall. Fog was widespread on the 6th & 27th. The month's temperature extremes saw 18°C at Compton (10th) and a low of -12°C at Braemar (21st).

British Eagle challenged BEA's monopoly again on the Manchester-Heathrow route, insisting there was a big demand for extra services on the route. They were appealing against yet another rejection by the Air Transport Licencing Board. If successful, they would operate fifteen flights a week in each direction until March 1966, increasing to eighteen flights thereafter. The route had so much potential, that a second operator could only stimulate extra growth. Passengers on the route increased from 76,000 in 1958-1959 to 315,000 in 1962-63, so a second operator on the route would not take traffic away from BEA.

International flights operated during the winter as follows:

AIR FRANCE - SE.210s operating twice-weekly (Mon/Thu), cargo flights four-weekly (Wed-Sat) with DC-4s.

AER LINGUS - Amsterdam (3 x weekly), Brussels (2 x weekly), Copenhagen (2 x weekly), Dusseldorf (2 x weekly), Frankfurt (2 x weekly) & Zurich (1 x weekly), all operated by Viscounts.

BEA - Amsterdam/Dublin/Dusseldorf/Paris & Zurich.

BOAC - B.707s operate five-weekly to New York (BA538/7). Bristol Britannias no longer operate to New York, but still serve Montreal (3 x weekly) and Toronto (2 x weekly). CL-44 N228SW leased from Seaboard World now operates the airline's cargo flights thrice-weekly to Montreal/New York.

KLM - Viscounts operated twice-weekly (KL149/150) with one of these flights operating onwards to Dublin (KL151/2). Cargo flights operated five-weekly with Douglas DC-3s.
SABENA - Once-weekly to/from New York with B.707s (SN545/6). The direct Brussels flight now operates three-weekly (SN621/2 Thu) & (SN623/4 Mon/Sat). Cargo flights continue twice-weekly (Wed/Fri) with Douglas DC-3s.
SWISSAIR - Operated twice-weekly from/to Zurich (SR706/7) with CV-440s until 15th December. From 22nd December, a second flight was added (SR718/9), operated by SE.210s.

Equipment changes were Air France (AF898): L-1049 F-BGND (85th/20th) & first visit Breguet 763 F-BASQ (22nd), KLM (KL019): CV-340 PH-CGI (6th/7th), DC-7 PH-DSG (16th), Martin's Air Charter DC-3s PH-SCC (20th) & PH-SSM (22nd) and Sabena (SN623): DC-6 OO-CTM (18th).

No ILS traffic was noted this month, but a couple of training flights were RAF Comet C.4 XR397 on its first visit (15th) & British Eagle Douglas DC-6 G-APON (30th).

2nd Aer Lingus introduced the Carvair onto its five-weekly mail/freight flight to Dublin (EI9212/7).

2nd Hiller UH-12E G-ASIG arrived at 1610 from Cambridge to become a temporary resident at Manchester. It would operate for the North Western Electricity Board on pipeline surveys throughout the area until the 11th February.

3rd The first Seaboard World CL44 to visit Manchester, was today's arrival of N123SW at 1638 from Frankfurt. The type had begun to replace the airline's Constellation fleet. In 1968, it was leased to short-lived British airline Transglobe as a passenger aircraft. The following year, it was purchased by another UK operator, Tradewinds, for cargo operations.

4th KLM Douglas DC-7 PH-DSC operated an outbound charter to New York, with the return being operated by PH-DSN (29th). Meanwhile PH-DSE (8th) called in en route Montreal-Amsterdam as KL062.

8th USAF Douglas C-117 12437 arrived at 2024 for a short stop, while routing RAF Mildenhall-Prestwick.

12th Wideroe's Nord 260 Broussard LN-LMG made its only visit today, arriving at 1520 from Stavanger. This aircraft, along with the airline's other two, was sold during 1964 due to technical issues.

14th Brazilian Air Force Douglas C-54G C54-2406 arriving at 1943 from Toulouse, was the third different aircraft to visit this year. It was picking up more HS.748 spares and stayed for three days.

16th Due to fog today, Ringway only recorded eight arrivals.

17th Flying Tigers L-1049H N6915C made the second of two visits, arriving at 1321 today from Amman to night-stop. Tragically another Constellation was lost on 24th December 1964, crashing shortly after takeoff from San Francisco on a flight to New York. The probable cause was an unexplained deviation from its departure course, into an area of rising terrain where downdraft activity and turbulence affected the aircraft's ability to climb sufficiently.

18th TMA added a 'new' Douglas DC-6, in the form of OD-AEG, which made its first appearance at Ringway today. It was operating a freight flight from Beirut, departing at 1333 for Frankfurt.

24th This month's light aircraft activity was confined to the end, with Beech 95 OY-DCP making its first visit on a round-trip from Tirstrup today. Heavier metal was provided by another visit by Falck Air Heron OY-ADV (26th) & Dove PH-FST (28th).

25th Braathens Douglas DC-4 LN-SUP was also a freight charter, arriving at 1403 from Kristiansand, before departing for Rotterdam.

26th USAF T-39 Sabreliner 10654 arriving at 0724 from Wildenrath, was also a first visit of type. It was the military version of North American's new corporate jet. The civilian version prototype, which carried the model number NA-265, made its first flight on 16th September 1958. It was named "Sabreliner" due to the similarity of the wing and tail to North American's F-86 Sabre. The type received its FAA type certification in April 1963, and over 800 Sabreliners were produced, 200 of which were T-39s.

26th Another US military visitor was USAF Douglas C-47 50940, arriving at 1102 today from Mildenhall, leaving later for Alconbury.

27th A brief interlude from this month's constant wind, rain and generally cloudy weather, came during the evening, when fog closed Heathrow Airport. With the arrival of twelve diversions, it turned into a BEA invasion, with Vanguards G-APEA, APEJ, APEK, APEL, APER, Comets G-APMC & APMD and Argosy G-APRM. There were a couple of first visits with Pan American B.707 N763PA at 2338 (PA100 from New

York/Shannon) and Intercontinental Airlines DC-6 N90703 at 2213 (from Dusseldorf), which was the sixth Douglas DC-6 aircraft to be built back in 1946.

29th Nord 1002 F-BGVU arrived at 1632 from Hawarden to night-stop, before its onward flight to RAF Wattisham, ultimately bound for the USA.

DECEMBER 1963

Following November's very wet conditions, December became an unusually dry month. For the first twelve days, the weather slowly changed from cyclonic to anticyclonic. Thereafter, high pressure dominated until the last few days of the month. A northerly airstream from the Arctic brought very cold weather from the 18th, when parts of Scotland and northern England had up to three inches of snow. This soon gave way to quiet, but cold weather. A brief depression passing through the UK on the 24th/25th was preceded by a foggy spell, lasting three days before the next frontal system brought freshening winds. The month's temperature extremes saw 13°C at Penzance (2nd) and a low of -14°C at Worksop (24th).

The year saw the number of inclusive tour passengers double to over 190,000, despite the continual use of turbine-powered equipment by the airlines.

Figures showed that Mercury Airlines carried more than 12,000 passengers during the year. However, the average weekly utilisation of their two Herons was rather low, at just less than sixteen hours each, with an overall average load-factor of only 64% which represented just ten passengers per flight.

The frequency for Manchester Director changed during the month from 124.8 to 121.35, and is still in use over fifty years later! The frequency for PAR radar approach also changed from 119.9 to 120.6.

Equipment changes were few with KLM (KL019): CV-340 PH-CGI (2nd), KLM (KL149): Electra PH-LLC (22nd).

No ILS traffic was noted again this month, but a couple of training flights were Derby Airways Argonaut G-ALHG (12th) and BEA Trident G-ARPE (18th).

5th Air France operated a couple of extra freight flights during December, from/to Paris-Orly, with L-1049G Constellations F-BGND (24th) & F-BGNG (today/31st).

6th By now Sabena were only operating two Douglas DC-7s, OO-SFB & OO-SFC, which were used as cargo aircraft. The latter called in at 2153 today from Brussels, en route to New York, and both soldiered on with the airline until 1968.

8th File today under 'what might have been'! Overnight fog with visibility down to ten yards locally in Southern England persisted throughout the day, but Ringway also suffered from the bad weather. Flights were generally unaffected, but there were no diverted flights. However, the events of the end of the month more than made up for today!

9th British United made the first of several visits during the month, operating trooping flights from/to Western Germany with their Douglas DC-6s, G-APNO (21st) & G-APNP (today, also 10th/11th/12th).

23rd For the next six days fog persisted in many parts of southern England. There were diversions into Manchester on four of these days, producing sixty-eight aircraft, the majority from Heathrow. Today saw eleven diverted flights during the morning, including EL AL B.707s 4X-ATB at 0858 (LY539 from Tel Aviv) & first visit 4X-ATC at 0836 (LY212 from New York); BOAC Britannias G-AOVF at 0854 (BA3295 from Bermuda) & G-AOVL at 0852 (BA3259 from Prestwick); first visit Comet G-APDG at 0847 (CE892 from Rome) & B.707 G-ARWE at 0843 (BA684 from New York) and KLM Electra PH-LLK at 0919 (KL119 from Amsterdam).

26th In amongst this evening's ten Heathrow diversions were five BEA Vanguards (G-APEC, APED, APEI, APEO & APER), and another Qantas B.707 making its first visit was VH-EBC arriving at 1944 (QF530 from New York).

27th Today broke the record for the number of diversions handled in a single day, thirty-seven in total. The very first diversion was arguably the best movement of the year, with PIA L-1049H Constellation AP-AJZ arriving at 0012 (from Beirut). There were just four more early morning diversions before a temporary improvement in the Heathrow weather, with BEA Argosy G-AOZZ at 0624, Pan American B.707s N727PA at 0708 (PA102 from New York) & first visit N728PA at 0655 (PA120 from Los Angeles) and another visit by EL AL B.707 4X-ATC at 0821 (LY252 from New York). By early afternoon however the diversions started to arrive, twenty-six in the next five hours, which included BEA aircraft Comets G-APMA, APMB, APMD & ARCO; Vanguards G-APEC, APEH, APEI, APEJ, APEL, APER & APET and Viscounts G-

AOHM, AOHR & AOHW. There were several other first visits, by Alitalia SE.210 I-DAXT at 1555 (AZ280 from Rome), Pan American B.707 N762PA at 1719 (PA001 from Frankfurt) and Sudan Airways Comet 4 ST-AAW at 1713 (SD118 from Rome).

28th Yet more diversions! Another ten arrived from Heathrow during a bout of late evening fog with more first visits, all Comet 4s, with Olympic G-APZM at 1813 (OA409 from Athens/Rome), MEA OD-ADS at 1839 (ME213 from Beirut) & East African Airways VP-KPK at 1943 (EC718 from Rome). Others of note were British Eagle Britannia G-AOVB at 2015 and British United Britannia G-APNA at 2154 (BR454 from Tenerife). Over the last three days Ringway earned an extra £2,000 in landing fees, and January would see many more diversions, with some big days ahead when the record number of aircraft handled in a single day was broken yet again.

31st BOAC Douglas DC-7 G-AOII, operating a cargo flight to Beirut (BA5615), was making its penultimate visit to Ringway.

18th December 1963 – A poor photograph in quality, but included because of its rarity. It shows Hawker Siddeley HS.121 Trident, Britain's newest jet airliner making its debut at Ringway. G-ARPE had been crew training at various airports during the day, when it arrived from Prestwick at 1633, before departing for Heathrow at 1720. (S.L Hall)

FIRST/LAST ARRIVALS & DEPARTURES 1963

First arrival: BEA Viscount G-AMOO @ 1031 from Belfast
First departure: BEA Viscount G-AMON @ 0731 to Liverpool
Last arrival: L-1049 Constellation F-BGNG @ 2239 from Paris
Last departure: BOAC DC-7F G-AOII @ 2307 to Beirut

Airport Stats 1963 (+/- % on Previous Year)		
Scheduled Passengers	930,000	+1.4%
Inclusive & Charter Passengers	190,000	+115.9%
Freight & Mail (Tonnes)	17,000	+14%
Movements	41,700	+3.7%

AIRPORT DIARY 1964

JANUARY 1964

Apart from the last few days, this month's weather was predominantly anticyclonic. Fog was a problem for the first ten days, but it was dry and cloudy throughout. The south saw up to twelve inches of snow, spreading north the following day, petering out as it went. An Icelandic deep depression brought milder, moister air from the Atlantic to western districts on the 18th, when a renewal of drizzle and fog spread to all districts overnight. Extensive fog persisting over the Midlands for a week, thickened most nights and was unbroken from South Yorkshire to Worcestershire from the 19th-23rd. The month's temperature extremes saw 14°C at Aber, South Wales (2nd) and a low of -13°C at Caldecott (14th).

Although BOAC operated the majority of transatlantic flights between Ringway and the USA & Canada, they were still irritated by the share of traffic being lost to their rivals, Sabena, so they decided to move against their competitor. The BOAC solution was quite simple; when the Belgian airline's Fifth Freedom rights came up for renewal in October 1963, they lodged an objection to any extension to these rights. BOAC claimed that Sabena's service created a 'material diversion of traffic' from its own route, which was clearly the case, but they ignored the history of the situation. Sabena began the route three years before BOAC, and had consistently used the most modern equipment available. They also operated a punctuality and customer satisfaction record second-to-none. The Tory government consequently made the decision to restrict Sabena's transatlantic services to two per week during the summer, and one per week during the winter. However, the airline found the situation totally unacceptable, and decided to withdraw their B.707 services through Manchester completely. Sabena had been operating ten flights a week from Manchester to New York in 1958, so the levels the British government were now asking them to operate under were deemed uneconomically viable. It was estimated this would mean a loss of around £50,000 a year for Manchester Airport, but this would be offset by the introduction of a three-times-weekly Caravelle service to/from Brussels, replacing the current twice-weekly flights operated by CV-440s.

After three years of discussions with the MoA, the airport committee has recommended that the city council break all financial ties with the ministry. The result of the agreement will be that the ministry will cease all grants and financial aid to the airport and Manchester Corporation will keep the profits (£71,000 in 1963). The alternative plan was for the corporation to increase its payments to the MoA. As a parting gift, the ministry has agreed to give the corporation £650,000 towards the £1.8 million needed for the extension of the main runway, eventually to 9,000ft.

Equipment changes were few with Air France (AF898): L-1049G F-BGNG (2nd), KLM (KL019): CV-440 PH-CGI (14th) and Sabena (SN623): DC-6 OO-SDC (20th).

ILS traffic noted during the month was RAF Beverley XB291 (24th/27th) and a solitary training flight, with BKS HS.748 G-ARRW (25th).

2nd British United operated further trooping flights from/to Western Germany this month, with Douglas DC-6s G-APNO (6th) & G-APNP (2nd/3rd/6th/7th/9th/10th/11th/13th/16th/18th/22nd).

2nd First visit Schreiner Airways Dove PH-SAA began this year's foreign light contingent. However, most of the foreign light activity was confined to the end of the month, with first visit Commander 680 F-BJUP (25th), PA-23 Apache D-IMKU outbound to Cologne (27th) and Commander 560 SE-EDX (31st) on its only visit.

4th Helio Super Courier G-ARMU was a first visit of type. Designed in 1949, it was a Short Takeoff and Landing aircraft, first manufactured in 1954 with more than 500 being eventually built. G-ARMU became a resident at Ringway from June 1966 until October 1968, when it was sold in Eire as EI-ATG.

4th Fog forming widely became dense in parts of central and southern England. Twenty-nine diversions arriving from a variety of airports were mainly from Heathrow. The first was BEA Vanguard at 1317 from Dublin, one of seventeen from BEA during the day. Despite the quantity there were only four foreign arrivals, including two first time visits by KLM Electra PH-LLD at 1908 (KL135 from Amsterdam) & Pan American B.707 N760PA at 2133 (PA100 from New York).

5th The fog affecting Heathrow continued into the morning, and produced another four diversions. One of these was the first visit of Pan American B.707 N701PA at 0654 (PA058 from Chicago).

6th The New Year started with three Avro Anson visits; VL351 (today - MPMAG Andover/Scampton), VP518 (7th - MPMAH Hawarden/Andover) & VL337 (10th - CSM77 f/t Odiham).

14th Further fog in the south had the cash tills ringing again! Thirty diversions arriving today from 0830-1746 were mostly from Heathrow again. The fog, which was at its thickest from early morning until late afternoon, produced a little more variety than ten days ago, with plenty of first visits from SAS SE.210 SE-DAF at 1050 (SK513 from Stavanger), Pan American B.707s N706PA at 1112 (PA101 from Frankfurt) & N724PA at 1139 (PA724 from Bermuda), Alitalia SE.210 I-DABI (AZ288 from Milan), United Arab Comet SU-ALM at 1442 (UA787 from Frankfurt), Qantas B.707 VH-EBD at 1452 (QF731 from Frankfurt) and finally EL AL Britannia 4X-AGD at 1627 (LY231 from Tel Aviv/Athens).

14th BOAC Douglas DC-7F G-AOII made its final visit to Manchester today, on a further cargo flight to Beirut (BA5616). This aircraft and G-AOIJ had been sold by 1965, with G-AOII going to SAS as OY-KNE and G-AOIJ being sold in the USA as N16465.

19th A couple of early Heathrow diversions were Swissair SE.210 HB-ICZ (SR700 from Zurich) & Alitalia Douglas DC-7F I-DUVE at 0025 (AZ976 from Milan). Further fog in the evening produced yet another Pan American B.707, when N717PA made its first visit at 2202 (PA100 from New York). BOAC Britannia G-AOVM (BA3376 from Khartoum) also diverted in at 2206, with the Sultan of Tanganyika and his entourage onboard. This East African state would later merge with Zanzibar, to form the United Republic of Tanganyika & Zanzibar, which became Tanzania eventually.

20th USAF VC-47 51116 made the first of three visits this year, operating from/to its base at Brussels.

21st Yet another bumper day for diversions! Of the twenty-five arrivals during a twelve hour period from 1000, all but three were from Heathrow, and they included several notables worthy of a mention. There were six SE.210 Caravelles; Swissair's HB-ICU at 1024 (SR100 from Zurich) & HB-ICS at 1501 (SR110 from Zurich); two SAS first visits with SE-DAA at 1300 (SK513 from Stavanger) & LN-KLI at 1355 (SK501 from Copenhagen); and two from Alitalia with I-DABI at 1454 (AZ280 from Rome) & I-DABT at 1401 (AZ288 from Genoa) which was a first visit. Also remarkable were the six diverted Pan American flights, three of which were first visits, with B.707s N715PA (PA058 from Chicago), N719PA (PA120 from Prestwick), N761PA (PA101 from Frankfurt) & DC-8 N802PA (PA056).

21st Lebanese cargo airline TMA made four visits to Ringway this year. Arriving today was Douglas DC-6 OD-AEG on its second visit, night-stopping on a freight flight from/to Beirut via Frankfurt.

22nd A single diversion this morning from Heathrow was another Pan American flight, with DC-8 N812PA making its first visit at 0737 (PA106 from Boston).

24th Fog at Woodford this time produced RAF Vulcan B.2 XM610, the third Vulcan to land at Ringway. Arriving at 1318 today (Avro 8), it departed for Woodford the following morning at 1211.

24th French Air Force Noratlas 75/62-KS, f/t Le Bourget, was a first visit of type. These would be fairly frequent visitors to Ringway during the next three decades.

27th Kar-Air CV-340 OH-VKM (AY5043 from Glasgow) made its only visit, operating a charter on behalf of Finnair. In March 1964, it was transferred to Finnair, serving them until its sale in Canada in 1973.

FEBRUARY 1964

Low pressures over the south dominated, except for some high pressure on the 18th-21st and it was dry, but dull. The month's temperature extremes saw 15°C at Letchworth (27th) and a low of -14°C at Nairn (25th).

Equipment changes this month were <u>KLM (KL019)</u>: CV-440 PH-CGI (21st) and <u>Swissair (SR718)</u>: SAS SE.210s LN-KLP (29th) & SE-DAC (22nd).

ILS traffic included USAF C-133 56-2006 (14th), PA-23 Aztec G-APYK (19th) and camouflaged RAF Vulcan B.2 XM645 (27th). Training flights were operated by BEA Trident 1s G-ARPF (4th) & G-ARPE (7th).

3rd This month's foreign light arrivals began today with a first visit by Commander 560 F-BJEV. Others were Beech 58 N9605Y (20th), Heron OY-ADU (25th/27th), Commander 680 D-ILUX also on its first visit (27th), and lastly PA-23 Apache D-IMKU (29th).

4th The second BEA Trident 1 visit was G-ARPF, arriving from Heathrow on crew training duties. Another, G-ARPE (7th), was also crew training, carrying out numerous ILS approaches without actually landing.

4th USAF Douglas C-47 76207 was a first visit, operating from/to its RAF Lakenheath base. A much more interesting US military visitor would make its only appearance at Ringway ten days later.

4th Royal Navy Sea Devon XJ321 (Navair 745 from Lee-on-Solent) made its first and only visit this year. Other UK military aircraft this month were Pembrokes WV748 (5th) & XL954 (17th); Devon VP972 (20th) and Anson VM369 (28th).

7th Prototype HS.748 G-ARRV, arrived as a weather diversion from Woodford, and returned there the following day at 10.00.

8th Slow to clear overnight fog in the south resulted in seven Heathrow diversions, but none of any great interest. BOAC B.707 G-APFB arrived at 0648 operating a Nigeria Airways flight (WT910 from Lagos/Rome) and although BOAC Comets were not too common to Manchester, G-APDH diverted in at 0938 (BA130 from Cairo).

14th Another ILS visitor was the welcome sight of USAF C-133 Cargomaster 56-2006, en route to Lajes AFB, Azores.

16th The next five days of snowy weather produced few diversions, but three today were: Heathrow (BEA Viscount G-AOYP), Gatwick (BUA Britannia G-APNA) & Birmingham (BEA Viscount G-AOYG).

22nd The Cessna 336 Skymaster, a push-me-pull-you concept, made its first visit to Manchester when G-ASLL arrived, operated by TV personality Hughie Green. The first of its type onto the UK register, it made frequent visits until July 1968 when it was sold. Green, who flew for the Royal Canadian Air Force during World War II, would fly the judges of his recently resurrected game show, 'Opportunity Knocks', between venues all over Britain. Also, he was involved in an incident in West Germany last year in April 1963, when he was fired upon by a Soviet aircraft, whilst flying in a Berlin air corridor on his way to a personal engagement at RAF Gatow in West Berlin.

29th The month ended on a cold and foggy note, and although Heathrow was affected by fog early and late today, only four diversions arrived, with nothing of note amongst them. Leeds provided two diversions (Aer Lingus F.27 EI-AKF & BKS HS.748 G-ARRW), and Castle Donington provided two Derby Airways Dakotas, G-AMSZ & G-ANTD, both diverting in late evening.

29th Newcastle-based Tyne Tees Aviation operated three DC-3s for IT, ad hoc, and freight operations. One of these Dakotas, G-APUC, operated a return flight to Newcastle today. The airline would make three more visits during the year, and their last appearance at Manchester would be DC-3 G-AMNV (22nd Oct 1964). They continued operations until January 1965, when they went into liquidation.

MARCH 1964

Cold, dull and wet was the synopsis for March, with troughs of low pressures from the Atlantic giving unsettled weather. Mid-month saw significant snowfalls in Scotland, Yorkshire and central England and little sunshine throughout. Worthing and Ross-on-Wye recorded their dullest March since 1900. The month's temperature extremes saw 16°C at Sellafield (20th) and a low of -8°C at Dundeugh, Castle Douglas (7th).

The main 06/24 runway is to be extended by 400ft, at an estimated cost of £54,000. This will be the first stage in the proposed extension to 9,000ft, which calls for an extra 400ft at the north eastern end and 1,100ft at the south western end. This first stage will bring the length to 7,900ft.

Still no first visits from any scheduled service operators this month and no equipment changes either. From the 2nd March, BOAC replaced Bristol Britannias with B.707s on their Canadian flights (inbound BA608-Sundays and outbound BA607- Mon/Thu).

ILS traffic this month included RAF Vulcan B.2 XM646 (20th) and Air Ferry C-54 G-ASOG (23rd). Training flights were operated by BOAC B.707s G-ARWD (30th) & G-ARWE (11th).

1st It was the final day of Britannia operations by BOAC, with G-AOVH operating the final Britannia transatlantic flight through Manchester. The type had been operating the majority of North Atlantic flights since being introduced in April 1959. For a number of years, the Britannia and BOAC had a bad reputation for overflying Manchester in semi-adverse weather conditions. Many BOAC captains adopted a 'high and mighty' attitude in relation to Manchester's 'Runway Visual Range'. Visibility had to be at least two kilometres before they would even consider making an approach. However, the Britannia did provide a reliable service once flight crews became familiar with the aircraft, and had overcome Manchester's varying weather conditions and the relatively short main runway.

3rd Of the four foreign flights this month, Commander 500 F-BFRB today and Beech 95 D-GBIE (11th) were first visits. Apart from the Dornier (18th), the only other foreign visitor was Beech 80 D-ILDA (19th).

10th HS.748 G-ARAY, arriving at 2237 today, was returning from its South American tour via Keflavik. It cleared customs and night-stopped, before departing back to Woodford the following day.

10th Bell 47 GAPTH called in for fuel at 1715. This helicopter was based at Knutsford Services, operating police patrols covering the M6 Motorway.

10th TMA Douglas DC-4F OD-ADK, f/t Frankfurt was a freight charter, eventually bound for Melbourne.

11th BEA operated its first revenue earning Trident flight (G-ARPG), on an ad hoc substitution of a Comet 4B service from Heathrow to Copenhagen.

11th Cessna 310 G-APNJ arrived at 1639 from Liverpool. Apart from a few local flights, it remained tucked away inside the south side hangars, before finally departing to Birmingham on 23rd September.

17th Having overcome Tottenham Hotspur in December, Manchester United now faced Sporting Lisbon in the quarter-finals of the Cup Winners' Cup. Hopes were high of reaching the semi-final, after beating the Portuguese side 4-1 at Old Trafford in February. The team flew out today for the second leg aboard Air Links Hermes G-ALDA (returning 19th), but after a disastrous night in Lisbon, United crashed out of the competition, having been comprehensively thrashed 5-0!

18th Dornier Do.28 D-IBEL was the second example to visit. Arriving at 1741 from Dusseldorf, it was on demonstration to United Steel, who eventually took delivery of a Dornier (Do.28 G-ATAL) in August 1965.

29th As well as BEA introducing the Trident into full service this month, BOAC commenced VC-10 operations today, when G-ARVJ flew from Heathrow to Lagos.

31st Boeing 707 OO-SJF (1205/1300 SN545 BRU-JFK) was Sabena's final transatlantic flight from Manchester. They had pioneered transatlantic travel at Ringway, with their Douglas DC-6Bs. They provided Manchester's first scheduled transatlantic flight, were the first airline to operate a daily service, and the first to use jets across the Atlantic. However, the UK government would only permit them two services per week, which meant Sabena had no choice other than to withdraw. Having said this, the airline would introduce a three-times-weekly night-stopping service from/to Brussels, with SE.210 Caravelles from next month.

APRIL 1964
The month began with a large pressure and it was cloudy again, with more rain than March. The first four days were very cold, with London experiencing its coldest April since 1911. Conditions worsened from the 8th and for the rest of April. The month's temperature extremes saw 22°C at Gillingham (27th) and a low of -7°C at Alwen, North Wales (7th).

Although the Minster of Aviation was still to fully approve the £1.8 million runway extension, work began this month.

Sabena introduced SE.210 Caravelles onto their evening Brussels services, resulting in plenty of first visits, with OO-SRA (29th), OO-SRB (3rd), OO-SRD (8th), OO-SRE (1st), OO-SRF (24th) & OO-SRG (17th).

ILS traffic noted this month included RAF Vulcan B.2 XM647 (2nd) and BKS HS.748 G-ASPL (7th).
International flights were operated during the summer as follows:

AIR FRANCE - Thrice-weekly to Paris with SE.210s, increasing to six-weekly between July and September. Cargo flights operated four-weekly with Douglas DC-4Fs/L-1049s.

AER LINGUS - Amsterdam (5 x weekly), Brussels (3 x weekly), Copenhagen (2 x weekly), Dusseldorf (3 x weekly), Frankfurt (3 x weekly) & Zurich (1 x weekly), all operated by Viscounts.

BEA - Amsterdam/Dublin/Dusseldorf/Paris & Zurich, with summer routes to Barcelona/Palma & Milan.

BOAC - Were now operating B.707s on their New York/Montreal & Toronto services - New York (BA538/7) five-weekly increasing to daily from 1st May. Montreal/Toronto (BA607/8) three-times-weekly. Leased CL-44 N228SW operated cargo flights three-weekly to Montreal/New York (BA065).

KLM - Operated to Amsterdam four-weekly with Viscounts (KL149/150), one of these flights operates onwards to Dublin (KL151/2). Also a five-weekly DC-3 cargo flight to Amsterdam (KL019/020).

SABENA - The evening Brussels service is increased to thrice-weekly with SE.210 Caravelles. Ostend operated June-September four-weekly with a mix of CV-440s & DC-6s. Dakotas are used four-weekly on freight flights (SN191/2).

SWISSAIR - In April and October SR706/7 operated twice-weekly with CV-440s. From 15th May-28th September, flights operated thrice-weekly with a mix of SE.210s, Convair CV-440s & CV-990s.

1st SE.210 OO-SRE operated the first flight of Sabena's new three-times-weekly service from/to Brussels (SN623/4).

1st PA-23 Apache OY-DCC (also 10th) was the first corporate aircraft to be operated by the Danish toy manufacturer, Lego. Making its first visit today, it appeared regularly until June 1965, before it was sold later the same year. Other light aircraft during the month were PA-23 Apaches OY-FAV (15th) & D-GARY (24th) and Twin Bonanza D-ILLI on its first visit to Manchester (16th).

2ⁿᵈ April 1964 - The 1964 season would see Mercury Airlines operating its largest scheduled network to date, but also its last. To cope with these extra services, they took delivery of their first Dakota today, G-AMSN. Throughout the summer it would operate from other airports, such as Birmingham & Liverpool, and provide services from Manchester to the Isle of Wight & Ostend. (MA Archive via Ringway Publications)

5ᵗʰ Irish operator Aer Turas began operations in 1962 as an air taxi service from Ireland to the UK, with single Dragon Rapide EI-AML. Earlier this year they added an ex-Nigeria Airways Dakota, EI-ANK, which made its first visit today operating a cargo flight from Dublin. Although in the early days they would operate both passenger and cargo flights, they quickly concentrated their efforts on freight. On the 17ᵗʰ, Rapide EI-AML made its first visit from/to Dublin.

6ᵗʰ RAF Anson TX182 (also 7ᵗʰ) was one of thirteen Anson flights operating through Ringway during the month, but most remained unidentified.

14ᵗʰ Trans-Canada DC-8s began the first of a series of charters, operating throughout the summer, with the last on the 17ᵗʰ October. CF-TJO arriving at 0816 today (TC016 from Vancouver) was also a first visit. Plenty of others followed, with CF-TJA (31ˢᵗ May), CF-TJB (2ⁿᵈ June), CF-TJD (3ʳᵈ October), CF-TJG (17ᵗʰ June), CF-TJH (3ʳᵈ July), CF-TJI (18ᵗʰ May) & CF-TJP (1ˢᵗ July).

15ᵗʰ German-based RAF Pembroke XL931 arrived at 1036 today from Northolt, departing later for RAF Wildenrath. Delivered to the RAF in 1958 and scrapped at Wildenrath twelve years later, this was the aircrafts only visit to Ringway during its relatively short career.

21ˢᵗ Douglas DC-3 EI-ACE had the dubious honour of being used for the final Aer Lingus DC-3 flight through Ringway, operating cargo flight EI4200/1 from/to Dublin. The airline had purchased a number of war-surplus Douglas DC-3/C-47 Dakota aircraft, and commenced services through Manchester on 1ˢᵗ July 1946, with Dakota EI-ACT calling at Manchester en route from Dublin to Amsterdam. During daylight hours, these aircraft were 36-seater passenger airliners, but by night they were hastily converted into an all-cargo configuration. Sometimes there were up to three 'Dak' flights a night, providing around eleven tonnes of cargo capacity in each direction across the Irish Sea. The cargo varied from Post Office mail, to mushrooms, footwear, unfinished wool fabrics, kosher meat products and even greyhound dogs. The return loads were made up of mail, newspapers and every conceivable type of general freight. Although Fokker F.27s or Vickers Viscount would be used occasionally, the flights continued to be Dakota operated right up until today. The company's three Carvairs, which had been used occasionally since March 1963, would now exclusively operate all mail and cargo flights for the airline.

22nd Today, Aer Lingus B.720 EI-ALB commenced the first of several flights during the year, to/from New York, with most operating outbound via Shannon.

25th Caledonian began their summer programme from Ringway today, with Douglas DC-7 G-ASHL operating outbound as CA957 to Palma. Other aircraft used during the year were DC-7s G-ARYE, G-ASHL, G-ASID & G-AOIE, with the latter replacing G-ASIV which returned to Sabena at the end of 1963. The airline also leased two Sabena Douglas DC-6 aircraft, OO-CTN & OO-CTK, for the summer season as G-ASRZ (f/v 29th May) & G-ASTS (25th June) respectively.

25th Wardair DC-6 CF-PCI (WD317 Sondre Stromfjord/Keflavik) made the first of two visits this year today, with the second being on the 7th May (WD323 from Sondre Stromfjord).

26th Britannia G-AOVG made its first visit to Ringway today, on a charter from Amsterdam with its new owners, British Eagle. A number of ex-BOAC aircraft purchased by the airline earlier this year were G-AOVA/AOVB/AOVC/AOVE/AOVF/AOVM/AOVN & AOVT. Another Britannia, G-AOVO, crashed in January 1964 on approach to Innsbruck. All of these could be seen during the summer of 1964, operating inclusive tour flights, with the exception of G-AOVF which had been converted into a freighter.

27th Cessna 310 N1028Q arrived at 1542 from Warton to operate a demonstration flight for prospective south side interested parties!

MAY 1964

The weather was of a westerly cyclonic type for the first two weeks, with a series of troughs and ridges crossing the country. The next week was anti-cyclonic, but returned to low pressures with winds changing to easterly. On the 29th, thunderstorms accompanied by torrential rain caused flooding in central and northern England, which continued across many parts of the country for the next two days. The month's temperature extremes saw 27°C in various spots in southern England (17th) and a low of -2°C at Cairngorm (14th).

The government finally gave their approval for the runway extension. Negotiations had been ongoing since January 1961, when the city unsuccessfully submitted a scheme to the ministry to extend runway 24/06 to 10,500ft by crossing the Bollin Valley. The first stage, which began last month, involved adding 1,100ft at the south-western end. Work will also include adding 400ft of hard packed earth at the northeast end. The main Wilmslow-Altrincham road, which runs close to the end of the runway, will be carried in a tunnel under the extension. A grant of £650,000 would be made available by the government towards the cost of the extension. Under the terms of the agreement reached earlier this year, the city would get no more cash for capital works, but they would be allowed to retain all profits made at the airport.

The following could be seen during the summer months operating ITs to various destinations: Adria Airways (Dubrovnik/Ljubljana), Aviaco (Barcelona/Palma), Balair (Basle), Braathens (Bergen), BKS (Genoa), British Eagle (Nice/Ostend/Palma/Perpignan/Rimini), British United (Stavanger), Caledonian (Barcelona/Palma/Rimini/Valencia), Channel Airways (Ostend), Condor (Munich), Dan-Air (Basle/Bordeaux/Dinard/Munich/Ostend/Perpignan/Tarbes), Derby Airways (Ostend/Wick), Euravia (Barcelona/Genoa/Newquay/Nice/Palma/Perpignan/Pisa/Rimini/Valencia/Venice), SAM (Rimini), Spantax (Barcelona/Palma/Valencia), TASSA (Barcelona/Palma) & UTA (Perpignan).

The only scheduled first visit was Aer Lingus (EI9212): Carvair EI-ANJ (19th). Equipment changes were KLM (KL151): DC-7 PH-DSP (24th) and Sabena (SN623): CV-440 OO-SCP (3rd).

The only ILS traffic noted this month was Queen's Flight HS.748 XS789 (16th). Two training flights were operated by British Eagle Douglas DC-6 G-APON (24th) & BOAC B.707 G-APFC (25th).

1st Euravia began another extensive summer charter from Ringway today, with L-049 Constellation G-ARVP operating their first flight to Palma. They were operating an identical fleet to 1963, but all of their Constellations would be replaced by Britannias for the start of the 1965 summer season. The Constellation was deemed too small for many of the airline's routes, so a number of ex-BOAC Britannia 102s would be purchased. Their last visits are as follows:

G-AHEL	9th August	Sold November 1964 to Britair as 5Y-ABF
G-AHEN	18th October	Withdrawn April 1965, broken up May 1965
G-ALAK	23rd September	Sold August 1965 to Ace Freighters
G-ALAL	5th October (diversion)	Sold February 1965 to Ace Freighters
G-ARVP	3rd October	Withdrawn April 1965, broken up May 1965
G-ARXE	6th October	Withdrawn May 1965

2nd Dan-Air was another airline with a busy IT programme from Manchester, with all flights being operated by Airspeed AS.57 Ambassadors. Today's first was a rotation to Amsterdam with G-AMAE. Others during the summer were G-ALFR, ALZN, ALZO, ALZX, ALZY & AMAH.

3rd The first Martin's Air Charter DC-7 seen at Ringway was PH-DSO, arriving on a return flight from Amsterdam today. Purchased from KLM in March this year, it served until October 1968, when it was withdrawn at Stansted. For the next twelve years it was used by Stansted Fire Service Training School, still in the airline's old colours.

3rd Beech 65 LN-IKB made it first visit at 2144, direct from Hanover, where it had been on static display at the annual air show. It was made available to prospective south side buyers to view, and left on the 5th.

4th Belgian Army Dornier Do.27 OL-D02 arrived at 1736 today from Southend. In 1960 twelve Dornier Do 27J-1 single engine aircraft were acquired by the Light Aviation branch of the Belgian Army. They were used as a six-seat communications base hack, and for free-fall parachute training. Although these aircraft served with the Light Aviation until March 1977, OL-D02 was the only one to visit Ringway.

4th Derby Airways only operated summer schedules to Ostend and Wick with Dakotas, so Argonaut visits during 1964 were fairly limited. They were mainly used for occasional sub-charters, ad hocs or trooping charters and one such troop flight was operated today by Argonaut G-ALHG, inbound from Gutersloh.

8th French airline UTA made its first visit today, with DC-6 F-BHEF operating a round-trip from Toulouse. It departed on the 10th, two days later than envisaged due to engine trouble. From the 13th June to 19th September, the airline also operated a weekly IT flight to Perpignan, with Douglas DC-6s F-BGOB/BGTY/BHEE/BHEF & BHMS.

8th Another French visitor was Air Force Beech C-45 Expeditor 765, arriving at 1447 from Villacoublay. This aircraft was also present until the 10th, probably in connection with the unserviceable UTA DC-6.

10th RAF Pembroke WV704 (Rafair 5361) arrived at 0914 from Crosby-on-Eden, clearing customs before departing to Northolt. Other RAF flights during the month were Anson TX213 (26th/27th/28th) and Whirlwind XP349 (22nd), which operated from Platt Fields Park to RAF Valley.

10th Spantax had a similar programme to last year, with DC-7 EC-ATR operating the first flight outbound to Palma. In between they had added a second DC-7, EC-ATQ (f/v - 17th May), which was formerly with Sabena as OO-CFF.

10th Balair began a weekly Basle charter today with Douglas DC-6 HB-IBZ, with flights operating until 20th September. Also used were Douglas DC-6s HB-IBR (f/v 28th June) & HB-IBU.

11th Braathens operated an ad hoc charter from Gothenburg, using Fokker F.27 LN-SUE which was also a first visit. From the 17th May until the 20th September, a weekly Bergen flight was operated with F.27s LN-SUA, SUE, SUG, SUN, SUO & SUW (f/v 5th July).

14th Smiths Aviation HS.748 G-ASJT carried out various ILS approaches, landings and touch-and-goes between 1056 and 1648 today. This aircraft, which was delivered in October 1963, was used for developing the company's latest instruments and their SEP6 Autopilot system, as well as demonstration tours of Europe and the United States.

20th KLM Douglas DC-7F PH-DSE arrived at 0628 direct from Miami, with an unusual and varied cargo. Included aboard this Noah's Ark flight were eight porpoises, a family of boa constrictors and the gift of a palm tree from the City of Miami. They were all in connection with the opening of Morecambe Oceanarium, the first of its kind in Europe. Brantly G-ASHD operated by Pontin's was also present, before departing for Morecambe with food for the dolphins.

22nd Beagle 206 G-ARXM, arriving at 2302 today from Dusseldorf, was a first visit of type. It left for Goodwood the next morning, but unfortunately it was written off two days later following a fatal accident at Wisborough Green, Sussex. The seven-seat twin-engine liaison and communication aeroplane was built by Beagle Aircraft Limited at Shoreham Airport & Rearsby aerodrome. This particular aircraft (designated B.206Y), was the second prototype and slightly bigger, with a larger span and extra seating. Two aircraft were built for evaluation by the Ministry of Aviation. To decide which aircraft would replace the Avro Anson, a competition had been held at RAF Northolt in March 1963, to choose between the Beagle 206 and the de Havilland Devon, which resulted in twenty Bassets being ordered for the RAF. The first delivery to RAF communications squadrons was made in May 1965. The first civil ordered aircraft (G-ASWJ) was delivered in May 1965 to Rolls-Royce Limited at Hucknall. When the company needed the room at Rearsby to build the new Beagle Pup, production of the B.206 ended with their eightieth aircraft.

23rd Adria Airways began their summer programme, with Douglas DC-6A YU-AFD operating to Dubrovnik. Flights operated to Dubrovnik and Ljubljana until the 4th October, with DC-6s YU-AFC/AFD/AFE & AFF.

24th Today's appearance of British Eagle Douglas DC-6 G-APON was very interesting. It arrived from Heathrow at 1454 to carry out numerous ILS approaches on a crew training detail, but the following month it was sold to Zantop as N6814C.

24th Canadian Pacific Airlines made five visits to Ringway during the year, the first of which was operated today by Douglas DC-8 CF-CPF from Toronto, departing to Stansted. Two more DC-8s making first visits would be CF-CPH (31st August) & CF-CPJ (21st July). The airline was an original delivery customer of the DC-8, receiving their first DC-8-43 on 22nd February 1961. At this point, the colourful orange scheme the airline was best known for was another four years away. In 1968, Canadian Pacific Airlines was renamed CP Air by the parent company, which led to the orange scheme already being used by the Canadian Pacific Corporation's other subsidiaries, such as CP Rail and CP Hotels.

25th Aviaco returned to Ringway today, for the first of their series of IT flights, again with their L-1049G Constellations. Flight AO1220/1 from/to Palma operated on Mondays until the 7th September, with the following same aircraft being used again this year: EC-AIN/AIO/AMP/AMQ/AQM/AQN & ARN.

28th Although BOAC had ceased operating Bristol Britannias on scheduled transatlantic services, resulting in a number being sold, they were still operating G-AOVH/AOVJ/AOVK/AOVL/AOVP/AOVR & AOVS. One of these, G-AOVL, arrived from Heathrow today on a charter to New York via Prestwick (BA3577).

28th A stubborn bank of fog affecting Heathrow well into the morning, netted the airport eighteen diversions. First visits were Kuwait Airways Comet 9K-ACE at 0807 (KU047 from Geneva), Austrian Viscount OE-LAH at 0817 (OS5213 from Salzburg), Pan American DC-8 N817PA at 0904 (PA056 from Boston) & Swissair DC-8 HB-IDA at 0918 (SR103 from Chicago). A few others of note were Pan American B.707 N758PA at 0730 (PA058 from Chicago), KLM DC-8 PH-DCI at 0912 (from New York) & Qantas B.707 VH-EBC at 1151 (QF735 from Frankfurt).

30th Spanish operator TASSA began their second IT programme from Ringway, with Douglas DC-6 EC-AVA. Also used were Douglas DC-6 EC-AUC and DC-7s EC-AVP (f/v 20th June) & EC-AXP (f/v 11th July).

30th May 1964 - Heron OY-AFO arrived at 1247 for pre-customs clearance, prior to its delivery to Falck Air. This was the last DH.114 Heron off the production line, and used for ambulance and scheduled flights between Beldringe, nr Odense and Copenhagen-Kastrup. In March 1968 it returned to the North West to take up residency at Ringway as G-AWDT, operating for the Nuclear Power Group. (Dave Peel collection)

30th May 1964 - New Irish operator Shannon Air made their debut at Manchester, with their sole aircraft Douglas DC-4 EI-ANL, from/to Shannon. This former Northwest/Trek Airways and Luxair aircraft would only make two further visits, before the airline folded in 1966. However, it would spend a further ten years on the Irish register, operating for Aer Turas as EI-APK. (Lloyd Robinson)

31st German airline Condor commenced a weekly late-night flight to Munich until the 20th September. Operated by Vickers Viscounts, D-ANOL was used on the first service. Others used during the summer were D-ANIP (f/v 7th June), D-ANUN (f/v 14th June) & D-ANUR (f/v 26th July).

JUNE 1964

June's weather was mainly cyclonic until the 21st, with troughs or depressions over the UK. The rest of the month was dominated by high pressure, extending from the Azores. Southeast England saw frequent thunder and heavy rain during the month, with Worthing experiencing the wettest June since records began in 1887, although it became dry and sunny towards the end. The month's temperature extremes saw 27°C at Gillingham (27th) and a low of -4°C at Cairngorm (20h).

Ringway officials urged the French government to reconsider the decision to halt scheduled flights to Nice, three weeks before they were due to start. After approving a twice-weekly British Eagle service from Manchester to Nice, they withdrew permission saying it would not attract sufficient traffic.

The number of foreign light aircraft purchased in the UK during the last three years, was more than double those manufactured in Britain. The Americans had a big lead over the British in 1961, with an established light aircraft industry, and the French and others were also making serious inroads into the UK market. Despite the setting up of the Beagle Company, there was no imminent improvement in the sales of British-made aircraft. Beagle were concentrating on building up a strong and satisfactory after-sales service for the home market, before starting deliveries abroad. The three models exported were the Airedale, the Terrier and the new 206. This was not enough however, and more British firms were urged to start designing and constructing aircraft for this blossoming market.

Scheduled first visits this month were Sabena (SN623): OO-SRC (19th) & Swissair (SR728): CV-990 HB-ICF (28th). Equipment changes were KLM (KL149): DC-7s PH-DSN (20th) & PH-DSC (27th).

No ILS traffic was noted this month, and the only training flight was BOAC B.707 G-ARRB (2nd).

1st In 1964 there weren't many privately operated airliners, but one such example arrived at 1537 today from Gatwick. It was Douglas DC-6 N100J, which was operated by Inter American Minerals until 1968, and would eventually operate for the Mexican Air Force for nearly thirty years before its retirement in 2003.

5th USAF Convair VT-29B 17899 made its first visit, arriving at 1026 today from RAF Northolt. These converted T-29s (based on the Convair 240) were used for transporting staff. This particular VT-29 was based at RAF Mildenhall until its retirement and subsequent preservation at Duxford in 1975. USAF Douglas C-47 48913 (11th) also made its first visit, arriving from Northolt and departing for Ramstein.

6th KLM DC-8 PH-DCH made its first visit arriving from Amsterdam in full Viasa colours, departing to New York via Prestwick. Another KLM/Viasa DC-8, PH-DCM (10th July), also operated a New York charter.

6th June 1964 - Channel Airways operated up to eight flights weekly to Ostend during the summer, mainly with the endangered species that was the Vickers Viking! The airline had just three of these aircraft at this point, G-AJFR/APOO & APOP. Also used during the summer were Viscounts G-AMOA, G-APZC and Douglas DC-4 G-ARYY. Note the 1964-vintage vehicles! (MA Archive via Ringway Publications)

7th Italian charter airline SAM (Societa Aria Mediterranea), began their summer IT programme, operating three flights f/t Rimini, MQ428/9 (fortnightly), MQ432/3 via Prestwick & MQ454/5 with DC-6s until the 2nd September; with the same aircraft as last year: I-DIMA/DIMD/DIME/DIMI (today)/DIMP & DIMU.

8th SE-ECS became the first foreign registered PA-30 Twin Comanche to visit Ringway, operating Malmo/Cardiff today. Others during the month were Beech 80 D-ILGU (9th), Beech 58 N9605Y (16th), Beech Bonanza F-BJRZ (17th), Beech 65 D-ILDA (18th/20th), & PA-23 Apache D-IMKU (23rd). However, the most interesting arrival was German monoplane Putzer Elster D-EDUF from Luton (29th).

16th Transair Sweden Douglas DC-6 SE-BDI operated a charter f/t Malmo today (TB233/4). It was the airline's first visit to Ringway since operating a summer IT programme in 1962.

17th BEA Helicopters S-61 G-ASNM operated a demonstration flight in between its arrival from Fort Dunlop and its departure to Harrogate. BEA Helicopters were formed as an independent company in 1964, and on the 1st May inaugurated the first service between Penzance and the Scilly Isles, with their new Sikorsky S-61s. In July 1965, the airline expanded into offshore oil support flights. Their S-61s were the backbone of the fleet, until being eventually phased out during 1986.

20th RAF Anson TX230 made its first visit today, night-stopping f/t Ternhill. Again, this was one of the numerous unidentified Anson flights during the month.

21st Two DHC-3 Otters, N127F & N128F, arrived during the evening on a fuel stop. Owned by Atlantic Helicopters, New York, they had recently served with the United Nations in the Congo, but were returning to Canada for resale. They left for Prestwick the next morning, suggesting they had limited fuel endurance.

22nd Douglas DC-3 TU-TIA arrived at 1621 from Keflavik, in full Air Ivoire colours. This aircraft had been operated by Pacific Northern, and was on delivery routing Seattle-Abidjan via twenty-five refuelling stops!

22nd Caledonian DC-7 G-ARYE departed at 2327 (CA167) bound for Leopoldville, a distance of 4,100 miles. Up to this date, this was the longest non-stop flight operated from Manchester.

23rd Due to the unavailability of DC-4 G-ARYY, Channel Airways had to draft in three aircraft to cover two Vikings (G-APOO/APOP) and Bristol 170 G-AICH.

24th Ten weather diversions from Heathrow this morning produced two first visits, with BOAC Comet G-APDI at 0933 (BA937 from Rome) and Lufthansa B.707 D-ABOD at 0937 (LH823 from Dublin).

28th Saturn began the first of a series of transatlantic charters, when DC-7 N90804 (f/v) arrived at 1920 from Gatwick, ultimately bound for New York. Flights operated until the 2nd September and the following DC-7s were also used: N90773, N90774, N90778, N90802 (f/v 24th July) & N90803 (f/v 21st July).

30th Iberia began a weekly scheduled night-flight to Barcelona/Palma (IB782/1) until the 22nd September, utilising L-1049G EC-AMQ on the inaugural flight.

JULY 1964

Although the month was a mainly dry, with some rain early on, the North West recorded an inch of rain on the 8th. High pressure took charge mid-month, resulting in below average temperatures. The temperature extremes saw 29°C at various places in the southeast (17th) and a low of -1°C at Balmoral (6th).

Equipment changes were KLM (KL149/151): DC-7s PH-DSC (11th), PH-DSD (4th), PH-DSL (18th/19th), PH-DSP (25th) & Electra PH-LLD (26th) and Swissair (SR706): DC-8 HB-IDC (3rd).

GCA/ILS traffic noted this month was RAF Vulcan B.2 XL384 (9th) & USAF C-130E 63-7832 (25th).

1st Mooney D-ELER, en route Southend-Inverness, made an emergency landing at 1115 due to a fuel shortage.

1st Anson G-AHKX, operating for Meridian Airmaps, arrived from Leeds to night-stop. It set course for Sheffield early the next morning for a local aerial survey, and appeared again on the 13th from Shoreham. It was based for the next two days undertaking more aerial surveys, including shots of the airport.

2nd Two first time visitors were Air India B.707 VT-DJJ (AI107 Heathrow-New York) collecting extra passengers, and B.707 VT-DNZ (AI106 New York-Heathrow 23rd) dropping in with extra passengers.

4th July 1964 - This was the final year of Connie operations by Euravia. G-ALAK began life with Aer Lingus in 1947, but served with them for less than six months, before being purchased by BOAC the following year. After retirement by Euravia, it was bought by Ace Freighters of Coventry, who operated it for just over a year. From 1968 to 1971, it was registered in Bolivia and Peru, before being broken up at Miami in late-1971. (Hubert Parrish)

5th Bolkow 208 Junior LN-TVI landed at 1503 today from Ostend, and stayed until the 11th. Yet another first visit of type, it was basically a Flygindustri MFI-9 Junior made in Sweden. It was also produced under license as the Bölkow Bo 208. It was powered by an air-cooled Continental A-75 engine, producing 56 kW (75 hp), driving a two-bladed variable-pitch propeller. The shoulder wings were forward swept, to place occupants ahead of the spar for visibility, and also used a tricycle undercarriage. The first example to be UK-registered was Biggin Hill-based G-ASAS in August 1962.

5th Martin's Air Charter DC-7 PH-DSO was drafted in on behalf of Caledonian, due to the unavailability of one of their own DC-7s. It operated CA957/8 f/t Palma, CA977/8 f/t Shannon & CA1027/8 f/t Barcelona, before positioning back to Amsterdam.

7th Sterling Douglas DC-6 OY-EAO made the first visit by the Danish charter airline, at 2010 on an inbound passenger charter from Copenhagen. DC-6 OY-BAU operated the return flight on the 4th August.

8th Beech 95 N9404Y f/t Luxembourg, which made its first visit today, would make one more appearance in February 1965. Other arrivals this month were PA-23 Apache's OY-FAV (12th) & EI-ANI (23rd), Commander 680 OO-SID (13th/14th), MS.880 Rallye F-BKKV (14th), PA-24 Comanche F-BLGY (18th), Twin Bonanza D-ILLI (25th) and Beech Marquis D-ILCA (30th).

9th Pan American operated the first of two transatlantic charters this year, when B.707 N714PA arrived at 0934 today on an inbound New York flight. B.707 N704PA (3rd September) operated the outbound flight to New York via Shannon.

9th Again due to the unavailability of a DC-7, Caledonian chartered Flying Enterprise Douglas DC-7 OY-DMS to operate CA1027/8 to/from Barcelona.

10th The only two US Army U-6 Beaver flights this year, both arrived this month. 58-2003 from Southend today, departed to RAF Leuchars the next morning, and 55-3299 routed Prestwick-Gatwick on the 15th.

11th Balair DC-6 HB-IBZ was sub-charted by Caledonian today, operating CA911/2 to/from Rimini.

11th Douglas DC-7 N8208H arrived from Palma at 0751, using the callsign 'EC-AXP'. It was eventually re-registered as such, having recently been purchased from National Airlines.

14th BEA cargo flight BE4902/3 operated by Skyways York G-AGNV, was the last visit by an Avro York. On 8th October 1964, it was flown to Staverton and donated to the Skyfame Museum. It was preserved in the colours of the famous York LV633 "Ascalon", the personal transport of Prime Minister Winston Churchill. According to local press, the York landed just 50ft short of the runway. Its C of A expired on 6th May 1965, having logged 18,100 flying hours. It was later moved to RAF Brize Norton and Shawbury, until it found its final resting place in the RAF Museum Cosford, forming part of the current "Cold War" exhibition.

17th Wideroe's Douglas DC-3 LN-RTA operated f/t Torp on a freight charter. After service during the Second World War, the aircraft came to Flugfelag Islands as TF-ISD and later LN-SUK with Braathens. It was then bought by Riis Flyrederi in September 1962 as LN-RTA, and leased to Transair Sweden during March/April 1963. After this it was leased to Martin's Air Charter, Loadair and finally Wideroe. It was broken up at Oslo during 1971, and used for fire practice until 1976 when it was burnt out.

18th TASSA DC-7 EC-AXP, which had recently arrived from Birmingham and was parked on Gate 6, had an engine fire and was declared unserviceable. Travel agency officials spent the day desperately searching for a substitute aircraft. Angry passengers besieged the Mercury Travel desk, demanding compensation for time lost on their 60-guinea holiday!

18th Flying Tigers L-1049H Constellation N6917V arrived at 0217 from Stockholm, later departing for Shannon. A second aircraft, L-1049G N7121C (9th August), landed from Gander on three engines.

18th Ex-KLM Douglas DC-7 PH-DSM, purchased by a new German operator Sudflug as D-ABAD in August 1963, made its first visit to Ringway today operating flights on behalf of Spantax.

19th As a result of TASSA DC-7 being unable to depart, more than eighty passengers finally left for Palma today, 21 hours late aboard DC-4 G-ARXJ. The irate passengers had staged a 'sit-down', and refused overnight accommodation at a Buxton hotel, alleging they had been "imprisoned" in the airport departure lounge. This was the third time that TASSA had suffered major delays. The previous week (12th) DC-7 EC-AXP left 24 hours late, and the week before (6th) DC-6 EC-AVA left 42 hours late.

20th USAF Douglas C-47 15619 made a brief visit from RAF Bovingdon, departing for Bitburg.

22nd This was the final year that US airline Capitol would operate Constellations into the UK, being superseded into the jet age with their new Douglas DC-8s. The arrivals of L-1049Hs N5402V (today) & N5401V (31st) and L-1049G N4903C (11th August) from Shannon to Amsterdam, would prove to be the final ones into Ringway.

25th July 1964 - Trans-Canada (later Air Canada), was another airline operating fairly regular charters during the 1960s from Ringway to Canada. DC-8-42 CF-TJE is seen above on its second visit, departing at 1325 today as TC026 to Prestwick/Toronto. (MA Archive via Ringway Publications)

28th Westair Cessna 310 N8052M arrived from Liverpool at 1227, later departing to Blackpool. In between, it performed a 50 minute demonstration flight.

31st Swissair operated an extra flight today, with SE.210 HB-ICR. This aircraft had been leased from Air France (F-BJTJ), and was making the first of three visits during 1964 before returning to Air France.

AUGUST 1964

High pressure dominated, bringing mostly dry weather during the month. A depression on the 19th brought a sharp fall in temperature, with parts of England 7°C below normal. It was very cold at night, with both air and ground frost a common occurrence. A southerly airstream at the end of the month, brought in some hot temperatures and uninterrupted sunshine across the UK. The month's temperature extremes saw 32°C at Cromer (28th) and a low of -2°C at Lincoln (31st).

Scheduled first visits were Air France (AF960): SE.210 F-BJTQ (22nd) and Swissair (SR706): DC-8 HB-IDD (7th). Equipment changes were KLM (KL149/151): DC-7 PH-DSD (1st) and Electras PH-LLF (2nd) & PH-LLK (9th).

RAF Vulcan B.2 XL835 (20th) was noted performing a couple of approaches, and BOAC B.707 G-APFL (14th) was seen crew training f/t Heathrow.

2nd Luton-based Autair (known as Court Line in January 1970), had made very few visits to Ringway so far during the 1960s. They were operating a varied fleet of Ambassadors, Vickers Vikings & Dakotas. Positioning in from Luton at 2013 today, Ambassador G-ALZV departed to Basle on an ad hoc flight to Basle on the 10th. It also operated an inbound pilgrimage flight from Lourdes.

2nd Also operating an ad hoc charter today was Austrian Airlines Viscount OE-LAH as OB1487 to Salzburg, which also made the return flight from Salzburg (15th) as OB1491. In May 1965, they commenced a weekly Salzburg IT charter.

4th This month's foreign light visitors kicked off today with PA-23 Apache OY-DCC (also 5th). Other arrivals were PA-28 Cherokee SE-ECB (5th), Beech Marquis D-ILCA (7th), PA-24 Comanche F-BLGY (17th), Commander 680 F-BILU (20th) and rounding off a busy month was Beech 95 OY-AOP & Cessna 182 OY-AEU (both 25th).

5th The Manchester Evening News reported that 21,000 spectators visited the airport's terraces, at a cost of 1s per head over the recent Bank Holiday weekend.

7th PH-DSL from Gander was the final KLM DC-7 passenger aircraft to visit Ringway. The airline's remaining aircraft had been sold by the end of 1964, but their cargo aircraft (PH-DSE/DSF/DSG/DSI) remained in service. Details of their final visits and subsequent fates are as follows:

PH-DSB	26th May 1962	Sold August 1962 as N9610Z
PH-DSC	11th July 1964	Sold May 1965 to Martin's Air Charter
PH-DSD	1st August 1964	Sold April 1965 as N382M
PH-DSH	7th September 1963	Sold July 1964 as D-ABAC
PH-DSK	7th June 1962	Sold October 1962 to Martin's Air Charter
PH-DSL	7th August 1964	Sold November 1964 to Martin's Air Charter
PH-DSM	16th October 1963	Sold August 1963 as D-ABAD (as per PH-DSH)
PH-DSO	3rd July 1963	Sold March 1964 to Martin's Air Charter
PH-DSP	25th July 1964	Sold November 1964 as D-ABAS
PH-DSR	4th September 1962	Sold October 1962 as N904ME

7th Dragon Rapide G-AGTM arrived at 1158 today from Blackpool, to perform a parachute display in the Middleton area of Manchester.

9th Two inbound New York charters by KLM produced two DC-8s making their first visits. PH-DCC arrived via Prestwick today and two weeks later PH-DCF (23rd) arrived direct, positioning out later to Heathrow.

10th KLM Douglas DC-7F PH-DSE operated a freight charter to Rangoon via Damascus.

13th Air India B707 VT-DJJ, arriving at 0902 today (AI106 from New York), paid a further visit en route to Heathrow.

15th UTA's weekly Perpignan IT flight was operated by Air Afrique DC-6B TU-TCJ (ex F-BGSL) today. It had been leased by the African airline since December 1963, but returned to UTA in November 1965. It served with them for another four years, until its withdrawal in January 1970.

18th Shannon Air's 'newest' aircraft, Douglas DC-7C EI-ANM, made its first visit today operating a charter from New York. In March 1965 the airline would add a second DC-7C, EI-AOC, but it returned to the leasing company in November the same year without ever visiting Ringway.

23rd Aer Lingus Carvair EI-AMR (EI9213) returned to Manchester at 2318, due to a suspected bomb onboard, having departed 20 minutes earlier.

25th First registered in 1947, Miles M.65 Gemini arrived at 1156 from Jersey for a lengthy stay, possibly an overhaul. It finally departed back to Jersey on the 12th October.

26th TMA Douglas DC-6Fs OD-AEG & OD-AEL were freight charters to Tokyo, initially departing to Brindisi.

26th BEA Trident 1 G-ARPG, the third to visit Ringway, operated demonstration flights to Jersey and Belfast.

26th Newly-registered Cessna 182 G-ASRR made its first visit today. Arriving from Blackpool and departing later to Great Yarmouth, it was operated by the comedian Jimmy Edwards.

26th Swedish Air Force Dakota 79005 made its second visit to Ringway today, arriving at 0936 from Filton. Its first visit was way back in June 1960. Delivered to the Air Force in April 1956, this aircraft was written off at Nykoping in October 1974.

27th RAF Pembroke C.1 WV755 (c/s MPGQW) made its only visit during the decade today, night-stopping on a return flight from RAF Wildenrath. It served its entire life based in West Germany, until it was struck off charge in March 1972.

28th Aer Lingus had continued operating transatlantic charters throughout the summer, with their three Boeing 720s. Today their first Boeing 707, EI-AMW, made its first visit to Ringway, operating IN5904 from New York.

29th Spitfire G-ASJV arrived at 1249 today from Elstree, and returned there the following morning, after performing a high speed run along the main runway. It was one of a batch of 44 Spitfire LF.IX aircraft built by Vickers-Armstrong at their Castle Bromwich factory during early 1943, eventually becoming MH434. It served with the RAF until 1945, and became one of 48 sold to the Belgian Air Force, serving until 1954. In 1956 it was civil registered as OO-ARA, serving as a target tug, and undertaking other Army co-operation duties until 1962, when it was replaced by Gloster Meteors. After another period of storage, it arrived at Stansted on 29th June 1963, after being sold to Simpson Aero Services at Elstree.

SEPTEMBER 1964

Apart from a period during the third week, high pressure dominated and produced sunny, dry and generally warm weather. The month's temperature extremes saw 28°C at Gillingham (11th) and a low of -3°C at Kielder Castle (21st).

There was much speculation in the local media that another runway may be needed by 1970 if terminal passengers continued to grow. Although no plans had been drawn up, the airport was aware of the need for a 6,000ft-7,000ft runway by the early 1970s. A runway parallel to runway 06/24 was not considered feasible due to the amount of land required, so another plan was being considered to extend one of the cross-runways, with 02/20 being the most likely alternative.

The only equipment change this month was KLM (KLO19): DC-7 PH-DSF (24th).

GCA/ILS traffic noted was USAF C-130B 61-2638 (10th) performing two GCAs and overshoots, French Air Force Dakota 60521 (14th) & BEA Trident 1 G-ARPC (29th).

1st Dornier Do.27 OY-ABU made its first and only visit to Ringway today, night-stopping from Brussels. It was written off at Kalmar, Sweden in August 1967. Other first visits were Twin Bonanza F-BLEG (9th) clearing customs before departing to Lindholme, Cessna 310 SE-CXX from Blackbushe (17th), Commander 560 N1015 from/to Denham (24th) and Cimber Air PA-23 Aztec OY-BAA (30th), which stayed for two days from/to Esbjerg.

2nd Air France began operating Breguet 763 aircraft on their four-weekly cargo flights, with F-BASV making its first visit today. Another, which was also a first visit, was F-BASU (25th/30th). Further flights were operated by F-BASV (4th/11th/16th/18th) and F-BASV (4th/11th/16th/18th).

6th Three KLM Douglas DC-8s making their first visits during the month started with today's arrival of DC-8F PH-DCS, the airline's first pure-freighter. Only delivered at the end of July, it was to operate a freight flight to Rome the following morning. The second was passenger DC-8 PH-DCO, arriving from New York via Prestwick, and finally PH-DCN (24th) operated outbound to New York.

11th Autair Viking G-AHOY positioned from Luton to operate a passenger charter to Gothenburg, before returning there following morning.

12th Austrian Airlines were present again this month. Viscount OE-LAL operated another inbound charter from Salzburg today, returning to operate the outbound on the 20th. The following week, Viscount OE-IAM (27th) operated as OB1591/2 from/to Basle on behalf of Balair.

13th Due to Caledonian's equipment problems, Interocean L-749 Constellation LX-IOK paid its first visit, sub-charted to operate Palma flight CA915/6. It was the former BOAC and Skyways G-ANUP, purchased by Interocean in July 1964. Its tenure with the Luxembourg outfit was very short-lived, as it was damaged beyond repair in October 1964 at Addis Ababa.

20th Flying Enterprises' Douglas DC-7 OY-DMR, *John Foltmann II*, made its only visit to Ringway today, arriving on Caledonian flight CA954 from Valencia, departing as CA1027 to Barcelona. Looking resplendent with its white and silver fuselage, it also sported a blue tail with a red logo.

26th A mass troop movement took place today, with eighteen flights departing for Dusseldorf and Brussels. Involved were Dan-Air Ambassadors G-ALZN/ALZY/AMAH; Derby Airways Argonauts G-ALHS/ALHY; Caledonian DC-6 G-ASRZ & DC-7 G-ASHL, and British United Britannias G-ANCD & G-ARXA.

27th Fog was extensive countrywide for the next three days, but today was the most disruptive from the travellers point of view. All but two of today's sixteen diversions were from Heathrow. Just two were non-British, and the only first visit was Pan American B.707 at 0913 (PA002 from New York).

28th Cessna 172 PH-RPL arrived at 1511 from Lympne for maintenance, returning there on 1st October.

29th Fog at Heathrow produced another seven diversions, including D-ABOC landing at 0715 (LH821 from Montreal), the second Lufthansa B.707 to visit Ringway. The most notable diversion was BOAC VC-10 G-ARVJ at 0908, which was operating a Nigeria Airways flight (WT908 from Kano). It was BOAC's first Vickers VC-10, one of eleven Standard VC-10s delivered to the airline during 1964.

29th Today saw the last Channel Airways Ostend flight of the season, operated by Viking G-APOP. This also happened to coincide with the end of the airline's association with the Vickers Viking. By this time the only two aircraft still operating were G-AJFR & G-APOP. A third, G-APOO, made its last visit to Ringway on 5th August, and it was withdrawn from service on the 18th August. The withdrawal of the airline's Vikings was hastened during 1964, by introduction of certain restrictions concerning the operation of the type from

Southend, which made it too impractical to continue. G-AJFR (last visit 20th September) was withdrawn during October 1964 and G-APOP flew its very last flight for Channel Airways on 4th January 1965 from Basle to Southend.

27th September 1964 - Captured amid an impressive back-drop of two BEA Comets, one BOAC Comet (G-APDO) and an Alitalia Caravelle (I-DABI), this photograph also features a number of young spotters – is that you? TASSA Douglas DC-7 EC-AVP is seen having recently diverted in from Palma due to fog at Gatwick. Although the airline had a weekly IT flight from Ringway in 1965, this would be the aircraft's final visit, as they ceased trading in August 1965 due to continuing losses. (Hubert Parrish)

30th Fog affected nearly thirty flights this morning, including the arrival of BEA Helicopters Sikorsky S-61 G-ASNM. It was due to leave with twenty-three members of the local government commission and Lancashire County Council for a 'bird's eye view' of south Lancashire and Merseyside, but it was delayed nearly five hours due to fog and low cloud.

OCTOBER 1964

The dry and sunny conditions at the end of September continued into October, but broke down around the 5th, when the next ten days became unsettled with rain, occasionally heavy. On the 9th October, winds increased to storm force in the English Channel. A gust of 94kt at Jersey airport was the highest ever recorded in the British Isles during October. From the 16th, it became generally more settled and milder. The month's temperature extremes saw 23°C at Eastwick Lodge, Essex, (5th) and a low of -7°C at Lincoln (13th).

By the end of last month, the airport had handled more than one million passengers, 1,091,151 to be exact, an increase of 11% on last year's figures. Movements also increased by 10% to 36,486.

A new service planned for next April, was a once-weekly car ferry flight to Salzburg, Klagenfurt & Vienna, operated by Austrian Airlines with a Carvair chartered from British United Air Ferries. However, it was postponed due to difficulties in obtaining satisfactory terms for the hire of a Carvair. The airline was hopeful that flights would start in 1966, but they never took place.

Just one scheduled first visit this month was <u>Air France (AF872)</u>: Breguet 763 F-BASN (9th). Also just one equipment change was <u>Sabena (SN623)</u>: CV-440 OO-SCP (7th).

Plenty of GCA/ILS traffic was noted this month, including Thai Airways HS.748 HS-THB (1st), RAF Vulcan B.2 XM654 (9th), Air Ceylon HS.748 4R-ACJ (9th/14th) & USAF Douglas C-118 51-7646 (26th). Training flights during the month were BOAC B.707 G-APFD & BEA Trident 1 G-ARPF (both 2nd).

1st October 1964 – Philips Dove PH-ILI arrived at 0951 today on a day-stop from/to Gatwick. One of many aircraft operated by the Dutch electronics giant down the years, its last visit to Ringway was 13th September 1966, before being sold the following year as OO-WIP. (Geoff Ball)

3rd RAF Avro Anson C.19 VM385 (c/s MPMJV), operated by the Northern Communications Squadron based at RAF Topcliffe, made its first and only visit on a round-trip from White Waltham. It was struck off charge in October 1965, and used for fire fighting at Topcliffe.

6th Mercury Airlines was one of the first to operate into the new airport at Middleton St. George (Teeside) today. Heron G-ANCI operated the inaugural flight of their five-times-weekly service from Manchester, but after just a few weeks on the 31st October, they ceased flying and placed their aircraft into storage.

9th Only the second HS.125 to visit Ringway, was G-ASTY, arriving for a brief stop from Hatfield to Glasgow. It was delivered on the 8th February 1965 to Swiss charter company, Chartag, as HB-VAH.

10th This year's only Auster visit was today's arrival of Hunting Surveys Auster J5P G-AOGM f/t Blackpool. It was becoming a disappearing type, as far as Ringway was concerned. This particular locally based example met its end on 19th September 1970, when it was damaged in a hangar fire at Squires Gate.

12th PA-23 Apache HB-LBT, arriving at 1228 from Luton, was the first of two foreign light aircraft making first visits during the month. The other was Beech 55 D-ILPU (27th) from Hanover, which stayed for two days.

18th G-AHEN operated the last Euravia Constellation flight from Ringway, landing at 2033 from Barcelona, departing at 2122 to Luton. Earlier this year on the 16th August, the airline was officially rebranded Britannia Airways.

26th Two USAF aircraft today were Douglas C-118 51-7646 on a crew training flight through Manchester performing an approach and overshoot; and Convair VC-131 54-2822 f/t RAF Northolt on its first visit.

26th Transair Sweden Douglas DC-6 SE-CCY arrived at 1422 with the Djurgardens football team for an Inter-Fairs Cup first round first leg game with Manchester Utd, who comfortably beat the Swedish side 6-1.

27th Pan American DC-8 N812PA, arriving at 1003 today (PA102 from New York), was the only aircraft of note amongst six fog diversions from Heathrow.

28th The first Transair Sweden DC-7 aircraft to visit Manchester was SE-BDO, one of ten purchased from Eastern Airlines this year. It arrived today to take the Djurgardens football team back to Stockholm.

29th Another memorial presented by the airport, was a concrete statue in the form of a symbolic winged man, paying tribute to Manchester's famous aviation pioneers, Alcock & Brown. It was unveiled today by the Lord Mayor of Manchester.

29th Mercury Airlines G-ANCI appeared two minutes earlier than its scheduled arrival time today, touching down at 1908 from Newcastle, operating its final service.

NOVEMBER 1964

Apart from a period of occasional heavy rain from the 11th - 17th, high pressure was firmly in charge with mainly dry and mild weather. On the 26th a cold front moved south-eastwards throughout the country, and brought snow to all areas. The month's temperature extremes saw 17°C at Hawarden (19th) and a low of -9°C at Corwen, North Wales, (10th).

After going into liquidation last month, the aircraft formerly operated by Mercury Airlines started to leave Ringway, starting with Dakota G-AMSN (12th) and Herons G-AOZN (13th) & G-ANCI (19th). Their schedules would be operated the following summer by British Midland Dakotas (Newcastle) and Dan-Air Herons/Doves (Exeter/Bournemouth/Isle of Wight), pending a decision by the ATLB as to who will operate their routes on a more permanent basis. With effect from the 2nd, Dan-Air took over the Teeside/Newcastle flights temporarily, operating three-times-weekly (with Dove G-ALVF & Heron G-AOZM) until mid-December, when it was terminated again.

International flights were operated during the winter as follows:

AIR FRANCE - Twice-weekly to Paris with SE.210s. Cargo flights operated four-weekly flights and reverted back to Douglas DC-4Fs.

AER LINGUS - Amsterdam (2 x weekly), Brussels (2 x weekly), Copenhagen (2 x weekly), Dusseldorf (2 x weekly), Frankfurt (2 x weekly) & Zurich (2 x weekly), all operated by Viscounts.

BEA - Amsterdam/Dublin/Dusseldorf/Paris & Zurich.

BOAC - Daily to New York (BA538/7), Montreal/Toronto outbound (BA607) operate four-weekly and inbound (BA610) three-weekly. All services operated by B.707s routing via Prestwick. Leased CL-44 N228SW operated cargo flights once-weekly to Montreal/New York (BA065).

KLM - Operated to Amsterdam three-weekly with Electras/Viscounts (KL149/150), one operating onwards to Dublin (KL151/2). Also operating is a five-weekly DC-7 cargo flight to Amsterdam via LHR (KL001).

SABENA - The evening Brussels service operates three-weekly, with SE.210 Caravelles (SN623/4). Dakotas are used four-weekly on freight flights (SN191/2).

SWISSAIR - Operated once-weekly from/to Zurich (SR706/7) with CV-440s, increasing to twice-weekly from 22nd December. From 19th December, a third flight was added (SR718/9), also with CV-440s.

Scheduled first visits this month were KLM (KL149): Electras PH-LLF (4th) & PH-LLE (18th). The only equipment change was Sabena (SN191): DC-6 OO-CTK (27th).

There was plenty of GCA/ILS traffic during the month. Noted was Heron CR-GAT (7th), Thai Airways HS.748 HS-THC (12th/14th), BEA Trident 1 G-ARPJ (12th) & HS.748 XS791 (14th/20th).

1st Widespread overnight fog persisted throughout the day in many places across the country. Heathrow was only affected from early evening, when a number of late evening diversions arrived. Three first visits produced were Finnair CV-440 OH-LRE at 2042 (AY5344 from Paris-Orly), Alitalia SE.210 I-DABM at 2039 (AZ296 from Milan) & Qantas B.707 VH-EBL at 2054 (QF530 from New York).

2nd KLM introduced DC-7s onto their Amsterdam freight services, and Electras on one of their passenger flights. These were originally purchased for intercontinental flights to Africa and the Middle East, but were rapidly replaced on these routes by their Douglas DC-8s. As a consequence, Electras were now turning up on more European routes.

5th Beech 95 SE-EEX arriving at 1111 today from Vasterias was the only foreign light aircraft making its first visit this month.

9th The airport was completely blanked out by fog all day, with not a single arrival or departure. Amongst the many diversions away was Flying Enterprise DC-7 OY-DMS, which eventually made it into Ringway two days later, when it positioned up from Birmingham to operate an outbound charter to Copenhagen.

10th Riley Turbo-Exec 400 N1472V made the first of three visits towards the end of 1964, having been delivered earlier in the month to Keegan Aviation. It started out life as a standard De Havilland Dove, but has been much modified. It now features a swept fin and rudder, two Lycoming IO-720 engines and a colourful scheme. It will be used for a European sales tour, while Luton-based McAlpine Aviation established a conversion line to modify more Doves to the same standard. The first three aircraft to be converted to Riley Doves were ex-South African Air Force examples G-ASUV/ASUW & ASUX.

6th November 1964 - The swansong for the Bristol 170! Dan-Air began operating a second late-evening freight service from/to Heathrow during the winter on behalf of BEA. Aircraft used throughout this period were their two remaining aircraft, G-AINL & G-APLH. (MA Archive via Ringway Publications)

11th L-1049G F-BGNI arriving at 0841 today (AF050 Gander-Orly) was the last visit by an Air France Constellation. The airline had ceased operating the type on their cargo flights out of Ringway last June.

11th Spantax DC-7s EC-ATQ (arriving at 1139 from Brussels) and EC-ATR (arriving at 1142 from Jeddah) were both operating MoD flights, when they diverted in from RAF Brawdy due to the weather.

16th Canadian Pacific operated a winter charter today (also 23rd), with DC-8 CF-CPH (CP590/571 Montreal/Prestwick). Also brightening up a winter's day was night-stopping Kar-Air Douglas DC-6 OH-KDA (AY5383 from Helsinki). From 1977 to 1981, this aircraft would become a regular sight at Manchester, operating on behalf of Finnair.

17th RAF Pembroke C.1 XK885 made its first visit to Ringway, arriving at 1054 today (CEM52) from RAF Andover. First flown in 1956, this aircraft spent its early life based in the Far East, before returning to the UK in 1962. It served with the RAF until 1975, when it was loaned to the A&AEE at Boscombe Down, then used for training at St. Athan. It is now preserved and on display at the Gatwick Aviation Museum.

17th Dornier Do.28 G-ASUR arrived at 1649 today from Denham, before departing two days later for Worksop. It is owned by Mr. William Wallace, who hopes to start flights between Hull and Manchester and was in the region for discussions with the airport and local authorities.

17th Today was the last movement at Ringway by a Handley-Page Hermes. G-ALDA had made various visits during the summer operating ad hoc charters, but this afternoon it arrived at 1637 with engine trouble en route Belfast-Hanover. It was the last Hermes in the world to fly commercially, and the chapter closed on this British-built aircraft when it undertook its very final flight in December 1964. Listed below are the Hermes aircraft that visited Ringway during the 1960s, together with their last visit dates:

G-ALDC	Falcon Airways	8th October 1960	Written off at Southend 9th October 1960
G-ALDE	Air Safari	16th October 1961	Broken up at Bournemouth during 1962
G-ALDG	Silver City	16th September 1962	Withdrawn and broken up late-1962
G-ALDI	Silver City	16th September 1962	Withdrawn and broken up late-1962
G-ALDL	Air Safari	30th July 1961	Withdrawn at Stansted 1962
G-ALDM	Air Safari	26th September 1960	Broken up at Bournemouth during 1962
G-ALDP	Silver City	23rd September 1962	Withdrawn at Stansted during 1962
G-ALDT	Silver City	24th September 1961	Broken up at Southend during 1963
G-ALDU	Silver City	23rd September 1962	Withdrawn at Stansted during 1962

18th The latest aircraft operated by McVitie & Price was Commander 560 G-ASYA, which made its first visit to Ringway today.

20th A regular visitor to Ringway since August, was Beech 95 OY-AOP, which arrived today to take up residency. Owned and flown by local businessman Mr Eric Raffles, it was re-registered the following month as G-ASZC and first flew as such on 5th January 1965.

21st Martin's Air Charter DC-7 PH-DSO arrived at 2215 from Palma, operating a sub-charter on behalf of Caledonian.

24th Canadian Air Force Bristol 170 VC8699 arrived at 1215 today on a tech stop, routing Gatwick-Prestwick. Operated by No.137 Transport Flight based at Langar, Notts, it was sold in 1967 and converted to civil standard, before eventually being delivered to Wardair as CF-WAE in July 1968.

25th Five of this morning's nine fog diversions from Heathrow, were Boeing 707 aircraft. Included was EL AL 4X-ATC at 1022 (LY212 from New York), which had been in previously, and Qantas B.707 VH-EBF making its first visit to Manchester at 1117 (QF747 from Cairo).

29th G-AOVL became the final BOAC Britannia to visit Manchester, operating an extra Prestwick/Toronto flight as BA607R. Their remaining aircraft were disposed of during 1965, and made their last visits as follows:

G-AOVH 3rd September 1964 (BA3763 Heathrow/New York) To Caledonian March 1965
G-AOVJ 20th October 1964 (BA3808 Prestwick/Heathrow)   To Caledonian April 1965
G-AOVK 29th August 1964 (BA3734 Prestwick/Heathrow)   To British Eagle May 1965
G-AOVL 29th November 1964 (BA607R Heathrow/Prestwick) To British Eagle April 1965
G-AOVP 8th July 1964 (BA3633 Heathrow/Prestwick)   To Lloyd Intl April 1965
G-AOVR 31st July 1964 (BA3775 New York/Heathrow)   To British Eagle April 1965
G-AOVS 30th September 1964 (BA3793 Heathrow/Gander)   To British Eagle August 1965

30th BOAC Comet 4 G-APDG (BA4307) operated a charter from/to Heathrow today, but their association with the Comet was coming to an end. G-APDT (BA237 from Milan - 11th Dec 1964) was their last to visit Ringway, diverting in due to fog at Heathrow. Also in December, the first to leave the fleet was G-APDR, following its sale to Mexicana as XA-NAZ.

DECEMBER 1964

It was a cold month, with occasional snow and some mild and stormy periods. High pressure was only really in charge from the 17th to 23rd. On Christmas Eve, an arctic blast brought snow to northern areas, which continued in the north and east on Christmas Day, before reaching all areas by Boxing Day. The year ended with sunny intervals, scattered showers, and strong winds. The month's temperature extremes saw 15°C at Tavistock (8th) and a low of -15°C at Caldecott (10th).

Sabena will increase their Brussels service up to four-weekly from April. They had hoped to increase to daily during the summer months, but it didn't happen. The airline also stated that the withdrawal of their transatlantic flights was only temporary. Also from April next due to extra demand, cargo flights would be increased to five-weekly.

Just a single scheduled first visit this month was KLM (KL149): Electra PH-LLL (23rd). Equipment changes were Sabena (SN623): CV-440 OO-SCV (30th) and Swissair (SR706/718): SE.210 HB-ICW (19th) & CV-990 HB-ICE (22nd).

GCA/ILS traffic noted this month was USAF Douglas C47 0-51133 (4th), HS.125 G-ASTY (8th) performing a GCA approach before setting course for Hatfield, & Smiths Aviation HS.748 G-ASJT (9th). Training flights were BEA Argosy G-APRM (1st), BOAC B.707 G-ARRB (11th) & BKS HS.748 G-ASPL (12th).

10th In amongst four late evening weather diversions from Heathrow, was BOAC Comet G-APDI at 2156 (BA4314 from Ottawa), with PM Harold Wilson and his entourage onboard. Also during the evening were four British Midland Dakotas, arriving in the space of twenty minutes, due to fog at East Midlands. These were G-AGJV & G-ANTD from Leeds, G-AOFZ from Ringway, and G-AMSX from Ostend.

11th Following on from last night's diversions, another twenty arrived throughout the day, with all but one from Heathrow. Disappointingly BEA Trident 1 G-ARPK at 1907 (from Stockholm) was the only first visit and all but three were UK flights. Included was Lufthansa Viscount D-ANAD at 1704 (LH224R from Frankfurt), Swissair CV-440 HB-IMK at 1732 (SR114 from Basle) & HB-ICZ at 2120 (SR102 from Geneva). The fog was eventually blown away by an extremely vigorous low pressure, sweeping across the country bringing heavy rain and flooding in places.

14th It was generally a very quiet month for foreign light aircraft. Today's appearance of Beech 95 F-BMRB, which stayed for two days, was the only first visit.

16th Beech R18 G-ASNX, which cost £103,000, had been delivered through Prestwick earlier in the year on the 31st March, for the American-owned Cameron Iron Works. Varying from the others seen in the UK at the time; it made its first appearance today on a flight from Rotterdam. Although it left the UK-register in 1969, it made no further visits to Ringway after December 1965.

16th December 1964 - BKS HS.748 G-ASPL had arrived the previous evening from Amsterdam, due to fog at Leeds. The airline, which became Northeast Airlines in November 1970, operated five HS.748s from 1962 to 1968. (Bob Thorpe)

23rd Air Ferry Viking G-AOCH arrived at 1442 operating a passenger charter from Dinard, departing at 1625 back to Manston. This aircraft would make one further visit (11th July 1965) from/to Manston, before being purchased by Invicta in April 1968.

FIRST/LAST ARRIVALS & DEPARTURES 1964

First arrival: Swissair CV-440 HB-IML @ 0012 from Zurich
First departure: Air France L-1049 Constellation F-BGNG @ 0021 to Paris
Last arrival: Aer Lingus F.27 EI-AKE @ 2238 from Dublin
Last departure: Aer Lingus F.27 EI-AKE @ 2306 to Dublin

Airport Stats 1964 (+/- % on Previous Year)		
Scheduled Passengers	1,027,000	+10.4%
Inclusive & Charter Passengers	221,000	+16.3%
Freight & Mail (Tonnes)	18,900	+11.1%
Movements	45,300	+8.6%

AIRPORT DIARY 1965

JANUARY 1965

High pressure during the first and last week brought in sunny, but cold weather. In between, troughs of low pressure crossed the UK. The county basked in unbroken sunshine for first three days, but the fourth brought snow to many places. A deep depression on the 13th brought heavy rain to northern England and gusts up to 80kts. Central England/South Wales were heavily affected by snow on the 18th & 21st, but the pattern changed again on the 24th, when winds became light and fog was an increasing problem with hard night frosts. The month's temperature extremes saw 14°C at Wye (5th) and a low of -12°C at Houghall (30th).

Aer Lingus announced they would operate their four new BAC 1-11 aircraft on their continental routes from Manchester in May. Four aircraft were ordered, with the first being delivered in April. They were introduced onto Dusseldorf (13th May), Zurich (25th May), Frankfurt (7th June), Copenhagen (7th June) and Brussels (8th June). The airline predicted this would generate an increased revenue of up to 30%.

Just a single scheduled first visit this month was KLM (KL149): Electra PH-LLI (6th). Equipment changes during were Sabena (SN191): DC-6 OO-CTM (7th), (SN623): CV-440s OO-SCM (17th) & OO-SCN (10th) and Swissair (SR718): SE.210s HB-ICT (9th) & HB-ICZ (16th).

Plenty of GCA/ILS traffic was noted again this month, including Thai Air Force HS.748 HS-TAF (7th/11th/19th), RAF Vulcan B.2 XL351(12th), HS.748 XS792 (20th), Braathens F.27 LN-SUG (21st) performing a touch-and-go f/t Leeds & HS.748 XS793 (23rd). The only training flights were BEA Trident 1 G-APRM (8th) & BKS HS.748 G-ARRW (9th).

3rd The year started well with the arrival of the first notable visitor, 1946-vintage Percival Proctor G-AHBD at 1345 today from Blackpool, departing later for Barton.

4th Wardair Douglas DC-6 CF-PCI, arriving at 1832 (WD101 from Edmonton), was on a fuel stop en route to Amsterdam.

5th January 1965 – KLM Douglas DC-7 is preparing to depart on a much delayed flight as KL001 to Heathrow/Amsterdam, towards the end of a cold period, about to change to milder weather. (Geoff Ball)

6th The first visit by new UK cargo airline, Ace Freighters, took place today with the arrival of Douglas C-54F G-ASEN on a freight flight from Le Bourget. The airline was set up on 1st March 1964 with DC-4 G-APEZ, and a second aircraft, C-54F G-ASEN, was added in November 1964.

7th Comet G-ARCP, arriving at 1352 today from Rome with an unserviceable engine, was a weather diversion from Heathrow. Other diversions during the afternoon included MEA Comet OD-ADT at 1524

(ME205 from Beirut) and a couple of first visits with BOAC VC-10 G-ARVM at 1346 (BA1020 from Bahrain) & Syrian Arab DC-6 YK-AED at 1324 (RB403 from Damascus/Munich), which departed six hours later back to Damascus via Paris. It would be another eight years before this airline appeared again.

8th BEA Trident 1 G-ARPM was present for most of the morning crew training, operating f/t Stansted.

11th Interocean Airways Douglas DC-4 LX-HEP arrived at 1727 to operate the first of several freight charters to Bremen during the month. It would make one further visit to Ringway on 12th April 1965, before being withdrawn and broken up at Luxembourg during July 1967.

13th British Eagle Britannia G-ARKA (EG244 from Georgetown/Bermuda) was operating an inbound trooping flight.

15th Another Interocean Airways making its first visit was Carvair LX-IOH, one of two operated by the airline. This aircraft also operated cargo flights to Bremen, and today's visit was the first of three during January. In June 1965, it was sold to Compagnie Air Transport as F-BHMU for operation as a car ferry.

18th This year Ringway saw a great flurry of different Belgian Air Force C-119 Packets, but interestingly there were no further visits during the decade. The purpose of today's arrival of CP-9 at 1238 (OT-CAI), routing Cologne-Brussels, was to ship out engine parts on behalf of Rolls Royce. Others making their first visits this year were CP-10 (30th November), CP-11 (17th June), CP-22 (20th May), CP-27 (13th July), CP-40 (12th April) & CP-43 (20th December).

20th Dan-Air Ambassador G-ALZO (also 29th) was used on the BEA freight flight, replacing a Bristol 170.

21st Avions Fairey Bristol 170 OO-FAG made its final visit to Manchester, on a round-trip from Gosselies. It was sold as I-SATC later in the year, flying Fiat spares around Italy before being withdrawn a year later.

21st Belgian-airline Sabena, which carried over 11,000 passengers between Manchester and Belgium last year, had their new booking centre in Peter House, Oxford Street, opened today by the Lord Mayor of Manchester. From April, the airline will increase their Caravelle services from three to four flights a week.

22nd BEA Viscount G-AOYO 'lost its way' on the runway, and forced KLM DC-7 PH-DSI (KL001 from Amsterdam) to overshoot, whilst operating the airline's evening cargo flight. The Viscount, inbound from Belfast with sixty-six passengers, missed its exit off the runway and as the KLM DC-7 was close behind, the pilot was forced to go round.

24th The airport was closed due to snow from 2009 to 1321 the next afternoon. Prior to closing, Ringway took a number of diversions from local airports, including three from Dublin, Air France SE.210 F-BJTA at 1123 on a charter flight, TMA Douglas DC-6F at 1442 & BEA Viscount G-APJU at 1623.

25th LIAT HS.748 VP-LII arrived at 1755 from Lympne due to fog at Woodford. It began its long delivery flight two days later, initially departing for Stornaway.

25th Work was completed on further lengthening work on Runway 24/06 today, adding an extra 400ft at the north eastern end.

26th The first Schreiner Airways Fokker F.27 to visit was PH-SAF, day-stopping on a charter f/t Amsterdam. They would operate regular IT flights to the Dutch bulb fields, which were very popular during the 1960s.

28th Fire crews were on standby for the arrival of BEA Vanguard G-APEM, with 130 passengers onboard. Inbound from Heathrow with one of its four engines feathered, it landed safely at 1248. Its inner port engine had stopped after losing oil during its flight.

29th Royal Navy Sea Prince WF138, arriving on a round-trip from RAF Brawdy, barely stayed ten minutes.

FEBRUARY 1965

Apart from a stormy period around the 12th/13th, the month was dominated by anticyclones over or to the west of Britain, which brought dull and rather cold, but mainly dry conditions. The month's temperature extremes saw of a high of 10°C and a minimum of -5°C locally, and 4°C at Wye (5th) and a low of -12°C at Houghall (30th) over the rest of the UK.

With the major airlines planning more than sixty new scheduled jet flights a week, Manchester Airport was facing its greatest ever increase in traffic this year. Flying times would be reduced, capacities doubled, and new passenger and freight routes including new jet flights, would be introduced. A boom in holiday flights and business travel between Manchester and London sent the number of passengers handled at the airport during 1965 up to 1.5 million. BEA estimated there would be an increase of 18-22% on traffic carried during the year by all airlines. They had gone into the package market this year for the first time, and allocated thousands of seats out of Manchester. BEA also introduced the Trident on their five-times-weekly Paris flight. There would also be a twice-weekly flight by Iberia with Caravelles to Barcelona & Palma, which was introduced last year when the airline operated the service with 80-seater Constellations.

Scheduled first visits this month were KLM (KL149): Electra PH-LLH (10th) which have all visited Ringway; and Sabena (SN623): SE.210 OO-SRI (17th).

GCA/ILS traffic noted was Canadian Air Force C-130 10306 & USAF C-130 21791 (both 2nd), HS.748 YV-C-AMC Aeropostal (4th/5th) and BEA Trident 1 G-ARPB (17th). Training flights were BEA Comet G-ARGM (19th) & Trident 1 G-ARPM (24th).

8th BUA BAC 1-11 G-ASJI landed at 1612 today, to operate a local flight for travel agents from/to Gatwick. It was a first visit of type for this newly British-built aircraft, flying in on a demonstration run before its route proving programme, which included continuing flights to Genoa, Jersey & Malaga until it had clocked up 200 hours. It would then be given a Certificate of Airworthiness to commence commercial operations with BUA next month. The airline hoped to introduce the BAC 1-11 on feeder services from Manchester to Gatwick by the end of the summer, with up to three flights a week linking up with their international services One of the new features of this aircraft, was an auxiliary power unit built into the tail, keeping its systems running whilst on the ground, meaning a faster turnaround!

11th TMA Douglas DC-6F OD-AEL arrived at 2336 today from Brussels. It departed the following evening on an outbound freight flight to Cairo via Brindisi.

17th Not an exciting month for visitors, but Avro Anson C.19 TX209 of Western Communications Squadron paid its first visit today, arriving at 1440 from RAF Wyton. Another making its first visit was C.19 TX196 (25th) f/t Binbrook, which served in Amman during the 1950s, but is now based at RAF Wyton.

18th February 1965 – Since October 1961, British United had been contracted by the MoD for transport flights from Ringway to several points in West Germany. These were operated by Vickers Viscounts and occasionally DC-6s, but from April 1965 they would gradually be replaced by BAC 1-11s. Viscount G-APTB is seen here on a quiet Thursday afternoon 'resting' prior to its departure back to Hanover. (Geoff Ball)

22nd Sabena Douglas DC-7F OO-SFB arrived at 1049 on a tech-stop, en route Gander-Brussels.

26th Former Balair DC-4 HB-ILC, which was purchased by Air Ferry in March 1963 as G-ASFY, made its first visit today in British markings on a cargo charter to Bremen. In 1967/68 it would operate along with other Air Ferry aircraft, namely Lufthansa's recently introduced cargo flights from Manchester.

27th G-ARPM (BE4032/7 f/t Heathrow), was the first Trident 1 operating a scheduled service from Ringway.

MARCH 1965

The very cold weather at the end of February continued into the first week of March. The first few days brought heavy snow to many parts, before dry, cold, but sunny weather took over. On the 19th, a trough became stationary over southern England, which brought dull and wet weather over the next five days. Northern England had snow, heavy at times with Buxton recording 14 inches on the 22nd. Finally, March ended on an exceptionally warm note, with plenty of sunshine. The month's temperature extremes saw 25°C at Wakefield (29th) and a low of -21°C at Corwen (3rd).

Manchester became the first major UK airport to have 'on-tap' fuel, provided by the largest hydrant fuelling system in Britain, operating directly underneath the parking spots. Instead of being met by a fuel bowser, aircraft were now 'plugged-in' to underground pipelines. Although the system was laid during construction of the new £2.5 million terminal building, problems with water and sand seeping into the miles of pipeline had taken two years to resolve.

Lancashire County Councils' plan to turn Burtonwood into an international airport was thwarted by the National Coal Boards intention to extract the coal located under the base at nearby Bold Colliery. The council claimed Burtonwood should be developed because Speke and Ringway weren't located near enough to main roads and rail networks. They also added that extensive surveys would be required if mining under Burtonwood's runway was possible.

Just a single scheduled first visit again this month, with BEA (BE4902): Argosy G-ASXL (2nd). Canadian Air Force C-130 10307 (2nd) & British United BAC 1-11 G-ASJF (26th), both performed a touch-and-go.

2nd   BEA's latest Argosy, series -200 G-ASXL, made its first visit to Ringway today. The three series -100 aircraft currently in service (G-AOZZ/APRM & APRN) were merely stopgaps, until they took delivery of the five -200s ordered in 1964. Of these two would be lost in crashes, G-ASXL in July 1965 and G-ASXP in December 1967, so G-ATTC would be ordered as a replacement for the lost aircraft.

3rd   LTU Caravelle D-ABAF, operating to/from Manchester due to snow at Speke Airport, was bringing Cologne supporters in for their match with Liverpool FC. The aircraft was in basic Finnair colours, and although its previous identity of OH-LEA had been crudely scrubbed out, it was still visible.

4th   British Midland Herald G-ASKK made its first visit today, positioning in from East Midlands to operate a charter to RAF Wattisham.

7th   Fog at Heathrow provided Ringway with six diversions during the morning. Included were two first visits with East African Airways Comet 4 5H-AAF at 1041 (EC712 from Cairo) & BOAC VC-10 G-ARVA at 0916 (BA116 from Rome). There was also a first visit of type, with the arrival of Lufthansa Boeing 727 D-ABIC at 1104 (LH220 from Frankfurt). This aircraft, which was less than a year old, departed empty to Heathrow during the afternoon.

9th   PA-23 Aztec OY-AFE, arriving from Stavanger, was the first of two light aircraft first visits during March. The second, 1948-Nord 1101 Noralpha F-BFUZ (29th), would become G-ATHN later in the year.

12th   RAF Devon C.2 VP955 (CDS52 from Northolt) which was making its first visit since July 1962, would make just one more appearance during the decade, in February 1966. The following day (13th), Devon C.2 (MPJMY from Woodvale) made its first of three calls on Ringway during the 1960s. Another RAF first time visitor was Pembroke WV741 (18th), which arrived at 1126 as 'AGD52' from RAF Andover.

15th   BEA had to cancel a late night departure flight from Heathrow, and leave forty-eight passengers stranded, due to the airport's refusal to stay open later than its current closure time of 23.00 for runway work. Flight BE4060, which had been delayed at Heathrow from its regular departure time of 20.40 due to cross-winds at Manchester, had been given a revised departure time of 22.15 from Heathrow, meaning it would arrive at Ringway after the airport had closed.

16th   Two Belgian Air Force aircraft present at Ringway during the month were both first visits. Pembroke RM-2 (OT-ZAB) operated from/to Brussels today, and Fairchild C-119 CP-44 departed for Le Bourget (17th). The Belgian military were quite rare visitors, until 1976, when they became fairly regular taking out HS.748 parts.

18th   British United G-ASJF (also 20th/24th/26th/27th/28th), was the second BAC 1-11 to visit, arriving at 0931 from Wisley on the first of numerous training flights during the month.

21st   BKS HS.748 G-ATAM made its first visit to Manchester today, diverting in from Heathrow at 2105 due to fog at Leeds. It positioned back to Leeds the following morning.

22nd Fog affecting airports in the north produced a few interesting diversions, including two Dan-Air Dakotas, G-ALXK & G-AMPP, both originally destined for Liverpool. Former BOAC Britannia G-ANBK now operated by BKS, also appeared at 0910 from Heathrow, due to the weather at Newcastle.

25th Cessna 337 N2147X (also 28th) was technically a first visit of type. Basically an uprated Cessna 336, it was the UK company demonstrator, operating from/to Blackpool and carrying out a local demonstration in between.

31st Air France 'temporarily' withdrew their four-weekly freight service to Paris, with the last being operated today by Douglas DC-4F F-BBDD (AF886/7). They said the reason for this, was the lack of available aircraft to switch the flight back to an after-midnight operation, when overnight work on Ringway's main runway would be completed in April. They also said they would rather withdraw the service until an aircraft for night operations becomes available, but in the end it became permanent. However, the airline was able to carry extra freight on their passenger service, when increased to five-weekly from April.

31st Dan-Air operated the final Heathrow freight flight on behalf of BEA this evening, which coincided with Bristol 170 G-APLH making its final visit to Manchester. This aircraft had the notoriety of being the only one in the airline's history that was purchased from new. It left the fleet in 1968, when it was sold to Thomas Lamb Airways, Canada, as CF-YDP. Their other Bristol 170, G-AINL, which had made its last visit to Ringway on the 11th March, was also sold to Thomas Lamb in 1968 as CF-YDO.

APRIL 1965

The fine weather at the end of March continued, with unbroken sunshine and temperatures as high as 20°C, but by the 6th this had broken down to give cool and showery weather for the rest of the month. The month's temperature extremes saw 22°C at Huddersfield (3rd) and a low of -7°C at Kielder Castle (2nd).

Ringway made a profit of £26,513 in the year ending 31st March 1965. The spectators had contributed no less than £30,000 to the airport's coffers!

Scheduled first visits were by new Argosies again: <u>BEA (BE4902/4)</u>: G-ASXM (14th) & G-ASXN (1st). International flights operated during the summer as follows:

AIR FRANCE - Five-weekly to Paris with SE.210s, increasing to six-weekly between July and September. Cargo flights were terminated at the end of March.

AER LINGUS - Amsterdam (up to 5 x weekly), Brussels (up to 3 x weekly), Copenhagen (up to 3 x weekly), Dusseldorf (up to 3 x weekly), Frankfurt (up to 3 x weekly) & Zurich (1 x weekly), all operated by Viscounts. From the 8th June, BAC 1-11s were introduced on the Frankfurt route.

BEA - Amsterdam/Dublin/Dusseldorf & Paris, with summer routes to Barcelona & Palma operated on both a scheduled and inclusive tour basis.

BOAC - Daily to New York (BA538/7), Montreal/Toronto outbound (BA607) operated five-weekly and inbound (BA610) twice-weekly. All services operated by B.707s, routing via Prestwick. Leased CL-44 N228SW operated cargo flights back to three-times-weekly to Montreal/New York (BA065).

IBERIA - From the 1st June, served Palma twice-weekly with SE.210 Caravelles, with one via Barcelona.

KLM - Operated to Amsterdam up to four-times-weekly with Viscounts, one of these flights operates onwards to Dublin (KL151/2). Also a five-weekly DC-7 cargo flight operated from/to Amsterdam (KL019/020).

SABENA - The evening Brussels service now night-stops and has been increased to four-times-weekly with SE.210 Caravelles. Ostend operated June-September three-weekly with Douglas DC-6s. Dakotas were used on five-weekly cargo flights.

SWISSAIR - Twice-weekly flights to Basle and Zurich, operated by SE.210s/CV-990s. From the 18th May-28th September, a Tuesday CV-990 flight was added (SR728/9).

1st BOAC inaugurated services by a Super VC-10 today, when G-ASGD flew from London to New York, before continuing on to San Francisco.

2nd The fine and sunny weather experienced by the UK meant that early fog was a problem. Nine flights arrived from Heathrow, with the first being CSA IL-18 OK-NAA at 0338, which was also a first visit of type. It was carrying members of the World Philharmonic Orchestra. The freight onboard included a large quantity of musical instruments, required for their morning rehearsals in London. Although the musicians spoke little English, the crew's command of the language was more tuned in to the requirements of Air Traffic Control. Upon their arrival at Manchester, it was soon realised that their coaches were not designed for the transport of cumbersome musical instruments, so with the aid of a spanner several seats were removed from the coaches to make room. Once onboard they sped away southwards towards their destination, leaving behind a neat pile of abandoned coach-seats in the airport car park, brightly lit by a shining moon! There were three further first visits, starting with BOAC VC-10 G-ARVF at 0916 (from Rome), which was the fourth East African Airways Comet 4 to visit. Second was 5X-AAO at 0948 (EC716 from Benina) and lastly, Capitol Curtiss C-46 N66326 at 1026 (LH936 from Dusseldorf). The latter was one of several aircraft based in Germany, operating cargo flights throughout Europe on behalf of Lufthansa.

2nd Numerous UK military flights this month produced some first visits, starting with Army Beaver XP769 (Army Air 393 from Birmingham), at 1518. It was only the second UK example to visit Manchester. Valetta VX580 (5th) was on a flight from Le Bourget (Rafair 5424), and became the last of its type to visit Ringway. Several Ansons were also present, and produced first visits with VP520 (26th) & Anson TX195 (28th).

3rd Trident G-ARPM (BE4104/11 f/t Heathrow) had amongst its passengers, the Prime Minister Harold Wilson, who was ultimately returning to his local constituency of Huyton.

7th April 1965 - During the early part of the year, British United operated the BAC 1-11 on numerous proving flights from airports around the UK. Today, one such flight was operated by G-ASJJ, which was on its first visit to Manchester. A further aircraft, G-ASJJ, also made its first visit (16th). They also operated their first Ringway trooping flight with the BAC 1-11 (21st) with G-ASJJ (BR582/1 f/t Dusseldorf). (Geoff Ball)

8th An interesting mix of light aircraft making their first visits this month were PA-23 Aztec SE-EMA from Leeds to Malmo (today), Cessna 185 EI-AMT (9th), Jodel F-BMBL (12th) & Rallye F-BKLR (26th) which would become G-ATGG in July.

12th Several 18 inch high runway approach marking lights were either knocked down or blown over today, when BOAC B.707 G-APFE (BA607 from Heathrow) arrived at 0940. The pilot had made a low approach, but luckily none of the markers were damaged.

16th The Sequoia F.8L Falco which was designed in 1955 was an Italian-built single-engine, propeller driven aircraft, manufactured for private and general aviation use. The first example of such to visit Ringway was G-ATAK today. Although registered to an owner in Knutsford, it spent the rest of the year dividing its time between Manchester and Elstree, until it was based more permanently at Ringway during 1966.

25th BUA Herald G-APWE (JY585 from Blackpool) landed with a fire in the nose, which prevented its departure to Jersey for several hours.

12th April 1965 - The first of Aer Lingus' seasonal transatlantic charters was operated today by B.720 EI-ALA (IN5933 Dublin/Keflavik). Flights tended to operate on an irregular basis until the 31st October. Other aircraft used were B.720 EI-ALC and B.707s EI-AMW & EI-ANO, with the latter making its first visit on the 18th May. (Ken Fielding)

26th The end of era occurred today, when BOAC operated its final Britannia service, with G-AOVL in charge. Four days later it was leased to British Eagle, adding to their existing ex-BOAC Britannias.

MAY 1965

Although cyclonic weather patterns were in charge for most of the month, it was often cloudy with below average temperatures. There was some improvement in the second week, which was warm with long sunny periods. For the 16th/17th rain was widespread and occasionally heavy. The next two days recorded sleet and snow showers extending from the north as far south as East Anglia. The month ended on another cold note, with very little sunshine. The month's temperature extremes saw 29°C at Kensington (14th) and a low of -5°C at Alwen (20th).

As part of a cost cutting measure, BOAC announced they would be closing their passenger handling department at Ringway later in the year. Although they were handling around 50,000 passengers annually, they would hand over all of their ground operations to BEA.

The following could be seen during the summer months operating ITs to various destinations: Adria Airways (Dubrovnik/Ljubljana), Austrian (Salzburg), Autair (Genoa, Malta via Nice, Venice), Aviaco (Barcelona/Palma), Balair (Basle), Britannia Airways (Barcelona/Malaga/Palma/Perpignan/Rimini/Valencia/Venice), British Eagle (Nice/Ostend/Palma/Perpignan/Rimini), British Midland (Barcelona/Cork/Exeter/Ostend/Perpignan/Sandown/Valencia/Venice), British United (Malaga/Nice/Ostend/Palma/Perpignan/Rimini/Valencia/Venice), Caledonian (Barcelona/Palma/Shannon/Valencia), Channel Airways (Barcelona/Genoa/Malaga/Palma/Rimini/Valencia), Dan-Air (Basle/Biarritz/Lyon/Munich/Oporto/Ostend/Perpignan/Tarbes), Globe Air (Basle), SAM (Rimini), TAP (Lisbon) and TASSA (Barcelona).

Just one scheduled first visit during the month was BEA (BE4904): Argosy G-ASXO (5th). Equipment changes were KLM (KL149/153): Electra PH-LLK (10th/22nd) and Swissair (SR726): CV-440 HB-IMK (7th).

GCA/ILS traffic noted was USAF C-130s 63-7854 (19th) & 62-1788 (20th), and Heron CN-MAA (25th) on a test flight from Hawarden.

1st Dragon Rapide G-AHED arrived from Leavesden to perform a number of local photographic details until the 3rd.

1st Alitalia SE-210 I-DABV arrived at 2106 (AZ1290) with Inter Milan for their European Cup match with Liverpool, but were comprehensively beaten by the Reds 3-1. The same aircraft returned from Heathrow on the 5th to pick up the Italian team. Sensationally, when the teams met in Milan for the second-leg in front of 90,000 fans, Milan scored the three goals they needed to dump Liverpool out of the competition, who were agonisingly short of reaching their first European Cup final at the first attempt. Later on the game was the subject of a conspiracy theory, saying that 'dark forces' had been at work ensuring Milan progressed. A Liverpool director was quoted as saying "The game was evidence that a British team was never going to be allowed to win the European Cup". He was referring to a totally legitimate goal by Ian St. John being ruled offside, while two controversial Inter goals were allowed to stand.

6th The Excelsior with 264 beds became the airport's first hotel today, when it was officially opened by the Lord Mayor of Manchester.

6th Royal Navy Sea Devon XJ427 brought Commander Dan Duff, RN, and an inter-services party to Manchester. Commander Duff had played one of the most decisive roles in the Battle of Normandy in 1944, directing naval gunfire as part of Operation Neptune during the D-Day landings. Also in connection with this gathering were Ansons TX195 (f/t RAF Binbrook) & TX228 (f/t Hawarden).

7th Today's arrival of HB-IMK became the final visit of a Swissair Convair CV-440 (SR726/7), whilst substituting for a SE.210 Caravelle. Their services from Ringway over the next few years would be operated by a mix of CV-990s and SE.210s.

9th Britannia Airways began their first IT summer programme from Ringway today under their new identity, when Britannia G-ANBJ operated the first flight to Perpignan.

11th RAE Anson VS562 (Evergreen 83) arrived at 0939 from Boscombe Down. This communication aircraft for RAE Llanbedr was coded 'P' on the fuselage, identifying it as the prototype for the T.21 version.

11th Schreiner F.27 PH-SAD, arriving at 1041 today from Amsterdam, operated two local flights before its late night departure back to Amsterdam.

12th Having dispatched Borussia Dortmund and Everton in the previous rounds, Manchester United had now reached the quarter-final stage of the Inter-Fairs Cup, facing opponents RC Strasbourg away in the first leg at Old Trafford. The team flew out today aboard Autair Ambassador G-ALZZ, and returned the following evening victorious, having handed out another thrashing away from home 5-0.

14th Aviaco commenced their summer ITs today, with EC-AQN operating AO1112/3 f/t Barcelona. A Palma flight (AO1154/5) was added from the 29th. Six L-1049G Constellations used by the airline during the year were EC-AIO/AMP/AMQ/AQM/AQN & ARN. Missing was EC-AIN, which had crashed at Tenerife earlier this month on the 5th.

15th Air Links Argonauts G-ALHM & G-ALHT both made several return troop flights f/t Gutersloh. Later to become Transglobe Airways, the airline would only be seen at Ringway during 1965 operating ad hocs or sub-charters. In July, a Bristol Britannia (G-ATGD) was added to the fleet, complimenting the four Argonauts that were the backbone of their inclusive tour operation from Gatwick and various other airports, such as Newcastle and Teesside.

15th Adria Airways began their summer programme from Ringway, with Douglas DC-6A YU-AFC operating to Dubrovnik. Flights operated to Dubrovnik and Ljubljana until the 10th October, with DC-6s YU-AFC/AFD/AFE & AFF.

15th Viscount EC-AZK made the first of its four visits during the summer today, operating as AO1118/9 f/t Barcelona. Delivered to Airwork as G-ASED on 5th June 1959, it was immediately leased to Sudan Airways before returning to the newly formed BUA in December 1962. In April 1965 it was leased to Aviaco as EC-AZK, but returned to BUA in early November 1965.

15th Balair began a twice-weekly Basle charter today, with Douglas DC-6 HB-IBZ. Flights operated until the 25th September, and other aircraft used were Douglas DC-6s HB-IBR & HB-IBU.

15th British Eagle Britannia G-ANCG made its first visit today, on an outbound flight to Palma. This aircraft had been standing at New York-Idlewild ever since TSA ceased operations in 1962. It was cleaned up and prepared for delivery to British Eagle by Seaboard & Western Air Lines. It arrived at Heathrow (still in Argentine markings) on 23rd February 1965, joining LV-GJB (G-ANCF), which had been delivered to British Eagle on 16th January 1965. Both aircraft would be mainly configured for cargo carrying, but G-ANCG had the capability to be used as a passenger aircraft if required.

15th Caledonian began their IT summer programme today, operating CA147 to Palma, with DC-7 G-ASIV arriving from Biggin Hill Air Fair following its 'performance' there. Their fleet for the 1965 season consisted of Douglas DC-7s G-AOIE/ARYE/ASHL & ASIV, as their DC-6s had been sold by the end of 1964. Also added earlier in the year were Britannias G-AOVH/AOVI & AOVJ, which would visit Ringway during the summer, but only on transatlantic flights.

16th Cessna's latest model for UK distribution was the Cessna 411, which arrived from Biggin Hill today (also 20th) for a short demonstration over at the south side, before departing back to Cranfield. This aircraft, N7306U, which was part of a new generation of 'big little twins', had made its British debut in April, arriving from Brussels for UK distributors Rogers Aviation of Cranfield and Westair of Blackpool.

18th Manchester United's quarter-final second leg game with RC Strasbourg at Old Trafford was merely a formality. The French side arrived today aboard Balair DC-6 HB-IBZ, before leaving in the early hours of the 20th on Balair DC-6 HB-IBR, having earned a very creditable 0-0 draw. This meant their next opponents at the semi-final stage would be the Hungarian side, Ferencvaros, who would prove a much tougher nut to crack. The aggregate score over two legs was 3-3, meaning there would have to be a play-off, which unfortunately United lost 2-1.

18th Gregory Air Services were a Denham-based outfit, mainly operating in the air taxi market, although they had Dakota G-AKJH based at Newcastle for charters. This aircraft made the first of several visits over the next two years, arriving from Rotterdam today with football fans for the following night's game. In August 1968, it was sold in South Africa and eventually registered as VQ-ZJB.

19th RC Strasbourg fans did their team proud, by supporting them in large numbers. Martin's Air Charter provided four football flights, with DC-4 PH-MAE and three DC-7s, PH-DSC, PH-DSL & PH-DSO.

20th Britain's new 'bus stop jet', the BAC 1-11, failed to arrive today on a preview flight from Gatwick after hydraulic feed trouble forced G-ASJJ to return to Gatwick.

21st Although RAF visitors were scare during the month, two Pembrokes made their first visits to Ringway. The first, WV701 (JPK 36) at 1423 today from Liverpool, would only make one further appearance on 10th March 1967. The second, WV745 (MHF 55), was on a round-trip from RAF Andover on the 28th.

21st The first of two Netherlands Air Force F.27s appearing at Ringway this month, was C-1 (callsign PECAA) at 1248 today from Ypenburg, dropping off a group of military officials. They were collected two days later by another F.27, C-2 (callsign PECAB), positioning in from RAF Northolt at 1422, departing to Ypenburg thirty minutes later.

21st Cessna 310 VP-YUE arrived at 1623 from Glasgow and night-stopped. The following morning it continued on its delivery flight, initially bound for Le Touquet.

22nd Swiss operator Globe Air began a new weekly IT service to Basle. The first flight was operated by Herald HB-AAK and their other two Heralds, HB-AAH & HB-AAL, would also be used during the summer. This would be their only programme from Ringway, with flights ending on the 18th September.

23rd The first of Austrian Airlines' weekly IT flights to Salzburg began today, with Viscount OE-LAH. Continuing until the 19th September, their other three Viscounts, OE-LAK, OE-LAL & OE-IAM, were also used.

25th Air Canada also had a summer programme, although it was difficult to see a regular pattern of flights. Today's first operated by DC-8 CF-TJP arrived from Heathrow, and departed at 1934 as TC026 to Prestwick/Montreal. With flights operating until the 1st October, the numerous DC-8s being used were CF-TJA/TJD/ TJE/TJF/TJG/TJH/TJI/TJJ/TJO/TJP and finally TJQ (27th June), which was the only first visit.

29th Autair was yet another airline operating its first full programme from Ringway this year, starting with Ambassador G-ALZZ on the first flight outbound to Genoa. Other Ambassadors also used during the summer were G-ALZS & ALZV.

31st A new airline seen at Ringway for the first time in 1965, was Portuguese national carrier TAP. Their series of fortnightly late night flights to Lisbon provided much excitement and anticipation amongst the spotting fraternity. The main reason for this was the airline's use of their L-1049G Constellations. Just after midnight today, L-1049G CS-TLA arrived empty to operate the first IT flight to Lisbon. Their other aircraft making first visits were CS-TLB (9th August), CS-TLC (23rd August), CS-TLE (28th June) & CS-TLF (5th September). Only CS-TLA & CS-TLF made more than one visit, and the last flight was operated on 3rd October with CS-TLF. Although TAP did not return to Ringway for another fourteen years, their Constellations soldiered on until 1967, when all five were retired from service when sold.

27th May 1965 - Aer Lingus BAC 1-11 EI-ANE arriving from Dublin at 1242, operated two local flights for demonstration purposes, before departing to Copenhagen. The airline began full operations with the type from the following month with EI-ANE operating Frankfurt flight EI650/1 on the 7th June. (Geoff Ball)

JUNE 1965

The month of June was extremely disappointing. Apart from spells from the 2nd-3rd, 9th-11th and 19th-20th, it was predominantly unsettled with occasional rain and widespread gales on the 18th. The month's temperature extremes saw 26°C at Nottingham (11th) and a low of -2°C at Sutton Downham (4th).

Cyclists to Ringway were finally provided with their own parking facilities, when a 99 tubular metal bicycle holder was erected at the entrance to the spectator terraces.

Scheduled first visits this month were <u>Aer Lingus (EI642)</u>: BAC 1-11 EI-ANF (13th), <u>Air France (AF960)</u>: SE.210 F-BJTR (12th), <u>BEA</u>: Argosy G-ASXP (22nd) & Trident 1 G-ARPL (23rd), <u>Iberia (IB782/4)</u>: SE.210s EC-ARI (3rd), EC-ATX (8th), EC-AVZ (1st) & EC-AYD (22nd). Equipment changes were <u>KLM (KL149/153)</u>: Electras PH-LLC (26th), PH-LLD (5th) & PH-LLI (5th) and <u>Swissair (SR728)</u>: DC-8 HB-IDC (22nd).

3rd Aero-Nord Douglas DC-7 OY-ANA (OO921/2 & OO923/4) made the airlines only visit to Ringway, operating two flights today transporting lager to Copenhagen! In April 1969 this aircraft was sold to the Swedish Red Cross as SE-ERO for operations in Biafra.

3rd Once a common sight, but now quite rare, so it was good to see Sabena B.707 OO-SJD stopping off at Manchester en route New York-Brussels.

4th The College of Air Training based at Hamble has been visiting Ringway since 1963, with their growing fleet of PA-23 Apaches used for advanced pilot training, with 120 graduates passing through the college each year. During the last few years, they were mainly involved in training pilots to Trident standards, as apparently it was fairly easy to convert from a Piper Apache! The college claimed the success rate of conversion courses to the Trident was generally higher than those training under the responsibility of the airline. Two of their aircraft, PA-23 Apaches G-ARJW & G-ARJX, were present at Manchester today.

5th Lloyd International Douglas DC-6 G-ASTW operated a return flight to Ostend on behalf of British Eagle.

6th International Airlines DC-6 N1281 (also 20th June/18th July) operated flights to Amsterdam on behalf of Schreiner Airways. Built in 1954 and having operated for Flying Tiger and US Overseas, it was purchased by International Airlines in November 1964, and immediately sold to Foreign Air Transport Development. In 1965, it was based in Europe for charter work until September, when it was sold to Aaxico Airlines of Miami, Florida.

114

8th Douglas DC-7 N90774 operated the first of fourteen transatlantic charters by Saturn Airways during the summer, until the 20th August. Aircraft used were all DC-7s, N90773/N90778/N90802/N90803 & N90804. Four DC-7s also making their first visits were N951P (2nd August), N953P (11th August), N2281 (15th August) & N90801 (29th July).

9th British Eagle began a weekly series of flights to New York via Gander, originating at Heathrow, with Britannia G-ARKB operating today's first flight.

10th BEA Trident 1 G-ARPR, arriving at Heathrow operating BE343 from Le Bourget, was making the world's first fully automatic landing of a commercial airliner, carrying fare paying passengers.

10th Light aircraft Cessna 180 OY-ADH today and Cessna 336 LN-BIP (23rd) were both new to Ringway.

12th Hawker-Siddeley demonstrator Andover G-ARRV arrived at 1901 direct from Le Bourget, having spent the week on display at the Paris Air Show. It was parked on the south bay until the 14th, when it departed back to Woodford.

12th Beaver XP807 arrived at 1346 today (Army 396 from Middle Wallop).

12th June 1965 - Sabena operated the Dakota on freight flights to Brussels from April 1963-March 1967, when they were taken over by Douglas DC-7s, although the odd DC-3 still appeared up to October 1967. Seen here on a dull Saturday afternoon is OO-AWZ, awaiting its outbound cargo. (Geoff Ball)

13th Queen's Flight Heron XM296 (Kitty 4) arrived at 1439 today from RAF Benson, to collect George Brown, Deputy Leader of the Labour Party for transportation back to London.

14th Shoreham-based South Coast Air Services began a newspaper flight to Shannon today, with ex-Mercury Dakota G-AMSN. These flights continued almost nightly until the 5th August, when the airline ceased trading, but the following evening the flights were continued by Westpoint Dakota G-AMDB. Meanwhile, Dakota G-AMSN was parked up on the south side of the airfield with its SCAS titles removed, before departing to East Midlands on the 14th August.

15th An unidentified RAF Whirlwind (Tarnish Delta) arrived at 1636 today from/to Warton. It stayed around 25 minutes, disappearing in between time for a short local flight.

15th Canadian Pacific DC-8 CF-CPH made the first of only two visits during the year today, arriving from Gatwick before departing us CP573 to Prestwick/Toronto. The return operated on the 20th July, arriving at 0604 as CP572 direct from Toronto.

16th The Handley Page Hastings was a British troop-carrier and freight transport aircraft, designed and built by Handley Page Aircraft Company for the Royal Air Force. At the time it was the largest transport plane ever designed for the RAF, replacing the Avro York as the standard long-range transport. They had made occasional visits to Ringway during the 1950s, but today's appearance of WD491 at 1025 (BRR 62 from Strubby) was the first of the decade. Unfortunately, this aircraft was damaged beyond repair at RAF West Raynham on the 9th June 1967.

17th Due to late deliveries of the BAC 1-11, Aer Lingus had to sub-charter KLM Viscount PH-VIE, which was leased to the airline until late-July. It made several visits to Ringway, and today it operated Dusseldorf flight EI630/1. In July, Air France Caravelle F-BHRK was also leased, and could be seen at Ringway from the 23rd to the 30th July operating various international flights.

17th June 1965 - Two BOAC B.707s, G-APFK & G-ARWE, await their respective departures to New York & Montreal/Toronto. This scene would significantly change during the 1970s, when nose-in parking would be introduced, and further major expansion would include the building of a third pier and extended apron space. (Hubert Parrish)

17th RAF Shackleton T.4 WB819 called in at 2045 today from RAF Lyneham (callsign NEM 35) en route to RAF Kinloss.

19th Italian charter airline SAM (Societa Aria Mediterranea) began their IT summer programme today, this year operating just a single weekly flight (MQ846/7) f/t Rimini. Flights operated with DC-6s until the 18th September, with the same aircraft as last year, I-DIMA/DIMD/DIME/DIMI/DIMP & DIMU (today).

21st Emergency crews were on standby today, when Aer Lingus BAC 1-11 EI-ANE with 43 passengers onboard made an emergency landing, with a warning light in the cockpit indicating a faulty undercarriage. Luckily the aircraft touched down safely at 1526. An Aer Lingus official stated there was never any danger, as it was due to a faulty electrical system.

22nd What must have made a fantastic photograph, was the sight of three French Air Force Noratlas aircraft on the ground together, when 129/64-IC, 199/61-YD & 206/61-NI, all arrived around lunchtime from Glasgow. They departed to Cambridge within twenty minutes of each other, around 1730.

26th TASSA operated the first of several sub-charters today and also a sporadic series of flights from/to Barcelona, until their demise in August 1965. Douglas DC-6 EC-AVA & DC-7 EC-BAE were sub-charted during the weekend by British Midland, due to the lack of an available Argonaut.

26th The latest Aer Turas machine, Douglas C-54 EI-AOR, made its first appearance at Ringway as a passenger aircraft sub-charting a return flight to Ostend for British Midland. It would later become a pure-freighter, as the airline steered away from passengers to concentrate purely on cargo. Originally delivered to the USAF in 1944, and most recently with Air France, it was purchased by Aer Turas earlier this month, serving with them until as late as 1976.

20th June 1965 - From 1964 to 1968, Austrian Airlines would operate weekly summer charters to Salzburg, with their Vickers Viscounts. In March 1980, they returned again to Ringway to operate a twice-weekly schedule to Vienna with Douglas DC-9s. Here, Viscount OE-LAL is awaiting passengers for its return back to Salzburg. (Ken Fielding)

JULY 1965

Another disappointing month from a weather perspective. The first five days brought fine, sunny conditions, but the temperature gradually cooled off. Troughs then ran through the British Isles at regular intervals, with a particularly wet spell from the 10th-14th. A settled period took place until the 18th, when the country was subjected to more heavy rain, lasting right up to the 30th, when the country had fine and sunny day. The month's temperature extremes saw 25°C at Hoddesdon (14th) and a low of -2°C at Kielder Castle (17th).

Plans for a new road diversion at Manchester Airport, including a tunnel under the runway extension, are going ahead. As a first step in the £1.4 million scheme, compulsory purchase orders are being made on property on the Altrincham-Wilmslow road by Cheshire County Council. The new road, a diversion of the A538, will be two miles long, including the tunnel and its approaches. The plan will be laid before Manchester Corporation before the runway extension work begins. The compulsory purchase orders, which are subject to Minister of Transport confirmation, concerns gardens, farmland, part of the beds of the River Bollin and the stream at Cotterill Clough.

Scheduled first visits this month were BEA (BE795): Trident 1s G-ARPD (26th), G-ARPI (23rd), G-ARPJ (20th), G-ARPN (1st), G-ARPO (15th) & G-ARPT (25th), British United (BR572): BAC 1-11 G-ASJG (8th), Iberia (IB782/4): SE.210s EC-ARJ (8th), EC-ARK (6th) & EC-ARL (1st). Equipment changes were KLM (KL149/153): Electras PH-LLA (24th) & PH-LLD (17th).

1st BEA commenced jet services from Manchester, when Trident 1 G-ARPS departed at 0931 inaugurating a six-times-weekly service, serving Paris-Le Bourget. Today's initial flight carried the Lord Mayor of Manchester and a party of VIPs amongst the passengers, which took just 50 minutes, shaving 25 minutes off the schedule. As usual with these occasions, the E42 landing fee was waived!

2nd VC-10 G-ARVB arrived at 1206 today (BA1004 from Heathrow) on demonstration, undertaking a couple of local flights. However, this was not the first visit of type, as G-ARVJ had that honour diverting in due to fog at Heathrow on 29th September 1964. A further demonstration took place on the 9th, with VC-10 G-ARVF operating another two local flights.

3rd Piloted by the airline's managing director Britair L-049 Constellation 5Y-ABF arrived at 1638 to operate a rotation to Rimini on behalf of Britannia. The aircraft itself was formerly G-AHEL, which has served BOAC, Falcon Airways, Trans European & Euravia, but this was its only visit to Ringway with its new owners. In May 1966 it arrived at Shannon for storage, and was broken up during 1968.

4th Caledonian DC-7 G-AOIE had gone tech at Shannon the previous day, resulting in the airline sub-chartering Martin's Air Charter DC-7 PH-DSC for today's flights.

5th L-1049H N45515 would be the final Flying Tiger Constellation to visit Ringway. It was operating a cargo flight when it arrived at 1251 today from Gander, departing for Brussels the following afternoon.

5th A Canadian Pacific Britannia had not visited Ringway since 1962, but today saw the arrival of CF-CZW at 1724 from Winnipeg (CP378), leaving later for Toronto. Ironically this aircraft was not just a first visit, as it also proved to be the last Canadian Pacific Britannia to appear at Manchester.

6th July 1965 – BEA were now operating a fleet of five Argosy 222s to various European cities, as well as linking Glasgow, Manchester & Heathrow. However, this small fleet of Argosies were unprofitable and the type was totally withdrawn from BEA service by April 1970. They were replaced a number of Vickers Vanguards, that were converted to pure freighters and renamed Merchantmen. (Geoff Ball)

6th Langar-based Canadian Air Force Bristol 170 VC9699 diverted in at 1207 today with technical trouble, en route from Prestwick to Gatwick.

7th The first foreign registered Mooney to visit was SE-CMU, at 1829 today from Staverton to night-stop. Other first timers were Beech 95 OE-FSA (15th), Cessna 320 F-BKXT (20th) & Beech 58 OY-DPD (28th).

7th Sterling Douglas DC-6 OY-BAS (also 4th August) operated the first of four Wednesday charters during the summer as NB755/6 f/t Copenhagen, which was also a first visit. Other DC-6s used in this short series were OY-EAO (14th) & OY-BAT (11th August), with the latter also being a first visit.

8th Two Swissair DC-8 visits during the month were HB-IDC today, operating an extra Zurich flight (SR1470/1) and HB-IDB (21st) stopping off at Ringway as SR811 en route New York-Geneva.

8th The US military had been absent at Ringway for several months, but the US Army produced a new U-6A Beaver today, with the arrival of 37938 at 0952 from Leeds. It made a brief stop, before continuing onwards to RAF Woodvale. Another U-6A, 37939, arriving at 1512 on the 22nd July, was a tech diversion, en route from Birmingham to RAF Leuchars.

8th The first Royal Navy Sea Heron to visit was today's arrival of XR441 at 1029 from Sydenham (Navair 973). It was one of five acquired by the Royal Navy in 1961. Other military visitors included RAF Ansons TX209 (2nd) & VM325 (12th), Whirlwind XR486 (12th), Devons VP958 (30th) & VP962 (23rd) and another new Army Air Corps Beaver in the form of XP805 (16th).

10th Globe Air Herald HB-AAH finally made a smooth landing at 0228, after holding for more than 1½ hours due to undercarriage trouble, and one engine out of action. It was en route from Basle to Dublin, when it developed technical trouble. Having burned off all its excess fuel whilst holding, the passengers were ordered to remove any false teeth and spectacles, and to roll up their coats to make pillows for their heads. Six hours later the passengers left by coach for Holyhead, where they caught the afternoon ferry to Dublin, and the Herald returned back to Basle at 0129 after performing a test flight.

13th MS.760 Paris D-INGA was the first executive jet of the year, arriving from Cologne at 1325 today. Unfortunately this aircraft had visited previously, way back on the 28th May 1962.

14th The latest Heron for Falck Air, OY-DPR, was delivered today. Arriving from Hawarden at 1135, it stayed for just ten minutes to clear customs, before continuing on to Copenhagen. In February 1968, it returned to the UK and was intended for Imperial Tobacco as G-ASUY, but instead it was converted to an uprated-Riley Heron and sold to US operator Prinair as N554PR.

16th Polaris Air Transport Dakota LN-RTO arrived at 0058 from Kristiansand on a cargo charter. It was the first of two visits by this new airline to Ringway, with the other being Dakota LN-RTE (15th December). Polaris set up operations in 1964 with this single Dakota (ex-Starways G-AMPO), to operate cargo and passenger charters throughout Europe.

17th Sudflug Douglas DC-7 D-ABAD was sub-charted by Caledonian, who still had equipment problems operating their Shannon rotation CA145/6. This was its only visit, as it was sold in August 1968.

23rd Although there were two VC-10 demonstrations at Ringway earlier this month, today's arrival of VC-10 G-ARVM at 0940 (BA1008 from Heathrow) was probably the most important, as it was carrying BOAC's Chairman, Sir Giles Guthrie. The aircraft was put through its paces, showing what it could do to more than a hundred municipal administrators and pressmen during its sixty minute demonstration flight.

24th HS.748 G-ARAY arrived at 2228 from Keflavik for customs clearance and to night-stop. Returning to the UK after a five month lease to Lineas Aeropostal Venezuela (LAV), it would eventually leave for Woodford two days later.

25th *July 1965 - Looking a little tatty now it's more than twenty years old, is Douglas C-54 G-ARXJ. This aircraft and DC-4 G-APID were both leased to Dan-Air during the summer for passenger and freight work. Their visits to Ringway were mainly on troop charters or sub-charters. In the background, HS.748 G-ARAY can be seen sitting in the south bay, before leaving the following morning for Woodford. (Ian Hawkridge)*

28th Comet XK670 (also 28th September - same c/s and routing) operated by RAF Transport Command, was the latest to visit Ringway. Arriving from Aberdeen at 1153 (callsign JGR 299) today, it made a brief stop before continuing on to Bristol-Filton. Configured as a VIP transport aircraft, XK670 was another military Comet that was scrapped before its time.

31st The second Sudflug Douglas DC-7 to visit Manchester was D-ABAC, operating a number of Caledonian flights over the next two days. In 1965, the airline purchased six ex-KLM Douglas DC-7s due to extensive charter contracts with various travel agencies. In the following years, they grew to become the second largest German charter airline. In April 1967, Sudflug was the first German charter airline with traffic rights in the United States, initially for one year only. However, the purchase of two brand-new DC-9s and two second-hand Douglas DC-8s from Swissair, led them into financial trouble. The two DC-8s (D-ADIM & D-ADIR) were leased as planned in the spring, but delays on the delivery of their new DC-9s meant that for the duration of the 1967 summer season, other aircraft had to be leased to meet their contractual obligations. These lease costs contributed significantly to the economic decline of the airline. On the 2nd January 1968 they were taken over by their main competitor, Lufthansa, who fully absorbed them into their charter arm, Condor, eventually. During the same year, two employees of Sudflug left to form a new airline, Atlantis, and all aircraft operated by Sudflug were sold.

AUGUST 1965

Apart from a period from the 7th to the 17th when the weather became warm and sunny, the month was cool again and changeable. The month's temperature extremes saw 28°C at Valley (13th) and a low of 0°C at Alwen (9th).

Thirteen firms have been selected to tender for the job of building the £2m extension of the main runway. It is planned to extend runway 06/24 from 7500ft to 9000ft, to allow transatlantic jets to fly non-stop to America. Once work has started, it should take two years to complete.

Aiming to make Manchester Airport the hub of a jet network linking Scotland, Eire, Northern Ireland and the north of England with Europe; BEA will introduce their new Trident aircraft on at least three more routes from next April, including Amsterdam, Zurich and Dusseldorf.

Scheduled first visits this month were Aer Lingus (EI650): BAC 1-11 EI-ANG (2nd), Air France (AF960): SE.210 F-BJTS (22nd), BEA (BE795): Trident 1 G-ARPR (5th), British United (BR582): BAC 1-11 G-ASJE (13th), Iberia (IB782/4): SE.210s EC-AVY (12th) & EC-AXU (24th) and Sabena (SN623): SE.210 OO-SRK (20th) & (SN835): Douglas DC-6 OO-SDQ (14th). The only equipment change was Swissair (SR728): DC-8 HB-IDA (3rd).

The only GCA/ILS traffic noted this month was RAF Andover XS594 and Channel Airways HS.748 G-ATEH (both 24th).

2nd Ongoing delays to the departure of BR783 to Rimini, due to technical problems with the scheduled Viscount, caused a near mutiny amongst the sixty-seven passengers. The flight finally departed nineteen hours late, after the airline's latest Britannia, G-ANCH (ex-Ghana Airways 9G-AAG), made its first visit arriving from Gatwick to operate the flight.

4th Rhodesian Air Services Douglas DC-4 VP-YTY arrived from Salisbury via Malta to collect a load of Canberra spares. This aircraft would later turn up running guns to Biafra. In 1970, it was also the aircraft that evacuated Colonel Ojuwku and his staff when Biafra surrendered to the Federal Nigerian Forces, an event immortalised in the opening pages of Frederick Forsyth's novel 'The Dogs of War'.

4th Sir Giles Guthrie, BOAC's chairman, was back in Manchester again. This time it was to open the airline's new freight terminal in an action-packed thirty minute schedule. Although the terminal wasn't finished, BOAC staff learned to grab their chairman when they could! A member of staff commented how difficult it was to pin Sir Giles down, and by the time the building was ready he could be anywhere in the world. With this in mind, they collared him between briefly stepping off B.707 G-APFM, which arrived at as 1113 (BA607 from London), and joining the flight again half an hour later bound for Canada. During this time, he not only opened the new terminal, but also inspected BOAC's passenger and operations department. The new terminal would handle the airline's proposed six-weekly B.707F flights between Manchester and the USA & Canada.

7th Aer Turas Douglas C-54 EI-AOR began operating flights on behalf of Cambrian, due to the loss of Viscount G-AMOL, which had crashed on approach to Liverpool-Speke last month on the 20th July, following a flight from Ronaldsway airport, Isle of Man. Both crew members and two people on the ground were killed.

7th   A new Canadian airline to Ringway was Nordair, with the arrival of CF-NAL on its first visit at 0646 today from Toronto via Gander. It was one of the four L-1049H Constellations they bought during 1964.

7th   The United Steel Companies, one of a growing number of light aircraft operators based on the south side, had accepted a six week delivery delay of their new executive aircraft, Dornier Do.28 G-ATAL. This was due to the wrong radio equipment being fitted originally, and having to be changed. The aircraft finally arrived at 1803 today, direct from the Dornier aircraft factory at Bremen, flown in by a Dornier company pilot.

9th August 1965 – Capitol Airways replaced their Constellations on transatlantic charters with a number of DC-8-31s. Seen above is N4904C, which made its first to visit Manchester today, and the return flight on the 3rd September. (Geoff Ball)

11th   Early morning fog in the south produced eight diversions overall, but the only highlights were two first visits by MEA Comet OD-ADQ at 0622 (ME215 from Coulommiers) & BUA VC-10 G-ATDJ at 0816 (BR104 from Entebbe).

13th   Royal Canadian Air Force Lockheed C-130E 10316 was the first Canadian military Hercules to visit Ringway. Arriving at 2203 today from Bardufoss on a freight charter, it stayed until the 15th when it departed for Prestwick.

15th   The newest Douglas DC-7 for Shannon Air was EI-AOC, which burst a tyre on landing whilst making its first visit to Manchester. After its arrival from Gatwick, with a British United callsign (BR779) to operate a freight charter, it was grounded for two days undergoing repairs before eventually returning to Gatwick.

17th   TASSA operated their final flight from Manchester today, when DC-7 EC-BAF arrived at 0009 from Barcelona, later positioning to Copenhagen. They became the first Spanish casualty of the cut-throat inclusive tour industry, by ceasing operations completely later in the month.

27th   Only the third HS.125 to visit was D-COME, arriving at 0909 today from Dusseldorf. It became the first of many HS.125s passing through Ringway for customs clearance, before proceeding to Hawarden for maintenance.

28th   KLM DC-7 PH-DSI arrived at 0936 from Amsterdam to operate a freight charter to Benina, Libya.

12th August 1965 - Another new machine for Ferranti was Bell 47J G-ATFV, which made the first of many visits to Ringway today, operating from/to Knutsford. Operated by the Wythenshawe based electronics firm until late 1969 it made its last visit on 27th June 1968. (MA Archive via Ringway Publications)

14th August 1965 – Royal Canadian Air Force Canadair C-2 North Star 17515 was the only one to visit Ringway, seen above arriving at 1454 today on a round-trip from Gatwick. These aircraft were unpressurised, and used on a variety of transport duties. They were also notorious for the high level of cabin noise, caused by its Merlin engines. They had all been withdrawn from active service by the end of the year, with this aircraft eventually destined for preservation. (Ken Fielding)

15th August 1965 - Still wearing the company's old colours, Caledonian DC-7 G-ARYE is seen here in its final year of operation with the airline. It made its last visit on the 3rd October, and became one of six purchased by the fast-expanding German airline, Sudflug. (Malcolm Taylor)

SEPTEMBER 1965

It was confirmed during the month that Manchester would be linked by air for the first time with the industrial heart of America. BOAC were due to receive two brand-new Boeing 707-336C all-cargo aircraft. With operations planned to start in November, initially with four-weekly flights eventually increasing up to six-weekly, serving Montreal & New York. Plans to extend to Boston, Chicago, Detroit & Philadelphia at a later date were also made. In the first six months of 1965, 724 tonnes of freight had been exported to USA/Canada, compared to 581 tonnes (1964) and 370 tonnes (1963). The two Boeing 707s capable of carrying 40 tonnes, replaced CL-44 N228SW, which was currently operating the route, but limited to 30 tonnes. To speed up loading and unloading, goods were packed in 10ft long pallets, and stowed in the hold with the help of scissor-lift trucks. However, B.707F operations were put back to January 1966, so Flying Tiger CL-44s were used to operate all BOAC Cargo flights from November 1965 to January 1966.

Holiday fares between Manchester and America would be slashed next year, under a new international agreement. Prices for a 21-day holiday could be as little as £115, for the hotel, most meals and flights on scheduled services. A differential in summer and winter fares would also be abolished, but the new agreement from the 1st April next, would not embrace passengers who were not holidaymakers.

Scheduled first visits this month were Aer Lingus (EI652): BAC 1-11 EI-ANH (10th), BEA (BE795): Trident 1s G-ARPA (9th) & G-ARPP (1st) and Iberia (IB782/4): SE.210 EC-AYE (14th). The only equipment change was Sabena (SN623): CV-440 OO-SCV (17th).

GCA/ILS traffic noted during the month was HS.748 G-ARAY (16th) making the first appearance at Ringway of an RAF Dominie, XS712 (18th) and HS.125 G-ASSI (20th).

3rd HS.125 D-COME arrived at 1033 from Hawarden today for pre-customs clearance, before returning to Dusseldorf after work with Hawker-Siddeley.

4th Dan-Air DC-3 G-AMSS was also drafted in during the month by Cambrian, to cover for the loss of Viscount G-AMOL. It was first noted today operating several round-trips to Ronaldsway.

10th September had been lacking in interesting movements so far, apart from diversions and foreign lights, so today's first visit of Beech 65 HB-GAZ got the month off to a good start! Other first visits were Philips latest hack, Heron PH-ILO (22nd); PA-23 Aztec F-BMSF (23rd) & Beech Marquis F-BLLP (24th).

17ᵗʰ Pan Am operated the first of four late season transatlantic charters this year, when DC-8 N813PA arrived on its first visit at 1206 today from New York, returning via Shannon. All other flights from/to New York were also operated with the following Boeing 707s: N717PA (16ᵗʰ October), N726PA (28ᵗʰ September) & N725PA (10ᵗʰ October).

17ᵗʰ The first Canadian Air Force Yukon to visit Ringway was 15928, arriving at 1348 from Halifax. The CC-106 Yukon was the military version of the Canadair CL-44, and since 1962 they had operated twelve aircraft. Six different aircraft would visit Ringway between 1965 and 1970. The CC-106 Yukons were retired in March 1971, and replaced by the Boeing 707 (CC-137). The Yukons might have served longer with the Canadian military but for two factors: (1) the need for an aircraft which could operate as an in-flight refuelling tanker; (2) the chronic shortage and high cost of spares, which was the reason the CL-44 had not gone into large scale production. All Yukons were sold to South American and African operators, as they could not be registered in Northern America or Europe since the Britannia windshields did not meet their new security standards. The CC-106 had the original Bristol Britannia windshield and upon its retirement from RCAF operations, the cost of conversion was estimated at $250,000 per unit, which precluded its use in North America and Europe on cost alone.

18ᵗʰ September 1965 - In 1965 British Midland moved their base from Burnaston to Castle Donington. Apart from their Dakotas, they were still operating the following three Argonauts, G-ALHG, G-ALHS (as seen above) & G-ALHY. The two factors hastening the withdrawal of these Argonauts was the introduction of more Vickers Viscounts to the fleet and probably more importantly, was the Stockport air crash on the 4ᵗʰ June 1967, which involved Argonaut G-ALHG. (MA Archive via Ringway Publications)

22ⁿᵈ Fog at Heathrow sent fourteen diversions into Manchester this morning, twelve of which were British. BOAC aircraft were B.707s G-APFJ at 0740 (BA684 from New York), G-ARRA at 0907 (BA7031 from Montreal), G-APFD at 0925 (BA568 from Montreal) & G-ARWE at 1102 (BA7083 from Boston); and the first Super VC-10 to Ringway, G-ASGD at 1019 (BA506 from New York) with 125 passengers onboard. Others of note were Olympic Airways Comet G-ARDI at 0755 (OA781 from Athens), Alitalia SE.210 I-DAXO at 0624 (AZ308 from Rimini) and Capitol Curtiss C-46 N68966, currently on lease to Lufthansa arriving at 0645 (LH936 from Frankfurt). A single diversion from Gatwick, making its second appearance, was British United VC-10 G-ATDJ at 0821 (BR104 from Entebbe).

24ᵗʰ KLMs latest DC-8 to visit Manchester was PH-DCG, arriving as an Amsterdam diversion at 0936 today (KL624 from New York).

25th Today was yet another occasion when Caledonian had no choice other than to sub-charter. This evening, Martin's Air Charter DC-7 PH-DSC arrived from Amsterdam to operate CA147/8 to/from Palma.

28th RAF Ansons were becoming fewer and further between, so it was surprising that today's visit of Anson C.19 TX160 was a first visit, arriving at 1102 from/to Andover as 'HEM 48'. It served with the Western Communications Squadron based at RAF Andover until July 1968, and would end its days with the fire service at Stansted.

30th The first German Air Force Noratlas to visit Ringway was GB+111, arriving at 1324 today on a training flight from Chalgrove. It departed the following morning to an unknown destination. These aircraft would become fairly regular visitors during the 1960s, generally operating training flights and usually night-stopping.

OCTOBER 1965

This month's weather was dominated by high pressure, apart from the first few days with widespread and occasionally heavy rain. The period from the 5th-25th was dry and predominantly sunny, with fog commonplace on most days. The fine spell came to an end on the 27th, as wind and rain swept through the country. The last couple of days were especially wet and stormy. The month's temperature extremes saw 26°C at Hampton (7th) and a low of -4°C at Gatwick (23rd).

British United were seeking permission to operate scheduled services linking Manchester with London, Birmingham and the Isle of Man. Earlier in the year, despite strong opposition from BEA, BUA obtained rights to operate flights to Gatwick from Manchester, but with the proviso they only carried passengers with onward connections with the airline, but this was rejected by BUA. This latest application meant that British United would use Manchester as an optional stop on their Isle of Man to London services. The new service would have been in direct competition with BEA on the London and Birmingham routes, and with Cambrian Airways on the Isle of Man link.

Both BOAC and Qantas, along with the Manchester Chamber of Commerce, were evaluating the possibility of services from Manchester to Australia. Any new service would have been incorporated as a stop on their round-the-world services, but unfortunately this all came to nothing!

The results will be finalised by the end of the year, but Manchester Airport is well on the way to achieving another record breaking year. Up to the end of September passenger numbers were up 8% on the same period last year, standing at 1,112,735, so with three months to go there is little doubt that last year's passenger total of 1,324,092 will be broken.

Scheduled first visits were BEA (BE795): Trident 1 G-ARPU (11th) and Iberia (IB784): SE.210 EC-ATV (7th).

GCA/ILS traffic noted during the month was confined to two HS.748s on test flights out of Woodford, with G-ARAY (12th) & Lineas Aeropostal Venezuela (LAV) YV-C-AMY.

1st There were plenty of VC-10 first visits this month, beginning today with British United G-ASIX at 0538 (BR848 from Bahrain), diverting in due to fog at Gatwick.

2nd Twice in two days! BUA VC-10 G-ASIX made another visit today, diverting in again from Gatwick (BR812 from Aden). It was accompanied by several BOAC B.707 diversions from Heathrow, with B.707 G-APFB at 0940 (BA684 from New York), G-ARRB at 1003 (BA604 from Montreal) & G-ARWD at 1008 (BA512 from New York).

2nd EC-AIO became the final Iberia L-1049G Constellation to visit Manchester (AO1112/3 from/to Barcelona). Six of their seven aircraft would continue in service throughout 1966, but they were sold en masse to American company International Aerodyne in May 1967, for onward sale in South America. The seventh Connie, EC-AIN, crashed at Tenerife on 5th May 1965. Their last visit dates to Ringway are as follows:

EC-AIN	28th September 1964	
EC-AIO	2nd October 1965	Sold as N8023
EC-AMP	31st July 1965	Sold as N8021
EC-AMQ	24th September 1965	Sold as N8022
EC-AQM	10th July 1965	Sold as N8024
EC-AQN	28th August 1965	Sold as N8025
EC-ARN	24th July 1965	Sold as N8026

3rd US Army Beech U-8D Seminole 0-76093 arrived at 1219 today. Based on the Twin Bonanza, this was the first military version to visit, operating from/to its base in Stuttgart. A second aircraft, 0-76040, arriving later in the month on the 22nd, was on a late night flight from Stuttgart.

5th Today was a sunny and unusually warm, with temperatures reaching 23°C in the afternoon. During the morning there were eight Heathrow diversions, but the only one of interest was BOAC Comet G-APDS at 0824 (KU045 from Le Bourget), which was on lease to Kuwait Airways.

6th October 1965 – The first diversion this morning was this excellent Dakota, in the form of JAT Douglas DC-3 YU-ACD. Arriving at 0859 from Brussels operating a cargo flight, it was originally destined for Dublin. A second aircraft, YU-ACA, would make two visits to Ringway during 1968. (Bob Thorpe)

6th Today proved to be the ideal day for Ringway. With a clear blue sky and good visibility, it was the only major airfield in the entire country, except for Prestwick, that was unaffected by fog. However, because of this widespread fog, most UK bound aircraft remained grounded throughout Europe. In the end Ringway did handle nineteen diversions from a variety of airports, but none from Heathrow. The pick of these were BUA VC-10 G-ATDJ at 1107 (BR104 from Entebbe) on its second visit, and PA-24 Twin Comanche HB-OVW at 1620 from Berne.

8th Eight days into a month becoming dominated by diversions, there were two more today. Arriving were BUA VC-10 G-ASIW at 0703 (BR848 from Bahrain) and Beech Marquis F-BKOP at 0859 en route from Nantes to Dublin, which were both first visits.

9th German-based Curtiss C-46 N9893Z arrived at 0711 on a freight flight on behalf of Lufthansa. Capitol Airways, who operated the aircraft, had received the contract to fly Lufthansa's entire night-time European cargo network in 1964. They committed five aircraft to the operation, an arrangement that lasted until 1969. Over this period, Manchester saw the occasional visit by these venerable aircraft.

10th Martin's Air Charter DC-7 PH-DSO positioned from Amsterdam to operate CA147/8 to/from Palma on behalf of Caledonian.

10th Cessna 411 G-ATEY arrived at 1037 today, on delivery direct from the factory at Wichita, Kansas via Shannon, eventually bound for Rogers Aviation at Cranfield. This became the first Cessna 411 onto the UK register. It served with several owners until September 1975, when it was sold in the USA as N34JH.

12th The first Ace Freighters Constellation visit was G-ANTF at 2012 today from Coventry, collecting its cargo for an outbound departure the following morning to Sydney via Brindisi. This ex-Qantas and Capitol L-749 was operating in bare metal, with Ace Freighters titles and a 'black ace' on the tail. It also made a name for itself on 8th March 1966, carrying out a perfect wheels-up landing at Aden. The captain managed to feather all four engines, and position them to avoid damage before touchdown. A fire breaking out in the nose was quickly extinguished, and after minor repairs it returned to the UK.

13th The unpleasant business of searching for buried bodies on the Pennine moors, resulted in a number of aircraft being used as liaison flights to the scene, transporting police etc. Amongst those operating from Manchester was Brantly B.2B G-ATFG today and Cessna 172 G-ATGO on the 15th. Resident PA-28 G-ARVS was also used and another resident, Auster G-AGXN, took part in photographic sorties over the area today and again on the 23rd.

13th Another freight charter involved the only visit of Transmeridian DC-7BF G-ATAB. Positioning in at 1724 today from Southend, it departed two days later on a livestock charter bound for Algiers. It would replace the airline's two C-54s, G-APID & G-ARXJ, but in turn they were replaced by two Douglas DC-7CFs, G-ATMF & G-ATOB, in early 1966.

14th Hundreds of passengers were affected again, when their flights were forced to land at Manchester due to fog at London. Amongst the eight diverted aircraft were three Boeing 707s, BOAC example G-ARRC at 0749 (BA684 from New York) and two Pan American aircraft making first visits, N405PA at 0745 (PA058 from Chicago) & N729PA at 0757 (PA056 from Boston). Amongst the others were British Eagle Britannia G-AOVA at 0725 (EG929 from Istanbul) and another visit by BOAC Super VC-10 G-ASGD, which landed at 1022 (BA506 from New York). The fog, the worst of the autumn so far, had blanketed parts of southern England, but Manchester managed escaped the worst of it.

14th Today saw two types making first visits and several other interesting movements. Beechcraft's latest large twin, the Beech 90, was represented by D-ILMA on its only visit as it was written off in August 1969. The second was the executive jet, North American Sabreliner N911Q, which day-stopped from/to Heathrow. Also today was another Rhodesian Air Services Douglas DC-4, with VP-YYR operating from/to Salisbury via Malta, collecting more Canberra spares. Finally three RAF transport aircraft were Varsitys WJ892 & WL634 and an unidentified Valetta, all routing from Ballykelly to RAF Strubby. The Valetta night-stopped and was the last one to land at Ringway.

18th Dove D-IFSC operated by the German flight inspection unit, arrived at 1427 for customs clearance. It was eventually bound for maintenance at Hawarden.

21st Ringway was finally affected by fog. BOAC Boeing 707 G-APFB (BA538 from New York/Prestwick) was delayed at Prestwick for over two hours awaiting an improvement in the weather.

21st The French entrant into the growing executive jet market was the Dassault-Breguet Mystère 20 (later to be known as the Falcon 20). A total of 473 Falcon 20s and 35 Falcon 200s were built by the time production ended in 1988. Today's first visit was provided by F-BMSH at 0859 from Le Bourget, clearing customs prior to its departure to Warton.

22nd Manchester played host to numerous weather diversions again, totalling eighteen throughout the day, thirteen of which were escaping the fog at Heathrow. All were British, and the only one not from BEA or BOAC was British Eagle Britannia G-ARKB at 0903 (EG113 from Bahrain). Amongst the BEA contingent was Trident 1 G-ARPG at 0933 (BE'PG from Paris). BOAC sent in SVC-10 G-ASGF at 1014 (BA506 from New York) on its first visit and no less than five Boeing 707s! These were G-APFC at 0838 (BA684 from New York), G-APFK at 0947 (BA672 from Bermuda), G-APFN at 1232 (BA562 from Boston) which landed as a full emergency with less than twenty minutes fuel having held for a considerable time over Daventry, and finally G-ARRA at 1118 (BA568 from Montreal). B.707 G-APFO which had operated our own Montreal flight BA610, and was due to position back to Heathrow, landed back at Manchester after a failed attempt to return to Heathrow, as did G-APFC. Finally BKS Britannia G-ANBH diverted away from Newcastle during the evening, landing at 1929 from Heathrow.

24th The last Caledonian summer IT flight was operated by DC-7 G-AOIE (CA148 from Palma), which was also the only Caledonian DC-7 to make it into 1966. Their other three were disposed of as follows:

G-ARYE	Last visit 3rd October	Sold February 1966 to Sudflug as D-ABAR
G-ASHL	Last visit 3rd October	Returned in October 1965 to Sabena as OO-SFK
G-ASIV	Last visit 20th November	Sold February 1966 to Sudflug as D-ABAK

24th The first Queen's Flight HS.748 to visit Ringway was XS790, arriving at 1632 from Heathrow on a short trip before continuing onwards to RAF Leuchars. Delivered in July 1964, it served with the RAF and later the Royal Aircraft Establishment right up until its withdrawal in 1997.

22nd October 1965 – G-ASGF became the first Super VC-10 to visit Ringway, thanks the inclement weather prevalent in the south during October. No less than six VC-10s also made their first visits this month. In April 1966, the type would become a familiar sight at Ringway, when it began daily New York flights, replacing Boeing 707's. (Geoff Ball)

26th In a month dominated by bad weather in the south, the airport broke the record for the most London diversions handled in single day. Thirty-two were from Heathrow and a single early morning flight from Gatwick was British United VC-10 G-ASIX at 0546 (BR812 from Aden), returning soldiers to the UK on leave. The first session produced first visits by TAP SE.210 Caravelle CS-TCB at 1056 (TP450 from Lisbon), BOAC SVC-10s G-ASGB at 0651 (BA684 from Seattle) & G-ASGC at 0803 (BA504 from New York) and BEA Trident 1 G-ARPA (BE'PA from Geneva). Other morning diversions included BOAC B.707s G-APFD at 0625 (BA600 from Montreal), G-APFL at 0724 (BA562 from Montreal) & VC-10 G-ARVJ at 1158 (BA272 from Lagos). However, it was the evening session that produced the most diversions, putting the airport at full stretch with twenty more arrivals, all before midnight. Included were more first visits by Alitalia SE.210 I-DABS at 2121 (AZ290 from Milan) & VC-10 G-ARVL at 2027 (BA231 from Khartoum).

26th Arriving for demonstration today from Charleroi was SIAI S.250 I-ZUAR. The next day PA-28 Cherokee-lookalike, SIAI S.205 I-SIAA, also arrived from Charleroi for demonstration. Tragically I-ZUAR crashed eleven days later.

26th BEA Vanguard G-APEE would make its last visit to Ringway, as it crashed at Heathrow the following morning in the early hours, shortly after its third attempt to land in thick fog, killing all seventy-two onboard.

27th Two more diversions arriving in the early hours from Heathrow were Iberia SE.210s EC-ATV at 0142 (IB292 from Palma) & EC-ATX at 0119 (IB562 from Barcelona). A third, BOAC VC-10 G-ARVJ arriving at 0215 (BA272 from Lagos/Manchester), diverted back to Ringway due to Heathrow's closure following the Vanguard accident.

29th Iberia Dakota EC-ASF arrived at 1107 from Nantes for fuel en route to Glasgow. Another Dakota, Dan-Air's G-AMSS (30th), was noted with 'Double Your Money' written on the sides, advertising an extremely popular game show at the time, hosted by Michael Miles.

31st CL-44 N228SW which has been leased to BOAC, made it last visit today. The airline's freight service is now being temporarily operated by Flying Tiger CL-44s until BOAC's B.707F freighters are delivered.

NOVEMBER 1965

Although the month began on a stormy note with snow showers, a quiet spell from the 3rd-7th soon followed. Easterly winds took charge from the 11th, with occasionally heavy snow and low temperatures. Apart from a brief respite on the 18th, the pattern continued until the end of the month. Severe blizzards swept across northern England during the nights of the 26th/27th & 28th/29th, with many roads blocked by snowdrifts. In the Durham area they were reported as high as 15ft deep. The month's temperature extremes saw 18°C at Newport (1st) and a low of -11°C at Santon Downham (15th).

British Eagle, one of Britain's largest independent airlines, was seeking permission to operate between Manchester and Liverpool to Rotterdam and Frankfurt. British United also put in an application to serve Rotterdam from Manchester. If successful, British Eagle would operate their new BAC 1-11s on the route. Meanwhile, the airline was given the go-ahead to operate the type on flights from Manchester to Casablanca, Nice, Perpignan, Rabat, Luxembourg, Rimini & Forli.

Scandinavian Airlines System (SAS) announced they would introduce a twice-weekly Caravelle service between Manchester and Copenhagen from next summer.

The landing fees from the 297 aircraft that had diverted into Manchester so far this year, produced £17,000 worth of extra revenue for the airport.

International flights were operated during the winter as follows:

AIR FRANCE – Three-times-weekly to Paris with SE.210s.

AER LINGUS - Amsterdam (2 x weekly), Brussels (2 x weekly), Copenhagen (2 x weekly), Dusseldorf (2 x weekly), Frankfurt (2 x weekly) & Zurich (1 x weekly), all operated by BAC 1-11s except for Amsterdam.

BEA - Amsterdam/Dublin/Dusseldorf & Paris.

BOAC - Daily to New York (BA538/7) & Montreal/Toronto (BA610/607) three-weekly, all services operated by B.707s, routing via Prestwick. Flying Tiger CL-44s took over the Montreal/New York cargo flights (BA065) now three-weekly until 9th January. From 12th January, frequency increased to five-weekly with B.707Fs, now also routing via Prestwick.

KLM - Operated to Amsterdam twice-weekly with Electras/Viscounts (KL149/150), one of these flights operates onwards to Dublin (KL151/2). Also now operating a five-weekly DC-7 cargo flight to Amsterdam via LHR (KL019/020).

SABENA - The evening Brussels service continues four-times-weekly with SE.210 Caravelles. Dakotas operate four-times-weekly on the airlines cargo flights. Introduced in November was a Friday evening DC-6F service (SN195/6) f/t Brussels, but via Shannon on the outbound.

SWISSAIR - Once-weekly f/t Zurich (SR844/5) with CV-990s, increasing to twice-weekly from 22nd Dec.

Scheduled first visits this month were BEA (BE795): Trident 1 G-ARPW (21st), BOAC (BA065): Flying Tiger CL-44s N447T (17th), N449T (14th), N454T (24th), N1001T (5th) & N1002T (10th) and British United (BR572/582): BAC 1-11s G-ASJA (17th), G-ASJB (18th) & G-ASTJ (21st).

No GCA/ILS traffic was noted this month. A number of training flights operated the first for several months, with BEA Argosy G-APRM (10th/20th), Comet G-APMC (18th) & BOAC B.707 G-APFB (12th).

1st British United started the first ever direct air service between Manchester and Southampton. The first today was operated by Herald G-ATHE. They were four-times-weekly during the winter, increasing the next summer to twice-daily. Apart from the summer holiday traffic, there was also considerable business traffic. Around 30,000 people a year travel from the North West to Southampton to board cruise liners.

2nd Morton Air Services were regular visitors to Ringway, but from today they began a three-times-weekly scheduled service to Oxford and Bournemouth. The inaugural flight was operated by Heron G-AOXL.

4th Douglas DC-7B N774R, which arrived at 2227 from Heathrow and departed for Lyons on the 7th, was equipped as a travelling showroom for the IBM Corporation.

5th Today's visit of N100IT was one of seven different CL-44s used by Flying Tigers during their temporary operation of BOAC's transatlantic cargo flights. The entire section of the CL-44 tail section was hinged, and could be opened using hydraulic actuators to load large items quickly. An inflatable seal at the hinge-break enabled cabin pressure to be maintained, and eight hydraulic-operated locks assured structural integrity. The tail could be opened from controls within it in ninety seconds. The flight controls at the joint were maintained by a system of push pads.

5th Britannia G-ANCD (also 16th) was used on Dusseldorf troop flight BR582/1, rather than the customary BAC 1-11.

8th RAF Whirlwind (registration unknown) operated from/to Warton as 'Tarnish Delta'. This helicopter is used by BAC as a 'watch-aircraft' for aircraft making test flights over water.

13th Cessna 320 N4102M operated two round-trips from Blackpool today. The Cessna 320, which was developed from the Cessna 310, has super turbochargers to give the aircraft a high altitude capability.

15th Last present in November 1960, USAF C-47 0-48686 arrived at 0918 from Brussels, and stayed for three days. Also present today was RAF Pembroke WV753 (JVR 02 f/t White Waltham).

18th SAS DC-7 SE-CCA arrived at 1325 (DK1763 from Copenhagen) with the Danish Prime Minister onboard. He was attending various local engagements, before returning home the following afternoon.

18th Heathrow fog provided a late evening flurry of diversions, but the only aircraft of note was Qantas B.707 VH-EBI (QF530 from New York) at 2125, making its first visit. BOAC G-ARVI (BA112 from Johannesburg/Rome) had amongst its passenger's twenty-two boys from the Vienna Boys Choir, flying from South Africa at the start of their UK tour.

22nd Air France B.707 F-BHSB (AF4221 from New York) arrived at 0837 to drop off the Czechoslovak Philharmonic Orchestra, plus their instruments.

22nd Canadian Air Force C-130 10310 arrived at 1320 from Kinloss on a training flight. It landed, taxied slowly and departed to Gatwick, all in the space of ten minutes!

25th Mystere 20 F-BMSS orbited over Burtonwood and north of Ringway for about an hour prior to landing. This was second of its type to visit, conducting range tests.

25th Aero Commander N390GA arrived at 1327 from Kinloss on its first and only visit. In June 1966, it was re-registered as G-ATWN, operating for Alan Mann Racing. In 1968 it passed to Elliott Brothers (later Marconi-Elliott Avionics) based at Rochester until December 1976, when it was sold in South Africa as ZS-KAU.

29th Aero-Nord Douglas DC-7 OY-ANB was the second and last of the airlines DC-7s to visit Manchester. It arrived at 1151 today (AN909/10) from Billund, and stayed until the 2nd December. In 1966, the airline merged with Swedish-outfit Osterman Air Charter to form Internord.

DECEMBER 1965

Although it was a wet month, there was more than average sunshine almost everywhere. On the evening of the 13th, the rain moved away and winds fell light, leading to extensive fog persisting in many places the following day, but it was soon swept away. On the 15th more than four inches of rain was recorded within a 24 hour period in mid-Wales and daytime temperatures were as high as 13°C, and Kew had the mildest December night since records began in 1871. The last week was cold with snow at times, but New Year's Eve saw temperatures rise as another trough swept across the UK, bringing wind and rain. The months temperature extremes saw 15°C at Faversham (17th) and a low of -12°C at Chapel en le Frith (28th).

More good news from British United! They were given the go-ahead to operate the first ever car ferry from Manchester next year. The government told the airline they could press on with plans to use their Carvairs on a service linking Manchester with Rotterdam. It was thought that the route would become a catalyst for many more air ferry services, linking Manchester with other continental cities. Flights would operate at a frequency of four per week, commencing on the 1st April next year. They would also introduce twice-weekly flights from Manchester to Blackpool, costing around £2 16s return for the 28 minute flight. The airline had operated these flights in the past, which were mainly used by passengers in transit, but in 1966 they also hoped to attract holidaymakers for a trip to the seaside. Finally, Exeter would be added for the first time next year as an extension of its weekday Southampton flights.

BOAC planned to introduce new Super VC-10s onto their Manchester-New York services from next April. This would be the first time the 139-seater aircraft had operated from any point in the UK outside London.

BOAC/Flying Tigers provided the only scheduled first visits, with <u>BOAC (BA065)</u>: Flying Tiger CL-44s N446T (8th) & N453T (23rd). The only equipment change was <u>Swissair (SR844)</u>: DC-8 HB-IDA (22nd).

GCA/ILS traffic noted during the month was HS.125 G-ASSI (2nd) & LIAT HS.748 VP-LIN (3rd). Training flights were operated by BKS HS.748 G-ASPL (1st) & British Eagle G-AMOE (16th).

1st Hawker Siddeley hack HS.125 G-ARYC operated a return trip to Bristol-Filton. Delivered in March 1962, it was used on company business until March 1970, when it was sold to Rolls-Royce.

3rd TMA Douglas DC-6 OD-AEG arrived at 2008 from Frankfurt, departing three hours later for Calcutta via Heathrow on a cargo flight.

6ᵗʰ Lightning punched a hole in British United BAC 1-11 G-ASJC inbound to Manchester, whilst on a trooping flight (BR572 from Dusseldorf). The aircraft, with seventy-one passengers onboard, landed safely at 1256 and departed empty at 1530 to Gatwick for damage assessment.

9ᵗʰ Helped by strong tail winds, two BOAC aircraft broke the airline's own records for transatlantic flights. A Super VC-10 cut 1 hour 9 minutes off the scheduled New York-Heathrow time today, by completing the journey in 5 hours 26 minutes. B.707 G-APFG (BA606 from Montreal), which landed at 0639 with 98 passengers, cut just over an hour off the scheduled time, making the flight in 4 hours 52 minutes.

11ᵗʰ Dove D-IFSC arrived at 1110 from Hawarden for pre-customs clearance, before returning to Frankfurt.

11ᵗʰ Braathens F.27 LN-SUG operated from/to Oslo on a seamen's charter.

13ᵗʰ Air India B.707 VT-DNY stopped off at 0741 (AI116 from New York) en route to Heathrow.

14ᵗʰ The airport broke the record again for the most diversions in single day, for the second time in three months. The thirty-six diversions consisted of thirty-three from Heathrow and one each from Birmingham, Luton & Gatwick. Off-duty staff were called in to help with the flight chaos, when thick fog affected the southern half of the country, reducing visibility down to 200yds. Manchester however was bathing in winter sunshine! Most of these flights terminated at Ringway, where arrangements had been made to take the passengers by surface transport to London. What was also remarkable was that all the diversions arrived within an eight hour period, starting with Caledonian Britannia G-AOVH at 0632 (CA318 from Damascus). A combination of lack of parking space and the improving weather at Heathrow meant that BEA Trident 1 G-ARPG (BE'PG from Zurich) at 1450 was the final one. Numerous first visits in arriving order were SVC-10 G-ASGH at 0916 (BA684 from New York), SAS DC-8 SE-DBC at 1105 (SK501 from Copenhagen), TAP SE.210 Caravelle CS-TCC at 1114 (TP450 from Lisbon), Qantas B.707 VH-EBB at 1132 (QF751 from Athens), BOAC VC-10 G-ARVK at 1205 (BA124 from Rome), Alitalia SE.210 I-DABR at 1248 (AZ288 from Milan) & Lufthansa B.727 D-ABIQ at 1333 (LH226 from Cologne). Others of note were Pan American B.707s N727PA at 0903 (PA056 from Boston) & N763PA at 1330 (PA101 from Frankfurt); SAS SE.210 SE-DAF at 1401 (SK513 from Stavanger) and South African B.707 ZS-CKC at 1405 (SA222 from Prestwick). Autair Ambassadors G-ALZS & G-ALZW diverted from Luton and Heathrow respectively, and BEA took up valuable parking space with Argosy G-ASXN, Tridents G-ARPG/ARPR & ARPW, Vanguards G-APEB/APEC/APEF/APET & APEU and Viscounts G-AOHR/AOYM/AOYT & APOX.

15ᵗʰ LN-RTE was the second Polaris Air Transport Dakota to visit Manchester, operating a further seamen's charter, inbound from Kristiansand.

16ᵗʰ Alitalia DC-8 I-DIWE diverted in from Heathrow at 0731 (AZ639 from New York). At this time Europe's major flag carriers had full rights, exercising them to operate flights to the USA & Canada via UK points such as Heathrow and also Prestwick. These rights were also exercised by Sabena, who had operated quite happily through Manchester until March 1964, when government restrictions made them withdraw from the New York route.

18ᵗʰ Cessna 337 G-ATJO arrived at 0929 today from Shannon on its delivery flight, departing later for Rogers Aviation at Cranfield.

FIRST/LAST ARRIVALS & DEPARTURES 1965

First arrival: Air France DC-4F F-BBDK @ 0717 from Paris-Orly
First departure: BEA Vanguard G-APET @ 0755 to Heathrow
Last arrival: Aer Lingus EI-AKD @ 2232 from Dublin (Birmingham diversion)
Last departure: Aer Lingus EI-AKD @ 2320 to Dublin

Airport Stats 1965 (+/- % on Previous Year)		
Scheduled Passengers	1,098,000	+6.9%
Inclusive & Charter Passengers	250,000	+13%
Freight & Mail (Tonnes)	23,700	+25.3%
Movements	47,300	+4.4%

AIRPORT DIARY 1966

JANUARY 1966

One of Latin America's biggest airlines, Aeronaves de Mexico (Aeromexico), was considering operating a new service linking Manchester with Mexico City and Acapulco. No decision would be made until a full assessment of the demand and the economics of such a service had been completed. Under a two year agreement, BOAC and Aeromexico would start flights between London and Mexico City, with BOAC commencing services in April. But BOAC wanted to operate into the famous holiday resort of Acapulco. In return Aeromexico wanted to operate into London, as well as another point, possibly Manchester. Although many northern businessmen travelled to Latin America and could use Mexico as a stopping-off point, passenger demand from this sector in itself is unlikely to justify a service, but the Mexican airline may decide that the demand as a whole from northern Europe might make it worthwhile.

The airport made a record breaking profit of £222,875 in 1965, making it a boom year for passengers carried, freight, and aircraft movements. Landing fees netted £641,862, freight handling charges £321,526 and passenger service charges £92,833. Spectators on the roof terraces and piers brought in a further £30,526.

British Rail planned to introduce 100-mph trains in April, once the upgrade of the west coast main line was fully completed. As part of the 1955 British Rail modernisation plan, work began in 1959 to electrify the line between Liverpool, Manchester & Crewe to London which would eventually introduce the Inter-City branding and see journey times reduce to a mere 2½ hours. Naturally, this made BEA a little nervous, so they announced an extra Heathrow rotation from April. The airline was carrying over 400,000 passengers a year on the route, one of the busiest in Europe. The extra service would be operated by Vickers Vanguards, but calls to use Tridents were rejected, citing that the time saving would be negligible.

The month began with the first few days predominantly mild but windy with thundery showers, until high pressure took charge from the 4th, lasting for the best part of two weeks. During this period the temperatures became increasingly cold, with snow in most parts on the 11th. The cold spell had broken by the 20th with a spell of freezing rain, followed by widespread, dense fog and drizzle throughout much of the country. January ended again on a mild, wet and windy note. The month's temperature extremes saw 14°C at Penketh (28th) and a low of -19°C at Elmstone, Kent (19th).

Scheduled first visits this month were <u>BOAC (BA065)</u>: B.707s G-ASZF (13th) & G-ASZG (26th). The only equipment change during the month was <u>Sabena (SN623)</u>: CV-440 OO-SCS (23rd).

Plenty of GCA/ILS traffic was noted during the month. From Woodford was HS.748s YV-C-AMF (5th) & Channel Airways G-ATEJ (25th); RAF Vulcan B.2 XJ781 (14th) and Andover XS595 (18th), also HS.125 G-ASNU & Ghana Airways Viscount 9G-AAU (both 29th), the latter in the UK for maintenance at Wymeswold, and finally BAC President G-ARCN (31st). Training flights were operated by BEA Trident G-ARPH (14th), British Eagle Britannia G-ANCF (23rd) & BEA Argosy G-ASXM (26th).

8th Air India B.707 VT-DJJ called in at 1319 (AI111 from Heathrow) en route to New York via Prestwick.

10th Braathens F.27 LN-SUD arriving at 1640 from Edinburgh, was the latest of the Norwegian airline's F.27 to visit, leaving later for Oslo.

10th A very rare visitor today was Hawker Siddeley Dove G-ANMJ, from/to Holme-On-Spalding Moor.

13th BOAC introduced their brand new B.707 freighters today, on their services to Canada and the USA, each with a 36,000-kilo capacity. They replaced leased CL-44s of Seaboard Western and latterly Flying Tiger, which had operated since October 1963.

14th When BEA Trident G-ARPH touched down operating this evening's Paris flight (BE795); it became the first aircraft to make an automatic landing at Manchester.

18th Transglobe Britannia G-ATLE (ex-Canadian CF-CZC), the second of four that would be eventually operated by the airline, arrived at 1753 from Gatwick to operate a flight to Bahrain/Singapore on behalf of British United.

19th Aer Lingus Fokker F-27 EI-AKC, en route from Birmingham to Dublin, was forced to make an emergency landing at 1027 due to a feathered engine.

20th Ace Freighters Douglas DC-4F G-APEZ positioned from Coventry to operate a cargo flight to Stockholm the following morning.

9th January 1966 – Pan Am operated the first of numerous charters this year with N721PA, which positioned in from Istanbul. Departing with a full load to New York via Prestwick, the return flight operated on 28th January with B.707 N760PA. During 1966 the airline also entered the 'affinity-group' market , realising it not only had the potential to earn them money, but also prevented numerous B.707 & DC-8 aircraft from sitting around idle at the weekends. (Geoff Ball)

15th January 1966 – DH.104 Dove G-AMZN was based at Ringway from August 1965 to April 1972. It was already twelve years old by the time it was purchased by Richard Johnson & Nephew, locally-based manufacturers of iron, steel and copper wire whose roots could be traced back to 1773. (Geoff Ball)

20ᵗʰ Three weather diversions during the afternoon, BUA Britannia G-APNA at 1415 (BR852 from Istanbul), MEA Comet OD-ADS at 1457 (ME205 from Beirut) and Swissair SE.210 HB-ICR at 1500 (SR804 from Zurich), were just the pre-cursor to what would follow over the next two days, when much of the country was affected by dense fog.

21ˢᵗ Belgian International Air Services (B.I.A.S.) was set up in 1959, with its headquarters in Antwerp and Brussels. They mainly operated passenger and cargo air charter flights from Brussels to the former Belgian colonies in Central Africa. Today, the airline's DC-6 OO-ABG arrived at 2344 from Rotterdam to operate a cargo flight to Brussels. On 18ᵗʰ February 1966, it took off from Brussels operating a cattle flight bound for Milan. The flight was routine and the aircraft was cleared for a standard ILS approach to runway 35R. Runway visibility was given as 250m. The plane crossed the runway threshold deviating 8° to the right and continued along the runway for 2400m before striking trees and crashing into flames. The subsequent accident report concluded that the probable cause was attributed by the pilot's failure to adhere to the company's landing minima, and his belated decision to execute the missed approach procedure.

21ˢᵗ Today saw the start of a busy few days, with fog affecting operations at Heathrow. Fourteen flights arrived from Heathrow and Birmingham, mostly from BEA with just one 'foreign' airline, Aer Lingus Viscount EI-AKO. The first diversion, BOAC SVC-10 G-ASGF at 0925 (BA684 from New York) was also a first visit.

22ⁿᵈ Twenty-seven diversions today provided plenty of variety, with all but two from Heathrow. Two DH.Comets within three minutes of each other were East African 5X-AAO at 1008 (EC712 from Cairo) & Kuwait Airways Comet 9K-ACE at 1011 (KU049 from Kuwait/Frankfurt). Two Qantas B.707s making their first visits within seven minutes of each other were VH-EBA at 1250 (QF759 from Frankfurt) & VH-EBQ at 1257 (QF739 from Athens). South African Airways B.707 ZS-CKC at 1504 (SA214 from Rome) had visited before. Four SE.210 Caravelles diverting in were Air France F-BLKF at 1116, SAS LN-KLP at 1322 (SK513 from Stavanger), Alitalia I-DABV at 1213 (AZ288 from Rome) & I-DAXA at 1542 (AZ280 from Rome) which was a first visit. The second SAS DC-8 was SE-DBA at 1148 (SK501 from Copenhagen), and finally the best of today's arrivals was Lufthansa Viscount D-ANAF at 1301 (LH1238 from Rome).

23ʳᵈ A further twenty-two diversions arriving today, again mainly from Heathrow, were predominantly BEA/BOAC aircraft. Lufthansa Viscount D-ANAF visited again, arriving at 1238 (LH238 from Basle), but the pick of the day was actually a diversion from Dublin, with the arrival of SAS Douglas DC-7 SE-CCI (SK9226) at 0741 operating a charter from Stockholm.

28ᵗʰ The Lord Mayor of Manchester visited the airport to unveil a plaque provided by members of the squadron in memory of 613-Squadron (City of Manchester) Royal Auxiliary Air Force Squadron. In connection with this, RAF Varsity T.1 WL671 had brought in the UHF equipment two days earlier for a flypast of six Gnats of the C.F.S. Arriving today for the ceremony was Devon VP956, and Varsity WL671 returned on the 2ⁿᵈ February to collect the equipment.

27ᵗʰ Aeropostal HS.748 YV-C-AMF diverted in at 1157 from Hatfield due to problems at Woodford.

31ˢᵗ Sabena B.707 OO-SJA arrived at 1010 from Oporto, carrying Benfica FC for their European Cup quarter-final first leg with Manchester United two days later. The Reds just about scraped through, edging out the Portuguese side 3-2, but would put the side under enormous pressure for the return away fixture against a side with such an impressive record in European football.

31ˢᵗ More diversions, again dominated by British flights. Of the twelve arrivals mostly from Heathrow, the only flight of note was Pan American B.707 N763PA at 1327 (PA001 from Frankfurt).

FEBRUARY 1966

The weather was cyclonic in character apart from the 11ᵗʰ-17ᵗʰ when pressure was high over Scandinavia and north of the country. Late January's mild weather continued into the first week, before colder weather dug in. By the 11ᵗʰ, wintry weather took hold of the UK, when mid-month daytime temperatures remained near to or below freezing with severe night frosts. Occasional snow was heavy, but by the 18ᵗʰ troughs associated with a deep depression brought rain to the south and heavy snow further north, which turned into rain. The month ended with frequent rain as a series of troughs and depressions crossed the country. The month's temperature extremes saw 16°C at Wrexham (5ᵗʰ) and a low of -20°C at Braemar (15ᵗʰ).

Despite objections by airlines and coach firms, British Eagle were authorised to operate from Liverpool & Manchester, onwards to Rotterdam & Frankfurt. The Frankfurt services didn't start until 12ᵗʰ June 1967 due to legal wrangling, and Rotterdam was never served, but British United began a car ferry operation in April.

Although the airport was granted permission to extend its main runway by 400ft at the eastern end to 9,000ft, it was put on hold due to the curbs on public spending announced last July. The work which eventually started in March 1967 would be completed by spring 1969. This included the compulsory purchase of land to divert the main Altrincham-Wilmslow A538 road through a tunnel under the runway.

Plenty of GCA/ILS traffic was noted again this month, including Andovers XS596 (2nd) & XS597 (16th/17th); Vulcan B.2 XM606 & HS.125 G-ASSM (both 3rd); Channel Airways HS.748s G-ATEJ (4th/7th) & G ATEK (18th); Shackleton XF711 (23rd) and HS.748s G-ARAY (23rd) & XS794 (24th). Training flights were operated by British Eagle Britannia G-AOVT (9th), BOAC B.707s G-APFE (9th) & G-ARRC (28th); BEA Argosy G-ASXM (12th), British Eagle Britannia G-ANCF (23rd), BEA Argosies G-ASXM (12th) & G-ASXP (19th); and finally HS.125 G-ASNU (24th). However the highlight of the 'non-visitors' was RAF Hastings WD480, which appeared on consecutive days (16th/17th). Although it didn't land, unusually it was recorded in the official ATC logs.

3rd A rare visitor to Ringway, was Brantly B-2A G-ASHD, owned by Pontins. New to the UK register in April 1963, it would only make two further visits, both in 1966 before crashing into the River Colne near Brightlingsea on 15th February 1967. During the Second World War, Fred Pontin was drafted to run tough workers' hostels in Bristol and Kidderminster, Worcs. During this time he came up with the idea that would make his fortune - turning old military sites into mass seaside holiday camps. The first opened in 1946 at Brean Sands, a derelict former American tank regiment base in Somerset, which he bought for £23,000. More camps quickly followed across the country, although on a smaller scale than those run by his rival, Billy Butlin. By the 1970s there were twenty-two Pontin's establishments across the UK, catering to a million Britons a year. There were also ten "Pontinental" centres abroad, offering a fortnight's holiday on the Mediterranean for £50. Sir Fred promoted his famed bluecoats as the organisers of the leisure industry he had created, while his rival Sir Billy relied on redcoats to run his camps. However, with the advent of cheaper foreign package holidays, the popularity of holiday camps began to wane. Sir Fred retired in 1978, after his company was taken over by the Coral Group, but he continued wheeling and dealing well into his eighties, with a scheme to take tourists to Disneyland, Paris. However, he was forced to change the name from Mouse Tours to Magic Tours, when the Disney organisation realised that his logo, 'Freddie Mouse', would be confused with their own 'Mickey Mouse'!

7th Lear Jet 23 N706L arrived at 1946 from Heathrow for demonstration to local firms. Amongst those interested were Geigy Co, Davy-Ashmore, United Steel Company and Northern Executive Aviation. The aircraft was also chartered by Sebastian De Ferranti for a business trip to London the following day.

9th It transpired that BOAC Boeing 707 G-APFE, arriving at 0957 from Heathrow to operate a crew training duty, was making its final visit. On 5th March 1966 (BA911) it was operating a scheduled service from San Francisco-Hong Kong via Honolulu and Tokyo, but had diverted to Fukuoka due to bad weather at Tokyo-Haneda. After staying overnight at Fukuoka, it eventually left for Tokyo, and the aircraft was prepared for the next leg to Hong Kong. At 1342 the crew contacted ATC requesting permission to start the engines and clearance for a VMC climb via Fuji-Rebel-Kushimoto. The aircraft left the ramp eight minutes later, and was instructed to make "a right turn after takeoff", departing Tokyo at 1358. After takeoff the aircraft flew over Gotemba City on a heading of approximately 298°, at an altitude of approx. 15,000ft and indicated airspeed of 320 to 370 knots. Trailing white vapor, the aircraft suddenly lost altitude and parts began to break away. Finally at an altitude of approximately 6,000ft, the forward fuselage broke away and then the mid-aft fuselage and the wing made a slow flat spin to the right, before crashing into a forest. The forward fuselage fell approximately 1,000ft to the west of Gotemba City and caught fire. The probable cause was attributed to the B.707 suddenly encountering abnormally severe turbulence over Gotemba City, which imposed a gust load considerably in excess of the design limit.

12th Emergency services were alerted when BEA Vanguard G-APED advised ATC he would be landing with one engine shut down. However, the aircraft carrying thirty-three passengers, landed safely at 0904.

14th RAF Pembroke XF798 (AUD 53) arrived briefly at 1030 from RAF Andover, departing for Carlisle.

17th USAF Douglas C-47 48715 made its first visit to Ringway since April 1962. Arriving at 1710 from Chambery, it later departed for Chateauroux.

18th Beech 90 D-ILMU arriving today and Cessna 337 D-GOFI (26th) were this month's only first time visiting foreign lights.

24th HS.125 G-ASNU was present for most of the day on crew training duties, but it didn't land. In October 1964, this aircraft had been sold to Fried Krupp as D-COMA (same owner as D-COME), but it returned to Hawarden in November 1965. The next month it was restored as G-ASNU for Gregory Air Taxis.

28th West German Air Force Noratlas GC+232 arriving at 1041 from Celle, was also operating a training flight. As was customary with their flights, the aircraft stayed overnight before departing to Oldenburg. The West German Air Force operated three units, LTG.61 (based Neubiberg), LTG. 62 (Celle), and LTG.63 (Ahlhorn), with 186 Nord Noratlas aircraft.

MARCH 1966

The mild end to February continued well into March, with rain occasionally heavy. From the 8th, a cold front moved through the country with rain, gales and some snow in places. The period from the 11th to the 21st was dominated by high pressure and was mainly dry, but thereafter the rest of the month experienced unsettled and stormy at times cooler weather. The month's temperature extremes saw 15°C at various locations (18th-20th) and a low of -8°C at Alwen (19th).

BOAC were planning to tap into the north's enormous business potential, by proposing to establish a jet service between Manchester and the Far East, linking Ringway with cities such as Frankfurt, Beirut, Tehran, Bombay or Calcutta, Bangkok and Hong Kong. These plans were in the very early stages, and any flights would not begin before next year, with frequencies possibly operating three-times-weekly. These services would have been boosted by the large amount of freight being exported from Manchester via London to the Far East.

Scheduled first visits were Aer Lingus (EI208): Viscount EI-AOE (17th) & Swissair (SR844): CV-990 HB-ICG (2nd). Equipment changes were Sabena (SN623): DC-6 OO-CTN (23rd) & CV-440 OO-SCL (27th).

Plenty of GCA/ILS traffic noted during the month included HS.125s VH-ECE (6th/15th) & G-ATOW (19th). From Woodford were HS.748s G-ATMI (15th/29th), G-ARAY (18th) & Andover XS594 (18th). Training flights were operated by British Eagle Viscounts G-AOCB (19th), G-ATDR (19th) & G-ATDU (29th), all from/to Liverpool.

4th Air France B.707 F-BLCC made its first visit, arriving at 1333 operating a return charter to Paris-Orly.

4th A couple of diversions from Heathrow this morning, produced BOAC SVC-10 G-ASGA on its first visit at 0832 (BA500 from New York) and KLM DC-7F PH-DSG at 0919 (KL003 from Amsterdam).

9th Aircraft involved in taking Manchester United fans out to Lisbon, were BKS Britannia G-ANBD and British Midland Argonauts G-ALHG & G-ALHY. The team itself flew out today aboard Schreiner Airways DC-7 PH-SAE, returning the following evening. Those fortunate enough to travel, saw the Reds put on a tremendous show away from home, beating Benfica 5-1 in the quarter-final second leg of the European Cup, having already beaten the Portuguese side 3-2 at home in February. At the time it was hailed as the best performance in Europe by an English side. Also today were two British Eagle Britannias, G-AOVF & G-AOVT, operating outbound charters to Tunis.

11th RAF Hastings WD480 made another appearance this month, operating a touch-and-go at 1307 today (callsign MPDXK), en route Jersey-Birmingham. On the afternoon of the 15th, it made a ten minute stop en route from Edinburgh to Farnborough, also operating as 'MPDXK'.

18th Interocean Airways C-54F LX-IAL made its final appearance at Ringway, arriving at 1807 on a freight flight from Woensdrecht, later leaving for Shannon. Sold in May 1966 as LN-KAF, it never flew again and was eventually scrapped.

20th More early morning fog at Heathrow produced four arrivals, BOAC B.707 G-APFJ at 0733 (BA600 from Toronto), VC-10s G-ASGA at 0740 (BA500 from New York) & G-ARVF at 0834 (BA120 from Rome) and lastly BEA Comet G-ARGM at 0822 (from Athens).

20th Having been based at Ringway since 1961, Beech 35 EI-ALL operated for the final time as such on a flight from Blackpool. It would emerge from the south side hangars on 18th July, newly registered as G-ATSR.

21st RAF visitors this month included today's first visit of Devon C.1 WB535, routing from RAF West Raynham to Wattisham (callsign ASO 99). Also today was C.19 Anson TX219 (Hawarden/Andover) which made the first of three visits this year, before being struck-off in April 1967. Two further first visits were Navy Sea Devon XJ319 (24th) & Sea Heron XR442 (28th). Also on the 28th another C.19 Anson, TX209, operated from/to RAF Andover.

28th March 1966 – By 1966, visits by Sabena CV-440s were drawing to a close. They would only appear as an occasional equipment change on Brussels flight SN623/4, such as the visit here of OO-SCL. The very final one to visit was OO-SCQ, exactly twelve months later on 28th March 1967. (Geoff Ball)

28th March 1966 - A fine shot of Avro Anson G-APHV outside the freight hangar. Owned by Survey Flights, it passed to Southampton-based Kemps Aerial Surveys in 1969, who operated it until 1973. (Bob Thorpe)

23rd PA-23 Aztec HB-LAB arriving at 1830 from Brussels was the first of two foreign light aircraft making first visits during March. This aircraft was eventually sold to an Irish operator in the early-1970s, registered as N80WT. It later became EI-AUV and was a frequent visitor during this period. On the 31st another Cessna 411 demonstrator, N4952T, operated a return flight to Leavesden.

24th Today marked the first SVC-10 operation from Manchester, when G-ASGC (BA606 from Montreal) landed at 0722. From the 1st April, the type took over the New York flights operating daily as BA538/7.

24th Beagle 206 G-ATKP, which was operating a round-trip from Gatwick, attempted to depart at 1910, only to return fifteen minutes later as a full emergency with undercarriage trouble.

25th Cessna 337 D-GOFI, nearing Oldham NDB, suffered an engine failure and could not maintain height. He circled the beacon all set to crash land, when the controller pointed out he was only 14nm from Ringway. He managed to make it to Manchester and did several test flights, before returning to Germany the same evening.

27th By this time Ringway's north/south runway (02/20), was only used occasionally by light aircraft, but due to this evenings strong crosswinds Aer Lingus Carvair EI-AMP touched down on Runway 20.

28th West German Air Force Noratlas GC+241, is the latest Noratlas to visit Ringway. Although operating a training flight from Birmingham to Oldenburg, it did not stay overnight.

29th As if having a Grumman Goose (G-ASCS) based at Ringway wasn't enough, it was now being graced with regular visits by Grumman Mallard G-ASXG, owned and operated by The Grosvenor Estates based at Hawarden. It would eventually become a semi-resident, splitting its time between Ringway and Hawarden until its last visit in December 1969, although it remained on the UK register until 1973 when it was sold in Canada.

APRIL 1966

The weather was mainly cyclonic, except for the last week when ridges of high pressure moved eastwards across the country giving short periods of fine weather. The first few days were sunny and cold with northerly winds, but on the 2nd more than a foot of snow fell over Scotland and northern England. This was followed by a period of mild, wet weather until the 11th when temperatures fell sharply again under an easterly wind, heralding a further ten days of wintry weather, with frequent snow, occasionally heavy. April ended with a mainly dry and sunny week, becoming very warm in the final three days. The month's temperature extremes saw 23°C at Stonyhurst (30th) and a low of-12°C at Cairngorm (14th).

BEA introduced Trident 1s on its existing routes to Dusseldorf, Amsterdam, Paris and Zurich, as well as on new routes to Copenhagen and Brussels. KLM increased the frequency of their passenger service to Amsterdam to four-weekly and up to five-weekly from May.

Having served the route since August 1957, Aer Lingus were no longer operating services to Brussels, since having had their licence withdrawn in February by the Belgian government. However, from April BEA took over the route with a three-times-weekly service, operated by Tridents.

International flights were operated during the summer as follows:

AER LINGUS - Amsterdam (up to 5 x weekly), Copenhagen (up to 3 x weekly), Dusseldorf (up to 3 x weekly), Frankfurt (up to 3 x weekly) & Zurich (1 x weekly), all operated by BAC 1-11s/Viscounts. New services to Cork and Shannon were introduced, operated by Viscounts and both twice-weekly.

AIR FRANCE - Three-weekly to Paris with SE.210s, increasing to six-weekly between June and September.

BEA - Amsterdam/Dublin/Dusseldorf & Paris with summer routes to Barcelona & Palma operated on both scheduled and IT tour basis. New Trident services were introduced to Brussels/Copenhagen and Zurich.

BOAC - Daily to New York (BA538/7) now operated by SVC-10s and Montreal/Toronto (BA638/7) five-weekly operated by B.707s. Cargo flight (BA065 Montreal/New York) operates five-weekly with B.707s.

IBERIA - 27th May-14th October, served Palma twice-weekly with SE.210 Caravelles, one via Barcelona.

KLM - Operated to Amsterdam four-times-weekly with Electras (KL149/150), with an additional flight (KL153/4) on Saturdays operated by Viscounts. Also a five-weekly DC-7 cargo flight operated from/to Amsterdam (KL019/020).

SABENA - The night-stopping Brussels service operates four-times-weekly with SE.210 Caravelles. Cargo flights operated five-times-weekly with Dakotas/DC-7s.

SAS - Began twice weekly on 1st April serving Copenhagen with SE.210s (SK537/8) extending onwards to Dublin.

<u>SWISSAIR</u> - Twice-weekly flights to Basle and Zurich, operated by CV-990s. From 17th May to 27th September a Tuesday CV-990 flight was added (SR842/3).

Scheduled first visits this month were <u>Aer Lingus (EI208)</u>: Viscount EI-AOF (2nd), <u>BOAC (BA537)</u>: SVC-10 G-ASGI (12th) and <u>SAS (SK537)</u>: SE.210s OY-KRA (6th), SE-DAG (8th) & SE-DAI (13th).

GCA/ILS traffic noted was HS.125s 9J-RAN (20th) & G-ATNO (26th), RAF Varsity WL679 (25th), Austrian Airlines HS.748 OE-LHS (22nd) and BKS HS.748 G-ARRW (28th) from/to Leeds. Training flights were operated by Autair HS.748 G-ATMI (2nd) and British Eagle Viscounts G-ANRS (11th) & G-ATDU (23rd).

1st   SAS started their first scheduled service from Manchester, with SE.210 Caravelle SE-DAC operating Copenhagen-Manchester-Dublin and return (SK537/8). Other aircraft used during the month were OY-KRA (6th/27th), OY-KRD (29th), SE-DAD (15th), SE-DAF (20th), SE-DAG (8th) & SE-DAI (13th/22nd). SE-DAC was leased out to Thai International as HS-TGI later in the year, but it crashed into the sea on approach to Hong Kong on 30th September 1967.

1st   Today also saw the introduction of the SVC-10 on BOAC's daily New York service. G-ASGD operated the outbound BA537, which operates to New York via Prestwick. This was also made possible by the installation of a special turning area at the end of the main runway.

3rd   German-based HS.125 G-ATFO, operated by Grundig, arrived from Nuremberg at 1440 en route to Hawarden for maintenance. It returned on the 13th for a brief customs clearance stop, before returning to Nuremberg. Also today Invicta Airlines began a series of twice-weekly flights from/to Rotterdam with DC-4s. G-ASPM was used on today's first flight, operating until the 29th May. Another HS.125, G-ASSM (14th), made its first visit diverting in due to snow at Birmingham.

4th   British Midland began a new weekday feeder service between Manchester and Newcastle. A Douglas DC-3 positioned in each morning from East Midlands to operate BD071/4 to/from Newcastle, before positioning back to East Midlands at the end of the day. Fares on the 118 mile route to Newcastle started at £5 10s one way. However, the service became short lived as by May it was down to three weekly flights and by June it had disappeared completely. The airline did maintain a presence throughout the summer with IT flights to various destinations with Argonauts, and also weekend flights to Sandown, Isle of Wight with Douglas DC-3s.

4th   Kar-Air Douglas DC-6 OH-KDB arrived at 1306 on a night-stopping passenger charter from Helsinki, leaving for Gatwick the following afternoon. Purchased by the Finnish airline in 1965, it would make one further visit to Ringway in March 1968, before being sold to Belgian operator Delta Air Transport in 1972.

4th   An unusual visitor today was Saab Safir G-ANOK, which arrived at 1132 from Edinburgh. Registered in 1954, it was operated by Edinburgh-based Galt Toys, who also had a factory in Cheadle. It was an occasional visitor until 1971, when it was sold to a private owner in Essex.

5th   This month saw further West German Air Force training flights through Manchester. Today, Noratlas GB+115 arrived at 1220 from Birmingham, and unlike last month's flight, this aircraft night-stopped. On the 21st, GC+234 arrived at 1533, night-stopping from Newcastle to Birmingham.

5th   Aer Lingus Carvair EI-AMP (EI9190 from Dublin/Liverpool) made an emergency landing at 2303 with the number 2 engine out of action.

5th   British Air Ferries began their car/passenger service to Rotterdam. The first flight was operated by Carvair G-ATRV, and others used during the month were G-AOFW/ASDC/ASKG & ASKN. Encouraging signs indicated it would be a success, with healthy advance bookings during March. The airport produced a new drive-in customs hall that acted as a car examination room, converted from a small auxiliary customs hall in the airport's domestic pier. The service would operate Monday-Thursday with each Carvair flight capable of carrying up to five cars and twenty-two passengers on each two hour flight.

6th   Cessna 310 G-ATLD (Flo Air 636 from Shannon) arrived at 0808 on its delivery flight, leaving later for Cranfield.

6th   Not often used as a diversionary airfield for Warton, Ringway played host to two from there during the day. Commander 680 F-BJEV, a regular visitor to Warton, diverted in at 1537 from Paris-Orly. Also from Orly arriving at Ringway at 1036, was the only visit of a French Air Force Sud-Ouest SO.30P Bretagne, serial number 26 (callsign F-RAFU). Operated by the French military in the medium transport role, it was a twin-engined mid-wing cantilever all metal monoplane that saw service until the late 1960s.

7th Dan-Air Ambassador G-ALZX arrived at 2002 on a night-stopping flight from Le Bourget before departing the following morning to Lyon. It was its last visit, as on the 14th it was damaged beyond repair in a landing accident at Beauvais.

8th Sterling DC-6 OY-BAS arrived at 1053, operating the first of two charters to Dusseldorf. The second operated on the 12th, with DC-6 OY-EAO.

12th Schreiner Airways DC-7 PH-SAE was again trusted to transport Manchester United FC to a European away match. This time it left for Belgrade for the semi-final first leg with Partizan Belgrade. United returned on PH-SAE two days later, having lost the match 2-0. This left much to do for the return match at Old Trafford the following week. Also today was the visit of Fred Olsen Curtiss C-46 LN-FOR (also 6th June), which arrived at 1657 from Gatwick, and stayed just over an hour before leaving for Edinburgh.

14th Another Ace Freighters aircraft making its first visit with its new owners was L-749 Constellation G-ALAL. Arriving at 0529 from Stuttgart, it left later for Prague on a freight charter. This was the first of four visits by this ex-Euravia aircraft this year, before the airline ceased trading in September 1966.

14th Snow in April is not particularly unusual, but it was persistent through much of country today, falling intermittently for the next 48 hours. It closed Heathrow for a short period in the afternoon, when eight diversions within an hour produced three first visits, EL AL Boeing 720 4X-ABB at 1418 (LY451 from Tel Aviv/Turin) which departed direct to Tel Aviv at 0009 on 15th as LY452, South African B.707 ZS-DYL at 1418 (SA218 from Frankfurt) and SAS SE.210 LN-KLN at 1429 (SK505 from Stockholm).

16th Canadian Air Force Dakota 662, operated by the No.1 Air Division based at Sollingen, arrived at 1313 on its only visit. RCAF No. 1 Air Division, consisting of twelve fighter squadrons located at four bases, was established to meet Canada's NATO air defence commitments in Europe. Two bases were located in France (Merville & Grostenquin) and two in West Germany (Zweibrücken & Sollingen). These wings were part of a group of bases which also included US and French installations, all of which came under the jurisdiction of NATO's Fourth Allied Tactical Air Force (4 ATAF) which in turn was commanded by Allied Air Forces Central Europe (AAFCE). Canadian squadrons were originally equipped with Canadair Sabre day fighters. One squadron of each wing however would be replaced by the all-weather CF-100 in 1956. The Sabre squadrons were replaced by CF-104 Starfighters in 1962. After the RCAF left France in 1967 and were reorganized and consolidated with Canada's other two services, No. 1 Air Division was replaced by No. 1 Canadian Air Group, with headquarters at Lahr, West Germany. Another Canadian Air Force visitor, Beech C-45 Expeditor 1521 (23rd), arrived on a night-stop at 1147 from Zweibrucken.

18th JAT CV-340 YU-ADL arrived at 1935 from Belgrade via Frankfurt, with the Partizan Belgrade team for their semi-final second leg match with Manchester United. The local spotting fraternity had ample opportunity to 'bag' the frame, as it was present until the 21st. Unfortunately, Partizan proved a tough nut to crack, and although United won the match 1-0, it wasn't enough and they went out 2-1 on aggregate.

19th Federal Air Office Dove HB-LAS arrived at 1245 from Le Bourget for customs clearance, before departing for maintenance at Hawarden. It was used for calibration duties until its withdrawal in 1972 and onward sale in the UK as G-AZPG. Operating for Biggin Hill-based Fairflight Charter, it was withdrawn at Southend in November 1976 and broken up in 1979.

20th Cessna 337 G-ATPU was another aircraft passing through Ringway on delivery. Arriving at 1324 from Gander and departing for Cranfield later, it would eventually be based in Kuwait.

20th New Irish airline, Hibernian Air, operate three Dakotas. EI-APB made its first visit today, EI-APJ (f/v 4th June 1967) and EI-ARR (f/v 18th June 1967). They would become fairly regular visitors to Ringway, until the airline ceased trading in September 1967.

21st Another new RAF Devon to visit was VP957, arriving at 1011 from Woodvale (callsign LNU31). It was also the aircraft's only visit to Ringway during the decade.

21st Sabena had recently purchased a number of Cessna 310s for pilot training. The first of these to visit was OO-SEE today (also 25th), operating Brussels-Shannon via Ringway and return.

25th BOAC Cargo at Manchester broke two records today. The first was B.707F G-ASZF (BA5010) arriving at 0847 from New York with a 35 tonne load of fibreglass curtain material, the heaviest consignment of cargo to Manchester in a single load. The second was achieved by unloading the cargo in thirty minutes, instead of the one hour allotted for the task. The load was eventually destined for the textile firm Friedland & Co, based in Princess St, Manchester.

15th April 1966 – SAS began operations to Copenhagen during the month, with their SE.210 Caravelles. The type would operate the airline's twice-weekly flights, later increasing to three-weekly until 1974 when they were replaced by Douglas DC-9s, which under different variants would operate right up until 2013. (Geoff Ball)

20th April 1966 – British Air Ferries Carvair G-ASDC 'Pont du Rhin' is seen here creating a lot of activity work during the turnaround of its return to Rotterdam. Later named 'Plain Jane', it continued in service with the airline until 1979, although its car ferrying duties were long behind it by this time. An unsubstantiated story was that when it was stripped of its exterior paint to operate as a freight-only aircraft in a pure bare metal scheme, it was said to have gained an extra 10% payload space! (Geoff Ball)

26th BOAC began direct services to Canada from Manchester. Previously the flights began/terminated at Heathrow, but from today the airline started a four-times-weekly service to Montreal & Toronto via Prestwick, increasing to up to six-weekly by June with B707 G-ARWE operating the inaugural BA638/7 flight.

27th April 1966 – Arriving from Glasgow at 1451 today, was OK-BYU, the first Russian designed aircraft to visit Ringway. This twin piston-engined Avia 14 was basically a Czech-built Ilyushin Il-14M. Owned by the Czech government and carrying the Czech Minster of Trade, it departed the following day for Heathrow. (MA Archive via Ringway Publications).

28th Britannia Airways began this year's IT programme a little earlier than normal; with Britannia G-ANBE operating an outbound flight to Barcelona. Other Britannias used during the summer were G-ANBA/ANBB/ANBD/ANBF/ANBI/ANBJ/ANBL & ANBO, with flights operating until the 15th October.

MAY 1966

The warm and sunny end to April didn't continue, and soon broke down into cool, changeable conditions with heavy showers. There was a spell of warmer weather from the 12th-17th with long sunny periods and increasingly warm temperatures before cooler weather took hold again, with considerable rain on the 24th-25th. An anti-cyclone, eventually centring over Britain gave the UK generally dry and sunny weather for the remainder of the month. During the last three days the sunshine was almost unbroken over most of England and Wales, with temperatures about 5°C above average. The month's temperature extremes saw 27°C at Camden Square (2nd) and a low of -4°C at Santon Downham (29th).

After a lengthy battle, which included objections by three other airlines, Cambrian Airways has finally been given the go-ahead to operate services from Manchester to Cork. Flights will not commence however until next April, when they hope to operate up to three weekly flights. Aer Lingus will begin flights during the month on a summer only basis, but Cambrian plan to make the service an all-year-round operation.

A seamen's strike towards the end of the month saw an unprecedented demand for passenger and cargo space. Aer Lingus were carrying 25% more passengers between Manchester and Dublin. All three of Cambrian Airways daily flights to the Isle of Man were full, and the cargo being handled between Manchester and Ireland increased fifty-fold. Dan-Air and several other UK carriers flew daily flights to Belfast, which had escalated by mid-June, flying three to four times daily with urgent provision. The National Union of Seamen's strike over a reduction of working hours became so bad that a National Emergency was declared, but by the 28th, a week after the industrial action began, the situation was resolved.

Swissair announced the plan to introduce the Douglas DC-9 onto their Manchester-Zurich route in November. The DC-9 would operate the weekly late-night flight SR844/5.

The following operated summer ITs to various destinations: Adria Airways (Dubrovnik/Ljubljana), Austrian (Salzburg), Autair (Rimini), Aviaco (Barcelona/Palma), Balair (Basle), Britannia Airways (Barcelona/Genoa/Ibiza/Malaga/Palma/Rimini/Valencia/ Venice), British Eagle (Barcelona/ Newquay/Ostend/Rimini/Venice), British Midland (Genoa/Oporto/Palma/Tarbes/Venice), Caledonian (Barcelona/Palma/Perpignan/Valencia), Dan-Air (Basle/Biarritz/Dinard/Genoa/Munich/Ostend/ Perpignan), Itavia (Rimini), Luxair (Luxembourg) and SAM (Rimini).

Scheduled first visits were Aer Lingus (EI216): Viscount EI-AOG (14th), BEA (BE795): Trident 1 G-ARPX (28th), BOAC (BA537): SVC-10 G-ASGE (4th), British Air Ferries (VF251): Carvair G-ASHZ (3rd) and SAS (SK537): SE.210 SE-DAH (4th). One equipment change was Sabena (SN623): CV-440 OO-SCV (31st).

GCA/ILS traffic noted was confined to RAE Varsity WL679 (3rd/12th/24th/25th) & Austrian Airlines HS.748 OE-LHT (24th). Training flights were operated by British Eagle Viscount G-AOCB (7th) & BKS HS.748 G-ASPL (12th).

1st Lloyd International DC-4F G-ARWI arrived at 1845, operating a cargo flight from Gatwick, originating in Hong Kong. At the time the airline was operating two Britannias (G-AOVP & G-AOVS) and their sole DC-4 G-ARWI. The two Britannias would operate IT flights from Glasgow and Gatwick, as well as frequent charters to the Middle East. G-ARWI spent a considerable amount of time parked up at Gatwick, before being eventually sold in December 1968.

1st Adria Airways began their summer programme from Ringway today, with Douglas DC-6A YU-AFD operating to Dubrovnik. Flights operated throughout the summer to Dubrovnik and Ljubljana with DC-6s YU-AFC/AFD/AFE & AFF. On the 8th October, their final flight of the season was operated by YU-AFD, and they would not return to Ringway the following year. In February 1968, Adria Airways ceased all operations pending a decision on their future. Meanwhile the country's main tour operator, Yugotours, awarded this year's contract to national carrier JAT. However, Adria Airways was 'reborn' as Inex-Adria the same year, after purchasing a DC-9 to supplement their three Douglas DC-6Bs.

2nd Sabena operated two more training flights through Ringway, with Cessna 310s OO-SEE and first visit OO-SEH. Arriving during the evening within eight minutes of each other, they departed before midnight.

3rd The first of two new West German Air Force Noratlas to visit this month was GC+104, which arrived on a night-stop from Northolt, leaving for Birmingham the following morning. The second was GB+232 (12th), also night-stopping on a training flight from East Midlands to Oldenburg.

5th Commander 560 D-IBEF (today), Beech 95 D-GENA (15th) & MS.885 Rallye EI-AMG (26th) were the only light aircraft making first visits during May.

5th Air Canada began their summer programme of flights to Montreal and Toronto today, when DC-8 CF-TJB departed as AC036 to Montreal via Prestwick. Flights operated until the 18th October, with DC-8s CF-TJA/TJC/TJD/TJE/TJF/TJH/TJI/TJP & TJQ.

7th Dan-Air commenced this year's IT flights from Manchester today with Ambassador G-AMAH outbound to Ostend. They operated until 23rd October, with G-ALFR, ALZN, ALZO, ALZY, AMAE, AMAG & AMAH.

9th Twelve weather diversions descending on Manchester this morning were all BEA, BOAC or British Eagle flights. The only first visit amongst them was BOAC VC-10 G-ARVI at 0940 (BA118 from Frankfurt).

11th British Eagle commenced their summer IT programme, operated by Viscounts to various European destinations. They also operated numerous transatlantic charters with Bristol Britannias to the USA and Canada. Today's first flight to Halifax, Nova Scotia was operated by G-AOVT. Other Britannias used during the summer were G-AOVB/AOVC/AOVE/AOVG/AOVK/AOVL/AOVM/AOVN/AOVT/ARKA/ARKB & ARXA.

13th Pan American B.707 N718PA made its first visit on the inaugural flight of the airline's summer series of charters to New York, the last of which was on the 11th October. Aircraft used throughout the season were B.707s N409PA (f/v - 27th August), N412PA (f/v - 19th June), N701PA, N720PA & N725PA and DC-8s N802PA & N813PA.

13th Early morning fog at Heathrow produced eight more diversions, including two first visits by Air France B.707 F-BHSD at 0640 (AF4212 from Montreal) & BOAC VC-10 G-ARVH at 0700 (BA201 from Amman).

4th May 1966 – Autair began a weekly IT flight to Rimini today, using their two HS.748s, G-ATMI & G-ATMJ, with flights operating until the 14th September. (Geoff Ball)

9th May 1966 - USAF Douglas VC-47s made occasional visits to Ringway throughout the 1960s. This particular aircraft, 0-51116, arrived from Brussels to clear customs on a sunny morning en route to RAF Valley. It would make its final appearance on 4th March 1970, before eventually being ferried back to the States in 1972, arriving with a mere 5,000 hours on the clock. (Graham Davies)

14th May 1966 – Luxair began a series of late night weekend flights to Luxembourg today. Aircraft used were Fokker F.27s LX-LGA, LX-LGB (f/v - 21st May) & Viscount LX-LGC as seen here. It had recently been delivered from Hawker Siddeley, and was still wearing basic Pakistan International colours. (Geoff Ball)

20th May 1966 – Although the era of the Vickers Viking was drawing to a close, they still made occasional visits to Ringway. Here, Invicta example G-AHOY was operating a round-trip from Rotterdam. It made its final visit on 19th September 1967, and was withdrawn the following March. (Bob Thorpe)

13ᵗʰ Caledonian also began their IT summer programme, with DC-7 G-AOIE arriving from Dusseldorf to operate CA117 to Barcelona. Their sole Douglas DC-7 G-AOIE would operate most flights, but Britannias (G-AOVH/AOVI/AOVJ/ASTF/ATNZ) would operate a weekly late-night flight to/from Valencia and some occasional transatlantic charters.

14ᵗʰ Aviaco commenced their summer ITs today, by now replacing L-1049 Constellations with SE.210 Caravelles. During the summer they would operate two flights to Palma (Sat - AO1006/7-Sun & AO1010/1) and two flights to Barcelona (Sat - AO1100/1 & Sun - AO1104/5).

17ᵗʰ Pacific Western DC-7 CF-PWM operated a one-off charter from/to Vancouver via Keflavik as PW601/2. Although purchased from KLM in 1962, it was still wearing their cheatline, but with Pacific Western titles and logo. It would make two further visits in 1967, before it was sold in 1969 as N22CA, following delivery of their first Boeing 707. Pacific Western operated a further flight from/to Vancouver with DC-6 CF-PCI (23ʳᵈ/15ᵗʰ June/30ᵗʰ June), which had been leased from Wardair for the summer.

20ᵗʰ Italian charter airline SAM (Societa Aria Mediterranea) began their IT summer programme. DC-6 I-DIMB operated today's first flight, and similar to last year the airline operated just a single weekly flight f/t Rimini (MQ834/5). DC-6s used until the 30ᵗʰ September were I-DIMA/DIMD/DIME/DIMI/DIMP & DIMU.

21ˢᵗ RAF Hastings WD495 (EWG07) & WJ331 (EWG65), arrived from RAF·Colerne during the morning to operate two return flights to Jurby, before departing to Colerne. This was another British-built aircraft whose days were numbered, as they would be completely replaced by the Lockheed C-130 Hercules which would start to be delivered to RAF Transport Command. Also today was MEA Comet OD-ADR (ME025), night-stopping from Heathrow, before departing to Belfast in the early hours the following morning.

21ˢᵗ The first of Aer Lingus' seasonal transatlantic charters was operated today by B.707 EI-AMW (IN5933 to Montreal). Again they operated on an irregular basis until 1ˢᵗ November. Other B.707s used were EI-ANO & EI-ANV.

22ⁿᵈ Italian operator Itavia returned to Manchester after an absence of three years, to operate three weekly late-night flights f/t Rimini. They now operated three Handley Page Heralds, I-TIVA, TIVE & TIVU (f/v - 12ᵗʰ June), which all made regular visits during the summer, until the final flight on 25ᵗʰ September.

25ᵗʰ Balair began a twice-weekly Basle charter today, with Douglas DC-6 HB-IBU. Flights operated until the 6ᵗʰ October and other aircraft used were Douglas DC-6s HB-IBR & HB-IBZ.

26ᵗʰ Transglobe began a short series of flights to/from Tarbes, with the last operating on the 3ʳᵈ June. Aircraft used were Bristol Britannias G-ATGD (f'/v - 26ᵗʰ May) & G-ATLE.

28ᵗʰ The first of two aircraft worthy of note today, was the first visit of Fred Olsen Curtiss C-46 LN-FOP, operating a freight flight to Tirstrup. The second was Dragon Rapide G-AGTM, arriving at 1701 from Netheravon. It left over an hour later to perform a parachute drop over the Congleton area, before setting course back to Netheravon. This was the only visit to Ringway by a Rapide during 1966, a far cry from the start of the decade, when it seemed that hardly a day went by without one visiting!

29ᵗʰ Perpignan was an extremely popular destination during the 1960s, as the airport served many holiday resorts in the South of France. Several airlines flew there during this time including the latest, Air France, who began a weekly scheduled service (AF870/1). SE.210 Caravelle F-BJTP was given the honour of operating the first flight, but the service only lasted one season and did not return in 1967.

29ᵗʰ Transmeridian leased DC-7 G-ATOB earlier this year, which made the first of several visits during 1966, operating a cargo flight to Damascus today. It was returned to Trans World Leasing in December 1967, and was eventually sold as VR-BCT. Their second leased DC-7, G-ATMF, made its first visit on 25ᵗʰ June operating a freight flight to Kano. Both aircraft were operated in bare metal.

29ᵗʰ Schreiner Airways began a series of regular summer charters from/to Amsterdam. Two flights operated by Fokker F.27s PH-SAN & PH-SAP today were both first visits. These aircraft operated the flights until 21ˢᵗ September, along with a third F.27, PH-SAD, which was also used.

30ᵗʰ College of Aeronautics Avro Anson G-AHIC made the first of two visits this year, arriving at 1304 today from Blackpool, leaving later for Morecambe. It made a brief second visit on 21ˢᵗ July before departing on a photographic detail over Glossop. It would make a final visit on 14ᵗʰ March 1967, before being stored and then scrapped at Strathallan in the early 1970s.

JUNE 1966

Talks took place during the month between the airport, BOAC and a number of independent airlines, such as BKS, Cambrian Airways and British Midland, to persuade more of them to operate further feeder services into Ringway. Because of 'appalling' congestion at Heathrow, BOAC wanted to build up a worldwide network of services from Manchester to Africa, the Middle East and the Far East. Links to places such as Tehran, Bangkok and Beirut, which had previously been mooted. Cities such as Tel Aviv, Nairobi and Johannesburg were also being considered. Detailed studies were also taking place on the possibility of operating to Hong Kong, where many northern companies had export interests. Frequencies to New York and Montreal could be increased whilst adding services to places, such as Boston and Chicago. The airline also added that if the airport could persuade smaller airlines from the Midlands, Tyneside, Yorkshire and the north to operate from Ringway, it would accelerate their ambitious expansion plans.

The warm and sunny end to May continued until the 3rd June, with more than thirteen hours of daily sunshine in many places. From then on, it was a mix of sunny and warm, then cool, wet and occasionally thundery weather. The month's temperature extremes saw 29°C at Southampton (9th) and a low of 0°C at Santon Downham (30th).

Scheduled first visits this month were <u>Aer Lingus (EI602)</u>: Viscount EI-AOH (2nd), <u>British Air Ferries (VF251)</u>: Carvair G-APNH (28th) and <u>Iberia (IB784)</u>: SE.210 EC-BBR (3rd). Equipment changes were KLM (KL149): Schreiner Airways F.27 PH-SAP (22nd), <u>Sabena (SN623)</u>: CV-440s OO-SCL (7th/12th), OO-SCN (6th), OO-SCQ (1st), OO-SCS (5th) & OO-SCT (27th) and Swissair (SR844): DC-8 HB-IDA (8th).

GCA/ILS traffic noted during the month was HS.125s VH-ECE (1st), G-ATPC (4th) & G-ATPD (26th) and RAF Andover XS600 (23rd/25th) & Austrian Airlines HS.748 OE-LHT (24th). Two training flights operating on the 20th were BEA Argosy G-ASXM & BOAC B.707 G-APFH. Finally, Canadian Air Force CC-106 Yukon 15932 (8th) did a touch-and-go at 1036 en route from Prestwick to Brussels.

2nd UAT Douglas DC-6B F-BGSL arriving at 0857 on a passenger charter from Le Bourget night-stopped before positioning out to Edinburgh the following morning. It had been a regular visitor earlier in the decade, but this was to be the aircrafts last visit, as it was withdrawn at the end of 1969.

4th RAF Abingdon-based HS.748 XS794 made its first visit today, arriving from Edinburgh to operate a return flight to Little Rissington, before leaving for Edinburgh again. Another first visit was HS.748 XS789 from Newcastle at 1128 (10th). Operated by the Queen's Flight, it had a royal visitor onboard.

5th BOAC Cargo B.707F G-ASZF (BA5014 from Montreal) set a new record of 5 hours and 38 minutes, touching down an hour ahead of schedule. It was carrying 28 tonnes of car paint-spraying kit.

5th Today saw the very last visit by an Aer Lingus Fokker F.27, when EI-AKA was put in charge of the evening Dublin Mail flight, EI9212/3. The airline had seven delivered during late 1958/early 1959, serving alongside their Dakotas and Viscounts, but they were now being replaced by ex-KLM Viscounts.

5th The first of Austrian Airlines' weekly IT flights to Salzburg began today, with Viscount OE-IAM. Continuing until the 11th September, their other three Viscounts, OE-LAK, OE-LAL & OE-IAM, were also used.

6th This month's West German Air Force training flight was operated by Noratlas GC+239, which arrived at 1427 from Birmingham, and left for Northolt the following morning.

8th Two Avro Anson visits today, began with Western Comms C.19 TX177 at 1538 from its base at RAF Andover, which left ten minutes later for RAF Cosford. The second, C.19 TX192 from RAF Binbrook, was operating a return flight to RAF Valley. Both had been withdrawn by November and July respectively.

8th Belgian International DC-6B OO-GER arrived at 2336 from Brussels, with passengers from the cancelled Sabena flight SN623. Sabena staff had gone on strike on the 29th May, demanding an 18% pay increase, but following the company's refusal to meet their demands they began a campaign of 'unannounced strikes of unspecified duration'. The airline was forced to sub-charter aircraft and use administrative personnel to do the jobs of flight crews. OO-GER itself was formerly ex-Lloyd International G-ASTW, operating for the Belgian airline until it was sold as TN-ABR in April 1970.

9th This month's contingent of light aircraft making their first visits to Manchester, were Cessna 172 EI-AOK today, PA-23 Aztec F-BNOP (16th), Beech Marquis F-BKOP (17th) and PA-28 Cherokee SE-EIO (19th).

11th Fog at various airports produced ten diversions, but the only one of note was Newcastle diversion BKS Britannia G-ANBK at 0809 from Rimini, which diverted in again the following evening from Heathrow.

14th June 1966 – Tor-Air Curtiss C-46 SE-CFE (also 23rd) was operating an inbound cargo charter from Tirstrup. It was sold as 9Q-CZG in June 1967, but by 1970 it had been withdrawn. Note the period fuel bowser! (Bob Thorpe).

25th June 1966 – Global Presentations DC-7 N774R was on charter to Rank-Xerox, and painted in their scheme. The Union Jack flag seen sticking out the top of the flight deck wasn't due to Rank being patriotic, it was because the aircraft had been impounded by HM Customs! The orange and white boards are obscuring a length of strong chain, with one end firmly padlocked to the left main undercarriage leg and the other padlocked to the end of Pier A. It was finally allowed to depart three days later. (Ken Fielding)

28th June 1966 – Transair was a new Canadian operator to Ringway. This evening's visit of Douglas DC-7 CF-TAY was the first of four appearances over the next four weeks. It is seen here in the gathering gloom, having recently arrived from Winnipeg via Gander. (Geoff Ball)

30th June 1966 – Lear Jet 23 N365EJ arriving at 2047 today from Brussels, became the second of its type to visit. Operated by the Lear Corporation, it departed less than an hour later to Birmingham. (Geoff Ball)

11th Transair Sweden DC-7 SE-ERB (TB253/4) arrived at 1021, operating a passenger charter from Malmo. Purchased in 1964, it would make one further visit (27th June 1968) before its withdrawal in August 1969 and being scrapped later.

12th More early morning fog this time affecting the Irish Republic, produced three Aer Lingus diversions, BAC 1-11 EI-ANF and Boeing 720s EI-ALA at 0837 from New York & EI-ALC at 0733 from Boston.

17th Braathens produced two Douglas DC-6s during the month, both first visits. Today, LN-SUT positioned up from Gatwick for an outbound passenger charter to Bergen and on the 26th LN-SUH arrived at 1949 for the return flight.

19th Army Air Corps Scout XT616 (Army 335), arriving for fuel at 1646 en route Farnborough-Prestwick, was a first visit of type. The Westland Scout formed the backbone of the Army Air Corps throughout the 1960s and well into the 1970s. The first Scout flew on 29th August 1960 and an initial order for 66 aircraft followed a month after its first flight. Engine problems delayed the introduction of the Scout until 1963, and even when it entered service there were still problems with the engines, with notoriously low hours before a service. By 1964 however, the engine life had improved to two/three engine changes per 1,000 flying hours. The Scout AH Mk 1 was operated by the Army Air Corps on general light work, including observation and liaison. About 150 Scout helicopters were acquired for the Army Air Corps, who operated them up until 1994.

20th HS.125 HB-VAN arriving at 1815 from Cologne, eventually bound for maintenance at Hawarden, dropped in for pre-customs clearance. It returned from Hawarden four days later, again to clear customs before returning to Cologne.

24th Caledonian was having problems with serviceable Britannia aircraft. They were due to operate an affinity charter to Toronto, but when Britannia G-ATNZ finally arrived to operate flight CA1301, it was running over ten hours late. Meanwhile, Barcelona flight CA117 which should have departed at 2130 the same evening, didn't leave until 0731 the following morning operated by Douglas DC-7 G-AOIE. On the 25th, with various aircraft running late, the airline chartered MEA Comet OD-ADS to operate their evening departure to Valencia, returning at 0612 on the 26th.

26th On the same day that Caledonian sub-chartered MEA Comet OD-ADS, Luxair produced their only visit to Ringway of L-1649 Starliner LX-LGZ, due to Viscount LX-LGC going tech at Luxembourg. It arrived at 2334 and departed exactly an hour later. The airline operated three Starliners, with the others being LX-LGX/LGY, which were usually employed on a weekly service to Johannesburg, with stops at Palma and Luanda or Lisbon. All had been withdrawn from service by January 1969. LX-LGZ, which was sold as ZS-FAB in July 1967, was withdrawn from use in September 1969 and scrapped in mid-1970.

30th Transportflug Douglas C-54 D-ABAG operated a return flight from Belfast due to the continuing Irish shipping strike.

JULY 1966

Aer Lingus' network of BAC 1-11 flights from Manchester to the continent was attracting thousands of extra passengers from the northwest. The airline's report for 1965-66 showed 30,000 passengers flew between Manchester and six European cities, an increase of 14%. The busiest route at the time was Manchester-Amsterdam with 11,588 passengers, while Dusseldorf and Frankfurt saw passenger increases of 85% and 62% respectively.

The Air Transport Licensing Board granted BEA permission to operate the first scheduled air link between Manchester and Inverness, effective from 1st April 1968. A BEA spokesman said that if by 1968 the traffic potential justifies a service, then the current Heathrow-Inverness flight would call at Manchester, but the service never took place.

The warm and sunny weather at the end of June lasted until the 4th when, apart from a period from the 12th-16th and the 22nd-24th, anticyclonic weather dominated with wet and frequently thundery weather. In the month when the World Cup took place in England, the temperature extremes saw 28°C at Moreton Morrell, Warwickshire (23rd) and a low of 0°C at Caldecott, Oxfordshire (15th).

Scheduled first visits this month were <u>Aer Lingus (EI601)</u>: Viscount EI-AOI (13th), <u>BEA (BE795)</u>: Trident 1 G-ARPZ (4th) and <u>SAS (SK537)</u>: SE.210s LN-KLH (20th) & OY-KRF (13th). The only equipment change was <u>Swissair (SR844)</u>: DC-8 HB-IDC (27th).

GCA/ILS traffic noted was HS.125s G-ATPB (4th), G-ATNT (7th), G-ATXE (16th/17th) & VQ-ZIL (16th); COPA Panama HS.748 HP-432 (15th) & Venezuelan government HS.748 0111 (28th) and Heron CN-MAA (15th) on a test flight from Hawarden. The only training flight was BEA Argosy G-ASXP (21st).

2nd The first of seven early fog diversions produced L-1049H Constellation CF-NAM at 0437 (ND092 from Belfast) as a Stansted diversion, the second and final Nordair Connie to visit. Also of note were four British Eagle Britannias (G-AOVB/AOVE/AOVK & ARKA) diverting in from Heathrow in less than two hours.

4th With a couple of exceptions, most first time visiting light aircraft this month were Swedish! Cessna 210 SE-CYZ (today), PA-23 Aztec SE-ECF (11th), Cessna 182 SE-ETE (15th) & PA-23 Aztec SE-EOE (21st).

5th French Air Force Douglas C-54 '10358' (callsign F-YCKG) arrived at 1855 from Glasgow, departing for Cambridge the following evening. This aircraft served with the L'Armée de L'Air right up until 1975.

5th Sterling began a short series of flights from/to Copenhagen today with Douglas DC-6s. OY-EAR operated the first flight with others being operated by OY-BAT (13th) & OY-EAR (2nd August/10th August).

6th Registered in 1953 and the only DHC-2 Beaver to appear on the UK register, was G-ANAR arriving at 0953 on a round-trip from its base at Birmingham. It remained British registered until 1971, when it was sold in Canada as CF-CNR. Also today was RAF C.19 Anson TX209 from RAF Andover to operate a round-trip to RAF Catterick.

7th HS.125 G-ATNT which overshot on a test flight from/to Hawarden was in bare metal with "100th aircraft" titles. It was delivered to the USA via Prestwick ten days later.

7th Another good military visitor this month was USAF C-130 55-0017 at 1351 on a flight from Stuttgart.

8th 1966 was the year that England hosted the World Cup finals. The tournament had begun the previous day when England was held to a 0-0 draw with Uruguay at Wembley. There were only two group matches to be held at Old Trafford, which didn't produce any extra flights. However, the West German team were based in Yorkshire for their forthcoming group matches, which was the reason for the first visit of Lufthansa Boeing 727 D-ABIT arriving from Heathrow, returning there after a mere thirty minutes.

12th Globe Air Herald HB-AAL was drafted into service to operate a much delayed Balair flight, departing at 0801 to Basle. This would be the final visit by the Swiss airline. On the 20th April 1967 Britannia HB-ITB was operating a flight from Bangkok to Basle, stopping at Colombo, Bombay & Cairo. Rather than fly to Cairo, they elected to stop at Nicosia instead. They were cleared to land at runway 32, but were too high so the approach was abandoned and a left circuit was entered to position for a new approach. While executing a low circuit, the aircraft collided with the ground. All but four of the 130 passengers and crew perished. This signalled the end of the airline, as they ceased trading soon afterwards.

12th Beech 65 D-ILSU arrived at 1626 from Stuttgart, with a number of wealthy spectators for the West Germany v Switzerland match. This gave them three hours to get to Sheffield, which in 1966 may not have given them as much as time as they thought! It made a further visit on the 23rd July, this time with possibly the same spectators for that day's match with Uruguay.

15th The United States Army made a rare appearance today, when U-6A Beaver 53-7929 arrived at 1054 from Wethersfield to operate a flight to Arbroath. Another US military visitor was VT-29B 0-15135 (21st), arriving at 1019 operating from/to Northolt.

16th In stark contrast to World Airways, who were using modern jets on their transatlantic services, Saturn Airways were still soldiering on with Douglas DC-7s. They began the first of a series of transatlantic charters today, with DC-7s N90778 & N90802 departing to New York. Further outbound flights operated on the 18th July (N90773), 23rd July (N90802), & 24th July (N90804). The return flights operated on the 6th August (N90773) & 10th August (N90778). They would return in 1967, but from then on only to operate the occasional ad hoc charter.

17th BEA found itself suffering from a shortage of Vanguards due to technical problems, so the airline chartered BOAC B.707 G-APFI to fly 120 passengers up from Heathrow, arriving at 1345 as BA7950.

19th American outfit Trans International Airlines (TIA) made its first visit today, operating brand new DC-8-55CF N3325T on an ad hoc flight from New York and a further inbound from New York the next day.

20th Two RAF visitors both arrived to make return flights to other bases. C.1 Devon VP974 made its first visit arriving at 0857 from its base at Topcliffe to operate a return flight to Leuchars, while C.19 Anson arrived at 1100 from Henlow to operate a return flight to Bassingbourne.

11th July 1966 – F-BHSR was the fifth Air France B.707 to visit Ringway. It arrived at 1610 from Paris-Orly to pick up a number of passengers bound for New York. It's seen here over the threshold of runway 24, with Jackson's Brickworks in the background. (Bob Thorpe)

12th July 1966 – The World Cup provided two first visits to Ringway today. Malev Ilyushin IL-18 HA-MOH, which was also a first visit of type, arrived at 1336 from Basle with Swiss football supporters for their match with West Germany. Perhaps they shouldn't have bothered, as the Swiss were convincingly thrashed 5-0! (Geoff Ball)

12th July 1966 – Falcon 20 HB-VAP (also 23rd) f/t Cologne was another football related movement. It was written off on 1st October 1967, when it ran out of fuel short of Goose Bay, Newfoundland. (Geoff Ball)

16th July 1966 – Today saw the first visit by World Airways, when B.707 N376WA arrived on an ad hoc charter from Oakland at 0751. Despite operating Boeing 707s since the early-1960s, the airline had shown little interest in the North Atlantic charter market, preferring to use their new aircraft flying Pacific charters for the United States military forces. But by now they had realised that the much expanded 'affinity-group' market was worth more of its attention. (Geoff Ball)

16th July 1966 – Schreiner Airways Dakota PH-DAC was making a fuel stop en route from Amsterdam to Belfast. During the summer, their F.27s and occasional DC-7s could be seen, but PH-DAC made a refreshing change. It was sold to Delta Air Transport as OO-VDF in October 1967. (Geoff Ball)

22nd July 1966 - A poor quality photograph, but worthy of inclusion. Heli-Union Alouette F-BNKZ arrived at 0938 today from White Waltham, en route to Edinburgh. This helicopter starred in the cult 1967 TV Series "The Prisoner", starring Patrick McGoohan. Arriving in Port Merion on 14th September 1966 (where the filming took place, and re-named the "The Village" in the series), it was used for most of the aerial pictures in the series. She was bought by RBA Helicopters on 16th January 1967, and registered as G-AVEE. However, it continued its role as a TV star, appearing in episodes of "The Avengers", "The Champions" & "Man In A Suitcase", which were all filmed in 1967-68. (MA Archive via Ringway Publications)

21st Laker Airways was formed in February 1966 as a contract-hire and ad hoc charter operator, founded by former managing director of British United, Freddie Laker. They had taken delivery in April of two Britannia 102s, G-ANBM & G-ANBN. The former aircraft, G-ANBM, made its first appearance at Ringway today with its new owners operating a crew training flight. Arriving at 1821, it departed eight minutes later to Gatwick. This aircraft operated Laker's first commercial service on 29th July 1966.

22nd Having departed at 2243 for Munich, Dan-Air Ambassador G-AMAH was forced to return at 2321 amidst a full emergency, but landed safely.

22nd Aer Turas purchased ex-BKS Bristol 170 G-AMLJ this year, which was re-registered EI-APC. Today, it made its first visit operating an Aer Lingus mail/freight flight. It would become a fairly regular visitor to Ringway through the 1960s, operating sub-charters for Aer Lingus, Lufthansa and also in its own right.

23rd Martinair Douglas DC-7 PH-MAK, operating a Dublin rotation on behalf of Aer Lingus, made the first of several visits throughout 1966, mostly for Aer Lingus. Only purchased in March 1966, this aircraft did not serve long with Martinair, as in early 1967 it was sold to Spanish operator TAE.

23rd Caledonian DC-7 G-AOIE departed to Barcelona (CA117) last night, but had failed to return having gone tech, leaving several flights to be covered. Sabena DC-6 OO-CTN positioned from Brussels to operate t/f Perpignan (CA119/120), but the surprise of the evening was Conair Douglas DC-7 OY-DMT positioning from Copenhagen to operate t/f Palma (CA113/4). This was the first visit by the Danish airline, formed in 1965, which made very few visits to Manchester in their twenty-eight year existence.

24th Three Army Air Corps AH.1 Scouts, XP890 (Army 337), XP895 (Army 335) & XP896 (Army 336) called in for fuel in formation, en route from Farnborough to Macrihanish. A fourth Scout, XT616 (Army 333), arrived at 2017 from Colerne the following evening also en route to Macrihanish.

25th Cessna 337 G-ATSM arrived at 0102 (Flo Air 678) on delivery from the Cessna factory at Wichita. It departed at 0923 for Rogers Aviation at Cranfield.

27th This month's West German Air Force training flight was operated by Noratlas GB+242 today, arriving at 1435 from Ahlhorn. It did not stay overnight, but left later in the day for Birmingham.

29th All four Army Scouts heading for Macrihanish earlier in the month, XP890/XP895/XP896 & XT616, passed through again on their way south. All but XT616 left for Middle Wallop, which left for Farnborough.

30th Today saw the return of American charter airline, Overseas National, making their first visit to Ringway since June 1960. DC-8-55F N852F, arriving at 1406 from Gatwick leaving later for New York via Shannon, was a first time visitor. It also operated the return flight on 1st September.

AUGUST 1966

The weather was low pressure-dominated for the first two weeks. The 9th-13th was a particularly wet period in the north, culminating in thunderstorms with torrential rain on the 13th. Over three inches were recorded in northern England and southern Scotland, but the rest of August was mainly anticyclonic apart from the 20th-21st and the last three days. On the 29th (August Bank Holiday), fine weather gave way to thunderstorms that continued into the 30th, bringing floods to many southern areas. The month's temperature extremes saw 29°C at Camden Square (20th) and a low of -2°C at Balmoral (23rd).

Scheduled first visits were confined to just two this month, with Air France (AF960): SE.210s F-BNKA (12th) & F-BNKB (23rd). Equipment changes were also thin on the ground with Aer Lingus (EI9212): Aer Turas Bristol 170 EI-APC (1st/2nd/9th).

GCA/ILS traffic noted during the month was HS.748s Venezuelan government 0111 (3rd), LIAT VP-LIP (4th) & COPA Panama HP-432 (4th). Also on a test flight out of Woodford, was RAF Vulcan B.2 XJ823 (4th). Two aircraft that had the authorities chasing payment after performing touch-and-goes, were Smiths Aviation HS.748 G-ASJT (4th) & RAE Varsity WL679 (10th). Finally, there were quite a few HS.125s on test flights from Hawarden, with G-ATPE (12th), G-ATUU (9th), G-ATUV (12th/24th), G-ATUX (27th) & VQ-ZIL (14th).

3rd American Flyers made their first visit today, when L-1049 Constellation N9724Z arrived at 0052 from Dallas/Gander, later departing for Gatwick. The airline would make further visits to Manchester over the next few years, but today's arrival proved to be the final visit of a US-registered Constellation to Ringway.

8th Air France B.707 F-BHSL arriving at 0803 (AF4532 from New York) was another first time visitor.

8th Federal Air Office Dove HB-LAS passed through Ringway for the second time, en route for maintenance at Hawarden.

15th Cessna 172 G-ATAF arriving at 1446 today from Blackpool left to undertake a short photographic detail in the Mobberley area.

15th Quick thinking by airport firemen prevented a disaster that could have resulted in thousands of pounds worth of damage. The emergency was first noticed from the fire station, when the number two port engine of Transmeridian DC-7 G-ATOB caught fire whilst taxiing for departure. The aircraft had arrived two days earlier, bound for Riyadh with a shipment of P.1. Lightning components, which formed part of a government contract to supply a number of the fighters to Saudi Arabia. It finally departed late the following day.

17th An early morning Gatwick diversion was British United VC-10 G-ASIX (BR812 from Aden), bringing more than a hundred servicemen back to the UK for their annual leave.

17th BEA was now operating three of the four Olympic Airways Comet 4Bs. The first of these, SX-DAK, made its first visit today operating BE4078/89 from/to Heathrow. The other two aircraft also made first visits as follows, SX-DAL BE4092/5 (21st) & SX-DAN BE4078/89 (22nd).

21st Today was the last visit by short-lived Ace Freighters, when L-749 G-ALAK arrived at 1405 from Milan on a livestock charter, leaving later for Coventry. The airline was put into liquidation on 14th September 1966, which also marked the end of twenty years of British Constellation operations, with all six of the airline's Connies never seeing commercial service again. Apart from their three operational aircraft, they also took delivery of another three in early-1965 (G-ASYS/ASYT & ASYU), which never entered service.

26th This month's West German Air Force training flight was operated today by Noratlas GB+107, arriving at 1010 from Filton. After a short stay it left for Cologne.

28th August 1966 - Itavia Herald I-TIVE was one of five operated by the Italian operator between 1963 and 1973. Operating IT flights from Ringway in 1963 and 1966, the only Itavia Herald to visit after this date was I-TIVE, again on a football charter on 15th May 1969. (MA Archive via Ringway Publications)

28th KLM Douglas DC-8 arrived at 0211 (KL064 from New York) on a tech stop en route for Amsterdam.

31st RAF Whirlwind XP347 landed at the Manchester City Police playing fields, situated in a corner of Platt Fields Park, Rusholme at approximately 2020 today. It was carrying a seriously injured Army officer from Bangor, North Wales, who suffered a fractured skull and a broken neck after a misjudging a dive into the sea at Rhosneigr. After leaving the police grounds, it departed to Ringway for night parking, before returning to RAF Valley the following day as 'Pedro 22'. It was the second time this year that a helicopter had used the police grounds. Wessex XR523 had also landed there earlier in the year, on the 24th February around 1200, to ferry a female student to Stoke Mandeville Hospital after falling from a float during a University Rag Day.

28th August 1966 - A plane load of lucky passengers stop to pose for the camera, before flying off on their specially organised flight to New York, aboard Pan American B.707 N409PA. Note the inscription on the side of the rear fuselage 'JET CLIPPER A.I.M.C. SPECIAL'. (MA Archive via Ringway Publications)

SEPTEMBER 1966

Another disappointing month as far as the weather was concerned. The first half was again predominantly cloudy and wet, as frequent troughs and depressions swept eastwards. There was a spell of drier weather from the 7th-10th, and most of the second half of September was more settled again. The warmest period was the 19th-22nd, when afternoon temperatures reached 23°C in several places, but mist and fog formed at night. A shallow depression moved slowly eastwards over northern France, bringing heavy rain to southern parts during the last two days of the month. The month's temperature extremes saw 25°C at Manston (12th) and a low of -1°C at Santon Downham (19th).

The only scheduled first visit this month was <u>SAS (SK537)</u>: SE.210 SE-DAB (23rd), and there were no equipment changes.

GCA/ILS traffic noted during the month was HS.125 G-ATUZ (9th), RAF Andovers XS603 (12th), XS604 (23rd) & XS605 (14th/21st) and Canadian Air Force C-130 130303 (26th).

1st Although they had been in service since 1953, a new US Army type to Ringway was the Beech U-8D Seminole (military version of the Twin Bonanza). Mostly European-based, with some stationed at UK USAF military bases, U-8D 62-3841 arrived at 1233 today from Northolt for a brief visit before leaving for Castle Donington. Others this month were USAF C-131 54-2814 from/to Wiesbaden (29th) & Convair VT-29 51-7899 from/to Northolt (30th).

2nd Light aircraft making their first visits this month were with Beech 65 PH-ILS (another Philips aircraft) today, PA-23 Aztec SE-EIY (4th/7th) and Mooney HB-DED (29th).

6th September 1966 - Apart from Dan-Air, one of the other two UK operators of Airspeed Ambassadors during the 1960s was BKS, with the other being Autair. They operated five aircraft during 1960 (G-ALZR/ALZT/ALZW/AMAC & AMAD), none of which were regular visitors to Ringway. G-ALZR seen here was converted to a freighter in 1964, but the other four were passenger aircraft. It had been operating several return trips to Dublin over the last few days and is about to depart on its next Irish rotation. In November 1969 it was purchased by Dan-Air for spares. (Bob Thorpe)

17th September 1966 – Extremely smart looking Belgian International DC-6B OO-GER has recently arrived on a passenger charter from Munich. The airline founded in July 1959, offered mainly passenger and cargo air charter flights from Brussels Airport to the former Belgian colonies in Central Africa. A co-operation contract in 1967 with Sabena which lasted until 1975 saw BIAS operating scheduled commuter flights out of Brussels Airport. (Ken Fielding)

9ʰ RAF Whirlwind HAR.10 XP349 arrived at 1542 from Ely to take part in the Manchester show at Platt Fields Park. For the next nine days it left Ringway each morning for Platt Fields, and returned in the evening. On the afternoon of the 19ᵗʰ, it departed for RAF Valley.

10ᵗʰ Kar-Air operated an outbound passenger charter to Copenhagen with CV-440 OH-LRC (AY5814/5). It wasn't a first visit however, as it had visited previously in August 1963. The return flight was operated by CV-440 OH-LRF (AY5816/7) on the 19ᵗʰ September.

15ᵗʰ Polaris Air Transport CV-240 LN-KAP arrived at 1536 from Gothenburg, and was based until the 18ᵗʰ for crew training. The company operated passenger and cargo charters with three CV-240s from 1966-1969 (LN-KAP/KLT & KLU). They were renamed Mey-Air later in 1966 due to a change of ownership, but ceased trading in 1974.

16ᵗʰ There were two West German Air Force training flights this month. Today, Noratlas GC+238 arrived at 1001 from Celle and after a short stay left for Oldenburg. The second was Noratlas GB+250 (30ᵗʰ) at 1157 from Ahlhorn which also left for Oldenburg.

20ᵗʰ RAF Pembroke WV740 (AXZ 52) arriving at 1103 from/to RAF Andover was another first visit. This aircraft entered RAF service in 1955 and was based at Aden until 1959, when it returned to the UK. In February 1967 it returned to Aden when UK forces withdrew from the Yemen. It was later transferred to Bahrain until 1971, and finally in 1978 it spent the last nine years of its operational service based at RAF Wildenrath.

22ⁿᵈ PA-28 Cherokee 9J-RBP arriving at 1435 from Elstree was here unusually for maintenance with Fairey's, before departing to Elstree on 12ᵗʰ October. It would eventually become G-AVPV in June 1967.

22ⁿᵈ Royal Canadian Air Force Dakota KG634 arrived at 1430 from Wethersfield.

23ʳᵈ G-AINL arriving at 2322 from Gatwick became the last visit by a Dan-Air Bristol 170. By this point in 1966, the airline was operating two aircraft, this and G-APLH which were both sold in late-1968. G-AINL became CF-YDO and G-APLH (last visit 9ᵗʰ June 1966) became CF-YDP.

24ᵗʰ The final KLM Viscount visit took place today, when PH-VIG operated KL153/4. In late-1965, Aer Lingus had announced they were to purchase all eight KLM Viscounts.

24ᵗʰ Morning fog at Heathrow produced first visit Alitalia SE.210 I-DABZ at 0751 (AZ318 from Rimini).

27ᵗʰ Wearing a smart white, grey and black corporate scheme, Gulfstream 1 CF-MUR arriving at 1105 en route Gatwick-Prestwick was also a first visit of type.

30ᵗʰ Amongst four late evening weather diversions from Heathrow, was Douglas DC-4 VQ-ZEC at 2246, operated by Botswana National Airways. It had visited previously on 16ᵗʰ August 1955 as N88756 of Transocean Airlines based at Oakland, California. Also diverting in at 2230 from Gatwick was BUA VC-10 G-ATDJ (BR212 from Entebbe).

OCTOBER 1966

Further ambitious plans by BOAC were announced this month, when the airline's chairman said they were planning to link Manchester with Bermuda and the eastern Caribbean. They were also considering using hovercraft for operations in the Caribbean to pick up northwest passengers once they had landed, and whisk them off to one of the hundreds of islands in the area. However their plans were dependent on the runway extension, which should be completed by early 1969.

BEA announced plans to serve Malta from Manchester. It was initially thought that the airline would be unable to introduce flights before 1969, but due to the attractive nature of sterling abroad, they reshaped their plans and began once-weekly flights on 5ᵗʰ April 1967. The airline's Trident flights to Amsterdam, Brussels, Copenhagen, Dusseldorf and Zurich introduced in April were under threat of withdrawal by the airline due to poor passenger loads. Brussels and Copenhagen in particular were struggling, and could pull the plug on BEA's future expansion plans. Load factors of 20% or 30% were a regular occurrence, but in the end route withdrawal was ruled out due to terms of the contract requiring a minimum of three years. However, good news from the airline this month was the plan to introduce a new freighter service to Dusseldorf and Frankfurt during November.

Under a new agreement announced during the month, the national airline of seven Middle Eastern countries will make Manchester their main diversionary airport when London-Heathrow is closed due to fog. Airlines involved were Iran Air, Royal Jordanian-ALIA, United Arab Airlines, Sudan Airways, Syrian Arab, MEA and Kuwait Airways.

Yet another disappointing month with unsettled weather dominating, apart from brief anticyclonic interludes. A small depression moving eastwards across southern England brought heavy rain; Bournemouth recorded more than 50mm of rain in two hours. The month's temperature extremes saw 22°C at Wincanton (4th) and a low of -7°C at Balmoral (5th).

Remarkably, October saw no scheduled first visits or equipment changes.

There was no GCA/ILS traffic noted this month, but a couple of training flights were BOAC B.707s G-APFJ (1st) & G-ASZG (24th), and PA-23 Apache G-ARJX (14th) from Birmingham performed a touch-and-go.

1st   Eight weather diversions appeared before 0300 this morning, three being first visits. British Eagle sent in two of their new BAC 1-11s, G-ATPL at 0241 (EG367 from Valencia) & G-ATVH at 0256 (EG537 from Palma), and Inter-Nord Douglas DC-7 SE-CNF arrived at 0055 from Gothenburg.

2nd October 1966 - This atmospheric shot catches CV-990 HB-ICC shortly after arriving on SR844 from Zurich. Swissair would operate their newly delivered DC-9s during the winter, but Coronados were used again during the summer on services out of Manchester from April to October 1967, when Douglas DC-9s took over the route fully. (MA Archive via Ringway Publications)

9th   Beech 55 SE-EKR (today) and Commander 500 D-IBAM (31st) were both first time visitors this month.

9th   Spantax Douglas DC-6 EC-AZX arriving at 1351 from Palma was a Birmingham diversion, in a year when Spantax did not operate a summer programme from Ringway. This was the aircrafts first visit, although in one of its previous incarnations it had operated with Sabena as OO-SDC. It would soldier on with the Spanish carrier until 1979, when it was sold as TI-A414B.

10th   Making a nostalgic departure from Manchester on a ferry flight back to Gatwick, was the last Caledonian DC-7 movement. G-AOIE departed as CA100 at 1113, having arrived the previous evening at 2207 (CA116 from Palma). It was eventually sold in May 1967 to Schreiner Airways as PH-SAX, but only operated one summer season in basic Caledonian colours before it was withdrawn. In March 1970 it was flown to Shannon, where it remained for many years.

11th   Three British military movements which arrived early afternoon and could be seen on the ground together before departing within five minutes of each other, were Royal Navy Sea Devon XJ324 (Navy 824 - Leuchars/Lee-on-Solent) and Varsities WJ890 (CHD 40) & WL634 (CHD 43) both from/to Strubby.

12th   Messenger G-AKIO arrived as crew ferry for the return of PA-28 Cherokee 9J-RBP back to Elstree.

12th October 1966 - Aer Lingus Carvair EI-AMR is seen making one of its final visits to Ringway, and Carvair EI-AMP operated the final Carvair flight through Manchester for Aer Lingus on 31st October. The type was originally ear-marked in 1962/63 to operate a car ferry service between Dublin, Cork, Liverpool, Bristol & Cherbourg, but after many unsuccessful attempts they transferred them to all-cargo, connecting Dublin with Manchester, Heathrow, Liverpool & Glasgow. On paper these three aircraft would solve all capacity problems, offering 7,500-kilos of freight per flight, but they proved to be a disaster for Aer Lingus due to continuous unserviceability problems with the Pratt & Whitney engines. Hardly a week went by without cancellations or serious delays, so they decided to withdraw the three Carvairs from service. Today was the final day of operation for all three aircraft. They remained withdrawn at Dublin until 1968, when they were all sold to Canadian carrier Eastern Provincial Airways. The third Carvair, EI-ANJ made its final visit operating as EI9208/9 on the 23rd October. (MA Archive via Ringway Publications)

22nd October 1966 - The Queen's Flight still operated four Herons at this point, which were gradually being replaced by brand new HS.748s. One of these, XS790, was making its first visit today, dropping off Prince Philip for a local engagement. (Bob Thorpe)

12th There were a further two RAF Varsity movements today, with WJ905 (CHD 38 f/t Strubby) and WL634 (CHD 40) which went tech and was stranded until its departure on the 14th. In between times WJ905 made several trips f/t Strubby with various bits, along with the military toolbox!

14th There were two West German Air Force training flights again this month, which both left for Oldenburg. Noratlas GB+246 arriving at 1034 today from Ahlhorn, made a short stay and Noratlas GB+243 from Northolt arrived at 1059 on the 28th.

20th Another 'last' this month, was the final operation of a British United DC-3 on schedules out of Ringway. With the withdrawal of their Oxford/Bournemouth services, Dakotas would no longer be seen at Manchester. Today's final flight was operated by G-AMYV, which was sold in November.

31st A new executive jet to visit Manchester, the Jet Commander N2100X, made a short visit today from/to Heathrow. The first 150 of these aircraft were built under licence by Aero Commander in the United States, before licence production was eventually passed to Israeli Aircraft Industries.

NOVEMBER 1966

Despite some foggy periods, the month was again mainly dominated by low pressure. The 7th-8th was foggy in northern and central areas, but away from the fog temperatures reached as high as 17°C. Another very foggy day was the 24th before another belt of frontal rain moved southeast across the country. The month ended stormy, with northwesterly gales and wintry showers in nearly all areas. The month's temperature extremes saw 18°C at Eastwick Lodge (7th) and a low of -12°C at Balmoral (11th).

BOAC handled a record amount of cargo in October, totalling 468 tonnes on its transatlantic flights, an increase of 83% on the same month last year.

BEA are now able to undertake maintenance on their based Trident aircraft, having invested in three giant noise bafflers at their maintenance base, installed at a cost of more than £20,000. Previously, there had been very few engine tests running due to residents' concerns over noise levels.

Channel Airways also applied to serve Malta from Manchester, but were rejected later, twice!

Northern Executive Aviation are hoping to run scheduled services between major towns and cities in the north and the Midlands, such as Preston, Nottingham, Wolverhampton and Sheffield by the middle of next summer. They recently placed an order for four new eight-seater BN-2 Islanders. G-ATCT flew in from Bembridge on the 2nd November, so that director and Chief Pilot David Antrobus could fly the aircraft for the first time. He said which cities would be linked had not yet been decided, but the plan was to offer an 'air bus' service to as many towns as practicable.

International flights were operated during the winter as follows:

AIR FRANCE – Three-times-weekly to Paris with SE.210s.

AER LINGUS - Amsterdam (3 x weekly), Copenhagen (2 x weekly), Dusseldorf (2 x weekly), Frankfurt (2 x weekly) & Zurich (1 x weekly), all now operated by BAC 1-11s.

BEA - Amsterdam/Brussels/Copenhagen/Dublin/Dusseldorf/Paris & Zurich.

BOAC - Daily to New York (BA538/7) with SVC-10s and Montreal/Toronto (BA637/8) three-weekly, all services operated by B.707s routing via Prestwick. Cargo flight (BA065 Montreal/New York) operates five-weekly with B.707s.

KLM - Operated to Amsterdam twice-weekly with Electras (KL149/150) and cargo flights continue five-weekly with DC-7s to Amsterdam via LHR (KL019/020).

SABENA - The night-stopping Brussels service operates four-times-weekly with SE.210 Caravelles. Cargo flights operated to Brussels three-times-weekly with DC-3s and twice weekly with DC-6/DC-7s via Shannon.

SWISSAIR - Operated once-weekly from/to Zurich (SR844/5) with newly-introduced DC-9s, increasing to twice-weekly from 21st December.

Only two scheduled firsts visit this month were BEA (BE5930): Argosy G-ATTC (22nd) & Swissair (SR844): DC-9 HB-IFA (4th). The equipment changes were Sabena (SN623): CV-440 OO-SCO (16th) & Swissair (SR844): SE.210 HB-ICU (11th).

No GCA/ILS traffic was noted during the month. Training flights were operated by BOAC B.707 G-APFL (3rd) & Dan-Air Comet G-APDO (29th).

1st The result of Aer Lingus withdrawing their three Carvairs meant that the airline was forced to use their Vickers Viscounts for mail and freight operations. Although EI-AOI (EI9190) & EI-AOH (EI9212) were used for this evening's flights, Aer Lingus were still presented with a major headache. Several convertible

Viscounts purchased from KLM were being operated as passenger aircraft by day and as cargo aircraft by night, but it was soon realised they were unsuitable for freight operations. Due to severe restrictions in cabin height and width, standard IATA pallets could not be accommodated, so specially manufactured small dimension metal and wood pallets were utilised, which became known as 'postage stamps'. As these pallets could not be interchanged with other carriers' equipment, Aer Lingus management decided that a recent order placed with Boeing for a number of B.737s should include four 'convertible' aircraft. In the meantime another Irish carrier, Aer Turas, would begin to play an important 'stopgap' role by providing Aer Lingus with the following aircraft to solve their short term cargo problems, Bristol 170s EI-APC & EI-APM and Douglas C-54s EI-AOR & EI-APK.

1st   Upper Heyford-based USAF Douglas VC-47 44-77214 arrived at 0932, later departing to Northolt. From 1945 to 1948 this aircraft served with the Royal Air Force as KP244. It ended its days in 1974, when it was scrapped, having previously served with the El Salvador Air Force.

1st   Cessna 310 OY-EGD operated by Egetaepper Air Services, made a first visit, day-stopping f/t Billund. They also operate Lear Jet 24 OY-EGE, which made its first visit at 0834 (30th) from Copenhagen.

1st   Danish airline Inter-Nord made its second visit today, when DC-7 OY-ANC arrived at 1014 from Birmingham, before departing for Prestwick the following morning.

2nd November 1966 - Britten-Norman began life in 1953 to convert and operate agricultural aircraft. They also produced hovercraft. Design of the Islander started in 1963. The first prototype, BN-2 (G-ATCT), first flew on 13th June 1965 and the second on 20th August 1966. Both aircraft had engines that were less powerful than the production versions. G-ATCT which arrived at 1148 today from Bembridge made a return flight to Barton on demonstration to Northern Executive. On the 9th November it was due to fly back to England following demonstration flights in Germany. It departed Emden and continued over the northern part of the Netherlands at 1500 feet above the clouds. Weather conditions in the Amsterdam Control Zone were IMC, so the air traffic controller advised the flight to divert to Eelde. At 1235 the pilot reported serious compass trouble. He circled the area and began to climb to FL60 and later to FL87 in an attempt to get on top of the clouds. The aircraft continued to climb to about 10,000 feet, where it would have encountered severe icing conditions. Control was lost and the airplane broke up in flight. It crashed into the Ringwiel, a small lake near Oudega. The cause of the crash was put down to the failure of the starboard wing, as a result of overstressing during a fast descent. The descent was presumably caused by loss of control under conditions of heavy icing and turbulence, when the aircraft was flown beyond the operating limitations stipulated in its Certificate of Airworthiness. (MA Archive via Ringway Publications)

3rd   BOAC SVC-10 G-ASGH (BA538 from New York/Prestwick) burst three tyres on landing this morning, but none of the 73 passengers were injured. It managed to turn off the runway before coming to a halt, and was unable to move until the tyres had been changed. It was later revealed that a further four tyres were unserviceable.

4th November 1966 – Swissair beat KLM today to be the first airline to operate the new Douglas DC-9 between Manchester and the continent. HB-IFA seen here was used on the weekly-evening Zurich flight SR844/5. The type would eventually replace the SE.210 Caravelle and CV-990 Coronado on flights out of Manchester. Dutch airline KLM would not introduce the DC-9 on its Manchester-Amsterdam flights until November 1967, before eventually replacing Lockheed Electras. (Geoff Ball)

4th   Overnight fog covering much of England, southeast of a line from Durham to Dorset during the morning, badly affected Heathrow. Twelve diversions with over a thousand passengers arrived during the morning, but freshening winds during the afternoon cleared the fog away, eventually bringing heavy rain. There was only one first visit with Ghana Airways VC-10 9G-ABO at 1020 (GH702 from Accra/Rome), but a few others of note were EL AL B.707 4X-ATB at 0848 (LY252 from New York) & East African Airways Comet 5X-AAO at 1013 (EC716 from Benina/Rome). These generated over £1,500 worth of landing fees, and off-duty staff were called to help cope with the extra flights.

4th   Fog at Heathrow provided BEA and Smiths Autoland with the opportunity to test the Trident with its 'blind-landing' system. The actual conditions at Heathrow were 'sky obscured' with runway visual ranges fluctuating throughout the day from 50-100yds. Trident 1 G-ARPB managed ten fully automatic landings, but each was followed by a ten minute struggle to find the way back to the threshold for its next departure!

7th   Ambassador G-ALZP made its first visit today arriving at 1656 on a round-trip from Gatwick. Delivered to BEA in 1950, it was sold to the King of Morocco in September 1960 as CN-MAK. It was acquired in November 1963 as a flying test-bed and sales demonstrator for the Decca Navigator Company, but sold to South Seas Airways as ZK-DFC in November 1971. It was not taken up however, and was parked at West Malling until it was broken up in September 1974.

8th   The next five days saw an invasion of Martinair (renamed in October) Douglas DC-7s. Mostly from/to Amsterdam, they were, PH-DSC (8th/10th), PH-DSL (9th), PH-DSO (9th) from Keflavik, PH-MAK (9th/11th) and finally PH-DSC again (12th) which night-stopped from Amsterdam and departed to Abidjan.

9th   Operating on a code-share arrangement with Lufthansa, BEA commenced a four-times-weekly freight service to Dusseldorf and Frankfurt. The first service was operated today by Air Ferry Douglas C-54 G-APNP. Further C-54 aircraft from Air Ferry also used during the month were G-APYK & G-ASOG.

14th   This month's foreign lights first visits were Cessna 411 D-IELB today & Beech 65 F-BMLD on the 30th.

18th   The second Transair Sweden DC-7 visit, was SE-ERG (TB1209) arriving at 1218 on a passenger charter from Copenhagen. Upon its withdrawal in August 1968, it only had eleven years service, and apart from Transair Sweden it only operated for one other airline, Eastern Airlines, from 1957 to 1965.

24th Clear skies the previous evening after earlier rain led to freezing fog forming over the Midlands and southeast England during the night. The fog persisted throughout the day in the south, although it cleared during the morning in most other districts. Ringway itself had a cool and cloudy day with medium visibility. Thirty-one diversions from Heathrow and three from Gatwick (BUA VC-10s G-ASIW, G-ATDJ & Dan-Air Comet G-APDO) kept airport staff extremely busy. The bulk of these diversions appearing mid-morning to mid-afternoon produced numerous first visits, with Alitalia SE.210 I-DABW at 1122 (AZ284 from Milan), Pan American DC-8 N803PA at 1251 (PA106 from Shannon), EL AL B.707 4X-ATR at 1428 (LY451 from Tel Aviv/Frankfurt), Alitalia SE.210 I-DABU at 1503 (AZ280 from Rome), Libyan Arab SE.210 5A-DAB at 1552 (LN105 from Geneva) & Pan American B.707 N416PA at 2129 (PA100 from New York). There were fewer BEA flights than on previous occasions and BOAC sent in B.707s G-APFC/APFN/ARWD/G-ASZF and VC-10s G-ARVF/ARVK/G-ASGD & ASGE. Apart from the first time visitors, there were plenty more foreign airline diversions, with Swissair CV-990 HB-ICE (SR812 from Geneva), Pan American B.707s N758PA (PA056 from Shannon) & N762PA (PA101 from Brussels), MEA Comet OD-ADQ (ME205 from Beirut), SAS SE.210s OY-KRG (SK501 from Copenhagen), SE-DAD (SK505 from Stockholm) & SE-DAI (SK513 from Stavanger) and Qantas B.707 VH-EBD (QF755 from Athens). Another diversion from Heathrow was South African Airways B.707 ZS-CKD (SA218 from Johannesburg) at 1342. This airline operated occasional charters to South Africa, and visited frequently due to bad weather at London.

25th This month's West German Air Force training flight was operated today by Noratlas GB+240, which landed at 0901 from Ahlhorn and departed for Birmingham.

28th Air France SE.210 Caravelle F-BHRU ran off the runway in snowy conditions, and got stuck in the mud just short of the Wilmslow-Altrincham main road. The airport had to close for nearly four hours, but fortunately none of the 52 passengers and crew was hurt.

29th Twelve hours after the Air France Caravelle skidded off the runway and became bogged down to its axles, it was finally towed back onto the runway and into the south bay. Air France Breguet 763 F-BASU arrived at 0419 from Paris-Orly with the necessary towing gear, which also marked the last Deux-Ponts visit to Ringway, although they still appeared at Heathrow occasionally. The very last Deux-Pont flight took place on a flight from Heathrow to Paris-Orly on 31st March 1971.

DECEMBER 1966

The introduction in April of the electrification of the Manchester-London rail link and the risk of bad weather saw the number of passengers on BEA's Heathrow route fall by 10% in November over the same month last year. In the period April-October when the improved rail link was launched, BEA carried 62,000 fewer passengers than the same period last year. These disappointing figures, which were slightly offset by strong inclusive tour and transatlantic figures, were a particular blow to the airport as they had recently announced a £6 million development programme, which by 1971 would call for a freight village, an extra pier to handle Boeing 747s and extra and expanded terminal facilities.

December was a generally wet and mild month over England, while Scotland was colder. A deep depression on the 1st brought gales and heavy rain through much of the day, with heavy snow on the Pennines and some snow at lower levels. Snow showers continued, but decreased in frequency and intensity over the next three to four days. Temperatures rose rapidly on the 5th to put England in a spell of mild and occasionally wet weather, lasting until the end of the month. Scotland was colder with occasional snow during this period, and even recorded a white Christmas! The month's temperature extremes saw 14°C at Bletchley (30th) and a low of -13°C at Carnwath, Lanarkshire (25th).

Scheduled first visits were Aer Lingus (EI9212): Viscount EI-AOJ (8th), British Air Ferries (VF251): Carvair G-ARSD (27th) and Swissair (SR844): DC-9s HB-IFB (2nd) & HB-IFC (30th). There were no equipment changes, but BEA/Lufthansa cargo flight (BE/LH2201) used DC-6 G-APNO (20th/21st/22nd/23rd/27th), C-54 G-APYK (1st/3rd/7th/8th/9th/10th/14th/15th/16th/17th) & C-54 G-ASOG (29th/30th/31st).

GCA/ILS traffic noted during the month was RAF Andover XS6010 (6th), Bahamas Airways HS.748 VP-BCJ (11th), RAF Vulcan B.2 XM572 (30th) and BKS HS.748 G-ARRW (30th).

1st Beech 90 D-INAW, registered in June 1966, made its first visit today, night-stopping from Gatwick. PA-30 Twin Comanche OY-DMC (17th/19th) was also a first visit, operating a return flight to Belfast.

3rd USAF VT-29 Sabreliner 61-0665 arriving at 1519 from RAF Alconbury, was the second of its type to visit, but the first military version. Its appearance was in connection with the reopening of Burtonwood.

12th Mallard G-ASCS arrived at 1444 from Tiree, and was then placed into storage at Fairey's. It made a test flight on 1st June 1967, but did not leave until the 6th November when it departed for Biarritz.

14th December 1966 – Both Aer Turas Bristol 170s, EI-APC & EI-APM (seen here), were frequent visitors this month operating extra cargo flights for Aer Lingus. Both would continue to visit Ringway into 1967, until EI-APM came to grief at Prestwick. (Geoff Ball)

19th Air India B.707 VT-DNY called in at 0805 (AI116 from New York) en route for Heathrow with a number of passengers for Manchester. A return flight was operated on 7th January with B.707 VT-DNY (AI111 Heathrow-New York).

20th Canadian Air Force C-47 KG455 arrived at 1517 from Ramstein. It was later re-serialled as 12924 and is currently preserved at Petawawa AFB, Ontario.

22nd This month's West German Air Force training flight was operated today by Noratlas GB+102, which landed at 1006 from Ahlhorn and departed for Oldenburg.

23rd There were several charters today returning servicemen home from West Germany. Aircraft involved were BUA Britannia G-ANCE, Invicta C-54 G-ASPN, Dan-Air Ambassador G-ALZO and Autair Ambassador G-ALZV. The return flights were operated on 1st January by G-ALZV (Hamburg), Invicta C-54 G-ASEN (Bremen) & BUA Britannia G-APNA (Hanover).

FIRST/LAST ARRIVALS & DEPARTURES 1966

First arrival:	Aer Lingus Carvair EI-ANJ @ 0008 from Dublin
First departure:	Sabena DC-6 OO-SDQ @ 0020 to Shannon
Last Arrival:	BEA Vanguard G-APEG @ 2253 from Heathrow
Last Departure:	BEA Trident G-ARPH @ 2357 to Zurich

Airport Stats 1966 (+/- % on Previous Year)		
Scheduled Passengers	1,112,000	+1.2%
Inclusive & Charter Passengers	291,000	+16.4%
Freight & Mail (Tonnes)	33,700	+42.1%
Movements	49,900	+5.4%

AIRPORT DIARY 1967

JANUARY 1967

After much speculation, BOAC announced flights to the Caribbean would be introduced from Manchester as an extension of its current Prestwick/New York flight. The service was inaugurated on 13th December 1967, with SVC-10 G-ASGD. It would fly on from New York four-times-weekly connecting with Antigua and Barbados, but unfortunately the start was delayed due to a two-day BOAC pilots strike.

Middle East Airlines were considering a Manchester-Beirut service. An exhibition held at the Grosvenor Hotel, Chester to gauge interest, included flying in a Lebanese chef to prepare local delicacies.

Helped by the introduction of Boeing 707 freighters, BOAC Cargo carried a record 4,332 tonnes of cargo across the Atlantic during 1966, compared to 2,500 tonnes in 1965.

The month began bright and cold, with wintry showers in northern and eastern England. There was plenty of sunshine, but frost at night. Despite a temporary return to milder weather, the cold was back by the 8th, and lasted a week before turning milder again. The UK was dominated by low pressure for the last week, bringing rain to most districts, with very mild temperatures to most places. The month's temperature extremes saw 14°C at Dartford (29th) and a low of -13°C at Carnwath, Lanarkshire (6th).

A single scheduled first visit was Aer Lingus (EI9212): Viscount EI-APD (1st). Equipment changes were BEA (BE823): Viscounts G-AOHV (20th) & G-AOYH (11th). Aircraft used on the BEA/Lufthansa cargo flight (BE/LH2201) were DC-6 G-APNO (12th/13th/14th) and C-54s G-APYK (11th/25th/26th/27th/28th) & G-ASOG (4th/5th/6th/7th/18th/19th/20th).

GCA/ILS traffic noted during the month was Aerotaxi HS.748 XA-SEI (10th) & Australian Air Force HS.748 A10-595 (18th) and plenty of RAF activity with Andovers XS610 (25th), XS611 (18th/27th) & XS612 (12th), Britannia XL636 (25th) and Shackleton XF708 (26th). Dan-Air Ambassador G-AMAH did a touch-and-go en route Gatwick-Newcastle (11th).

4th First time visiting RAF Pembroke WV749 (CRF 51), night-stopped on a return flight from RAF Andover.

4th Today's visit of Convair T-29D 52-5832 (Lakenheath/Upper Heyford) was the first of many US military flights over the next few months, in connection with the build up of staff and equipment due to the reactivation of Burtonwood for the USAF. The majority of these flights eventually transferred to Liverpool, but Ringway continued to be used until April, by which time Burtonwood was fully online with 24 hour customs and receiving its own flights, operated by U-8D Seminoles. Other flights were Beech U-8D Seminoles 56-3716 (23rd/27th), 58-3086 (13th/16th/18th) & 62-3841 (17th), Convair VT-29B 51-3816 of the 17th Air Force based at Ramstein (18th twice), Convair VC-131D 55-0294 with a group of top-brass generals (27th) and rounding off a busy month was C-47 0-51116 (27th).

10th Amongst the mass of USAF/US Army movements, was today's visit of C-124 Globemaster 52-0958 of the 63rd MAW. Arriving at 1828 from Frankfurt, it proved to be the final Globemaster movement at Ringway. It was bringing in around sixty troops, plus supplies, which were then loaded onto B.R.S. transporters for the journey to Burtonwood.

10th Aerotaxi HS.748 XA-SEI performed an ILS whilst on a test flight out of Woodford. It had returned off lease to the Mexican airline and was returning to BKS. It was restored to its original registration of G-ATAM the following day.

11th Two more RAF Pembrokes appeared today. Wildenrath-based C.1 XF799 arrived at 1247 (FWW 30) for major work with Fairey's and remained firmly locked away in the hangar until its departure back to Wildenrath. C.1 WV743 (FWW 80) arrived on the 25th May acting as the crew ferry.

20th US Army Sikorsky CH-34A 57-1742 arrived at 1655 from RAF Wethersfield, and left the following morning for Burtonwood where it would be based.

20th Air Ferry Douglas C-54 G-ASOG arriving at 1033 (LH2201), was on its final flight into Ringway. Operating the Frankfurt cargo service on behalf of Lufthansa, it left at 0119 on the 21st back to Frankfurt, but three hours later it hit some trees 2700m short of the runway at Frankfurt. The accident was attributed to the fact that the crew did not set the altimeters in the final approach according to the instructions in the operations manual. This error was aggravated by the fact that the final approach check list did not coincide with the altimeter setting procedure. In consequence the crew unintentionally flew below critical height and the aircraft collided with trees when the altimeters were showing approx. 200ft above the critical height.

18th January 1967 - Delivered new in November 1966, Jet Commander SE-DCK made its first visit, arriving at 1117 on a round-trip from Stockholm. This aircraft would only make one further visit to Ringway, in June 1968, as the following year the owners replaced it with another Jet Commander, SE-DCZ. (Geoff Ball)

24th Today saw the first visit of HS.125 demonstrator, G-ATSP, at 1737 on a brief stop from Hatfield. When the first flight of the BAC 1-11-500 took place on 30th June 1967, G-ATSP was engaged in photographic duties whilst flying along the south coast. It was sold as LN-NPE in April 1968.

31st SAS Douglas DC-7 OY-KNC arriving at 1609, positioned in from Copenhagen (SK9718) to operate a passenger charter to Oslo. This would be the final SAS DC-7 visit. The airline had operated sixteen passenger DC-7 'Seven Seas' aircraft since 1956, but all had gone by the end of 1967.

FEBRUARY 1967

Discussions were held about the possible extension of little used runway 02/20 at the western end from 3,000ft to 7,200ft. An estimate was received in May 1968, but unfortunately the plan did not proceed beyond the discussion stage and runway 02/20 itself was decommissioned in 1970.

Treffield International Airways, established as an airline in November 1966, were given approval to operate a series of holiday flights from Manchester to Barcelona, Ostend, Lourdes & Palma this summer.

Sudan Airways, who were flying three times a week into Heathrow, intended to add a fourth weekly flight in May. They were actively considering extending this flight to Ringway, due to the considerable amount of cotton originating from Manchester and being exported to Sudan.

Despite the mild and wet start, pressure rose on the 3rd with anticyclones in charge until mid-month. The weather patterns changed on the 15th, when the Scandinavian anticyclone moved, allowing troughs and depressions to bring rain into southwest England, accompanied by heavy rain at times and occasional thunder. The month's temperature extremes saw 15°C at Yeovil (20th) and a low of -8°C at Balmoral (13th).

Scheduled first visits this month were Aer Lingus (EI9212): Viscounts EI-AOL (21st) & EI-AOM (19th). Aircraft used on the BEA/Lufthansa cargo flight (BE/LH2201) were DC-6s G-APNO (1st/2nd/3rd/4th) & G-APNP (9th) and C-54s G-APYK (15th/16th/17th/18th) & G-ASFY (22nd/23rd/24th/25th).

GCA/ILS traffic noted was RAF Britannia XL658 (3rd), Andover XS595 (16th) & Bahamas Airways HS.748 VP-BCK (23rd). Training flights began again with BOAC B.707 G-ASZG (6th) & BEA Argosy G-ATTC (13th). With the introduction of ILS equipment, HS.125 test flights have been transferred to Speke.

3rd Carvair G-APNH was in charge of the final Rotterdam car ferry flight today for the final service. This was in line with the airline's intention to withdraw seven of their eighteen car ferry services by the end of February, due to falling passenger numbers. By October three aircraft placed into storage at Lydd were G-ANYB/AOFW & ARSD.

6th February 1967 - Seen parked during the afternoon outside the Fairey's hangar are (from left to right); PA-23 Aztec G-ATKW, PA-30 Twin Comanche G-ASYO & PA-23 Aztec LN-KAG, with the latter making its first visit before departing for Belfast later. (MA Archive via Ringway Publications)

6th Since the two big diversion days in November 1966, there was little fog affecting the south, but overnight it was dense and persistent in parts of the southeast all day. Eleven diversions descending on Manchester in two waves, early morning and late evening, only produced one first visit, with Pan American B.707 N703PA at 1115 (PA122 from Seattle). In fact all the others were BEA & BOAC aircraft, apart from Kuwait Airways Comet 9K-ACE arriving at 2026 (KU049 from Frankfurt).

6th HS.125 HB-VAN arrived at 0753 from Cologne for customs clearance, before proceeding to Hawarden for maintenance. It returned on the 11th at 1505 before leaving for Cologne.

13th The second Jet Commander visiting Ringway in as many months was N619JC, arriving at 0742 today for fuel en route Keflavik-Dusseldorf.

14th A cold Tuesday in February provided a variety of aircraft for anyone braving the elements of the terraces. Amongst the more interesting visitors were Commander 680 F-BFRB, Schreiner Airways F.27 PH-SAD, West German Air Force Noratlas GB+231, HS.125 G-ASSI, Heron G-ARTI, McAlpine Aviation Cessna 310 G-APUF and finally RAF Andover XS609 at 1640 (callsign MOSFR) from Northolt, which was operating a medical flight.

17th G-ARAY (Avro 2) arrived at 1743 from Woodford, ready for its departure to Rome on the 20th. Due to go on lease to Philippine Airlines, it was wearing their full colours.

20th Rank Organisation HS.125 G-ATZN landed at 1307 for fuel in the course of an instrument rating flight from/to Stansted.

25th After the frantic activity of US military flights in January, there was just one movement this month, by US Army U-6A Beaver 58-2004, at 1135 today from Brussels to clear customs, departing for Burtonwood.

MARCH 1967

BEA recently ordered eighteen new Super 1-11s for their Manchester-Heathrow services. In an effort to relieve pressure on engineering staff at Heathrow, they were considering the possibility of basing all Super 1-11s at Ringway, which would also mean the replacement of Tridents on all European flights. BEA favours the option of basing the 1-11 fleet at Jersey as it would be easier to integrate these into its network, but there was a question mark as to whether the Jersey authorities planned to extend the runway accordingly. Passenger figures dropped for the first two months, with 16% fewer than the same period in 1966.

Work began during the month on lengthening the main runway yet again, which would extend runway 24/06 by a further 1,100ft. This was a major undertaking, which included bridging the A538 Altrincham-Wilmslow road and creating four tunnels, two each for road traffic and pedestrians.

Gales and heavy thundery showers dominated the first half of March, thereafter an anticyclone sitting off the southwest coast took charge until the 23rd, bringing in dry and sunny weather. The weather pattern changed again on the 24th with a deep trough passing through the UK bringing in heavy rain, particularly to Scotland. The last few days saw a drop in temperatures, with wintry showers of hail or snow. The month's temperature extremes saw 19°C at Caledecott (21st) and a low of -7°C at Great Dun Fell (31st).

Scheduled first visits this month were <u>Air France (AF960)</u>: B.707 F-BHSH (22nd), <u>BOAC (BA537)</u>: SVC-10 G-ASGJ (13th) and British United (JY370): Herald G-AVEZ (8th). The BEA/Lufthansa cargo flight (BE/LH2201), apart from the 1st (G-APNP), was operated exclusively by C-54 G-ASFY.

GCA/ILS traffic was Bahamas Airways HS.748s VP-BCK (6th) & VP-BCL (20th), RAE Bristol 170 XG470 (14th) and RAF Comet XR398 (15th). The month's training flights were Dan-Air Ambassador G-ALZO (9th) and two first visits by Laker Airways BAC 1-11 G-AVBW (15th) & BKS Viscount G-AVED (29th).

2nd The third US-registered Cessna 411 to visit, N3256R, was Cessna's latest demonstrator. Again it was exhibited on the south side and made a local flight.

3rd Compagnie Air Transport Carvair F-BHMV brought the French rugby league team for a match against Great Britain the following day at Wigan. It operated from/to Toulouse and stayed until the 5th. After service with CAT (1965-1972), it was leased and then purchased by British Air Ferries as G-AREK. Withdrawn in February 1976, it languished for eighteen months at Southend until it was sold to another French operator, Uni-Air (1977-1979).

5th US Army U-6A Beaver 58-2030 arrived at 1656 from Brussels to clear customs, before departing for Burtonwood. The second CH-34A Chocktaw to visit, 56-4284, arrived at 1542 on the 27th from Harrogate and left four minutes later for Burtonwood.

7th This month's West German Air Force training flights were operated by Noratlas GB+246 today, which landed at 0958 from Ahlhorn and GB+244 (30th) from Birmingham to Oldenburg.

12th Britannia G-ANCH, which had been rolled out this morning from the British Eagle hangar at Liverpool in full Ghana Airways colours, succeeded in flipping over PA-22 Tri-Pacer G-ARGL as it taxied past during engine runs. The only occupant was the pilot, who was unhurt. G-ARGL was flown to Ringway on the 23rd May for repairs, before finally leaving on the 17th August.

14th The Royal Aircraft Establishment's Bristol 170, XJ470, made several ILS approaches on a sortie from/to Boscombe Down. Although serving the RAE since 1955, this was its only 'visit' to Manchester. In 1968 it was withdrawn and intended to be sold to Midland Air Cargo, but the deal collapsed and it was subsequently broken up several years later at Lasham.

15th Laker Airways BAC 1-11 G-AVBW, the first of three ordered by the airline, arrived at 1158 from Gatwick for crew training. Full commercial operations would commence from Gatwick in April and those from Manchester on the 2nd May, with a weekly flight from/to Palma (GK446/5). BAC 1-11 G-AVBX which was used on the first flight, was their second BAC 1-11 to visit Ringway.

18th Canadian Air Force C-130E 130320 was the third to visit, arriving at 2336 from Merville on a contract to export 131 tonnes of UN water drilling equipment to India. The machinery itself was manufactured and transported from a factory in Halifax. A second flight took place on 1st April with C-130E 130318. All landing and handling fees were waived by the airport.

21st USAF C-130s 61-2642 & 63-9810, which both operated from Mildenhall, were involved in the further transportation of equipment for Burtonwood.

APRIL 1967

New services inaugurated this month included a weekly Comet flight to Malta (BE859/8), a joint BEA/Swissair DC-4 freight service to Zurich and a three-times-weekly Cork service by Cambrian Airways.

BEA was also having teething problems with a new computerised booking system. Manchester has to link up with the main BEA computer, but a glitch in the system meant they were taking bookings for certain Heathrow flights down on the Manchester system as a Vanguard. The main BEA computer said the flights were operated by the much smaller Viscount, which resulted in several flights being overbooked. An official said that the change of aircraft had not been updated on the Manchester system.

Cardington had its coldest April night on record, with a minimum temperature of -7°C. The rest of the month was cool, cloudy and dry, with warm weather and prolonged sunshine at the end. The month's temperature extremes saw 22°C at Durham (28th) and a low of -12°C at Buddon Ness, Angus (1st).

International flights were operated during the summer as follows:

AER LINGUS - Amsterdam (up to 5 x weekly), Copenhagen (2 x weekly), Cork (4 x weekly), Dusseldorf (2 x weekly), Frankfurt (2 x weekly) & Zurich (1 x weekly), all operated by BAC 1-11s. Cork now operated throughout the year, with up to four-weekly in peak season. Shannon operated twice-weekly, increasing to three-weekly flights between July-August, both services with Viscounts.

AIR FRANCE - Three-weekly to Paris with SE.210s, increasing to six-weekly between June and September.

BEA - Operated Amsterdam/Brussels/Copenhagen/Dublin/Dusseldorf/Paris & Zurich with summer routes to Barcelona & Palma. A new once-weekly service to Malta (BE859/8) began in April with DH. Comets. Inclusive tour flights operated to Barcelona, Palma & Valencia.

BOAC - Daily to New York (BA538/7) with SVC-10s and Montreal/Toronto (BA638/7) four-weekly with B.707s which increased to daily between May-September. Cargo flight (BA065 Montreal/New York) operates five-weekly with B.707s with a new inbound Monday flight (BA068) from New York.

IBERIA - From 2nd June-15th October served Palma twice-weekly with SE.210 Caravelles one via Barcelona.

KLM - To Amsterdam four-times-weekly (KL149/150), with an additional flight (KL153/4 May-September) on Saturdays both with Electras. The DC-7 cargo flight operated f/t Amsterdam five-weekly (KL019/020).

LUFTHANSA - Twice-weekly cargo flight (LH942/3) to Dusseldorf/ Frankfurt with Air Douglas C-54s.

SABENA - Night-stopping Brussels service continued four-times-weekly with SE.210 Caravelles. Cargo flights four-weekly with Dakotas/DC-7s until June. B.727s operated twice-weekly from July (Wed/Fri SN197/8) and two more (SN193/4 Tue/Thu) continued with DC-7s departing to Brussels via Heathrow.

SAS - Continued twice-weekly serving Copenhagen with SE.210s (SK537/8), which extends on to Dublin.

SWISSAIR - Operated a once-weekly flight to Zurich from 29th May-18th September, increasing to three-weekly, with one flight operating onwards to Basle, all with CV-990s. A three-weekly cargo service to Zurich was introduced with Douglas DC-4s.

The only scheduled first visit this month was <u>Lufthansa (LH942)</u>: All-Air Douglas C-54 D-ADAB (4th) and there were no equipment changes during April.

GCA/ILS traffic noted was RAF Argosy XN816 (19th/20th) and the following HS.748s from Woodford: Australian Air Force A10-596 (19th/28th), Indian Airlines VT-DUO (19th/26th) & Bahamas Airways VP-BCM (22nd).

1st April 1967 – USAF C-130s 63-7853 and 63-7870 (seen here) both belonged to the 36th Troop Carrier Squadron. They were bringing in more supplies from Mildenhall for the re-equipping of RAF Burtonwood. As well as the airlift of equipment, there was also a considerable amount shipped in via Liverpool Docks. The final USAF C-130 to visit Ringway was 63-7824 on 8th August 1967, by which time Burtonwood was fully up and running. (Geoff Ball)

1st Britannia Airways began their summer programme slightly earlier, due to an intensive series of flights during April/early May to Beauvais & Rotterdam. The first IT flight was on the 13th May, when G-ANBA operated to Ibiza. Aircraft used this year were G-ANBA/ANBE/ANBF/ANBI/ANBJ/ANBL & G-ANBO.

5th Invicta Airlines and Channel Airways began a series of flights to the Dutch tulip fields, which were very popular during the 1960s and 1970s. Invicta began today with flights operating to Rotterdam throughout April and May with C-54s, G-ASEN/ASPM/ASPN & ASZT, and also some of the final visits by their Vickers Vikings, G-AHOW (21st), G-AHOY (12th/15th), G-AHPL (21st) & G-AIVF (28th/17th May). Channel Airways commenced on the 9th with Viscounts G-APPU/ATUE/AVHE/AVHK/AVIW & AVJL.

5th BEA introduced a new once-weekly service from/to Malta (BE859/8), with the first being operated by Comet G-APMC. Although regular visitors on Heathrow flights, this was the first time Comets were scheduled on flights from Ringway. Swissair also commenced a new three-times-weekly freight flight to Zurich (SR846/7) with DC-4F HB-ILD.

6th TMA operated two cargo flights to Beirut with Douglas DC-6s. Making their firsts were OD-AET today & OD-AEY on the 12th.

7th April 1967 - Cessna 310 OY-EGD made its first visit to Ringway, arriving from Finningley to clear customs, before departing for Dublin. Other light aircraft making first visits in April were Cessna 310 OO-SIK (4th), PA-23 Aztec F-BNFU (6th), Beech 65 N4260 (6th), Beech 65s HB-GAT (19th) & LN-NPP (27th) and the first foreign-registered Cessna 206 to visit, N4719F (24th). (Geoff Ball)

7th The first of two rare Beagle types to Ringway, was Beagle Airedale G-ASRK at 1635 today from Warton, departing on the 9th. Based at White Waltham, it was owned by Engineering Appliances (1964-1975) and was uncommon during the decade, after its initial visit on 22nd April 1965. The second, Beagle Terrier G-ASOM (24th) made its first visit since 4th June 1964, on a flight from Glasgow, departing later to its home at Halfpenny Green. After making several visits during the year, it was never to be seen again.

10th From today the MC-131As of the Aero Medical Service began a scheduled service on Mondays and Wednesdays, arriving from Ballykelly, Prestwick or Mildenhall, but always clearing to Mildenhall. Aircraft used were 0-25805 (24th/26th) & 0-25788 (10th/12th/17th/19th).

11th USAF T-39A Sabreliner 24460 arrived at 1005 from Stuttgart with three generals. US Army CH-34A 56-4284 was already waiting on the tarmac to whisk them away to Burtonwood.

16th British Eagle began their summer IT programme with a weekly flight to Palma, prior to next month's full schedules. Operated by BAC 1-11s, first visits were G-ATPJ (today - EG294) & G-ATTP (23rd - EG294).

17th Canadian Air Force CC-106 Yukon 15927 arrived at 1400 from RAF Manston on its first visit, departing just over an hour later to Gatwick.

27th April 1967 - USAF C-121A Constellation 080609 is seen here on the west side of the international pier, having arrived the previous evening from Brussels. It was carrying a number of senior US Army officials for an inspection of their Burtonwood facility and later in the day it made a short trip to RAF Shawbury. This aircraft served with the USAF from December 1948 to March 1968. It was also the penultimate Constellation to visit Manchester. (Geoff Ball)

30th April 1967 - Spantax began their summer programme with a return flight to Palma, operated by DC-7 EC-ATQ. They would operate flights to Barcelona, Ibiza & Palma with Douglas DC-7s, and from the 14th May CV-990 Coronados EC-BJC & EC-BJD (seen here), with the last flight operating on 15th October. Apart from the Douglas DC-7s used in previous years (EC-ATQ & EC-ATR), they also produced the following first visits, EC-BBH (f/v-7th August), EC-BBT (f/v-18th June), EC-BDL (f/v-7th May) & EC-BDM (f/v-7th May). Also used as aircraft changes were Douglas DC-6s EC-BBK (3rd June) & EC-AZX (7th October). (Bob Thorpe)

19th RAF Argosy XN816 made the first of two consecutive visits today, carrying out a number of ILS approaches. Twelve aircraft converted during 1967/68 to an airfields' aid calibration role and designated 'Argosy E Mk.1', were eventually assigned to 115-Squadron. Externally they appeared the same as the Argosy C Mk.1, apart for extra aerials on the port side of the nose. Internally they carried extra electronics and at least one aircraft, XR137, would carry an extra radome beneath the main one. The twelve aircraft converted were XN814/XN815/XN816/XN817/XN855/XP413/XP439/XP448/XP449/XR137/XR140 & XR143.

19th Cameron Steel Fairchild F.27 N172C arrived at 0935 from East Midlands to operate a rotation to Edinburgh. This aircraft, built under licence in the USA, was a frequent visitor to Ringway during 1967.

19th This month's West German Air Force training flight was operated today by Noratlas GB+116, which night-stopped from Bristol-Filton. It left the following morning to Cologne.

21st BOAC Cargo B.707F G-ASZG (BA065) was hit by lightning inbound from Heathrow in the early hours. Once landed, airport workers were told to keep away from the aircraft, as there may be dangerous rays coming from the aircraft's radar! It was carrying 24 tonnes of cargo when it was struck on the nose radome and port wing tip at around 4,000ft inbound. A spokesman from the airline later said there was no question of 'death rays' beaming out from the aircraft, it was just a standard precautionary measure.

27th In contrast to the quantity of American military flights, April only produced one UK military flight, with Army Air Corps Scout XR636 making its first visit at 1733 (Army 442) to night-stop from/to Farnborough.

28th Transair Sweden Douglas DC-7 SE-ERM positioned in at 2052 to operate an outbound passenger flight to Stockholm (TB1227). Having been delivered new to South African Airways in 1956, it was bought in March 1966 by Transair Sweden, but had been withdrawn less than two years later. The impact of jet aircraft on the industry was so great, that an aircraft with relatively low flying hours could become surplus to requirements in such a short space of time.

30th Caledonian also started their summer programme today, now operating exclusively with a fleet of six Bristol Britannias, G-AOVH/AOVI/AOVJ/ASTF/ATMA & ATNZ. Flights operated until the 29th October, which also included a number of transatlantic charters.

MAY 1967

BOAC increased their Montreal/Toronto flights to a daily service with effect from 1st May until 30th September, and five-weekly during October. All flights will be operated by Boeing 707s.

May was exceptionally wet with frequent thunderstorms. Low pressure was totally in charge, apart from a couple of days when weak high pressure calmed things down. The month's temperature extremes saw 26°C at several locations (11th) and a low of -7°C at Moor House (3rd).

The following operators could be seen during the summer months operating ITs to various destinations: Air Ferry (Basle), Austrian Airlines (Salzburg), Aviaco (Barcelona/Palma), Balair (Basle), Bavaria (Munich), Britannia Airways (Alicante/Barcelona/Ibiza/Palma/Rimini/Tarbes), British Eagle (Barcelona/Genoa/Ibiza/Lisbon/Newquay/Ostend/Palma/Perpignan/Rimini/Valencia/Venice), British Midland (Barcelona/Genoa/Venice/Palma/Oporto), Caledonian (Barcelona/Malaga/Palma/Perpignan/Rimini), Dan-Air (Barcelona/Basle/Biarritz/Dinard/Genoa/Munich/Ostend/Perpignan), Invicta (Ostend), Laker Airways (Palma), Luxair (Luxembourg), SAM (Rimini), Spantax (Barcelona/Ibiza/Palma), Trans Europa (Barcelona/Palma) and Transglobe (Dubrovnik/Ljubljana/Split).

Scheduled first visits this month were Lufthansa (LH942): All-Air C-54s D-ADAC (10th) & D-ADAD (31st) and Swissair (SR844): DC-9 HB-IFD (21st). Equipment changes were BOAC (BA065): Transmeridian DC-7F G-ATMF (15th) and Sabena (SN623): DC-6 OO-CTK (21st).

GCA/ILS traffic noted was a real mixed bag, with Zambian Air Force HS.748 AF.601 (10th), Lan Chile HS.748 CC-CEC (11th), RAF VC-10s XR806 (15th) & XV101 (18th), BKS Viscount G-AVIY (17th) and HS.125 G-AVGW (20th).

1st Viscount VP-BBW, which arrived at 0049 from Keflavik, was returning to the UK for Channel Airways having been leased to British Eagle. In July it was restored as G-APTA and leased again, this time to BKS. It made its first visit as such on 23rd September 1967, when it diverted in from Leeds.

1st The USAF medevac flights continued with MC-131As 0-25805 (today/22nd/24th), 0-25806 (8th/10th), 0-25788 (30th) & 0-25790 (17th). The Burtonwood-based CH-34A Chocktaw 56-4284 also made several visits (2nd/22nd/23rd/24th).

5th May 1967 – Britannia G-ANBM made its first visit with its new owners, Treffield International, seen here on the first of its summer flights out of Manchester, departing for Barcelona. It was also meant to operate weekly flights to Ostend and Palma, but only made three further visits with the airline. The aircraft became unreliable, so much so that a number of companies terminated their contracts with Treffield, and by July they had filed for bankruptcy. (Bob Thorpe)

14th May 1967 – Air India B.707 VT-DNZ called in to pick up extra passengers en route from Heathrow-New York (AI115). A further flight operated on 31st May with B.707 VT-DVA (seen here), which made its first visit calling in at 1134 whilst operating New York-Heathrow as AI104. (Geoff Ball)

1st   The month was ushered in by squally showers and thunderstorms with lightning, which hit three aircraft this morning. BOAC SVC-10 G-ASGC (BA538 from New York/Prestwick) was struck at around 4,000ft inbound, which caused a twelve inch split in the nose cone, blacking out the airborne radar. It was damaged badly enough for the airline to bring up replacement SVC-10 G-ASGD from Heathrow to operate the outbound New York flight. BOAC B.707 G-APFO outbound to Prestwick as BA637 was also hit, but no damage was reported on landing at Prestwick. Finally a Cambrian Airways Viscount (registration unknown) was also hit, making the short hop over from Liverpool to operate an outbound Isle of Man flight.

2nd   Fred Olsen operated their first Douglas DC-6 flight into Ringway, with night-stopping LN-FON, which left on a cargo charter to Gothenburg. Built in 1958 for United Airlines, it was the third DC-6A for Fred Olsen. Until 1973 it was mainly used for SAS Cargo services, but it also operated ad hoc charters worldwide. In January 1977 LN-FON was sold as 9Q-CMG and withdrawn from use in 1984.

4th   This month's light aircraft making their first visits were Beech 65 D-ILBO (today), PA-23 Aztec F-BOET (12th), PA-30 Twin Comanche D-ECWA (14th) which operated a local flight the following day before departing on the 16th, and finally the first Finnish light aircraft to Ringway, PA-24 Comanche OH-PIE (22nd).

5th   British Eagle began their full summer IT programme, and provided further BAC 1-11 first visits by G-ATPH (27th May) & G-ATPI (2nd June). All of the airline's European destinations, with the exception of two weekend Viscount flights to Ostend, were operated by BAC 1-11s. From the 17th July to 1st August, a series of Britannia flights to/from New York also operated. On the 12th June the airline introduced a weekday scheduled flight to Frankfurt, and Newquay was also added as a new summer-only destination.

6th   This year's Yugotours summer programme would be operated by Transglobe. However, the first couple of flights were operated by JAT. SE.210 YU-AHA positioned in from Belgrade to operate today's first flight to Ljubljana and SE.210s YU-AHB (7th) & YU-AHE (14th) both operated round-trips from Dubrovnik and all were first visits.

6th   World Airways began an extensive series of transatlantic flights today, with first visit B.707 N372WA arriving empty from Brussels, departing to New York via Gatwick. Flights operated until the 22nd October with B.707s N370WA (f/v-17th August), N371WA (f/v-7th July), N373WA (f/v-2nd June), N374WA (f/v-20th May) & N375WA (f/v-19th May).

7th   Dan-Air was still operating Airspeed Ambassadors to various IT destinations this year, but today they began a twice-weekly charter from/to Barcelona with DH. Comets. Used during the summer were ex-BOAC aircraft G-APDJ/APDK & G-APDO. Operations with Ambassadors began on the 13th, with a flight to Ostend. Aircraft used this year were G-ALZN/ALZO/ALZY/AMAG & AMAH. One missing from this year's roll call was G-ALFR, which had been withdrawn earlier this year in March.

8th   Global Presentations DC-7 N774R arriving at 1533 from Gatwick, was making its third and final visit to Manchester. It was bringing the Beach Boys into Manchester as part of their UK tour, with their name proudly emblazoned on the upper fuselage. This aircraft had become derelict at Bangkok by 1975, where it was ultimately broken up.

8th   Transair Sweden operated a further two passenger charters during May. Today, DC-7 SE-ERK operated from/to Copenhagen (TB1224) and SE-ERA (11th) operated outbound to Malmo. In a similar fate to SE-ERM, both aircraft had been withdrawn by the end of 1968.

10th   Balair began a three-times-weekly Basle charter today, with first time visiting Fokker F.27 HB-AAU. The flights operated until the 1st October, and other aircraft used were Douglas DC-6s HB-IBR, IBU & HB-IBZ plus F.27s HB-AAV (f/v - 5th July) & HB-AAW (f/v - 19th July).

10th   XV268 was the first of two Army Air Corps Beavers making their first visits during 1967, arriving at 1242 today operating f/t RAF Valley (Army Air 176). The second, XP825 (1st August) arrived from Belfast and left for Old Sarum.

11th   Air Canada began their summer programme of flights to Montreal and Toronto today, although there were considerably fewer than in previous years, with just eight flights. DC-8 CF-TJH departed as AC036 to Montreal via Prestwick. Flights operated until the 23rd October with DC-8s CF-TJA/TJC/TJD/TJH/TJL & TJP.

13th   Transglobe began their first summer series of flights from Manchester today, to Dubrovnik, Ljubljana & Split. The airline had recently ordered six Canadair CL-44s from Seaboard World, five of which would be convertible passenger/cargo models, while the sixth would be a pure freighter. Deliveries of these did not begin until April 1968, so they would operate the 1967 summer programme with their four Bristol

Britannias G-ANCC/ANCH/ATGD & ATLE. During the year these four aircraft covered 2,597,000 revenue miles, achieving an average utilisation of over 2,000 hours per aircraft.

13th British Midland began what would be the start of an ill-fated summer programme, when Argonaut G-ALHY positioned from East Midlands to operate the first flight to Barcelona. Also used were the airline's other two Argonauts, G-ALHG & G-ALHS, but after the tragic events of the 4th June involving G-ALHG, the remaining two aircraft would not see out the summer. G-ALHS made its final appearance on the 30th July on a return flight to Ostend, and G-ALHY on the 20th August also on an inbound flight from Ostend. By this time, most of the airline's IT flights had been taken over by Vickers Viscounts.

14th Luxair began this year's series of late night weekend flights to Luxembourg today, which operated until the 17th September. Aircraft used were Fokker F.27s LX-LGA, LX-LGB & PH-FSG leased from Schreiner Airways. Although Viscount LX-LGC was still in service, it did not appear during 1967.

14th Pan American began the first of another extensive series of transatlantic charters, until the final flight on the 16th October. Today's first was operated by B.707 N721PA, and others used throughout the season were B.707s N403PA (f/v - 8th October), N409PA N410PA (16th October), N415PA (f/v - 6th August), N417PA (f/v - 4th August), N421PA (f/v - 29th July), N423PA (f/v - 3rd September), N/01PA, N/04PA, N723PA, N724PA, N759PA (f/v - 22nd July), N760PA & N764PA (f/v - 8th July) and also N804PA (f/v - 26th September).

14th Another unremarkable month for diversions, but today did produce the first visit by Air Spain, with the arrival of Britannia EC-BFL at 0238 today. (JA126 from Palma). Founded in 1965, but not starting full operations until this month, Air Spain was operating three former UK-registered Britannias, EC-BFJ/BFK & BFL. Although they became occasional visitors, they would not begin regular flights into Ringway until 1972.

17th HS.125 aircraft passing through Ringway for customs clearance en route for Hawarden were becoming a regular feature. Today's latest example, D-COMI, operated by German industrial giants Krupp, made its first visit arriving at 0845, eventually bound for maintenance at Hawarden. It returned from Hawarden on the 24th, again to clear customs, before returning to Dusseldorf.

17th In December 1965 Air Ferry purchased the two British United Douglas DC-6s, G-APNO & G-APNP. These were mainly used for long range cargo charter work, but this summer they were employed as passenger aircraft. Today, they began a twice-weekly late night charter flight to Basle, which operated until the 3rd October.

17th RAF Pembroke WV705 (KHW 59) arrived at 1125 from RAF Wildenrath with a crew to give fellow-Pembroke XF799, which had been present since the 11th January, a test flight.

21st Six months after Swissair introduced the Douglas DC-9 to Manchester, KLM sent in their first aircraft, PH-DNB, which arrived from Amsterdam at 2229 to operate a passenger charter to Stuttgart. Delivered in April 1966, it served the airline until 1982 when it was leased out to British Midland as G-BMAG. The return flight operated on the 25th with another new aircraft, PH-DNA.

23rd Aviaco commenced their summer IT programme f/t Barcelona (AO1120/1) with SE.210 EC-AVY. From the 18th June a return flight to Palma was introduced (AO1014/5), also with SE.210 Caravelles.

23rd The Netherlands Air Force operated the first of three Fokker F.27 flights this month, with C-7 today (f/v - also 28th) & C-2 (26th) f/t Ypenburg. This Dutch Air Force base was a civilian airport until 1955, when it was turned into an air base. After 1968, it was mainly used as a VIP airport for politicians and the royal family. It was decided to close the air base in 1982, but it was not abandoned by the air force until 1992. Among the last aircraft using the airport were military cargo flights bound for Kuwait during the Gulf War. Very little remains of the airport today, the former air traffic control tower being a notable exception.

24th Once a common sight at Ringway, but by now today's visit of RAF Avro Anson C.19 TX160 (FUY 45) at 1144 from RAF Odiham was a major event. Another lean month for British military visitors was rounded off on the 28th, with the first visit of an Army Air Corps Sioux, when XT172 (Army 349) arrived at 0937 for a short stay en route from Larkhill to Carlisle.

26th Pacific Western DC-7 CF-PWM operated a one-off charter from Vancouver via Keflavik (PW713), positioning out later to Amsterdam. A return flight operated on the 14th July as PW742 routing via Sondre Stromfjord. The airline would return to Ringway in 1968 operating the occasional B.707 charter.

19th May 1967 – Trans-Europa Companía de Aviación SA (Trans Europa) was founded in July 1965 and began operations two months later using a single Douglas DC-7C (EC-BCH) for passenger and freight ad hoc charters from its base at Palma de Mallorca. EC-BCH inaugurated their first programme from Ringway today with a weekly Palma flight (TR816/7). A second DC-7, EC-BJK, is seen above the following week operating flight TR816/7, and from 10th July a fortnightly flight to Barcelona was introduced. (Geoff Ball).

28th May 1967 – Since BOAC disposed of it in 1962 and its subsequent sale to BKS, Britannia G-ANBK made just a handful visits to Manchester, but unusually it was pressed into service today by BEA to operate a scheduled flight to Jersey (BE3516). It would make three further visits as diversions, before its withdrawal in October 1969. (Graham Davies)

27th German-outfit Bavaria, another new airline to Ringway in 1967, began a twice-weekly IT flight today until September with Heralds D-BEBE (f/v-today) & D-BOBO (f/v-28th May), which operated until 16th September. Founded in 1957, Bavaria (Bavaria Fluggesellschaft Schwabe & Co) initially used light aircraft for air taxi work. Three Douglas DC-3s were acquired in 1960 and used until 1967, by which time their main business was carrying freight on behalf of Lufthansa. With increased passenger traffic, a Handley Page Dart Herald (D-BEBE) was added in 1964 and by 1966 two more Heralds (D-BIBI & D-BOBO) were added when they carried around 800,000 passengers. D-BIBI did not visit Ringway as it was returned to Handley Page earlier in the year, but Bavaria would continue to serve Manchester until 1973.

JUNE 1967

High pressure was in charge of the UK weather until the 18th; with generally sunny and very warm conditions prevailing. Once this pattern had broken down by the 19th, it became cooler with rain, heavy at times and there were thunderstorms from the 23rd-25th. During these storms, rainfall exceeded 5 inches in many places. At Aberystwyth, Cardiganshire, 1½ inches was recorded in 42 minutes and at Weybridge, Surrey, over an inch fell in as many minutes. Flooding was extensive in many parts of the country, particularly in northwest England. The month ended quiet and dry with 11 to 12 hours of sunshine. The month's temperature extremes saw 27°C at Worcester (14th) and a low of -2°C at Santon Downham (9th).

There were no scheduled first visits during June. Equipment changes were BOAC (BA065): Transmeridian DC-7F G-ATMF (1st/3rd/8th/10th) and Swissair (SR846): C-54F D-ADAB (23rd).

GCA/ILS traffic noted during the month was Lan Chile HS.748 CC-CEC (14th), and the first appearance at Ringway of the new submarine surveillance aircraft, Nimrod XV148 (16th), and RAF Andover XS643 (21st).

1st French Air Noratlas 29/63-BI was the first to visit Ringway since June 1965, arriving at 1211 today to night-stop on a return flight from Pau. Further Noratlas visits took place with '130' (18th November) & '47/63-BK' (29th December). Both flights night-stopped and operated f/t Pau.

2nd The departure of British Midland Argonaut G-ALHG to Genoa was delayed over two hours this evening, due to technical problems before finally leaving at 2315. It arrived back at Manchester at 0836 the following morning to day-stop before its next flight to Palma departing at 2229.

3rd Beechams HS.125 G-AVGW made the first of its six visits to Ringway today, prior to being written off. On the 23rd December 1967 as part of a training flight, a scheduled engine failure was simulated on takeoff from Luton. The aircraft failed to maintain height, struck the roof of the Vauxhall factory, caught fire and crashed. The two people aboard were killed. Another HS.125 making its first visit during June was G-ATPC (16th), operated by the Department of Trade and Industry, which arrived at 1317 from Heathrow.

3rd A British diplomat, who had recently been made to stand in the sun for over seven hours by the Chinese authorities, because he refused to bow to hundreds of Chinese officials and admit that the British were imperialists, arrived in Manchester this morning. He was on his way back from Hong Kong, where he was the British Consul in the Portuguese colony of Macao. His aircraft, B.707 G-ARRC (BA919 from Hong Kong/Zurich), had diverted into Ringway due to fog at Heathrow. There were six other fog diverts including SAM Douglas DC-6 I-DIMU at 0700 (MQ812 from Alghero) and World Airways B.707 N373WA at 0840 (WO373 from Toronto), both Gatwick diversions.

4th Sadly, British Midland Argonaut G-ALHG never made it back to Manchester on its delayed return from Palma. It crashed several miles short at Hillgate, Stockport (a place the writer knew extremely well, having lived there from 1979-1990). The approach to runway 24 passed over many densely populated areas and the loss of an airliner over one of these conurbations would have been the airport's and an airline's worst nightmare. The crew aborted the first approach of Argonaut 'Hotel Golf' to Manchester voluntarily, so it peeled off to the north for a second attempt. Shortly thereafter, the pilots were confronted with a severe power failure, resulting in the loss of two of the aircraft's engines. The Argonaut then began to sink below its recommended height and an emergency landing was requested. By the time "Hotel Golf" was passing over Bredbury, around five miles from touchdown, it was 800ft below the glidepath and had lost power in a third engine. The aircraft was now sinking unavoidably towards Stockport town centre, and it was becoming obvious to those monitoring the VHF broadcasts and to the onlookers that it would not make it. Within seconds a 'Mayday' call was transmitted, but soon afterwards the stricken aircraft ploughed into a patch of derelict land. Its text-book belly-flop landing was brought to a sudden and jarring halt by the brick wall of an electricity sub-station. Seventy of the eighty-four people onboard were killed. Only a skilled piece of flying by the pilot prevented an even worse disaster of possibly hundreds of casualties on the ground. The subsequent investigation highlighted two probable causes; poor flight-deck design and pilot error. The fuel system controls on the Argonaut were sited in a position where a fuel transfer could be initiated by accidental or unnoticed contact with the levers. This had occurred on the doomed 'Hotel Golf' but had escaped the attention of the pilots, who were thoroughly disorientated by their inability to locate the cause of their fuel-starvation problem. The Air Investigation Branch also commented on the shoddy materials used on the Argonaut's seats, which were highly inflammable and prone to collapse during a crash landing. Thirty-five of the seventy-two fatalities were directly attributed to the aircraft's seating. The airline's remaining two Argonauts, G-ALHS & G-ALHY, continued in service until the end of the summer season before being withdrawn.

5th The USAF medevac flights continued, with MC-131As 0-25787 (19th/21st), 0-25790 (26th/28th), 0-25805 (today/7th) & 0-25806 (12th/14th).

7th Dragon Rapide G-AHED arrived at 1357 from Leavesden, and was based until the 14th. It was engaged in photographic work for road construction on the Wirral and locked away each night in the Manchester Airport Agencies hangar, which was available for night-stopping aircraft. Also this month was a second Dragon Rapide, G-AIYR (19th), which arrived from Leavesden and departed towards Liverpool also on a photographic detail.

7th Cessna 401 G-AVKN arrived on delivery from Shannon at 0648 from the Cessna factory, departing for Rogers Aviation at Cranfield. It remained on the UK register until 2007 when it was sold in the USA.

9th RAF Avro Anson C.19 TX213 (CWM 48), operated by the Western Command Squadron, arrived at 1153 on a round-trip from White Waltham. After retirement from RAF service in August 1968, TX213 was sold as G-AWRS and operated by Kemps Aerial Survey Company, before becoming part of the Strathallan collection in 1974. It is currently preserved at the North East Aircraft Museum.

11th Today marked the final visit of Aer Turas Bristol 170 EI-APM. A fairly regular visitor since December 1966, it was written off the following day routing from Prestwick to Dublin. The flight itself was uneventful and the aircraft was cleared for a runway 17 approach and landing. The aircraft touched down at the threshold and bounced three to four times. The crew decided to carry out an overshoot, and the aircraft continued to climb, slowly turning towards the left. The bank angle increased until the port wing struck a house. The plane then hit the ground and an office block. The cause of the accident was put down to the pilot attempting an overshoot manoeuvre, following the stoppage of the port engine, at too low a speed (below the minimum control speed), resulting in an uncontrollable turn towards the airport buildings.

11th The first of Austrian Airlines' weekly IT flights to Salzburg commenced today, with Viscount OE-IAM. Continuing until the 17th September, the airline would also use Viscounts OE-LAH & OE-LAL.

12th British Eagle began their weekday flight to Frankfurt today. The first flight operated by BAC 1-11 G-ATTP finally gave Aer Lingus some competition on the route.

12th An interesting selection of foreign light aircraft first visits began today with PA-30 Twin Comanche SE-EOK. Others were Beech 95 HB-GBM (20th), Cessna 172 F-BOQD (23rd) & Cessna 337 N2396S (30th).

16th Italian charter airline SAM began their rather belatedly summer IT programme today, with DC-6 I-DIMU operating their first weekly flight to Rimini (MQ844/5), until the 15th September with DC-6s I-DIMB/DIMD/DIMI/DIMP & DIMU. It was their last summer programme until 1971. Between these times they disposed of their fleet of Douglas DC-6s and re-equipped with SE.210 Caravelles leased from Alitalia.

16th Beech 55 Baron N155AS, owned and operated by the Associated Spring Corp, arrived at 1924 today from Vagar. It stayed for two days before departing for Amsterdam.

17th The writing for Treffield International was by now well and truly on the wall. Their final two flights through Ringway operated today with Viscount G-ATVE (f/v) from/to Ostend and Viscount G-ATVR (f/v - 19th June) outbound to Tarbes. Earlier in the month, Britannia G-ANBM was returned to Laker Airways, and just as the season was building up to its peak, Treffield ceased operations on 23rd June 1967. Their two Viscounts ignored waiting passengers and were flown back empty to Castle Donington, before flying to Southend the following day. The airline's contracts were taken over by a variety of airlines including Autair, Cambrian & Channel Airways. The airline's founder and managing director, Lord Trefgarne, put the failure of Treffield down to insufficient capital to ride out a very difficult period.

5th June 1967 – The Stockport plane crash was extensively covered in an excellent book, 'The Day The Sky Fell Down' by Stephen Morrin, so the full story of this terrible disaster will be left there, but the above photo from the following morning shows the aftermath. Note there are still plenty of curious people looking on. The photo below shows the following day's frontage of a local newsagent on Middle Hillgate, Stockport. (Both Lloyd Robinson)

9th June 1967 – Air Canada, American Flyers, British Eagle, Caledonian, Capitol, Pacific Western, ONA, Pan American, Saturn and World Airways would all operate transatlantic charters during the summer of 1967, although one airline missing from last year was Aer Lingus. Today, a new addition was TWA, with the arrival of B.707 N18708 making its first visit to Ringway, operating an outbound flight to New York via Heathrow (TW8203). Further flights on 5th July and 2nd August both operated with N18708. The final flight took place on the 1st September with another first visitor, this time N8725T. (Geoff Ball)

18th Schreiner Airways operated the first of a series of charters to Amsterdam, although considerably less than last year. Fokker F.27 PH-SAD was in charge of today's first of eight flights (AQ221/2), with the last operating on the 26th September. Apart from PH-SAD, the only other Fokker F.27 used was PH-SAR (f/v - 10th September). On the 1st October, they made the decision to cease trading due to operating losses.

19th HS.125 HB-VAN arrived at 0730 from Cologne to clear customs, prior to its departure to Hawarden for maintenance. It returned in the opposite direction on the 24th, leaving at 1450 for Cologne.

20th Over 100 soldiers of the 1st Battalion Lancashire Fusiliers arrived back at Manchester this morning, over 80 hours behind schedule. Caledonian Britannia G-AOVH touched down at 0602 (CA524 from Halifax), after one of the longest delays to an aircraft that staff at Manchester Airport could remember. Once they had arrived, the weary troops were taken away on a fleet of coaches back to their barracks at Weeton, near Blackpool. They had been on a six-week exercise in Jamaica, where the catalogue of delays began. First, engine failure as the plane positioned out to Jamaica to pick up the troops forced G-AOVH to divert to New York for an engine change, which took 36 hours. On the return flight from Kingston it was scheduled to stop at Halifax, Nova Scotia, but its departure was delayed by a further 14 hours at Kingston due to fog at Halifax. When the Britannia reached Halifax, a technical fault delayed the aircraft further and spare parts had to be flown from Gatwick before it could finally depart for Manchester.

21st Possibly the best movements of the month were two Ilyushin IL-14s operated by Malev. HA-MAD arrived empty at 0314 today from Budapest (MA0028) and departed with a consignment of rabbits. A week later (28th), Ilyushin IL-14 HA-MAE departed to Budapest via Amsterdam, this time transporting pigs.

21st Only the fourth Lear Jet to visit Ringway, was LJ24 HB-VBB, arriving at 0932 today from Rome. It stayed overnight before its departure to Heathrow the following morning.

23rd Dan-Air Ambassador G-ALZY returned to Manchester less than thirty minutes into its flight to Biarritz with technical trouble, so the airline sent up a second Ambassador, G-AMAE, to cover the flight. The trouble did not end there, because it was forced to divert to Bordeaux due to bad weather. This meant the airline had no aircraft to cover the next rotation to Ostend, so a third Ambassador, G-AMAG, was again sent from Gatwick to operate this much-delayed flight.

24th Twenty-four hours after the collapse of Treffield, several flights had to be covered by other airlines. Iberia SE.210 EC-AYE was used for a flight to Valencia (AO1401). Laker Britannia G-ANBM departed for Perpignan and Belgian International DC-6 OO-ABE operated two return flights from Ostend.

30th Trans Union was a new French airline, operating a number of second-hand Douglas DC-4s & DC-6s. Douglas DC-6 F-BOEV arrived at 1719 today on a freight flight from Le Bourget, leaving empty for Manston. Another Trans Union aircraft, DC-6 F-BNUZ (28th July), arrived at 1227 operating f/t Le Bourget.

JULY 1967

Following the collapse of Treffield, Laker Airways took over most of their summer programme. They also bought out Liverpool-based tour company, Arrowsmith Holidays, who had been arranging IT holidays from the north of England for over twenty years. The takeover now meant that Laker BAC 1-11s would also fly IT flights from Liverpool.

Beech 35 G-ASFJ arrived by road after suffering cam-rod damage after a forced landing at Glenrothes, Fife. After an extended repair time, it finally undertook a test flight on 3rd November 1968, before departing for Liverpool the same day.

Anticyclones dominated the weather across England until the 12th; otherwise high pressure was in charge during July. The first week was characterised by cloud and rain, heavy at times. Around the 9th the conditions began to improve, with very warm weather, but frequent thunderstorms. On the night of the 13th, storms produced a fall of 64mm at Neston, Cheshire. The month ended on a cloudy and wet note, with thundery rain or showers in most areas. The month's temperature extremes saw 30°C at Watnall, Notts (17th) and a low of 1°C at Moor House (22nd).

Scheduled first visits this month were Sabena (SN197): B.727 OO-STB (5th). Equipment changes were Swissair (SR846): Trans Union DC-6F F-BOEV (19th) & Belgian Intl DC-4F OO-RIC (5th/21st/22nd).

There was a great variety and quantity of GCA/ILS traffic during the month. Test flights from Woodford were HS.748s Lan Chile CC-CEC (3rd/8th/10th), CC-CED (25th) & Falckair HS.748 G-11 (25th). Possibly the highlight of the 1967 ILS traffic was Austrian Air Force Vampire 5C-YA (3rd/6th). Others were RAF VC-10s XR807 (5th/6th/7th), XR810 (21st), XV101 (5th) & XV102 (21st/24th); Britannias XM519 (19th), XN404 (19th) and Andover XS644 (25th). Finally two HS.125s from Hawarden, G-5-12 (11th) & G-5-14 (14th), would eventually become G-AVRG & G-AVRI respectively.

1st Capitol Airways operated an ad hoc charter with DC-8 N4904C. It arrived at 1231 from Munich and departed for New York via Shannon.

2nd Pan American B.707 N760PA arrived from Heathrow at 1250, but its departure to New York was delayed over three hours, when its wing tip was damaged by a set of boarding steps.

2nd Chipmunk G-AORW, operated by British Midland (1959-1971), arrived at 1720 on a round-trip from Castle Donington with an Argonaut pilot! Built in 1950, this was the aircrafts only visit Ringway, although it still flies in 2014!

4th The USAF medevac flights continued with MC-131As 0-25787 (24th/26th), 0-25788 (today), 0-25805 (10th/12th) & 0-25806 (17th/19th/31st).

5th Sabena provided Ringway with its first scheduled Boeing 727 service today, with OO-STB operating a new twice-weekly freighter service f/t Brussels (SN197/8 outbound via Heathrow). A twice-weekly freight service directly serving Brussels (SN193/4) was still operated with Douglas DC-3 & DC-7 aircraft.

6th Cessna 337 G-AVJG arrived at 1610 from Shannon on delivery from the Cessna factory. It later departed for Rogers Aviation at Cranfield.

7th A very rare type to visit Ringway was the PA-18 Super Cub, when G-ARAN arrived at 1701 today from its home at Tollerton and stayed until the 9th.

9th BOAC SVC-10 G-ASGG finally made its first visit today (BA538 from New York/Prestwick), two years after its delivery. Until recently, it had been retained by Vickers for Autoland trials.

10th Danish operator, Sterling, now used a mix of Douglas DC-6s & SE.210 Caravelles. Two DC-6 flights (NB775/6 f/t Copenhagen) operated as part of their summer programme by OY-BAS (7th Aug) & OY-BAV today on its only visit. They would also use their Caravelles on Manchester flights for the first time, with first visits from (NB537/8 f/t Copenhagen), OY-STA (19th Jul/16th Aug/30th Aug) & OY-STB (2nd Aug).

1st July 1967 – The latest Canadian Air Force CC-106 Yukon to visit was 15930, arriving at 1306 from Manston. It can be seen in this shot just about to park up on gate 50 on Pier A. This would be the aircraft's only visit to Manchester, as in November 1971 it was sold and eventually became 9Q-CWK. (Geoff Ball)

11th July 1967 - American Flyers returned to Manchester today. Now operating four ex-Northwest Orient Electras as a stopgap until their recently ordered two Boeing 727-185C aircraft were delivered. N124US arrived from Tours via Brussels at 1538 operating a USAF charter and left for New York via Gander the following afternoon. The airline made three further visits during the year, with N122US (4th August/27th September) & N124US (6th September). (Geoff Ball)

14th July 1967 - Polaris Air Transport CV-240 LN-KLT, the second to visit, arrived at 1238 from Bremen on an ad hoc charter. The airline operated three CV-240s with this particular aircraft being withdrawn in June 1968 and then stored at Woenstrecht for eight years before being scrapped. (Bob Thorpe)

15th July 1967 - Today was the first visit of the new stretched DC-8. N8961T operated by US carrier TIA, arrived at 1425 from New York, later positioning to Brussels. Its first visit should have been yesterday, but due to fog at Manchester it diverted to Prestwick. It would make further visits on 17th July/25th July/6th Oct. A second DC-8, N8008F, made its first visit on 12th August, also inbound from New York. (Geoff Ball)

20ᵗʰ RAF Pembroke C.1 WV725 arrived at 0939 from White Waltham to operate a return flight to RAF Wyton. The final RAF Pembroke movement of 1967 was also a first visit, when C.1 WV735 (3ʳᵈ October) arrived at 1053 from Liverpool and also departed to White Waltham.

21ˢᵗ A quiet month for foreign aircraft visitors, but PA-23 Aztec F-BNTS provided July with a first time visitor.

22ⁿᵈ Dan-Air Douglas DC-7 G-ATAB arrived at 2348 today from Belgrade, and left the following evening for Tehran via Thessaloniki and Istanbul. Operating a cattle charter, this was the first of five visits since being purchased from Transmeridian last year. G-ATAB served with Dan-Air as a freighter until June 1969, and it was scrapped in June 1973.

25ᵗʰ July 1967 - Canadian Air Force KP221 Dakota had arrived the previous evening on a flight from Lahr. This fifth Canadian military DC-3 to visit Ringway was at one time based at RAF Northolt. (Geoff Ball)

28ᵗʰ The latest American charter carrier making their first appearance at Manchester, was ONA with the arrival of DC-8 N852F at 0945 from Prestwick, later departing for Shannon. The airline made three further visits this year with N851F (16ᵗʰ August/8ᵗʰ September) & N852F (1ˢᵗ September).

29ᵗʰ Yet another Air India flight routed through Ringway today, when B.707 VT-DVB (AI111 from Heathrow) arrived at 1308 en route to New York via Prestwick. A further flight with B.707 VT-DJI (AI104 from New York) operated on 14ᵗʰ August and both were first visits.

29ᵗʰ In amongst the numerous summer transatlantic charters, increasingly operated by modern jet airliners, were Saturn Airways who remarkably still operated Douglas DC-7s on these flights. Today, N90773 arrived at 2036 to operate an affinity charter to Rochester, New York the following evening. The return flight from New York on the 16ᵗʰ August was again operated by DC-7 N90773. This however was the last year of DC-7 operations by Saturn who would be seen in the UK during 1968 with their new DC-8 aircraft.

AUGUST 1967

British Eagle made applications to the Air Transport Licensing Board to operate cargo flights from Manchester and Liverpool, as well as Heathrow and Prestwick, to New York, Boston, Philadelphia, Washington, Detroit & Chicago. If successful, the service would have mirrored BOAC Cargo's transatlantic operations, but the plan would fail partly for this reason and the fact that BOAC would strongly oppose it. Caledonian also objected on the grounds that they also had plans to operate freight flights to ten US and Canadian cities. Unbelievably, British United joined in the scrap, by applying to operate a cargo flight. Transglobe were also seeking to operate passenger, cargo and mail flights from Manchester to Chicago, Los Angeles, San Francisco, Edmonton, Calgary & Vancouver.

Although the weather over southeast England was warm for the first few days, it was much cooler over the rest of the UK. From the 5th until the 19th, low pressure was in charge. On the 8th, violent thunderstorms accompanied by torrential rain broke over the northwest of England. Falls exceeding 75mm in three hours were recorded in parts of Lancashire during late afternoon/evening, bringing considerable structural damage and widespread flooding. On the 18th the weather pattern began to change, with a large high pressure bringing mainly dry and warm weather through the rest of August. The month's temperature extremes saw 30°C at Herne Bay (1st) and a low of 1°C at Santon Downham (20th).

The only scheduled first visit this month was Sabena (SN197): B.727 OO-STD (2nd). Equipment changes were Swissair (SR846): All-Cargo Douglas C-54F D-ADAB (12th), D-ADAC (11th/29th), Belgian Intl DC-4F OO-RIC (2nd/4th/5th) & Capitol Airways Curtiss C-46 N9892Z (16th).

There was another mixed bag of GCA/ILS traffic during the month. RAF aircraft consisted of VC-10s XR809 (2nd/7th), XR810 (14th) & XV104 (9th), Shackleton XF703 (17th) and RAE-operated Varsity WL679 (14th), HS.125 G-AVPE (22nd) & Fiji Airways HS.748 VQ-FAL (25th). HS.125 G-5-14 (9th) performed a touch-and-go and finally an unidentified Canadian Air Force C-130E (28th) also did a touch-and-go en route from Shannon. There was also a solitary training flight by BEA G-ARPM (2nd).

2nd August 1967 - August was the final month that the USAF operated their MC-131As through Ringway, as from September onwards these would route via Liverpool. MC-131A 0-25806 is seen here prior to its return to Mildenhall. Others during the month were 0-25787 (21st/23rd), 0-25788 (7th/9th) & 0-25805 (14th). (Bob Thorpe)

8th   USAF C-130 63-7824 arrived at 0834 from Frankfurt with a spare tyre for MC-131A 0-25788, which had burst one on landing yesterday.

9th   The scheduled, charter and IT flight companies plied their trade, and kept the airport busy. There were plenty of light aircraft movements as well, but very little of interest. However, two foreign light aircraft making their first visits this month were Cessna 310 OY-EGW at 0023 today from Reykjavik to Deventer and Beech 55 F-BMRB (30th).

9th   Not a common occurrence, but HS.125 G-5-14 did a touch-and-go at 1453 from Hawarden (Tibbet 53). It would eventually be registered as G-AVRD and later delivered to its new owner as HB-VAZ.

12th   A new Vickers Viscount for Channel Airways, G-AVNJ, arrived from Ostend to operate a return flight to Venice. At the time of its delivery to Channel, this aircraft was less than ten years old, but it operated its last service on 23rd October 1969, having clocked up 28,834 hours and 31,579 landings.

16th August 1967 - USAF Convair T-29B 51-7899 arrived at 0907, with six VIPs who would make a base inspection of Burtonwood. The party was collected by one of Burtonwood's resident US Army Sikorsky CH-34As, 64323, as seen above which was already on the ground awaiting its passengers. Unfortunately, this helicopter was lost in April 1968, when it crashed near Crawley, West Sussex. (Geoff Ball)

27th August 1967 - Martinair Convair CV-640 PH-MAL was the first of its type to visit Ringway. They were basically CV-340/440s with Rolls-Royce Dart engines with four-blade propellers in place of piston engines with three-blade propellers. The only two CV-640s to visit from 1967 to 1971 were PH-CGD & PH-MAL, both operated by Martinair. (Bob Thorpe)

16th Cambrian Airways DC-3 G-ALCC, en route from Manchester-Glasgow, was struck by lightning but the twenty passengers and three crew were unhurt. Earlier on the 7th August, G-ALCC had diverted to Liverpool shortly after leaving Manchester due to the shutdown of one engine, which delayed its onward flight to Glasgow by four hours.

16th Capitol Airways Curtiss C-46 N9892Z, which was based in Europe operating freight flights on lease to Lufthansa, arrived at 0342 operating Swissair flight SR846/7 from/to Zurich.

19th Another Ambassador flight with technical problems was G-AMAE, inbound this morning from Munich. The pilot reported to ATC that he had engine trouble, and although the aircraft landed safely it was out of action for over thirty hours, causing another major headache to the airlines busy weekend schedule!

27th Spantax flight BX075/6 (f/t Palma) was operated by TAE Douglas DC-7 EC-BEN today. A new Spanish airline to Manchester, they were set up in 1957 but did not begin flights until April 1967, operating with three Douglas DC-7s (EC-BCI/BEN/BEO). They intended to operate an ex-Air France L-1049 Super Constellation in 1966, but it was not taken up.

SEPTEMBER 1967

Pleasure flights were in question this month after a female employee was knocked down on the airport access road by Auster G-AOBV, returning from a 10 minute pleasure flight. Airport director George Harvey said it was just one of those unfortunate accidents. The pilot had not seen the woman as he was taxiing past, and she had ignored all the warning notices. Both had failed to observe the necessary caution, and as a result of a period of consultation, future flights would no longer be operated from Gate 41.

A succession of fronts and depressions moved eastwards during the first week. Heavy rain and gales were commonplace, but high pressure was mainly in charge until around the 17th when the pattern reverted back to changeable weather. The month's temperature extremes saw 24°C at Southend (28th) and a low of 1°C at Santon Downham (8th).

Scheduled first visits this month were KLM (KL151): PH-DND (18th). Equipment changes were Swissair (SR840): SE.210s HB-ICT (7th) & HB-ICZ (21st).

This month's GCA/ILS traffic was dominated by HS.748s from Woodford, with Hawker Siddeley's G-AVRR (5th/19th) & G-ATAM (19th/20th), Lan Chile CC-CEE (18th/21st), Fiji Airways VQ-FAL (5th) and Philippine Airlines PI-C1014 (12th/29th). Also RAE Varsity WL679 (7th/27th) and RAF VC-10s XR806 (29th) & XV102 (29th).

1st Martinair were drawing towards closing operations with their Dakotas, however DC-3 PH-MAA arrived at 1041 to day-stop on a return flight from Amsterdam.

1st West German Air Force training flights continued today, after an absence of several months. Another first time visitor, Noratlas GA+233, arrived from Filton at 1233, later departing for Erding Air Force Base, Bavaria. Used by the United States Air Force until 1957, when it was handed over to the reconstituted West German Air Force as a front line facility, where it hosted various F-104 Starfighter squadrons.

3rd Royal Navy Sea Prince WM756 was the third to visit Ringway. Arriving at 1134 today f/t Yeovilton, it was in overall blue colours with Royal Navy titles. Used as transport for the Flag Officer, Naval Flying Training, his flag and initials 'FONFT' were displayed on the nose.

8th Yet another prop with engine trouble was SAM Douglas DC-4 I-DIMP. After its scheduled arrival (MQ844 from Venice) it was then due to depart empty to Moscow, but after an hour into its flight it returned to Manchester with a shutdown engine. It finally departed on the 10th to Gatwick.

9th Having not operated a transatlantic charter all summer, Aer Lingus pitched in today with B.707 EI-APG (IN5876 from New York), making its first visit, although operating over 24 hours late. On departure from New York the pilot reported oil pressure difficulties, forcing his return. The 173 passengers onboard, members of a British University student association (BUNAC), were put up overnight in New York while replacement B.707 EI-APG was sent in to collect them. A second flight operated with B.707 EI-AMW (28th), also as IN5876 from New York. Also two diverted flights due to fog at Shannon on the 14th were B.707s EI-ANV (IN104 from Shannon) & B.707 EI-APG (IN124 from Chicago).

11th French Navy Flamant 314 (call sign F-YCKN) was en route to Edinburgh, but bad weather and low fuel reserves forced it make an emergency landing. Once refuelled, it departed an hour later for Edinburgh.

14th Philips latest aircraft is Beech 55 PH-ILP, which made the first of three visits during 1967 today. The Dutch CAA asked Philips to re-register Beech 55 PH-ILP to avoid continual r/t confusion with the company's

F.27 PH-LIP. Philips duly obliged and the Beech 55 was re-registered as PH-ILB at the end of 1967. Other first time visitors this month were Beech 55 SE-EKZ (today) arriving from Brussels to clear customs en route to Hawarden, Beech 95 SE-EEU (17th), Beech 33 D-EFTH (20th), Cessna 320 N6155Q (21st), Cessna 182 SE-CYL (21st), Beech 80 D-ILKE (25th), Beech 90 D-ILDB (27th) and Commander 500 N6537V (27th).

22nd September 1967 – Gulfstream N360WT operated by IBM, made a first visit of type today, arriving on a flight from Glasgow, later departing for Nice. The next evening it arrived at 1811 from Montpellier, departing again for Glasgow. After first rejecting an idea to develop the Grumman Widgeon as an executive transport, the company looked into producing an executive transport based on a turbine-powered variant of the naval utility transport, the Grumman TF-1 Trader. They had already determined that any new aircraft would have to be turboprop-powered, and the Rolls-Royce Dart engine was chosen. Further studies indicated that the Trader-based design would not sell, and they needed an all new design with a low-wing and room to stand up in the cabin. In June 1957 the design of G-159 was finalised, and Grumman started selling slots on the production line at $10,000 each. The initial customers worked with Grumman on the detailed design and avionics fit. The G-159 was named the Gulfstream, and the first aircraft registered, N701G, took off from Bethpage, New York on its maiden flight on 14th August 1958. By the 2nd May 1959, the aircraft was awarded a type certificate by the Federal Aviation Administration. (Dave Jones)

23rd Fog affecting Leeds and Newcastle early and late in the day resulted in five BKS flights diverting to Ringway. They were Viscounts G-APNF (twice), G-APTA, G-AVIY and Britannia G-ANBK. Also during the evening was the second Air Spain Britannia to visit, when EC-BJF diverted in from Birmingham,
25th One of the more unusual first visits this month was Nord Noralpha F-BGGH, operating from/to Lille.
26th Dutch airline Schreiner Airways operated its final IT from Manchester today (F.27 PH-SAR), having previously announced their intention to withdraw from the charter market.
27th Group Captain Ken Wallis brought his Wallis 116 Gyrocopter G-ARZB to Ringway to publicise the latest James Bond film, 'You Only Live Twice'. After shooting up a few aircraft for the press, Captain Wallis found himself upside down! This was due to a gust of wind, coupled with the fact that he opened up too quick on the recently installed larger engine. The resultant damage was estimated to take 36 hours to repair at a cost of £500.
28th The only visit during 1967 by an Inex-Adria Douglas, was today's appearance of DC-6 YU-AFC, arriving at 1336 from Ljubljana, departing on 1st October to Maastricht.

OCTOBER 1967

The country became affected by a foot and mouth epidemic this month, chiefly centred on the Welsh border and Shropshire. Airlines such as Aer Lingus took no chances, laying out a 'disinfectant' mat at the foot of the steps of all their aircraft; a measure set out by the Minister of Agriculture to make sure the disease did not spread into Ireland.

Autumn mists and mellow fruitfulness - not this month anyway! October was dominated by low pressure bringing very wet weather with complex troughs and fronts regularly sweeping through the country. On the 16th, the day's rainfall exceeded 50mm in most parts, with widespread flooding in the Midlands. Gales were severe in places and continued into the 17th with thundery showers spreading to all areas when the wind changed to a northwesterly direction. Snow was reported as far south as Ringway itself. The month's temperature extremes saw 21°C at Southampton (8th) and a low of -7°C at Cairngorm (18th).

Lufthansa hoped to begin a weekday service from Ringway to Frankfurt in 1968, but these plans are late due the Vietnam War delaying deliveries of the Boeing 737. Also announced were two new holiday destinations from Ringway next year to Tunis (British Eagle) and Tenerife (Dan-Air).

Only one scheduled first with BEA (BE859): Comet SX-DAO (25th) and no equipment changes. The GCA/ILS traffic was dominated by Woodford traffic again, Varig HS.748 (13th/20th), Philippine Airlines HS.748 PI-C1015 (20th) & RAF Nimrod XV147 (24th) and more RAF VC-10s: XR810 (24th), XV104 (3rd) & XV105 (12th).

1st Aer Lingus began using flight numbers for ATC purposes, rather than the aircraft registration.

1st A Lufthansa aircraft made a rare visit today, when B.707F D-ABUI (also 6th/15th) arrived at 2125 (LH971R from New York), en route to Frankfurt to uplift some extra cargo. All flights were on charter to the 3M Corporation, originally destined to operate into Birmingham but Lufthansa preferred to use Manchester. Also today was another visit by Air India, but different to their recent visits, B.707 VT-DVA (AI103B/102A) operated from/to Bombay via Rome.

2nd Cessna 172 Skyhawk PH-RPA arrived from Lympne for modifications and overhaul with Northern Executive. It made a local flight on 4th November and departed back to Lympne the following day. Another Cessna 172, PH-RPL, arrived from Lympne on 30th October for overhaul, departing on 2nd November. Both aircraft were operated by the Dutch police.

2nd HS.125 G-AVAI paid a visit today on a flight from Heathrow, on demonstration to Granada TV who operated Dove G-ARFZ. This was the first of four visits before it was sold in late-1968 as LN-NPA. However, it returned four years later when it was purchased by engineering company Brown & Root. It became an elusive visitor to Ringway thereafter, until it was sold again in 1980.

3rd The first of two new Falcon 20s to visit Ringway during 1967 was F-BNRE. It was operated by Dassault Aviation until early-1969, when it was sold to Fred Olsen as LN-FOD. The second, F-BOOA, operated by Europe Falcon Service, visited on 2nd November 1967 from/to Le Bourget.

6th TIA DC-8 N8961T brought the heaviest load to date into Ringway. Arriving at 0707, with 249 passengers and 12 crew from Salt Lake City via a fuel stop at Toronto, it was returning a party of Manchester Mormons from a conference there.

9th Formerly G-ATGK, Vargas Aviation Dove F-BORJ arrived from Le Bourget at 2059, and stayed until the 11th. It operated in France until 1975, when it was restored as G-ATGK with Fairflight Charter.

18th One of the more unusual weather diversions during 1967 was 1934-built Leopard Moth G-ACMA, which arrived at 1027 from Cranwell as a Coventry diversion. Another 'geriatric' visitor was 1948-vintage Miles Messenger G-AKKG (30th), which made the trip north from its base at Leavesden.

20th Uplifting newspapers in the early hours were Autair Ambassadors G-ALZV & G-ALZZ and British United Bristol 170 G-AMLP, all operating from/to Luton. The following morning the operation was repeated, this time with Autair HS.748s G-ATMI & G-ATMJ.

21st Apart from the Dutch Cessnas, some other foreign light aircraft making their first visits were PA-23 Aztec LN-NPD today, PA-23 Aztec HB-LDL (22nd) & Beech 55 HB-GCL (24th).

26th HS.125 HB-VAT arrived at 1106 on a short round-trip from Hawarden. On the 20th November another Swiss-registered HS.125, HB-VAY, night-stopped from Heathrow. Both aircraft were first visits. A third Swiss HS.125, HB-VAN (11th November), arrived from Hawarden to clear customs prior to its departure back to Cologne.

5th October 1967 - Douglas C-54 EI-APK made its first to visit to Ringway, but it is seen here departing on a positioning flight to Liverpool, having arrived on a charter from Ostend. Earlier this year, Aer Turas won a contract to operate cargo flights for Alitalia until their Douglas DC-9Fs were delivered. EI-APK made its last visit in February 1970, before eventually being sold as N6304D. It arrived at Malta in February 1977 for storage, but never flew again and ended its days on the fire dump during 1985. (Geoff Ball)

15th October 1967 - Operated by Martinair since 1966, seen making a smoky start is Martinair Dakota PH-SCC, with BKS Viscount G-AVED & Dan-Air Ambassador G-AMAH in the background. Having been operated by the airline since March 1966, PH-SCC was making its final visit on a flight from Amsterdam to Belfast. In 1970, it was sold to Delta Air Transport as OO-AVG. (Graham Davies)

22nd October – Apart from the RAF aircraft frequenting the ILS for training, the only other British military movement during the month was Royal Navy Devon C.1 XK896, operating from/to Exeter. (Geoff Ball)

NOVEMBER 1967

BEA plans to operate a weekly scheduled flight between Manchester-Gibraltar have been turned down. They also announced that their fleet of Super 1-11s will be maintained at Manchester. The Trident 1 aircraft currently being looked after by BEA Ringway would then be maintained at Glasgow.

With the ongoing month-by-month increase in cargo operations at Manchester, BOAC opened an extension of its existing cargo warehouse, formerly the old 613sq ft hangar attached to the original terminal. At an additional cost of £23,000, an extra 8,000sq.ft was added to the existing 5,400sq.ft of the export section and 1,850sq.ft to the import area. The official opening was Tuesday 12th December.

The unsettled, stormy and cold weather from October carried on into the first week. From the 9th-14th, high pressure covered much of the UK bringing sunny but increasingly fog, preceded by colder weather lasting until around the 24th. It was foggy on the 20th/21st in northern and central England. Ringway was badly affected, particularly during the latter part of November. BEA alone diverted over fifty flights to Liverpool during this period. The last week of the month brought a return to wet and windy weather. The month's temperature extremes saw 16°C at Dartford (11th) and a low of -8°C at Caldecott (18th).

International flights were operated during the winter as follows:

AIR FRANCE – Three-times-weekly to Paris with SE.210s.

AER LINGUS - Amsterdam (2 x weekly), Copenhagen (2 x weekly), Cork (2 x weekly), Dusseldorf (2 x weekly), Frankfurt (2 x weekly) & Zurich (1 x weekly), all by BAC 1-11s except for Cork (Viscount).

BEA – International services to Amsterdam/Brussels/Copenhagen/Dublin/Dusseldorf/ Paris & Zurich.

BOAC - New York daily (BA538/7) with SVC-10s, from 10th Dec. extends to serve Antigua & Barbados. Montreal (2 x weekly) & Toronto (3 x weekly) with B.707s, routing via Prestwick. Cargo flight (BA065 Montreal/New York) five-weekly with B.707s, also inbound Monday flight (BA068) from New York.

KLM - Operated to Amsterdam three-weekly with Electras/DC-9s. Cargo flights continue five-weekly with DC-7s to Amsterdam via LHR (KL019/020).

SABENA - The night-stopping Brussels service continued four-times-weekly with SE.210 Caravelles. Cargo flights operated four-weekly f/t Brussels, with the outbound via Heathrow (3 x B.727s & 1 x DC-7).

SAS - Continued twice weekly serving Copenhagen with SE.210s (SK537/8), which also extends onwards to Dublin.

SWISSAIR - Cargo flights continued a three-weekly service to Zurich with Douglas DC-4s. From the 16th December, a once-weekly passenger flight to Zurich (SR844/5) was introduced with Douglas DC-9s.

Only one scheduled first visit again this month was KLM (KL151): DC-9 PH-DNF (28th) and just one equipment change was Sabena (SN623): DC-6 OO-CTK (13th).

GCA/ILS traffic, more HS.748s on test from Woodford was Varig PP-VDN (3rd/8th/9th/10th/13th) and Philippine Airlines PI-C1016 (20th) & PI-C1017 (17th). Also during the month were RAF VC-10s XV104 (22nd) & XV105 (17th), HS.125s G-AWVA (15th) & G-AVDX (22nd) and finally Gulf 1 G-ASXT (20th).

1st November 1967 - Charrington United Breweries Piaggio P.166 G-ARUJ was a regular visitor from March 1962 until its final visit on 24th March 1971. It was sold the following month in April 1971, but officially withdrawn by 1972. In September 1972, its fuselage was spotted on a piece of waste ground in Ancoats, Gtr Manchester, complete with the wings and the engines dumped next to it! (Graham Davies)

4th Not a common airline to Manchester, but Lloyd International operated a freight flight to Malta with Britannia G-AOVP. Another airline operating a cargo flight was Norwegian-outfit Polaris Air Transport who used Dakota LN-RTO (7th) outbound to Kristiansand. Polaris also operated a passenger charter (22nd) with CV-240 LN-KAP f/t Bergen.

7th Twelve months after Swissair introduced the type onto services from Manchester, KLM introduced their Douglas DC9s (PH-DNB today) on their Amsterdam service (KL151/2). The passenger service now operates three-times-weekly, once with DC-9s and Electras on the other two flights. By April 1968, the Electra had been completely replaced by DC-9s, and the service upgraded to weekdays (KL153/4).

8th This month's foreign light aircraft contingent making first their visits were Beech 90 D-ILMO today, Commander 680 HB-GBW (16th) undertaking several flights to/from Coal Aston on behalf of United Steel and Beech 55 D-IHPA (27th).

13th British Eagle BAC 1-11 G-ATPJ (EG2563) left for Dubrovnik carrying Manchester United for their European Cup second round first leg game with Saravejo, which ended 0-0. The return leg took place at Old Trafford on the 29th which United won 2-1. The Yugoslavian side arrived at Manchester on a BEA flight from Heathrow.

14th Another first visit of type was today's arrival of the single-engined Aero Commander 200 N2965T. Available at a 'fly-away' price of around £17,000, this aircraft was operated by Atlantic Commander Ltd and based at Gatwick and would later become G-AWYH.

14th Shorts Skyvan G-ASCO arriving at 1433 today from Birmingham was also a first visit of type. The aircraft was on a demonstration tour of the UK, departing for Heathrow at 1702.

15th November 1967 - All-Air Douglas C-54s & DC-4s would operate Lufthansa's cargo service to Frankfurt until 24th January 1970, when they would operate in their own right with their B.737-200QCs. (Geoff Ball)

15th The second Fred Olsen DC-6F visit, was LN-FOM, on a cargo flight from Copenhagen to Prague.

18th Aer Lingus operated a mass exodus of newspaper flights to Dublin, rerouted to operate through Manchester due to fog at Liverpool, so they were not technically diversions. Aircraft used were Viscounts EI-AOL (EI924/5 & EI934/5), EI-AJJ (EI926/7), EI-AOG (EI928/9) & EI-AOM (EI930/1).

20th The airport was closed to arrivals and departures for over twelve hours during the day. By the evening the fog had lifted enough to allow seven departures, but still no arrivals.

22nd CAA HS.125 G-AVDX performed an ILS and overshoot on test from Hawarden. It had returned to the Hawker Siddeley factory earlier in the year for modification to Cat.2 instrument standard. In early-1968, it went on lease to Ferranti at Edinburgh for black-box flight trials, but would not appear at Ringway again until November 1970.

23rd Air Ferry DC-4F G-ARWI, leased from Lloyd International, arrived from Manston and stayed for two days before returning there. It returned to Lloyd in October 1968 and was sold on to the Nigerian Air Force, who operated it until its withdrawal in 1974.

26th Since the first visit of a Piper PA-28 Cherokee to Ringway in October 1961, numerous aircraft had visited since. However, today saw the first visit of an uprated aircraft, with the appearance of Piper PA-28R-180 Cherokee Arrow G-AVXF. With its improved Lycoming engine and retractable landing gear, it arrived at 1431 from Oxford during a round of demonstration flights at airfields around the UK. The following day it made ten 'local' flights before leaving later for Leavesden.

DECEMBER 1967

It was generally sunny, but frost became widespread and severe at night. Snow spread to all areas by the morning of the 9th and snow lay up to twenty inches deep in Wales. This lasted until the 11th when mild Atlantic air moved in. A fresh outbreak of northerly winds from the 15th to the 21st produced cold and sunny weather in between. The last week was cold with rain and snow. The month's temperature extremes saw 14°C at Durham (1st) and a low of -13°C at Wallingford (8th).

Scheduled first visits this month were KLM (KL151): DC-9 PH-DNE (19th), Swissair (SR844): DC-9 HB-IFE (30th) & HB-IFF (16th). There were no equipment changes during December.

This month's GCA/ILS traffic was RAE Viscount XR801 (5th) HS.748s PP-VDO (21st) & PI-C1018 (28th) and British Midland Viscount G-AVJB (28th).

195

3rd Canadian Air Force Dakota 10911 arrived at 1331 from Lahr, en route to Prestwick, while on the 30th, USAF Convair T-29B 51-7899 arrived at 1719 from Lakenheath and departed to RAF Northolt.

7th Dove CN-MBB arrived at 1226 from Hawarden to clear customs, prior to its delivery to the Moroccan government. As if that wasn't enough, another Moroccan Dove, CN-MBA, arrived on the 10th from Casablanca via Bordeaux, eventually bound for Hawarden for maintenance. Both aircraft were attached to the King's executive fleet.

8th This month was much better for diversions, but not as good as previous Decembers. Heavy snow across the country had closed Heathrow during the morning. Diversions to Manchester included the first visit of a SAS Douglas DC-9, with the arrival of LN-RLS at 1116 (SK501 from Heathrow). Others were KLM Electras PH-LLD (KL101 from Rotterdam) & PH-LLC (KL119 from Amsterdam) and BOAC flights G-APFB (BA692 from Bermuda), G-APFH (BA500 from New York), G-ARVH (BA118 from Frankfurt), G-ASGG (BA506 from New York) & G-ASGH (BA568 from Montreal).

11th HS.125 D-COMI arrived at 0947 from Dusseldorf. Eventually bound for maintenance at Hawarden, it dropped in for pre-customs clearance. It appeared on the 13th from Hawarden, again to clear customs before returning to Cologne.

13th Late evening fog produced three more Heathrow diversions, BEA Trident G-ARPD, Pan American B.707 N717PA at 2155 (PA100 from New York) & Balair DC-4F HB-ILU at 2347 (SR868 from Zurich).

14th Britten-Norman Islander demonstrator G-AVUB arrived at 1528 from Bembridge. It made quick local flight, before leaving again for Southampton. This aircraft would operate for Rolls-Royce, Herts & Essex Aero Club and Ford-based Miles Aviation, until its sale as OO-ARI in June 1971.

15th Pacific Western L-100 CF-PWO made its first visit today from Edmonton, leaving later with a consignment of cargo bound for Prague. It made four more visits before it was written off on 16th July 1969, after an attempted landing in low-lying mist at Cayaya, Peru. The starboard wing hit the ground and broke off and the aircraft veered off the runway. The cause of the accident was blamed on pilot error for landing in adverse weather conditions, and on the lack of specialised ATC staff at the airport.

16th Two pre-Christmas charters were World Airways B.707 N368WA outbound to New York, with the return flight on 14th January with B.707 N376WA; and Braathens F.27 LN-SUE arriving for a charter to Oslo, with the return flight on the 15th January with F.27 LN-SUA.

18th More fog provided Ringway with further diversions. This time it was Liverpool, Birmingham and Castle Donington's turn to be affected. However, there was nothing of interest amongst the nine arrivals, which were mainly BEA & British Midland flights.

21st Further snow at Heathrow brought in three BEA Trident flights within fifteen minutes of each other. Arriving this afternoon were G-ARPI (from Madrid), G-ARPS (from Milan) & G-ARPZ (from Copenhagen).

22nd The first Bell 206 Jet Ranger for Ferranti, G-AVSN, made its first visit today, arriving from Gatwick at 1526. It made two return trips to Knutsford and was a frequent visitor throughout 1968 and 1969.

FIRST/LAST ARRIVALS & DEPARTURES 1967

First arrival: BEA Vanguard G-APEG from Belfast @ 0115
First departure: BEA Vanguard G-APEG to Heathrow @ 0821
Last arrival: BEA Viscount G-APEX from Heathrow @ 2220
Last departure: BEA Viscount G-AOYG to Belfast @ 2242

Airport Stats 1967 (+/- % on Previous Year)		
Scheduled Passengers	1,069,000,	-3.8%
Inclusive & Charter Passengers	340,000	+16.8%
Freight & Mail (Tonnes)	33,400	-0.9%
Movements	50,900	+2.0%

AIRPORT DIARY 1968

JANUARY 1968

Aer Lingus and BEA flights between Manchester and Dublin lost more than £70,000 in cancelled bookings from mid-December. Flights were operating at 25% their normal schedules because of an Irish government ban on travel to the country due to the foot-and-mouth outbreak.

British Midland were granted a licence to operate a network of domestic flights from Manchester to Birmingham, East Midlands, Leeds and Edinburgh during the month, but they were never taken up.

BEA reported they carried 50,000 fewer passengers during 1967 than the previous year. The airline cited two reasons; firstly the loss of passengers to package tour operators, secondly, the £50 travel allowance imposed on UK citizens travelling outside of the sterling area in July 1966, which the airline claimed put off would-be holidaymakers. They had also applied to increase fares on domestic routes by an average of 15%. During an Air Transport Licencing Enquiry, BEA said that if the increases were granted, they would operate in the mornings and evenings to help channel off holiday traffic, and leave more seats for business travellers during the day. The increases would also be an important step towards making their domestic routes financially successful.

Channel Airways had applications turned down twice, to operate a scheduled service to Malta. This month also saw their application to serve Tenerife and Las Palmas turned as well.

The year began rather cold with a trough of low pressure, accompanied by rain and snow. Milder weather arrived on the 4th across much of England, with parts of Devon reaching 14°C during the afternoon. This contrasted with near freezing conditions in southern Scotland and northern England, where a foot of snow covered the lower hills. Mild and wet weather lasted until the 8th, when easterly winds brought heavy snow to the Midlands and central England. The 13th - 18th marked more wet, windy but mild weather, which changed again the following day when high pressure took control. Fog was a problem, persisting all day on the 23rd, but milder and wetter weather returned, lasting until the end of January. The month's temperature extremes saw 14°C at Winnington (14th) and a low of -14°C at Cromer (13th).

Scheduled first visits this month were Lufthansa (LH942): All-Air Douglas C-54 D-ADAD (2nd) and KLM (KL151): DC-9 PH-DNH (2nd). The only equipment changes involved BEA who used the following Viscounts on a number of European flights, G-AOHM (31st), G-APEY (29th) & G-APKF (25th).

GCA/ILS traffic noted during the month was British Midland Viscounts G-AVJA (2nd/17th) & G-AVJB (15th), Varig HS.748 PP-VDP (12th/26th), RAF VC-10 XV103 (16th) and Andover XS647 (19th). For the first time in many months, BOAC operated a training flight, B.707 G-APFD (29th).

7th Two youths stowed away aboard an evening Belfast-bound BEA Viscount. They were eventually flown back to Manchester and came down the aircraft steps with coats over their faces. They were then whisked away in a police van to the airport police station, where they were detained for several hours. They were only discovered hiding in a cloakroom, when aircraft cleaners boarded the plane at Belfast to prepare it for the return flight.

9th Thirteen diversions generated over £2,000 worth of landing fees, when heavy snow affected the southeast. The majority were from either BEA or BOAC, but foreign airlines included Swissair CV-990 HB-ICE at 1021 (SR800 from Zurich) & DC-9 HB-IFF at 1135 (SR810 from Geneva) and Olympic Airways Comet SX-DAO at 1614 (from Athens). Finally, SAS DC-9 SE-DBZ made its first visit at 1132 (SK501 from Copenhagen).

11th British Air Ferries Carvair G-ASHZ positioned from Southend to operate the much delayed Swissair cargo flight to Zurich (SR847). It returned on the 13th from Zurich operating inbound SR846.

12th Ringway has been used for several years for the delivery of varying sizes of Cessnas, but today the airport saw the first foreign registered light aircraft to do so. Cessna 421 F-BOXS, which arrived at 1409 from Reykjavik, night-stopped before continuing its flight onwards to Toussus-Le Noble.

17th Today's visit of Army Air Corps Beaver XP826 (Army 333 from Old Sarum) was the first of four flights during 1968, all first visits. The others were XP805 (29th July), XP820 (21st June) & XP825 (26th June). A couple more Army Air Corps aircraft making first visits this month were Sioux XT560 (29th) en route from Worcester to Warton & XT152 (31st) en route from Liverpool to Leeds as 'Army Air 148'.

19th Beech 65 F-BOOL was the first of two foreign light aircraft making their first visits this month. The other was Beech 80 F-BMSM (22nd), a Birmingham diversion.

21st After plenty of appearances on training flights, today saw the first RAF VC-10 to land at Ringway, when XV105 arrived at 1027 (RR2108 from Nicosia) due to fog at Brize Norton. The Royal Air Force VC-10s differed from standard VC-10s in several ways. A large freight door was fitted on the port side, the cabin floor was strengthened for military loads and an auxiliary power unit was fitted to enable operations away from normal VC-10 routes. The radio and navigation equipment were designed for "off-airways" regions and there was also provision for in-flight refuelling. These aircraft would be used primarily as troop carriers, capable of carrying up to 150 passengers.

23rd January 1968 – DH.Heron 2 G-ARTI made regular appearances throughout the 1960s. Its first visit was on 28th March 1961, and it's last on 23rd December 1969, before being sold in 1970 to Air Paris as F-BRSK. It was operated by Bristol-based E.S. & A Robinson, a UK paper, printing and packaging company who merged with John Dickinson Stationery in 1996, and became the Dickinson Robinson Group (DRG - hence the tail titles). They were responsible for such products as 'Sellotape' & 'Basildon Bond'. (Geoff Ball)

31st Dragon Rapide G-AJSL arrived at 1340 from Farnborough for a protracted stay at Manchester. After a one hour test-flight on the 12th May 1968, it finally departed for Birmingham on the 19th May.

FEBRUARY 1968

In less than three years, BOAC Cargo trebled its cargo out of Manchester. When the airline increased the frequency of their Montreal/New York flight up to three-times-weekly in April 1965, the service was being operated by a leased CL-44 from Seaboard World, and then Flying Tiger CL-44s. Around 100 tonnes a month was being handled at Manchester, with the ratio of cargo being 90-10 towards Canada. However, they were now handling around 300 tonnes a month, since the introduction of the B.707F, and the ratio of cargo for Canada and the USA was now evenly split 50-50.

For two shillings each (around 10p in today's money), you could buy a bottle of beer and a cheese sandwich from the airport's buffet. At this time the average salary for an information desk assistant was around £800 per annum!

February was at its most interesting during the first half of the month. When rain quickly turned to snow on the 4th, many roads in Scotland and northern England were blocked, with snow drifting in places as cold fronts moved across the country. Snow lay 15cm deep over much of Scotland, and up to 10cm in parts of northern England. Frost was widespread and temperatures as low as -8°C were recorded as far apart as Bournemouth and Eskdalemuir. During the next four days, the British Isles was covered by a complex area of low pressure. A snowfall of twelve to eighteen inches in parts of the Midlands on the 6th caused considerable disruption to traffic. The persistent cloud cover broke on the evening of the 7th, when night fog and frost became widespread. Freezing fog persisted in parts of central and northwest England throughout the 8th. The low pressure gradually drifted away, when it became less cold, with rain at times but mainly sunny. The latter part of the month was a mix of cold temperatures and sunny periods, but the last few days brought milder weather in from the Atlantic. The month's temperature extremes saw 13°C at Boxworth (14th) and a low of -12°C at Moor House (16th).

Scheduled first visits this month were BOAC (BA538): SVC-10 G-ASGL (22nd) and KLM (KL151): DC-9 PH-DNC (13th). Equipment changes again involved BEA, who replaced Tridents with Viscounts on several European flights, G-AOHM (1st) & G-AOYH (23rd) and also Swissair (SR846): Air Ferry C-54 G-ASFY (23rd/24th/28th).

February's appalling weather severely restricted GCA/ILS traffic this month. Noted were Philippine Airlines HS.748 PI-C1019 (16[2th]), RAF VC-10 XR810 (19th) and British Midland Viscount G-AVJA (26th).

3rd This morning's New York flight was terminated at Prestwick, when SVC-10 G-ASGI (BA538) got stuck in mud after managing to run off the main runway at Prestwick, which closed the airport for several hours.

4th Pembroke WV741 arriving at 1328 today (EAV 55 from Newquay), leaving later for Upavon, was the only RAF visitor during the month.

8th After a night of severe frost and freezing fog, temperatures at Ringway failed to rise above -2°C all day, preventing any arrivals before 1347.

9th Cambrian Airways began using flight numbers for ATC purposes, rather than the aircraft's registration.

10th A tightening up of procedures regarding the recording of aircraft movements by airport controllers began today. From now on, only the official aircraft type designator is referred to, for example, no longer will the Trident be referred to as 'Trid', but as the 'HS21'. Other slack examples were 'Dove' (now HS04) and 'Argosy' (now HS65)!

10th Beech 90 D-IBMA was a first visit, operating f/t Cologne. Also on the 25th was Italian PA-23 Aztec I-NEMJ arriving at 1815 from Le Bourget. It stayed for two days before departing for Castle Donington.

12th Falcon 20 D-CBAT, arriving at 0820 today from Cologne, was the first of six new Falcon 20s to visit Ringway during 1968. It operated on the German register until 1971, when it was sold to Omni Investments in December 1971 as N5CA.

19th Gatwick was badly affected by snow throughout the day, but produced no diversions. Liverpool was also affected by heavy snow, particularly during the afternoon, but aircraft were confined to Cambrian, British Eagle Viscounts and Dan-Air Dakotas G-AMPP & G-AMSU. Finally USAF MC-131 0-25790 arriving at 1552 from Prestwick, had also been prevented from landing at Liverpool, but it was actually flight-planned to be operated through Manchester.

20th Another fog affected day, with no arrivals prior to 1541. KLM DC-8F PH-DCS called in at 2357 (KL9270 from New York) to pick up freight from the cancelled KL019/020 flight and another KLM DC-8, PH-DCW (28th) diverted in at 0237 (KL674 from Montreal) due to fog at Amsterdam.

21st Dakota OO-AUX was the last of its type to be used by Sabena on their cargo flights out of Manchester. Since the airline introduced scheduled freight flights in April 1963, ten different Douglas DC-3s were used over the next five years. The aircraft used and their final visit dates to Ringway were:

OO-AUX - 21st Feb 1968	OO-AUY - 22nd Mar 1966	OO-AUZ - 7th Oct 1965
OO-AWG - 23rd Jun 1965	OO-AWK - 7th Sep1967	OO-AWM - 3rd Oct 1967
OO-AWN - 5th Oct 1967	OO-AWZ - 22nd Aug 1967	OO-CBU - 29th Jun 1967
OO-CBW - 27th Jul 1967		

23rd Airviews resident Auster G-AOBV returned from Rearsby, where it had a fresh coat of paint and its registration enlarged. Obviously pleased with the result, Bruce Martin the owner of Airviews did some local flying, culminating with a Precision Approach to runway 06. Strict procedure was followed by the controller, who calmly came on saying "Bravo Victor, do not acknowledge any further instructions, check your wheels down and welded!" However, this last remark did not draw any response. The standard reply would normally have been "Wheels down and locked".

23rd A first visit of type today was EP.9 Prospector G-ARTU at 1520 for a thirty minute stay from/to Barton. In 1954, Edgar Percival formed Edgar Percival Aircraft Limited at Stapleford aerodrome. His original company had become part of the Hunting Group and his first new design was the Edgar Percival P.9, a utility aircraft designed for agricultural use. It was a high-wing monoplane, with an unusual pod and boom fuselage. The pod and boom design allowed the aircraft to be fitted with a hopper for crop spraying. The pilot and one passenger sat together with room for four more passengers. The clamshell side and rear doors also allowed the aircraft to carry standard size wool, straw bales, oil drums or even livestock. Even when the hopper was fitted, a ground crew of three could be carried when moving between sites. The prototype (G-AOFU) first flew on 21st December 1955. After a demonstration tour of Australia, four aircraft were ordered as crop sprayers and an initial batch of twenty were built. Two aircraft were bought by the British Army in 1958 (XM797 & XM819). In the same year, Salmesbury Engineering Limited acquired the rights to the design and the company was renamed the Lancashire Aircraft Company, who renamed the aircraft the Lancashire Prospector EP.9. However, only six more were ever built. The two aircraft with the British Army were struck off charge and sold during 1961. XM797, which became G-ARTU made its only visit to Ringway today, as on the 6th September 1969, it crashed on takeoff at Old Warden. The other aircraft, XM819, was once owned during the late-1960s by a gang of international smugglers, who found it the ideal way to smuggle stolen furs and counterfeit Swiss francs between England and Belgium. Although the criminals were apprehended in 1969, the EP.9 ended up for sale in Belgium in 1972. Two more EP.9s to visit Ringway were G-AOZO (12th May 1973) & G-APXW (four visits during 1973).

28th British Eagle BAC 1-11 G-ATPJ (EG2563) left for Dubrovnik carrying Manchester United for their European Cup second round first leg game with Saravejo, which ended 0-0. The return leg took place at Old Trafford on the 29th which United won 2-1. The Yugoslavian side arrived at Manchester on a BEA flight from Heathrow.

MARCH 1968

As part of the celebrations planned to mark the 50th anniversary next year of the historic transatlantic flight by Alcock and Brown, it was announced that a replica Vickers Vimy would go on show. Built at a cost of £30,000, it will fly from Wisley and put on display from the 13th June to the 14th July. The public would be charged one shilling to see it.

An anti-cyclone to the west and southwest of the British Isles dominated the weather pattern until the 12th. From then until the 25th the weather was generally cyclonic in character, after which the country was split, high pressure in the south and low pressure in the north. It was particularly wet on the 26th when rainfall exceeded 100mm in many places and up to 165mm in some places in Scotland. Yet in most of England, southerly winds brought unusually high temperatures for the time of year. On the 29th, East Dereham recorded a maximum of almost 24.9°C almost equalling the highest previously recorded March temperature for the UK.

Scheduled first visits this month were Swissair (SR844): DC-9s HB-IFG (23rd) & HB-IFH (16th). Equipment changes were confined to Swissair (SR846): Air Ferry Douglas C-54 G-ASFY (2nd/6th/9th/13th/15th/16th).

The month's GCA/ILS traffic was Woodford-heavy again, with four different HS.748s, Philippine Airlines PI-C1019 (6th), Varig PP-VDR (12th/19th/21st), Lan Chile CC-CEG (29th) & Hawker Siddeley G-AVZD (12th/25th). Also RAF Comet XR396 (6th) and British Midland Viscounts G-AVJA (12th) & G-AVJB (25th/27th).

5th Enstrom F-28 G-AVUK, which arrived at 1216 from Staverton, later leaving on pipeline patrol survey work, was a first visit of type. This small, light piston-engined helicopter was given FAA type certification in April 1965. It used Lycoming piston engines, virtually identical to those found in general aviation fixed-wing aircraft. Operated by Twyford Moor Helicopters of Southampton, G-AVUK would eventually be operated by several companies before it was written off at Thruxton in December 1975.

11th The West German Air Force had recently undergone a change in their unit markings. The first aircraft of such to Ringway was today's visit of Noratlas 53+13. Arriving at 1002 from Ahlhorn, it departed for Erding.

12th British Eagle Britannia G-AOVN (EG3388) departed for Krakow with Manchester United for their European Cup quarter-final second leg game with Gornik Zabre. The first leg at Old Trafford took place on 28th February, which United won 2-0. Although United lost the second leg 1-0, it was enough to see them through into the semi-finals where Real Madrid awaited them. Also operating today was an outbound fans' charter to Krakow, operated by Britannia Airways Britannia G-ANBA.

2nd March 1968 – Lloyd International Britannia G-AOVS is seen here having recently arrived from Stansted, awaiting its cargo. It departed the following morning for Istanbul. Bought by IAS in January 1973, it later served with Redcoat until its withdrawal in October 1979 and was later broken up. The fuselage, however, still exists on the fire dump at Luton. (Bob Thorpe)

4th March 1968 - KLM operated several inbound freight flights from New York during the month. DC-8F PH-DCW is seen here having recently arrived as KL9272. (Geoff Ball)

12th Philips operated two outbound flights to Eindhoven today, both departing within ten minutes of each other. Beech 65 PH-ILS and Falcon 20 PH-LPS were used, with the latter making its first visit. This registration had previously been used by their Beech 18, which was sold at the end of 1965.

12th Hawker Siddeley HS.748 G-AVZD, which made its first flight last month, made the first of two ILS approaches this month today (also 25th). Next month it was used as a certification aircraft for Rolls-Royce Dart 8 engines for tropical trials at Asmara. Development trials on the aircraft ended this June, after which it was modified to standard RAAF fit and handed over to the RAAF at Woodford in August (1968). Ferried via Athens, New Delhi, Bangkok, Singapore, Denpasar, Darwin & Alice Springs, A10-601 arrived at the RAAF School of Air Navigation, East Sale, in September 1968. It served until its withdrawal from service in January 2004, and was preserved with the RAAF Museum at Point Cook on the 20th January 2004.

13th A variety of first time visiting foreign lights this month were Beech Marquis F-BLLR on a round-trip from Le Bourget today, Jodel DR.1050 EI-ARW & Beech 55 OY-DPZ (both 26th) and Beech 90 F-BFRE (27th).

14th Former South African Air Force Heron G-ASUY made the first of three visits in as many weeks today, arriving from East Midlands. Operated by Keegan Aviation since July 1964, it was sold to Puerto Rico-based Prinair as N554PR in April 1968.

15th RAF visitors had been thin on the ground in previous months, but March month produced four. Three of these arriving today were Comet C.4 XR397 (JRQ 46) at 1006 f/t RAF Lyneham which was also a first visit; Pembroke WV733 at 1733 (LBR 01) f/t White Waltham; and Devon C.2 VP968 (EQU 40) at 1857 from Leavesden, departing to RAF Bovingdon. The fourth arriving from White Waltham on the 29th was Pembroke WV735 (LLZ 02), which departed for Liverpool.

17th One of Hawker Siddeley's HS.125 demonstrators, G-AVOI, arrived at 2104 from Keflavik on its first visit. It left the following morning for Luton. It had been used by the Daily Express on a recent 'JET-SELL' mission to North America. It would be purchased by Trust House Forte in 1969, and make many more visits to Ringway until its sale in 1980.

18th KLM Electra PH-LLL departed on a wet Manchester afternoon on its final visit. The airline operated the Lockheed Electra for the final time on 29th March, with PH-LLD in charge. From April 1968, the service was upgraded to a five-weekly DC-9 operation.

23rd Aer Lingus Viscount EI-AOM made its final visit today, operating EI720/1 from/to Cork (1807/1844). The following morning on a flight from Cork to Heathrow (EI712) it crashed off the coast of Ireland thirty minutes into its flight, killing all onboard.

23rd Aer Lingus operated another mass exodus of newspaper flights to Dublin. Like the previous occasion this happened, the flights were rerouted to operate through Manchester. Aircraft used were the following Viscounts, EI-APD (EI920/1 & EI930/1), EI-AMA (EI924/5), EI-AOJ (EI926/7), EI-AOH (EI928/9) & EI-AOE (EI932/3).

29th The second French-registered Dove to visit Manchester, was F-BGOA, arriving at 1508 today from Castle Donington, departing later for Gatwick.

30th Cessna 337 G-AWCI arrived at 1202 from Shannon on its delivery flight. In keeping with all the other UK Cessnas delivered through Ringway, it departed for Cranfield for Rogers Aviation.

31st Britannia Airways began their summer programme with an outbound flight to Palma by Britannia G-ANBA. Aircraft used this year were G-ANBA/ANBD/ANBE/ANBF/ANBI/ANBJ/ANBL/ANBN & G-ANBO. Two of these worth mentioning are G-ANBD and G-ANBN, which were leased from BKS and Laker Airways respectively for the summer season, due to the late arrival of the airline's Boeing 737s.

APRIL 1968

Caledonian ordered three BAC 1-11-500s for use next year, operating direct from Manchester, Gatwick and Prestwick to a wide range of destinations in the Mediterranean and North Africa, on behalf of Global Tours, one of the country's largest tour operators.

The first week was mainly dull and wet but became colder with periods of sleet or snow and severe night frosts. From the 6th, pressure began to rise giving generally cold, dry and sunny weather. From the 15th-22nd, frontal troughs crossed the country bringing warm but unsettled weather with scattered thunderstorms, heavy at times. The month ended on a showery note, but the last two days were cold and very wet. On the 29th, RAF Brawdy recorded nearly 50mm of rain. The month's temperature extremes saw 26°C at Camden Square (21st) and a low of -11°C at Great Dun Fell (2nd).

6th April 1968 - Representing a new West German Air Force visitor type to Ringway was Convair CV-440 12+01, arriving to night-stop on a return flight to Cologne. It's seen in the April sunshine about to depart. Purchased in 1962, it served with the German military until 1973, when it was sold as N5DG. (Geoff Ball)

8th April 1968 - For the 1968 summer season, Dan-Air had a more extensive Comet programme, serving destinations previously unattainable by their Ambassadors, which were becoming infrequent visitors. G-APDK which arrived in the early hours from Palma, day-stopped before departing for Barcelona shortly before midnight. Also used during the summer were G-APDJ & G-APDO. (Graham Davies)

International flights were operated during the summer as follows:

AER LINGUS - Amsterdam (3 x weekly), Copenhagen (2 x weekly), Cork (up to 4 x weekly), Dusseldorf (3 x weekly), Frankfurt (3 x weekly) & Zurich (1 x weekly), all except Cork operated by BAC 1-11s. Shannon also operated up to three-weekly during the summer months with Viscounts.

AIR FRANCE - Three-weekly to Paris with SE.210s, increasing to six-weekly between July and September.

BEA - Operated Amsterdam/Brussels/Copenhagen/Dublin/Dusseldorf/Paris & Zurich with summer routes to Barcelona, Malta & Palma. Inclusive tour flights operated to Barcelona & Palma.

BOAC - Daily to New York via Prestwick (BA538/7) with SVC-10s, extending to Antigua & Barbados on Fri/Sat/Sun. Montreal & Toronto served five-weekly and daily from June with B.707s, routing via Prestwick. Cargo flight (BA065 Montreal/New York) operates five-weekly with B.707s and also an inbound Monday flight (BA066) from New York.

IBERIA - 1st June-12th October, served Palma twice-weekly with SE.210 Caravelles, one via Barcelona.

KLM - Operated to Amsterdam five-times-weekly (KL153/4) with Douglas DC-9s. The DC-7 cargo flight (KL019/020) operated from/to Amsterdam five-weekly until the 30th August. This flight was replaced from the 3rd September when DC-9Fs operated AMS-GLA-MAN-AMS Tue-Sat (KL005).

LUFTHANSA - Operated their cargo flight twice-weekly to Dusseldorf/Frankfurt with All-Air Douglas C-54s. From the 4th September, Aer Turas Douglas C-54s took over the route, operating six-weekly (LH934/5).

SABENA - The night-stopping Brussels service continued four-times-weekly with SE.210 Caravelles. Cargo flights operated four-weekly with B.727s f/t Brussels, with the outbound via Heathrow (SN197/8).

SAS - Operated twice-weekly serving Copenhagen with SE.210s (SK537/8), which also extends onwards to Dublin. From the 5th June, this increased to three-weekly when a Sunday flight was added.

SWISSAIR - Cargo flights continued a three-weekly service to Zurich with Douglas DC-4s (SR846/7). Passenger flights operated twice weekly to Zurich with DC-9s between 4th April and 30th September. One of these flights also served Basle.

Scheduled first visits were Air France (AF960): SE.210 F-BOHA (29th) and KLM (KL153): DC-9s PH-DNG (4th), PH-DNI (1st), PH-DNK (9th) & PH-DNL (3rd). There were no equipment changes during April.

GCA/ILS traffic noted this month was Lan Chile HS.748 CC-CEG (1st) & Varig HS.748 PP-VDS (19th/22nd/26th). Ringway seems to be back in favour judging by the number of HS.125s during April, with G-AVHA (2nd), G-AVXL (2nd), F-BPMC (18th/22nd), HB-VBN (25th) & G-5-14 (26th), British Midland Viscounts G-AODG (4th), G-ASED (8th), & G-AVJB (9th) and a solitary RAF VC-10 XV106 (10th).

1st BEA began a weekday service today to Edinburgh with Viscounts. The new schedule aimed at businessmen, departs MAN (BE4820) at 0800 and returns at 2055 (BE4839).

1st The Hiller UH-12 helicopter was not a common visitor to Ringway, but this month saw two examples making first visits, operated by Twyford Moor Helicopters, G-AVKX (today) & G-AVKY (17th). Both helicopters were regular visitors to the area, frequently calling at Bramhall Oil Terminal in connection with pipeline patrols.

3rd All Air Douglas C-54 D-ADAC went tech on arrival operating cargo flight LH942 from Frankfurt. It was towed to the Manchester Agencies hangar, where the port outer engine received attention and departed to Nice five days later.

5th Delivery flights of new Cessnas continued with Cessna 402 G-AWDM arriving at 1402 from Shannon (Flo Air 987), departing an hour later for Rogers Aviation at Cranfield. It was the first Cessna 402 to visit, and the first UK-registered example. Since the first twin-engined Cessna was delivered through Ringway, (Cessna 411 G-ATEY in October 1965), most were delivered through Manchester thereafter due to the handling agents being based there They were also responsible for shipping the single-engined Cessnas, normally flown to a port in the United States, usually New Orleans. They were then dismantled and crated over to the docks at Manchester, where they would be transported by road to Cranfield.

5th Invicta began a series of flights f/t Rotterdam until the 16th May, with today's first being operated by Viscount G-AOCC. Others used were Viscount G-AOCB and Douglas C-54s G-ASEN/ASPM & ASPN.

5th British Eagle began their final summer programme from Ringway, with Britannia G-AOVG operating a return flight to Tunis via Birmingham (EG941/0). The following Britannias operated the bulk of their operation, G-AOVA/AOVC/AOVG/AOVK/AOVL/AOVN/ARKA/ARKB & ARXA. These were supplemented by flights by their BAC 1-11s, along with a weekly Viscount flight to/from Newquay.

20th April 1968 - The Beech 35 Bonanza with its signature V-tail made it one the most distinctive private aircraft in the sky. Along with its combination elevator-rudder called a 'ruddervator' and retractable landing gear, also made it one of the most efficient. N9014S arrived from Prestwick and stayed for two days, before departing to Andover. In comparison, the basic aircraft it was based on also paid a visit, when Beech 33 Debonair D-EKVI arrived from Stuttgart to clear customs en route to Leeds today. (Geoff Ball)

20th April 1968 – Transglobe's first Cl-44, G-AWDK seen here, was delivered to the airline on 1st March. Arriving this morning from Gatwick with British United VC-10 G-ATDJ, both were open for public viewing during the day. Formerly with Seaboard World, G-AWDK had undergone major modifications to enable it to operate as a 170-seat passenger aircraft, which included the fitting of numerous windows. (Geoff Ball)

25th April 1968 – CF-CDL Otter (ex 64-441) was one of three ex-Norwegian Air Force examples passing through today. This and the other two, CF-XIL (61-423) & CF-XJM (ex 5329), all arrived from Rotterdam en route for Shannon, New York and ultimately Manitoba. However, the departure of CF-CDL was delayed for two days due to a faulty engine, which was convenient as the pilot had friends in the area! (Geoff Ball)

30th April 1968 – Caledonian B.707 G-AVTW set a number of records today. Departing Manchester as CA743 with 186 passengers and 7 crew bound for Toronto, it flew direct in an incredible 6 hours 55 minutes. Apart from being the longest non-stop flight ever made by a jet from Ringway, it was also carrying the largest number of passengers direct to Canada in one aircraft. It was also the heaviest at 132 tonnes, 20 below the aircraft's maximum takeoff weight. Earlier, the 186 passengers had been piped aboard to mark the airline's first group charter with a Boeing 707 from the UK. The passengers from various parts of the country were all members of the National Overseas Association, each paying £60 10s for the flight and staying in Canada for four weeks. Caledonian's new Boeing 707-320C was an improved version on BOAC's Boeing 707-336s that have improved fan engines for better performance. (Geoff Ball)

10th PA-31 Navajo G-AVZT was a first visit of type, operated by Lancashire-based communications company Plessey. Arriving at 1013 from Stansted and departing to Liverpool, it would make numerous more visits during the year. The only other PA-31 appearing in 1968 was G-AWED (f/v - 4th October 1968), newly purchased by Whitbread.

13th Laker Airways began IT operations from Manchester with BAC 1-11 G-AVBW in charge of the first flight. Each Saturday a BAC 1-11 operated the rotation GK705 Gatwick-MAN-Palma and return, which continued until the 11th May, when a BAC 1-11 became based for the summer. Also from June, they would operate regular charters to New York throughout the summer with leased Boeing 707 G-AWDG.

14th Sabena routed two New York-Brussels flights this month, with B.707 OO-SJE today & OO-SJA (15th).

14th Caledonian began their summer programme with Britannia G-ATMA positioning from Gatwick to operate CA141 to Ibiza. This year they would also use their newly-delivered Boeing 707s (G-AVKA & G-AVTW) on transatlantic charters, along with their Bristol Britannias (G-AOVJ/ASTF/ATMA & ATNZ). Two aircraft used during 1967, G-AOVH & G-AOVI, were sold to Monarch Airlines earlier in the year.

17th USAF Convair T-29 51-5135 arrived at 1808 from Chevres with a number of generals for another base inspection of RAF Burtonwood. US Army CH-34 Chocktaw 56-4323 arrived to collect them for the short trip, and returned with them the following morning. The T-29 night-stopped and departed to Bristol-Filton once the top brass had arrived.

22nd Spantax CV-990 EC-BNM arrived at 1132 with Real Madrid FC for their European Cup semi-final first leg match with Manchester United. The match took place on the 24th, which United did just enough to win 1-0, but would it be enough to see them into the final? The return leg would take place on the 15th May and witness a mass airlift of Manchester United supporters.

24th Aer Lingus operated three extra flights with supporters for the Manchester United v Real Madrid match, with Viscounts EI-AMA (EI5206), EI-AOE (EI5208) & EI-AJJ (EI5210).

30th Transmeridian Douglas DC-7 G-AWBI arrived at 2012 from Stansted, departing the following afternoon to Istanbul via Nicosia carrying NATO equipment. Another freight charter today was operated by TMA Douglas DC-6F OD-AEU, which also night-stopped and departed for Beirut on a military charter on behalf of BAC.

30th West German Air Force Noratlas 53+09 was the latest Noratlas to visit. It arrived at 0953 from Ahlhorn and left during the afternoon for Cologne.

MAY 1968

A new £131,000 fire station, designed for quick access onto the runway, complete with medical rooms for emergencies would be built. The Board of Trade will pay the bulk and Manchester Corporation the remainder. It would be constructed on the northwest side, at the southern end of the strip between runway 02/20 and the western taxiway. It will have eight bays, ancillary accommodation and a specially designed watchtower for maximum all-round visual cover of the airfield.

BEA were dissatisfied with their European network from Manchester. Not convinced it would develop into a viable proposition, the chairman threatened to axe the Trident services on more than one occasion!

The weather was disappointingly cold and cloudy for most of the month, with rain, except for the last few days when the high pressure began to take control bringing warmer and sunnier weather. The month's temperature extremes saw 24°C at Southampton (24th) and a low of -6°C at Santon Downham (8th).

Airlines seen during the summer operating various ITs were Aviaco (Alicante/Barcelona/Palma), Air Ferry (Basle/Perpignan), Austrian Airlines (Salzburg), Balair (Basle), Bavaria (Munich), Britannia Airways (Alicante/Gerona/Ibiza/Milan/Palma/Rimini/Tarbes), British Eagle (Newquay/Palma/Rimini/Tunis/Valencia), British Midland (Gerona/Munich/Oporto/Ostend/Palma/Venice/Zurich), Caledonian (Gerona/Ibiza/Palma/Rimini), Dan-Air Alicante/Barcelona/Ibiza/Palma/Tenerife), JAT (Dubrovnik/Ljubljana/Pula/Split), Laker Airways (Barcelona/Ostend/Palma/Tenerife), Luxair (Luxembourg), Spantax (Gerona/Palma) and Transglobe (Basle/Genoa/Lisbon/Malaga/Rimini/Venice).

Scheduled first visits this month were BOAC (BA538): SVC-10s G-ASGK (4th), G-ASGM (11th) & G-ASGN (15th) and KLM (KL153): DC-9s PH-DNM (10th), PH-DNN (6th) & PH-DNL (3rd). There were no equipment changes.

There was plenty of variety with this month's GCA/ILS traffic. Noted were Varig HS.748 PP-VDS (13th) & Philippine Airlines PI-C1021 (29th/31st), HS.125s G-AVHB (6th), 9J-RAN (14th) & G-AVOK (31st).

The Royal Air Force provided the following, VC-10s XV105 (2nd) & XV107 (15th), Comets XR398 (17th/30th) & XR399 (8th), Nimrod XV148 (10th) and Britannia XL659 (17th). Finally, British Midland Viscount G-APNE (3rd) and Dornier Do.28 G-ASUR (22nd).

3rd Fog in the south produced two diversions. First was Kuwait Airways Comet 9K-ACE at 0830 (KU047 from Geneva), followed by the first visit of British Eagle B.707 G-AVZZ at 0918 (GK184 from Niagara), diverting from Gatwick operating a flight on behalf of Laker Airways.

4th Fog again produced further diversions this morning. Aer Lingus B.707 EI-AMW (IN5902 from New York) diverted from Shannon along with five Heathrow diversions, BOAC VC-10/SVC-10s G-ARVM (BA562 from Boston), G-ASGB (BA130 from Zurich), G-ASGH (BA508 from New York), B.707 G-ARWD (BA672 from Bermuda) and Pan American DC-8 N812PA at 0817 (PA102 from New York).

4th Two vintage types made their only appearances at Ringway today. DHC-1 Chipmunk G-APYG operated by British Midland arrived at 1408 from Wolverhampton with a crew member and Miles Gemini G-AJOJ night-stopped on a return flight from Shoreham. This aircraft wouldn't be around much longer, as it looped at Ford airfield later in the year and was sent to the scrap heap. After the war many aircraft manufacturers went metallic, but Miles kept the faith and continued with wood and fabric. The downside however was their glued joints. After a number of major (some in-flight) and fatal failures of such joints, possibly the cause of G-AJOJ's accident, Miles had to undertake remedial work, which became cost prohibitive. The upshot was that Miles and Percival aircraft were wheeled out of hangars and shunted into the long grass. No-one wanted them and they had no value. In November 1968 the flying club at Ford wanted a bonfire party. What better than an aviation themed night, so the remains of various Miles and Percival aircraft, including G-AJOJ, were stacked one on top of the other. A gallon of AvGas later, a spectacular bonfire was offered up. No more wood and fabric aeroplanes taking up valuable space! The irony is that because so few survived, those remain today are highly valued and many latter day restorers would not bat an eyelid at the prospect of renewing a glued joint with modern adhesives.

4th Having made a couple of test flights at Ringway earlier in the year, HS.125 F-BPMC made its first visit f/t Le Bourget, in between operating t/f Hanover. In 1978, it was purchased by Group 4 Securities and re-registered G-FOUR. Another HS.125 first visit was G-AVJD (16th), which was on the UK register briefly. Having arrived from Keflavik at 2017 to clear customs, it stayed overnight, leaving for Hawarden the following morning. Later in the year it would depart Hawarden after being sold in Canada as CF-AAG.

6th Dan-Air Comet G-APDJ operated Manchester's first inclusive tour flight to Tenerife.

9th British Eagle Britannia 312F G-ANCF (EG3734) was operating a freight charter to Kano.

11th British United upgraded their scheduled services to Jersey by introducing the BAC 1-11 on weekend flights, complementing their weekday Viscount flights until September. G-ASJA operated today's first flight.

12th Still wearing the colour scheme of its previous owner, Dove OO-WIP made the first of its two visits to Ringway (also 10th July 1969). Arriving today at 0013 from Southend, it stayed until the following morning when it left for Luton. Formerly operated by Philips as PH-ILI, it was sold in Belgium in 1967.

12th Just two first visits by foreign light aircraft this month, were Beech 55s D-IEVA today & F-BPFN (16th).

12th Transglobe began their summer programme from Ringway today, with Britannia G-ATLE operating outbound to Malaga. The airline had an increased presence during 1968, operating to six holiday destinations until the 13th October. Britannias used were G-ANCC/ATGD/ATLE. CL-44s G-AWDK/AWGT would also operate transatlantic flights to New York and Toronto.

12th Auster Alpha G-AIGR arrived from its base at Castle Donington with a pilot to test-fly Rapide G-AJSL, which had been present for overhaul since the 31st January.

14th Today's visit of Lear Jet 23 HB-VBA from Milan was the first of three new Lear Jets to visit during 1968. The other two were HB-VBC (24th October) & HB-VBK (31st October).

16th Pacific Western B.707 CF-PWV made the first of three visits during the year (also 4th August & 8th September) operating flights from/to Vancouver.

18th World Airways began another extensive series of transatlantic flights, with today's first operating from Gatwick to Toronto with B.707 N368WA. Flights operated until the 20th October with the following B.707s, N368WA/N369WA (f/v - 14th June) /N370WA/N371WA/N372WA/N373WA/N374WA/N375WA & N376WA.

5th May 1968 - JAT had been awarded the IT contract from tour operator Yugotours, previously operated by Adria Airways. Destinations served were Dubrovnik, Ljubljana, Pula & Split, with Caravelles YU-AHA/AHB/AHE/AHF & AHG. Unfortunately the SE.210 proved unsuited to the 'stress and strains' of IT work. After many years of easy going scheduled work, the aircraft and airline became regularly beset by technical delays and would not return to operate a programme from Manchester until 1973. (Geoff Ball)

15th May 1968 - HS.125 G-ATWH flew into Ringway today on demonstration to Granada Television. The company was evaluating the aircraft as a possible replacement for their Dove G-ARFZ. G-ATWH was ultimately delivered on 9th October and Dove G-ARFZ was sold the same month. Although the HS.125 could make up to three trips a day from Ringway, it was actually based at Heathrow. (Geoff Ball)

16th May 1968 - One of the very early 'mass' uplifts of Manchester United fans took place over the next two days. Up to 2,000 fans were part of a giant airlift for the club's European Cup semi-final second leg with Real Madrid, the biggest exodus of football fans from Manchester up to this point. BEA Trident 1 G-ARPF flew out the players, officials and press, whilst the fans went out on the following: Britannia Airways Britannias G-ANBD/ANBF/ANBJ/ANBL/ANBN/ANBO, British Eagle Britannias G-AOVA/AOVC (seen here on the 16th operating a return from Madrid) /AOVN/ARXA & B.707 G-AWDG, British United Britannia G-ANCD, Caledonian Britannia G-ASTF, Dan-Air Comet G-APDJ and Laker Airways BAC 1-11s G-AVBY & G-AVYZ. The match had extra importance, as United would be defending a 1-0 victory from the first leg at Old Trafford. A favourable aggregate score would mean that they would make the European Cup Final taking place at Wembley on the 29th May. (Geoff Ball)

19th Aviaco and Spantax began their summer IT programmes from Ringway today. Aviaco continued using Iberia SE.210s for the flights, lasting until 29th October, which produced a number of first visits, EC-BDC (19th August), EC-BIC (10th June), EC-BID (30th September) & EC-BIE (2nd September). Spantax operated three-times-weekly to Gerona and Palma until the 6th October, with the final flight operating from Gerona as BX179 by Douglas DC-6 EC-AZX. Aircraft used during the summer were Douglas DC-7s EC-ATQ/ATR/BBT/BDL/BDM and CV-990s EC-BJC/BJD/BNM.

20th Pan American B.707 N723PA operated the inaugural flight of the airline's summer series of charter flights to New York, ending on 22nd October. Amongst the numerous Boeing 707s were the following first visits, N496PA (23rd September), N497PA (4th August), N702PA (22nd October) and N765PA (19th July).

24th Today marked the final visit of a RAF Anson. TX228 (JDT 50), arriving at 0937 from RAF Andover stayed for ten minutes, before departing RAF Ternhill. It returned again in the afternoon, before leaving for Andover again. Of the 11,020 built, by this time the Royal Air Force had only eighteen aircraft in service. C.19 Anson VL349 of Southern Comms Squadron made the very last flight by a RAF Anson on 28th June 1968. One figure that must be quoted on the varied and interesting history of the Anson is 164. This was the official number of turns required to raise an Anson's undercarriage before being fitted with something more modern than a crank beside the pilot's seat. In some instances the aircrew failed to get the wheels up before the destination was in sight, which meant putting the whole process in reverse!

25th Bavaria returned to Manchester to operate weekly IT flights to Munich. BAC 1-11s would operate twice-weekly on Sat/Sun & Herald D-BEBE would operate fortnightly, also on a Sunday. The three BAC 1-11s used were all first visits, D-ANDY (25th May), G-AVGP (26th May) & G-AWGG (31st Aug). The two British BAC 1-11s were intended for Channel Airways, but leased to the German airline during the year.

18th May 1968 - TABSO, the Bulgarian state airline, later to renamed Balkan Bulgarian, commenced the first of a series of fortnightly flights today to Varna, serving the Black Sea resort. Their summer programme would last until 5th October, with all flights operated by Ilyushin IL-18s. Aircraft used were LZ-BEK/BES & BET, all of which were first visits. This was the start of a long association for the airline with Ringway, which would last over thirty-five years. (Geoff Ball)

30th May – LOT Antonov AN-12 SP-LZB, arriving at 0018 today from Warsaw, was used to transport a brand new computer. Leaving for Warsaw via Copenhagen five hours later, it also marked the first appearance of this Russian transporter. It made a second visit on 13th February 1969 to collect another English Electric computer. (Geoff Ball)

26th EL AL Boeing 707 4X-ATC made a short stop at 1254 (LY1415 from Tel Aviv) en route to Heathrow.

26th Air Canada had been reducing their presence at Ringway over the last few years. However, they operated their only transatlantic flight today, when DC-8 CF-TJC arrived at 1437 (AC803 from Heathrow), before departing to Prestwick (AC037).

28th Balair would only operate a once-weekly Basle charter during 1968, which began today with Douglas DC-6 HB-IBU. Flights operated until 10th September with further Douglas DC-6s HB-IBR & HB-IBZ.

28th British Eagle Britannia G-AOVM (using Air France callsign AF5330), was involved in the export of £380,000 worth of computers to Czechoslovakia. It arrived at 0958 today from Heathrow, and departed with an English Electric 4-50 computer direct to Ostrava for installation in one of the states steelworks. This was the first microelectronic computer to be sold behind the iron curtain.

JUNE 1968

The airport was still on course for aircraft to be able to use the newly extended runway 24 by early next year. By November the 1,288ft tunnel would carry part of the redirected Wilmslow-Altrincham road under the runway, with the first cars passing through on the 15th November. In order for the runway to be extended, concrete containing coarse sand from Wrexham and stone from Buxton quarries was made on the spot. When the project ended a concrete train would have laid about 100,000 tonnes, after track was laid exclusively for this purpose. As well as telephones and fire hydrants within the tunnel, plans were also in place for the future installation of mechanical ventilation and possibly TV screens to inform airport control how much traffic was in the tunnel, and whether there were any problems.

Manchester Airport will be the new base for BEA's eighteen-strong fleet of BAC 1-11-500s. They had announced their intention to establish engineering facilities at Manchester, with a permanent night shift of fifty workers to be employed in time for the winter timetable commencing on the 1st November. By this time six of these aircraft will have been delivered for use on the Manchester-Heathrow services, flights from Heathrow to Germany and internal flights within Germany.

Apart from a fine, settled spell mid-month, the weather was generally unsettled. It started with heavy, thundery rain, broken on the 9th by an anti-cyclone bringing in warm long sunny spells. Cyclonic weather was re-established on the 18th with further rain spreading across the country. It was particularly heavy over southern England on the 27th; with falls exceeding 40mm. Widespread flooding was reported on the 27th/28th in the Midlands and southern and eastern England. On the 29th high pressure developed again, with a return to dry and sunny weather. The month's temperature extremes saw 29°C at Southampton (30th) and a low of 0°C at Cairngorm (28th).

Scheduled first visits were KLM (KL153): DC-9s PH-DNO (10th), PH-DNN (6th) & PH-DNP (22nd). It was another good month for GCA/ILS traffic. Noted was Varig HS.748s PP-VDT (10th/24th), PP-VDU (18th) & Philippine Airlines PI-C1021 (24th). Aircraft on test from Hawarden were HS.125s D-CHTH (10th/12th), G-AVXL (12th), G-AVOL (13th), G-ATWH (22nd), G-AVRH (25th) and Heron G-AVTU (11th). The RAF were represented by Nimrod XV147 (19th) and VC-10 XR806 (24th). Finally, also from Woodford was Hawker Siddeley Dove G-ARHW (25th).

1st British Eagle were the latest to ditch aircraft registrations as their ATC identifier and use radio callsigns.

1st Dragon Rapide G-AKIF arrived at 1541 today from Booker. It departed later that afternoon to perform a parachute drop at the Congleton show, before setting course back to Booker.

5th French Air Force Noratlas 20/63-BY (also 21st December), which night-stopped on a freight flight from Pau, was the only French military Noratlas visit during 1968. The West German Air Force also sent in a further Noratlas during the month, with 52+87 arriving at 1345 (6th) from Jever and departing to Erding.

5th Oxford-based PA-28 Cherokee N9759W kicked off this month's foreign lights making their first visits. The others were PA-23 Apache OY-DYW (11th), Beech 60 D-IHSK (17th) & PA-28 Cherokee N3659K f/t Wethersfield (23rd/29th).

7th Commander 680 G-AWCU made its first visit as such today. Formerly HB-GBW, it was purchased by United Steel earlier in the year, and operated with them until October 1970.

9th Luxair belatedly began this year's series of late-night weekend flights to Luxembourg until the 20th September. Aircraft used were Fokker F.27s LX-LGA, LX-LGB & LX-LGD (f/v - 7th July). This was the airline's final series of flights from Manchester, as they would not return until March 1995, when they commenced a weekday service to Luxembourg.

2nd June 1968 - BEA Helicopters Bell 206 Jet Ranger G-AWGU made the first of several visits this month. It was being used by Ferranti, presumably whilst their Jet Ranger, G-AVSN, was being serviced. This aircraft spent its sixteen years on the UK register with BEA, and later British Airways. In 1984 it was sold in Oman as A40-DC. All of their helicopters would eventually carry the airline's full and changing liveries. Three days later, another BEA Helicopters aircraft passed through, in the shape of Sikorsky S-61 G-ATBJ, en route from Gatwick to Aberdeen. (Geoff Ball)

5th June 1968 - Lufthansa used Capitol Airways Curtiss C-46 N9891Z on today's delayed LH942 cargo flight from Frankfurt, until recently resplendent in full Lufthansa colours. As the fifth Capitol C-46 to visit Ringway, it would make a further and final visit on 30th April 1969. Although owned by Capitol Airways, it was leased to Lufthansa from July 1964 to November 1969 and later sold to Buffalo Airways as C-FAVO. Another treat for C-46 lovers was Fred Olsen LN-FOP (7th), operating a cargo flight to Flesland. (Geoff Ball)

11th A very rare visitor to Ringway today was Percival Prince G-ALWH (its only other visit was 22nd January 1974). One of several operated by Decca Navigator, it day-stopped from/to Biggin Hill. This aircraft has an interesting history. Delivered to Shell Petroleum in 1950, it was flown by WWII pilot Douglas Bader before being sold in Venezuela later that year, then returning to Britain in 1953. It was used by the Sperry Gyroscope Company, then Decca Navigator based at Biggin Hill in 1961. This particular Prince was a short-nosed version, with an endurance of six hours flying time and range of around 1,000 miles. It was also the unofficial personal transport of Sir Edward Lewis, chairman of the Decca group. In November 1976 it was sold in the USA as N206UP and left Biggin Hill in early-1977 for Van Nuys, California. This fine aircraft was seen at Biggin Hill by the writer on 29th January 1977, looking forlorn in the cold wind!

15th African Safari Britannia 5X-UVH was making its first visit, impressive in a zebra-stripe livery. Arriving from Gatwick at 2357 to operate a return flight to Rimini as IK865, it departed to Gatwick. It returned again later in the day from Genoa before leaving again, this time as IK560 to Zurich.

15th Persistent fog in the south brought fifteen morning diversions to Manchester, mainly from Heathrow, but Gatwick, Luton and Birmingham were also affected. Seven BEA flights included two first visits by Trident 2s G-AVFB (BE'FB from Pisa) & G-AVFD (BE'FD from Lisbon). Others of note were BUA Britannia G-ANCE at 0441 (BR402 from Ibiza), BOAC SVC-10 G-ASGE at 0525 (BA130 from Entebbe) and Spantax CV-990 EC-BNM at 0555 (BX053 from Ibiza).

15th Also amongst the mornings diversions was the first visit by a new UK operator, Monarch Airlines, when former Caledonian Britannia G-AOVH arrived at 0445 (OM105 from Palma). In June 1967, Cosmos Tours formed Monarch Airlines to operate its IT programme from 1968 onwards. On the 5th April 1968, Britannia G-AOVI inaugurated Monarch's first commercial service, when it flew a load of holidaymakers from Luton to Madrid.

16th Channel Airways Trident 2 G-AVYE was the first of the airline's Tridents to visit Manchester, arriving at 0636 from Barcelona on diversion from Newcastle.

17th A dispute involving 340 porters, firemen and marshallers seeking pay parity with other airports, resulted in a staged strike this morning, which closed the airport for ninety minutes. A number of flights diverted to Liverpool, but most were able to hold until the airport re-opened, including SVC-10 G-ASGM (BA538 from New York/Prestwick) with Manchester City FC onboard, returning from an American tour. Pan American B.707 N715PA stopped over at Shannon until Manchester reopened, before eventually landing at 1216. Further walkouts by staff took place over the following weeks, causing further disruption to flights. The closures that took place later in the month and into July lasted a little longer than today's, which led the airport to run a number of flights from Liverpool. Coaches were laid on to ferry passengers between the two airports. Balair, British Midland and Bavaria switched their operations to Liverpool during this period. The dispute was finally ended on the 18th July, when normal workings were resumed.

19th Caledonian B.707 G-AVKA (CA943) broke the flight record between Manchester and Toronto again today, flying the distance in 6 hours 41 minutes, beating the previous record set on the 30th April, also by a Caledonian B.707. Onboard were 117 members of the Canadian Road Racing Association, returning to Canada after three weeks in Britain.

21st World Airways B.707 N368WA arrived at 2302 non-stop from Honolulu. The 7,200 miles distance was covered in thirteen hours, due to the benefit of a light load and a tail wind en route.

23rd Also operating their final summer programme from Ringway was Austrian Airlines, beginning a weekly Salzburg-MAN-Dublin and return IT flight, with Viscount OE-IAM in charge of today's service. Operating until the 15th September, duties were shared between Viscounts OE-IAM and OE-LAL. Similar to Luxair, Austrian Airlines would eventually return to Ringway to operate scheduled services in March 1980, when inaugurating a twice-weekly flight to Vienna.

24th The country's rail network was thrown into disarray by a work-to-rule and overtime ban by the National Union of Railwaymen (NUR). They had rejected a last minute pay and productivity offer by British Rail two days earlier. Extra flights were organised nationwide, one of which was Autair BAC 1-11 G-AWBL (also 25th), operating in the early hours from/to Luton. Others were Morton AS Dakota G-AMRA (27th), Autair Herald G-APWC (27th), Autair BAC 1-11 G-AVOF (1st July) & G-AOVP (3rd July). The rail strike lasted twelve days in total, causing massive disruption to the network. On the 5th July, the work-to-rule was called off following the NURs acceptance of British Rail's peace offer.

20th June 1968 - TMA would make occasional visits throughout the 1960s, operating freight charters to various destinations worldwide. Today, Douglas DC-6F OD-AER was making its only visit to Ringway, operating one such cargo charter to Jeddah via Rome on behalf of BAC. (Geoff Ball)

30th June 1968 - XR142 (also 2nd Aug) had the honour of being the first military Argosy to land at Ringway. Arriving at 1416 from Lyneham (RJX 03) on a brief stop before leaving for Edinburgh, it's seen above being handled by BEA. This aircraft was part of 114-Squadron based at RAF Benson, formed in October 1961. It was also the last RAF transport Squadron to operate the Argosy C Mk 1 and it disbanded at RAF Benson on 8th October 1971. (Geoff Ball)

27th Apart from crew training flights, UK military movements had been fairly scarce so far this year, but this afternoon two Army Air Corps Scouts, XT206 & XT849, arrived from Wythenshawe having been on display there during the day. They both departed for the Army base at Holcombe Brook, nr Bury. Another pair, XT206 & XT247 (30th & 5th/6th July), also arrived in formation from Heaton Park, leaving ninety minutes later for Driffield.

28th BEA Trident 1 G-ARPT made its final visit this evening (BE4128 from Heathrow), due to being damaged beyond repair on 3rd July. It was hit by BKS Ambassador G-AMAD, which had recently been converted to a horsebox, on a flight from Deauville to Heathrow. It was transporting eight racehorses owned by businessman William Hill and his five grooms. As it was landing on runway 28R the left wing dropped, and the wingtip and left landing gear touched the grass adjacent to the runway. The crew tried to increase power to go-around and climb away, but the bank angle increased and it hit two empty parked up BEA Tridents, G-ARPI & G-ARPT. It knocked the tail fin off G-ARPI and sliced off the entire tail section off G-ARPT. The Ambassador cart-wheeled following the impact, slid upside down and came up against the ground floor of the terminal building whereupon it exploded. Six people onboard died, including the flight crew, three of the grooms and all the horses. Two grooms were seriously injured, as were two people on the ground and a further 29 received slight injuries. G-ARPT was written off, but G-ARPI was subsequently repaired, only to be destroyed on the 18th June 1972 in the Staines air crash. All other Ambassadors were grounded pending the result of an inquiry. The starboard rod was found to be satisfactory, but rods from some other Ambassadors showed signs of cracking and failed when tested, similar to G-AMAD's port rod. The port flap operating rod had failed due to metal fatigue and although the mechanism had failed, the compensating mechanism between the two sets of flaps remained intact. The port flaps had retracted, but the compensator caused the starboard ones to extend further. The resulting asymmetry of lift resulted in the roll to port. The pilot probably tried to overshoot and set the flaps to the correct 10 degrees, but due to the mechanism design this was not sufficient to cause the starboard flaps to retract, which would have taken 25 seconds in any event. The Department of Transport's report concluded that whatever the pilot's actions, it was "doubtful" whether an accident could have been avoided. Afterwards all Ambassadors were fitted with steel reinforcements to the flap operating rods.

JULY 1968

Subject to government approval, Iberia hoped to begin twice-weekly flights to Madrid in November. If successful, the service would be operated by SE.210 Caravelles, complementing the airline's summer schedules to Barcelona and Palma.

Two charter airlines would have an expanded presence at Manchester in 1969. Laker Airways would operate flights to Ibiza, Palma and for the first time, Tenerife and Las Palmas. British United, operating scheduled flights to Jersey and Southampton and regular trooping flights to Gutersloh, Dusseldorf and Hanover, would have an extensive IT programme operated by BAC 1-11s next year.

BOAC announced another boost for Manchester with plans to operate a once-weekly service to Tel Aviv via Heathrow from next March. Typical fares would be £174 15s for a normal return flight with no restrictions or a 30-day excursion ticket for £117 14s. Next month they would reveal plans to operate twice-weekly to Johannesburg via Heathrow, but no dates had been finalised. Both services would be operated by VC-10s, but the latter route failed to materialise.

The weather for July was a 50/50 split, cyclonic during the first half and anti-cyclonic in the second. On the 1st, the British Isles lay between a depression over Iceland and another over the Bay of Biscay. During the early hours, rain brought down a fine multi-coloured dust over an area extending from Devon to Essex and northward to Derbyshire. The dust, which varied in colour from almost white to dark red, was probably associated with high level winds from Africa. The afternoon was hot in the southeast, but the southwest saw thunderstorms and torrential rain spreading northwards. Flooding was widespread across the UK and RAF Leeming recorded 35mm of rain in nine minutes. Devon was badly hit; with towns and villages flooded, and crops and property damaged. Parts of south Wales and Devon saw hailstones up to 7cm in diameter. The 10th saw further heavy rain and flooding, in parts ranging from Exeter, Birmingham and Peterborough. Seven people were killed by the floods and hundreds of bridges were washed away. At Chaw Stoke, Somerset, 175mm of rain fell, and falls of more than 125mm in the Bristol, Bath and Gloucester areas. By the 17th, the British Isles were under the influence of high pressure, which remained near or over the country until the end of the month. The month's temperature extremes saw 33°C at Camden Square (1st) and a low of 0°C at Moor House (25th).

Scheduled first visits during the month were Alitalia (AZ296): SE.210 I-DABA (29th), I-DABF (19th), I-DABP (15th) & I-DAXU (12th), BEA (BE4128): Trident 2 G-AVFE (18th) and Iberia (IB784): SE.210 EC-BIB (20th). There were no equipment changes this month.

Most of this month's GCA/ILS traffic involved aircraft on test flights out of Woodford, with plenty of variation. Noted were Lan Chile HS.748 CC-CEH (3rd), Varig HS.748 PP-VDV (26th), Philippine Airlines HS.748 PI-C1022 (26th), RAF Shackletons XF711 (4th) & WG533 (12th) and Vulcan B.2 XL391 (15th). Amongst the non-Woodford traffic was RAF VC-10s XV103 (3rd), XR810 (29th) & Britannia XN404 (25th).

1st JAT SE.210 YU-AHF arrived at 0012 from Pula with technical problems severe enough to delay its departure until the next morning. A second SE.210 YU-AHD, positioned from Split to operate the delayed outbound to Dubrovnik. JAT DC-3F YU-ACA arrived at 2004 from Belgrade via Brussels with spare parts.

1st Following on from the initial announcement in February, Alitalia commenced a twice-weekly service f/t Rome/Milan today, with SE.210 I-DABU (AZ296) operating the inaugural flight.

2nd Trans-Union Douglas DC-6 F-BOEX (also 30th) arrived at 2139 today on a return flight from Paris-Orly. This was the airline's fourth visit, with F-BOEX making its debut at Ringway. Purchased from Ansett-ANA in 1966, it served with the French airline until 1975, when it was sold to Delta Air Transport as OO-VFG.

4th The West German Air Force operated two training flights through Manchester this month. The first, Noratlas 52+85 arrived at 1555 today from Bristol-Filton and left the following day to Neubiberg. The second, 52+71 (23rd) also night-stopped from Hohn to Erding.

7th Glasgow-based Loganair made a rare venture south today, with Islander G-AVRA (also 12th/22nd) making its first visit on a day-stopping return flight from Glasgow. The airline had chosen to purchase two brand new B-N Islanders in 1967 due to delays in production of their first choice, the Dornier Do.28. Their only regular inroad into English airspace at this time was a nightly postal flight between Glasgow and Blackpool, which had been awarded earlier in the year.

7th Despite numerous appearances at Ringway on crew training details, RAF Britannia XL659 became the first to land. Arriving at 1251 today (RR6408 from Lyneham), it stayed for just over thirty minutes before departing for RAF Leeming. Also today was the second RAF Argosy, when XR139 arrived at 1814 (RR4464 from Lyneham), for a brief stop before departing for Edinburgh.

7th American-airline Universal made its first visit to Ringway today, operating Douglas DC-8-61 N802U on an ad hoc flight from Philadelphia, later departing to New York via Prestwick.

9th Aer Lingus operated the first of three summer transatlantic charters today with B.707 EI-ANO (IN5871 to New York via Shannon). The others were Boeing 707s EI-ANV (20th September - IN5878 from New York) and EI-APG (27th September - IN5878 from New York).

9th This month's new foreign light first visits started with Iona National Airways' Cessna 337 N5384S f/t Dublin today. The Irish operator took delivery of this aircraft in June, but never put it on the Irish register. Others were Jodel DR.1050 HB-EBK from Shoreham (14th), Beech 55 OY-DPK (21st), Cessna 172 SE-EAW & Beech 23 SE-EWW (both 26th) and Cessna 3120 F-BJHT (29th).

11th The latest Transair Sweden Douglas DC-7, SE-ERD, arrived at 1644 (TB206P from Malmo) to operate an ad hoc passenger charter back to Malmo.

17th Sabena Boeing 707 OO-SJC arrived at 1254 from Brussels en route to Shannon and New York.

17th BEA Super 1-11 G-AVMI arriving at 1737 from Wisley, was based until the 28th operating proving flights to places such as Birmingham, Shannon, Hamburg, Dusseldorf, Cologne, Hanover & Frankfurt. This was the first Super 1-11 to visit ahead of full operations by BEA, who would have an eighteen strong fleet eventually, which from a technical point of view would be based at Ringway. Although British Airways would transfer maintenance of their Super 1-11s to Heathrow in March 1977, they continued operating domestic and international services from Manchester right up until their retirement from service in 1992.

18th TIA Douglas DC-8-61 N8962T made its first visit, arriving at 1433 f/t New York. Another TIA DC-8, N8961T, was also present the following day, operating an inbound flight from New York via Gander.

22nd BOAC B.707 G-AWHU made its first visit, arriving at 1042 today for a two hour crew training detail. This aircraft was originally intended for Saturn Airways, but was purchased by BOAC due to the loss of G-ARWE, which was damaged beyond repair in a landing accident at Heathrow on 8th April 1968.

21st July 1968 - Amongst numerous Pan American Boeing 707 visits this summer, was a sole Douglas DC-8, with the arrival of N809PA at 0948 from Heathrow en route to Gander & New York. As well as being a first visit, it was also their last DC-8 visit, as all had left the fleet by the end of the decade. (Ken Fielding)

24th July 1968 - By now American Flyers had re-equipped their fleet, by replacing their four stopgap Electras with two brand new Boeing 727s. The first of these, N12826, made its first visit today, positioning in from Gatwick, departing the following morning to New York via Keflavik & Gander. Their second aircraft, N12827, made the first of its two visits to Ringway on 23rd July 1969. (Dave Jones)

27ᵗʰ RAF Rescue Whirlwind HAR.10 XP353 arrived at 1820 today from RAF Valley for fuel (Pedro 22), prior to departing shortly afterwards to conduct a search in the Macclesfield area. It returned from there later in the evening and departed for RAF Valley.

AUGUST 1968

BOAC's Caribbean flights will increase to daily from the 25ᵗʰ November. At the same time, it will also extend to cover Antigua & Georgetown, Guyana, making it the first South American link with Manchester.

The first five days of the month were mainly fine and warm, but low pressure took charge from the 6ᵗʰ, bringing rain, especially to southwestern districts which had not seen any for over three weeks. A more complex and vigorous low pressure became established over the next week, with thunderstorms and occasionally heavy rain. High pressure on the 22ⁿᵈ brought dry and warm weather until the 27ᵗʰ when more thunderstorms developed. The end of the month saw another deep low pressure take hold with rain in most districts and cooler northeasterly winds. The month's temperature extremes saw 30°C at West Camel, Somerset (23ʳᵈ) and a low of 1°C at Kielder Castle (10ᵗʰ).

Scheduled first visits this month were Alitalia (AZ296): SE.210 I-DABG (9ᵗʰ), I-DABL (16ᵗʰ) & I-DAXI (5ᵗʰ), BOAC (BA065): B.707F G-AVPB (28ᵗʰ), KLM (KL153): DC-9 PH-DNR (17ᵗʰ) and SAS (SK537): DC-9 OY-KGR (7ᵗʰ). Equipment changes were Aer Lingus (EI620/1): B.720 EI-ALC (10ᵗʰ), KLM (KL019): DC-9 PH-DNR (22ⁿᵈ) and Swissair (SR842): CV-990 HB-ICA (5ᵗʰ).

This month's GCA/ILS traffic noted was HS.748s PI-C1022 (1ˢᵗ), PP-VDV (14ᵗʰ/16ᵗʰ), PP-VDX (16ᵗʰ) & Australian Air Force A10-601 (21ˢᵗ). RAF Britannia XL635 (13ᵗʰ), VC-10s XV105 (29ᵗʰ), XV107 (28ᵗʰ) & G-ASNU (13ᵗʰ). Training flights were operated by BOAC Boeing 707s G-APFM (2ⁿᵈ) & G-APFK (9ᵗʰ).

7ᵗʰ Aer Lingus BAC 1-11 EI-ANG (EI651 from Frankfurt) declared an emergency when the pilot noticed the oil pressure warning light illuminate, indicating a loss of power, forcing him to shut down the port engine. The aircraft landed safely, but did not leave for another three hours whilst repairs were instigated.

11ᵗʰ Early morning fog at Heathrow produced two weather diversions today. The first, BEA Trident 2 G-AVFF arriving at 0522 (BE'FF) was a first visit and the third Trident 2 to appear at Manchester. The second was BOAC B.707 G-APFG at 0916 (BA676 from Bermuda/Miami). On the 19ᵗʰ, Pan American B.707 N705PA also made a first visit, diverting in for fuel at 1243 (PA705 from New York).

11ᵗʰ JAT had further technical problems with their Caravelles. YU-AHB which had left earlier in the day for Pula went tech on arrival there, which resulted in an interesting aircraft substitution; when Yugoslav government Ilyushin IL-18 YU-AIB appeared at 2300 on its first visit, departing an hour later for Dubrovnik.

12ᵗʰ RAF Devon C.1 VP960 made its first visit today, arriving at 1010 from RAF Wyton (BKK06), departing for RAF Shawbury ten minutes later. It returned later in the day from RAF Cosford, staying a mere six minutes this time, before leaving for Wyton.

12ᵗʰ HS.125s continued passing through Ringway for custom clearance, en route for Hawarden. Today's aircraft was HB-VAN, arriving at 1802 from Linz. It returned from Hawarden on the 17ᵗʰ, again to clear customs before departing to Maastricht.

14ᵗʰ RAF Rescue Whirlwind HAR.10 XP349 arrived at 0734 from Platt Fields Park for fuel, before returning to its base at RAF Valley. On the 13ᵗʰ December 1972 it was written off, after ditching into the Irish Sea off Holyhead harbour due to engine failure.

18ᵗʰ British Eagle Boeing 707 G-AVZZ was due to operate an outbound flight to Toronto, but it was stuck in Canada after being struck by a ground truck. Britannia G-AOVK (EG191) was dispatched from Heathrow to operate the flight, but it too became grounded when a fuel leak was detected. All 122 passengers were put in a Manchester hotel overnight, before finally leaving the following morning over eighteen hours late.

20ᵗʰ PA-24 Comanche G-ARYV landed at 0856 from Leeds, having declared a full emergency due to undercarriage problems. After extensive work, it finally left for Southend on the 26ᵗʰ October.

21ˢᵗ British United operated a rare transatlantic flight from Manchester today, when VC-10 G-ATDJ arrived from Gatwick, departing as BR1059 to Toronto.

22ⁿᵈ Another eight flights diverted into Manchester due to fog in the south beginning with Gatwick diversion BUA VC-10 at 0206 (BR1060 from Toronto) The remainder from Heathrow were a mixture of BEA (Tridents G-ARPJ, G-ARPZ & Vanguard G-APEJ) and BOAC (B.707s G-APFD, G-APFM & G-ARRC) aircraft.

7ᵗʰ August 1968 – L-100 9J-RBW arrived at 1850 today from Benina, and stayed until the 11ᵗʰ. It was operating the first of several flights by Zambian Air Cargoes over the next few months, transporting ventilation equipment. United Nation sanctions imposed on Rhodesia had impacted on Zambia, as their only link to the sea was via a Rhodesian railway line, so ZAC was to prove vital in keeping the Lusaka government alive. Their L-100s became a common sight all over Europe, including Manchester, picking up essential supplies for the besieged nation. (Geoff Ball)

17ᵗʰ August 1968 - Europe Falcon Service Falcon 20 F-BPIO arrived at 1234 today from Barcelona on a wet summer afternoon. In 1972, it was re-registered as F-BIHY when it was purchased by Hennessey, the purveyor of some of the finest French cognac! (Geoff Ball)

22nd August 1968 – Saudi Arabian Airlines Douglas DC-6A HZ-ADB had landed at 2006 the previous evening from Dhahran via Athens as SV6584. It was the first of three visits by the airline this year (also 25th Aug/24th Oct) all with HZ-ADB picking up BAC Lightning and Strikemaster spares being built at Warton. (Bob Thorpe)

27th August 1968 - Britannia Airways B.737 G-AVRM was due to carry out crew training at Luton and Stansted, but due to fog at both airports it came up to Manchester instead! A second aircraft, G-AVRL, made its first visit on the 27th October, prior to entering full revenue service later in the year. (Geoff Ball)

23rd Fog affected operations at Heathrow for the second morning running. Of note were two first visits by Kuwait Airways Comet 9K-ACA at 0901 (KU047 from Geneva) & East African Airways VC-10 5X-UVA at 0907 (EC710 from Athens). The final diversion of the month was yet another first visit, when RAF VC-10 XV107 (27th - RR2242 from Nicosia) arrived at 0946 on diversion from Brize Norton.

25th Just two European light aircraft first visits this month were Sabena Cessna 310 OO-SEF arriving from Ostend today to operate a round-trip to Oxford and Cessna 182 D-EFIG from Bournemouth (26th).

28th Today was the final operation for the time being of All Air being used on Lufthansa cargo flights. C-54 D-ADAC was in charge of today's flight, but from 4th September to 31st December, Aer Turas Douglas C-54s EI-AOR & EI-APK would be used, and the frequency was also increased to six-weekly.

31st Saturn Airways had retired their fleet of DC-7s by now and replaced them with brand new DC-8 aircraft, the first of which, N8956U, arrived at 0936 on an ad hoc flight from New York. This was the airline's only visit to Ringway during 1968. The following year did not see much improvement either, with just one visit again by N8956U on 12th September 1969 from Le Bourget to Keflavik.

31st Australian Air Force HS.748 A10-601 arrived at 1754 from Woodford to be based at Manchester until the 3rd September for crew training. Ringway was used as it was ideal for day and night operations and not subject to restricted ATC facilities as at Woodford. It flew two airways crew training sorties on the 1st September and two more on the 2nd, before returning to Woodford for pre-delivery checks on the 3rd.

SEPTEMBER 1968

It was being reported that aircraft spotters were to lose their vantage point on the old Wilmslow-Altrincham road, once the new road is open. However, the airport was hopeful that an alternative spot could be found. One option was to fence off part of the airport at the Wilmslow side, but at the opposite side of the airport where spotters had been congregating. They were looking into the possibility of making this position a picnic area, complete with car park. Discounting the terraces, this kind of facility would not become available for another thirty years!

The month began cool and rather wet with rain or showers and scattered thunderstorms. The 4th-9th was milder and drier, though rain spread across the country on the 5th. Thunderstorms broke again on the 10th, with heavy rain at times over the next few days. On the night of the 12th, Cockle Park, Northumberland recorded 57mm of rain. On the 14th, another fall of 57mm in just forty-two minutes was recorded at Purleigh, Essex. It was estimated that an intensity of this order could only be expected for just one day in 200 years. This led to widespread flooding in Kent, Essex, Surrey, Sussex and East Anglia. The rest of the month was unsettled as a succession of depressions moved eastwards across the country. The month's temperature extremes saw 26°C at Camden Square (23rd) and a low of -3°C at Balmoral (19th).

Just a solitary scheduled first visit this month was Swissair (SR842): DC-9 HB-IFI (16th). Equipment changes were BEA (BE795): Viscount G-AOYP (18th) and Sabena (SN197): Sobelair F.27 OO-SBP (11th).

GCA/ILS traffic noted this month were HS.748s from Woodford, Avianca HK-1408 (4th/5th), Mount Cook ZK-CWJ (6th/12th/23rd/24th), Australian Air Force A10-602 (13th/27th), HSA G-AVRR (13th) & Thai Airways HS-THD (24th). The Royal Air Force were represented by Comet XR395 (3rd), Nimrod XV226 (5th) and Britannias XL658 (18th), XM496 (26th) XM520 (12th) & XN398 (24th). Brazilian Air Force HS.125 VC93-2120 (3rd) turned up from Hawarden and finally British Midland Viscount G-APNE (26th).

3rd Philips Falcon 20 PH-ILF arriving at 1007 today from Eindhoven was the first of four biz-jets making their first visits this month. The others were a second Falcon 20, D-CALL (5th - HB329/330 f/t Le Bourget) and two HS.125s, N372CM (19th) & Maersk OY-DKP (12th).

3rd KLM amended their freight flights from Ringway today, now operated by Douglas DC-9s five nights a week (Tue-Sat), routing Amsterdam-Glasgow-Manchester-Amsterdam. The DC-7s operated these schedules for the final time on the 30th August, with PH-DSI (KL019/020). The remaining four DC-7s made their last visits as follows:

PH-DSE	9th August 1968	Sold February 1969 to Aer Turas as EI-ATT
PH-DSF	29th August 1968	Sold February 1969 to Aer Turas as EI-ATU
PH-DSG	21st February 1969	Sold April 1969 to Aer Turas as EI-ATW
PH-DSI	30th August 1968	Sold March 1969 to Aer Turas as EI-ATV

As seen above, the actual last KLM DC-7F to visit Ringway was PH-DSG on 21st February 1969. This operated KL005E from/to Amsterdam in place of the usual DC-9.

14th September 1968 - Two shots of 9J-REZ, the second Zambia Air Cargo L-100 to visit Ringway today. Further visits were operated by 9J-RBW (28th October) & 9J-REZ (11th November and the final visit on 20th January 1969). Seen below is the interior of L-100 9J-REZ. (Both Geoff Ball)

15th September 1968 - Transglobe Britannia G-ATGD had gone tech on arrival from Venice, which led to another visit by African Safari Britannia 5X-UVH, positioning from Zurich to operate outbound flight IK862 to Lisbon. G-ATGD departed the following morning to operate a round-trip to Malaga (IK863), but when it attempted to position back to Gatwick departing at 1819, it returned an hour later with more technical trouble, before finally leaving on the 16th. (Geoff Ball)

24th September 1968 – Royal Saudi Air Force C-130E 454 arrived at 1216 today (RSF454 from Rome) to pick more BAC Lightning and Strikemaster spares from Warton. These flights had previously been operated by Saudia DC-6 HZ-ADB. This was the first of many Saudi Air Force flights to pass through Manchester right up until 2011. The 'golden period' was from 1978-1997, when these flights terminated at Manchester, which were also ordnance related and included flights operating to/from the USA. (Geoff Ball)

28th September 1968 – German outfit Sudflug (c/s 'Bluebird') had now replaced their fleet of Douglas DC-7s with two leased DC-8s, D-ADIM & D-ADIR. Both made their first visits during the month. The first aircraft, D-ADIM arrived at 0935 (12th - SZ170 Zurich/Gander), and the second, D-ADIR, is seen here arriving today at 0929 for fuel en route to Frankfurt (SZ111 from New York). (Geoff Ball)

30th September 1968 - The end of an era occurred today, with the replacement of the Dakotas by Viscounts on the Cambrian Airways route to Bristol and Cardiff, thus ending twenty-nine years of scheduled services into Ringway by the Dakota. Today's final flight (CS247) was operated by G-AGHM. For a time the airport management toyed with the idea of placing a Dakota on permanent display outside the main terminal. An aircraft was chosen, but the idea was eventually and sadly rejected. This photo taken earlier in the month shows DC-3 G-ALCC operating the Monday morning only service, CS245, parked next to a company Viscount operating an Isle of Man flight. (Graham Davies)

3rd West German Air Force Noratlas 55+91 (DCN7718 from Northolt) was the first of this month's training flights, also 52+49 (24th September - DCN7956 from RAF Brawdy). Note they were now using a new callsign prefix of 'DCN'.

5th Emergency services were on standby for Lloyd International Britannia G-APNA, with 127 passengers onboard. It had radioed ahead to warn ATC that they may have lost of part of a wheel on departure from Toronto. The aircraft which was due into Manchester from Toronto via Niagara Falls would have flown on to the aircraft's base at Stansted under normal circumstances, but it was unable to due to fog there. In the end it landed safely at Ringway at 0759.

5th BEA Sikorsky S-61 G-ATBJ, which passed through Ringway in June en route to Aberdeen, reversed the routing today and arrived from Aberdeen at 1821, later departing for Penzance. The following day S-61 G-ASNM arrived at 2137 from Penzance, and also departed to Aberdeen, presumably replacing G-ATBJ.

6th Today's visit of Beagle Terrier EI-ASU was one of three foreign light aircraft making their first visits during September. The other two were Beech 90 D-ILGK (15th) & PA-23 Apache OY-BKI (21st) arriving from Groningen to clear customs en route for Newtonards.

7th Wardair made its first appearance at Ringway today, rather late in the season, with Boeing 707 CF-FAN (WD688 from Toronto) on its first visit. A second flight arriving at 1208 on the 26th (WD536 from Winnipeg) departed the following afternoon for Toronto. Although the airline made irregular visits over the next six years, they would not operate a full programme from Ringway until 1975.

8th Three hundred passengers were given a 'holiday within a holiday' today, when Laker Airways experienced aircraft problems. Passengers had spent the previous evening in a Manchester hotel, instead of a Spanish one. They were provided with meals, and taken on coach trips and cinema visits after BAC 1-11 G-AVBW developed technical problems. This caused a knock-on effect to their flying programme, affecting two return flights and six hundred passengers. The airline made several unsuccessful attempts to charter other aircraft, but in the end they had to wait for a spare part to be flown up from Gatwick.

16th Two military arrivals making their first visits today were, VC-10 XR809 (RR2778 from Brize Norton) on a trooping flight to Gutersloh and Army Air Corps Sioux XT563. Arriving from Platt Fields Park (Army 452), this aircraft stayed for two days before leaving for Carlisle.

18th Having made their first visit in June as a Luton weather diversion, Monarch Airlines made their first official flight from Manchester today, when Britannia G-AOVH arrived from Luton to operate a return flight to Dublin (OM254/5). This fledgling airline operated three second-hand Bristol Britannias, but in later years became a major force in the British charter market, although their first IT programme at Manchester did not commence until 1979.

19th Two BEA Super 1-11s arriving today on first visits to be based for further crew training duties, were G-AVMJ (based until the 11th October) & G-AVMK (based until the 13th October).

25th The latest Canadian Air Force CC-106 Yukon to visit Ringway, was 15926 arriving at 1028 today on a training flight from Mildenhall to Valley.

26th The month of September was turning into a good one for military visitors. Danish Air Force Douglas C-54 K-586, which arrived at 1124 today from Vaerlose with a royal party, was in connection with a 'Danish week' being staged in Manchester.

OCTOBER 1968

Another UK charter airline that will have a greater presence at Ringway next year is Channel Airways. From April 1969, they will be operating a series of flights to Beauvais and Rotterdam with Viscounts, and from May to October, to Palma, Barcelona, Milan, Valencia, Basle, Ibiza and Rimini with their new BAC 1-11, G-AWEJ.

The first few days of October were dull with rain heavy in the north, which died out by the 3rd as a high pressure ridge came in from the south, bringing dry and very mild conditions lasting until the 8th. Cool and showery weather, with occasional longer periods of rain lasted until the 20th when another anti-cyclone established itself over the UK. Fog formed in many places on the 21st, persisting in some places until the following day. Falling pressure on the 23rd brought freshening southeasterly winds, which cleared away the fog. The rest of the month remained mild with further rain, occasionally heavy. The month's temperature extremes saw 22°C at Southend (21st) and a low of -1°C at Kielder Castle (18th).

Scheduled first visits this month were <u>BOAC (BA538)</u>: SVC-10 G-ASGO (9th), <u>KLM (KL005)</u>: Martinair DC-9 PH-MAN (24th) and <u>Sabena (SN197)</u>: B.727 OO-STE (9th). There were no equipment changes during October.

A good start again with this month's GCA/ILS traffic were the HS.748s from Woodford, with Thai Airways HS-THD (2nd) & HS-THE (30th), Avianca HK-1409 (10th), Lan Chile CC-CEK (24th) and the latest Australian Air Force frame, A10-603 (24th). The only RAF aircraft noted was Britannias XL640 (2nd), XL660 (9th/16th) & XM519 (23rd). Finally HS.125s from Hawarden started with the second Brazilian Air Force aircraft, VC93-2121 (11th /plus a touch-and-go 25th), G-AWMY (24th) & G-AVRF (29th). Training flights were operated by BOAC B.707 G-AVPB (2nd), BEA Vanguard G-APEI & Argosy G-ASXM (both 8th).

1st Danish airline Sterling operated a passenger charter from Tirstrup with one of their new Fokker F.27s, OY-STO. They operated two F.27s (with the other being OY-STN), from 1968 to 1973, but they were not regular visitors to Ringway.

1st Today was the first visit by new Dutch operator Transavia, when Douglas DC-6 PH-TRA operated a cargo flight from/to Amsterdam. As the second charter company in the Netherlands after Martinair, they started out in 1966 when two Americans bought a dormant company, Transavia Limburg. This was based in Maastricht, and had three Douglas DC-6 aircraft available. The Dutch government were approached by the airline for a licence to operate out of Amsterdam and for the DC-6s, which was issued on 14th November 1966. Two days later the first commercial flight operated from Amsterdam to Naples and return, with the Dutch Ballet Orchestra and the Dutch Dance Theatre onboard. This was also the first flight under the new name of Transavia Holland.

1st Viscount G-AVNJ from Perpignan operated Air Ferry's final flight into Manchester, later leaving for Gatwick. The airline's holding company had announced earlier in the season that they would wind up operations at the end of the month, with all services being transferred to British United. Viscounts G-AVHE & G-AVNJ would go to Channel Airways, while C-54s G-ARWI & G-ASFY and DC-6s G-APNO & G-APNP would all be put up for sale.

1st With the introduction of more Comets into service with Dan-Air, visits by the airline's ageing Airspeed Ambassadors became increasingly rare as the year progressed. Today however, the airline began a series of charters to/from Luxembourg, operating throughout the month with G-ALZO/AMAE & AMAH.

2nd As reigning champions of the European Cup, Manchester United kicked off the defence of the trophy with a two-legged match with Waterford, which provided two extra Aer Lingus charters with Viscounts EI-AJJ (EI206A) & EI-AJI (EI5210). The Irish champions provided no resistance whatsoever, and were soundly beaten 10-2 on aggregate.

2nd The latest Cessna delivered through Ringway was Cessna 337 G-AWKR, landing at 1429 today from Shannon, leaving later for Cranfield. However, the aircraft was short-lived on the UK register as it was sold in Israel as 4X-AYD the following month.

3rd PA-24 Comanche F-BLOM, night-stopping on a flight from Southampton, made its only visit to Ringway today. Other first visits during October were Beech 55 SE-EKU (6th), Beech 23 OY-AOZ (18th), Cessna 337 D-GAFY (20th) and finally Cessna 402 OY-AHP (22nd) on the first of its two visits (with the other being August 1970). In 1971, OY-AHP was sold in Kenya as 5Y-ANJ, but two years later it found itself on the UK register as G-BAWZ.

3rd Army Air Corps Siouxs XT154 (JDU 69), XT186 (JDU 68) & XT243 (JDU64) all arrived with ten minutes of each other, from Barton at lunchtime today. They stayed for just under two hours, before departing in formation for Castle Donington.

6th The season's penultimate JAT flight, operated by SE.210 YU-AHF, arrived at 0142 today from Dubrovnik with one engine malfunctioning. The unit which was found to be beyond local repair left the aircraft and the outbound passengers stranded. Telexes bounced back and forth to Belgrade, but no suitable replacement was found. Yugotours found this unacceptable, and pressurised the airline into providing another aircraft. Finally at 1846, Yugoslav government Ilyushin IL-18 YU-AIB arrived from Split, and departed to Pula eighteen hours late. This was the second time this summer JAT had problems with SE.210 YU-AHF, with the first being on 1st July when DC-3 YU-ACA was called to the rescue again to fly in some spare parts.

12th October 1968 – It was proving to be a great year for piston-powered aircraft! Arguably the best visitor this year was Ebano Petroleum Douglas DC-6A XC-DUC, arriving from Marseilles at 1039 today for fuel. Whilst on the ground the crew decided to air their machine innards, and opened the front and rear cargo doors. This charitable action revealed two Alouette III helicopters, bearing the registrations XC-DUM & XC-DUN. This immaculate aircraft departed at 1559 for Shannon/Gander/New Orleans, eventually bound for Mexico City. (Above Bob Thorpe, below Geoff Ball)

22nd October 1968 - Royal Canadian Navy S2F Tracker arrived on a hazy morning from Lee-on-Solent. It was one of thirteen attached to the Royal Canadian Navy's Bonaventure, berthed at Portsmouth. However, this Tracker, along with three others, had been temporarily based at Lee-on-Solent. Remarkably, the same aircraft diverted in on 11th October 1969, when it gave up trying to land at Gatwick! (Dave Jones)

28th October 1968 – Jetstar N530G arriving at 0900 from Prestwick, was a first visit of type on a fuel stop departing to Tripoli an hour later. Registered in 1966, it was operated by Beta Aviation right up until 2004, when it was eventually scrapped, although the fuselage still survives at Conroe, Texas. (Geoff Ball)

7ᵗʰ With the problems of SE.210 YU-AHF still unresolved, more entertainment followed today when JAT's cargo DC-3, YU-ACA, made its second visit to Manchester. It was carrying a replacement engine and the new unit was fitted in a matter of hours. YU-AHF finally departed on a positioning flight to Belgrade at 0213 on the 8ᵗʰ. Predictably, this was final straw for Yugotours after all the problems they had already encountered with JAT during the summer, so their contract was not renewed. In 1974, they became regulars again on the airline's summer services to Dubrovnik, but eventually all of these aircraft had been phased out by 1978.

16ᵗʰ With the advent of Cambrian withdrawing Dakota services from Manchester at the end of September, movements by this venerable aircraft started to become scarce. However, there were two DC-3 movements today. The first was USAF C-47 0-49185 arriving at 0958 from Leeds. The second was Air Ulster DC-3 G-AMJU arriving at 1529 on a return flight from Belfast, bringing in supporters for an intercontinental cup match between Manchester United and Estudiantes de La Plata.

20ᵗʰ Britannia Airways began their winter programme, with Boeing 737s for the first time, scheduled to operate a once-weekly to Palma via Blackpool. G-AVRM was used on today's flight, and G-AVRL was also utilised during the winter.

24ᵗʰ RAF Hastings TG536 (AEU59) arrived at 1420 today on a flight from RAF Lindholme to RAF Leuchars. It would become the last of its type to land at Manchester, although there would be further visits by various aircraft on training flights, with TG500 (4ᵗʰ August 1971) & WD499 (17ᵗʰ July 1969/9ᵗʰ July 1971). The Hastings was developed as a long-range transport aircraft that served with both the RAF and the Royal New Zealand Air Force. The first prototype flew on 4ᵗʰ May 1946 and entered service in 1948. A total of 147 plus two production aircraft were built, which could accommodate thirty paratroopers or fifty fully equipped soldiers. Most of the Royal Air Forces' Hastings had been withdrawn by 1968, but several soldiered on until 1975, by which time they had been converted for weather reconnaissance use.

28ᵗʰ BKS, later to become Northeast Airlines in 1970, had operated up to five Airspeed Ambassadors since 1958. By now they were just operating just one, G-ALZR, used almost exclusively as a 'horsebox'. Today, it was operating one such flight to Dublin. It would make three further visits, with the last on the 2ⁿᵈ March 1969. On the 26ᵗʰ July 1969 during a flight from Paris-Orly, its nosewheel collapsed on landing at Gatwick. It was eventually ferried to Lasham and later broken up.

30ᵗʰ A very early example of a DH.104 Dove was today's appearance of G-ARGN, operating f/t Cranfield on the first of two visits during the year. In 1962 after a spell in Canada and the USA, it returned to the UK as G-ARGN. Three years later was registered to Rogers Aviation at Cranfield, but by December 1970 it was withdrawn and the fuselage ended up at Hatfield.

31ˢᵗ Fog affecting Liverpool throughout the morning produced nine diversions. The only aircraft of interest was the first visit of Beech 90 OY-BAL, arriving at 0920 from Sonderborg.

NOVEMBER 1968

BEA would launch a service linking Glasgow and Manchester with Dusseldorf from April 1969, initially with Comets. From May, the service would be extended to Berlin and also introduce their Super 1-11s. At the same time, the night tourist flights to Palma previously operated by Vanguards will now be operated at the weekends by Tridents, originating and terminating at Glasgow. Also on the subject of BEA, their Super 1-11s which will be used on joint BEA/Air France routes within Germany, were obliged not to wear the company's new national tail insignia, as Air France had objected to the Union Jack that is featured. Accordingly it has been left off their entire Super 1-11 fleet.

The first couple of days were mild and wet over most of England before moving away, and the winds changed to a northerly direction with hail showers and snow in northern England. Temperatures in all districts fell well below the average. High pressure taking charge on the 8ᵗʰ lasted for two weeks. This brought cloudy, cold and mostly dry weather with moderate winds from the south and east. On the 9ᵗʰ, winds became light and variable and overnight fog persisted over the Midlands throughout the day. From the 20ᵗʰ, mild weather returned with showers or longer spells of rain. The month's temperature extremes saw 18°C at Camden Square (1ˢᵗ) and a low of -12°C at Grantown-on-Spey (18ᵗʰ).

Seen during the winter operating ITs to various destinations were <u>Autair</u> (Palma), <u>Britannia Airways</u> (Palma), <u>British United</u> (Palma) & <u>Laker Airways</u> (Ibiza/Las Palmas/Palma/Tenerife). Included was British

Eagle's weekly Sunday flight to Palma, which operated once (3rd November) before the airline's unfortunate demise later in the month.

International flights were operated during the summer as follows:

AER LINGUS - Amsterdam (2 x weekly), Copenhagen (2 x weekly), Cork (2 x weekly), Dusseldorf (3 x weekly), Frankfurt (2 x weekly) & Zurich (1 x weekly), with the exception of Cork, all other flights operated by BAC 1-11s.

AIR FRANCE - Three-weekly to Paris with SE.210s (AF960/1).

ALITALIA - Operated twice-weekly to Milan and Rome, now with Douglas DC-9s (AZ296/7).

BEA - Operated services to Amsterdam/Brussels/Copenhagen/Dublin/Dusseldorf/Paris & Zurich with Tridents. Super 1-11s began to operate on certain flights to London-Heathrow.

BOAC - Daily to New York/Antigua & Barbados via Prestwick (BA538/7) with VC-10s, extending to Port of Spain & Georgetown on Tue/Thu/Fri/Sun. Boeing 707s operated to Montreal (1 x weekly) & Toronto (4 x weekly). Cargo flights outbound to Montreal (3 x weekly) & New York (6 x weekly), with the inbound from New York increased (4 x weekly).

BRITISH EAGLE - Operated a weekday flight to Frankfurt via Liverpool until 6th Nov; when the airline ceased trading.

IBERIA - Began a twice-weekly service to Madrid via Dublin with SE.210s (IB744/3).

KLM - Passenger flights operated to Amsterdam three-times-weekly (KL153/4) and cargo operations continued from/to Amsterdam five-weekly via Glasgow (KL005). Both flights were now operating with Douglas DC-9s.

LUFTHANSA - Operated their cargo flight five-weekly (LH934/5) to Frankfurt with Aer Turas Douglas C-54s/DC-4s. From January, All-Air Douglas C-54s took over the route once again (LH934/5).

SABENA - The night-stopping Brussels service continued four-times-weekly with SE.210 Caravelles. Cargo flights operated four-weekly cargo flights with B.727s f/t Brussels, with the outbound via Heathrow (SN197/8).

SAS - Operated three weekly flights serving Copenhagen with SE.210s (SK537/8), extending to Dublin.

SWISSAIR - Cargo flights continued with a three-weekly service to Zurich with Douglas DC-4s. From the 20th December, a once-weekly passenger flight to Zurich (SR842/3) was introduced with Douglas DC-9s.

With the introduction of DC-9s onto the Alitalia service to Milan and Rome, there were plenty of scheduled first visits, with Alitalia (AZ296): I-DIKB (8th), I-DIKJ (22nd), I-DIKL (6th), I-DIKM (1st), I-DIKN (29th) & I-DIKP (27th), BEA (BE4108): BAC 1-11s G-AVML (29th) & G-AVMO (28th), and Sabena (SN623): B.727 OO-STA (18th).

GCA/ILS traffic this month once again started with aircraft from Woodford, RAF Nimrods XV147 (20th/22nd) & XV226 (1st/13th/15th) and HS.748s HS-THF (27th) & Fiji Airways VQ-FBH (18th). RAF traffic noted during the month was Comet XR396 (5th) and Britannias XL635 (7th), XL658 (20th), XM518 (26th) & XM519 (26th). Also HS.125 LN-NPA (5th), British Midland Viscount G-ASED (20th) and Autair BAC 1-11 G-AWBL (25th). BOAC were out in force during November with the following Boeing 707s noted operating training flights, G-APFC (24th/26th/27th), G-APFJ (7th), G-APFD (10th/12th/13th), G-APFP (20th), G-ARRC (6th) & G-ASZG (26th).

1st Iberia began twice-weekly flights from/to Madrid with SE.210 EC-AXU (IB744/3). The flight continues on to Dublin. Part of the outbound cargo on this inaugural flight was 5,000 one day old chicks. Other aircraft used during the month were EC-ARK (20th), EC-ATV (29th), EC-AVY (13th/27th), EC-AVZ (8th) & EC-AYE (6th/15th/22nd).

1st F-BRHB was the sixth and final Falcon 20 to make its first visit this year. Operated by Europe Falcon Service, it arrived at 1434 today from Geneva.

2nd Arriving for maintenance with BEA today was Viscount G-AOYK, which arrived at 1405 from Heathrow. It had been on lease to Cyprus Airways since October 1965, and was wearing their full colours and titles. It left for Nicosia via Heathrow on the 14th November. In May 1970 it returned to BEA, and was then sold to Mandala Airlines as PK-RVK.

6th Formed in 1948 with converted Halifax bombers, Eagle (later Cunard Eagle and finally British Eagle) ceased trading today and took the aviation industry by surprise. Press and television interviews revealed an unawareness of the situation. British Eagle had become a familiar sight at Ringway, with a variety of aircraft including Vikings, Viscounts, DC-6s, Britannias, 1-11s and Boeing 707s. The airline's services ranged from domestic and European schedules to a wide range of charter and inclusive tour flights. During the second week of September 1968, the news began filtering through to Eagle staff, and it was just a matter of when it would happen. Also during September the airline closed its maintenance base at Liverpool, with the loss of around 400 employees. The servicing of their Viscount fleet was transferred to Heathrow, which also suffered a cut in its work force. The following month four Britannias were seen parked up at Liverpool. The main reasons cited were a fall off in holiday traffic, the £50 holiday allowance and the failure to secure an Australian immigration contract, coupled with a general decline in operations for the winter period. The final flight operating from Liverpool was Viscount G-ATDR (EG755 from Glasgow). Once landed, it was immediately towed to the hangar, together with the company's ground handling equipment and then sealed off by the police. The last flight from Manchester was operated by BAC 1-11 G-ATPH 'Salute', which flew the EG660/1 Frankfurt flight, departing at 1722 today for the final time bound for Liverpool.

9th Ringway only saw eight arrivals today due to persistent fog.

12th Aer Turas Douglas C-54 EI-APK departed at 1449 (LH935 to Frankfurt), only to return just over an hour later as a full emergency. It departed to Wymeswold on three engines for further attention on the 16th. Bristol 170 EI-APC arrived from Dublin to operate the flight for the next few days.

13th Belgian side Anderlecht came to Manchester for a European Cup second round first-leg game with Manchester United. The team arrived aboard Belgian International Douglas DC-6 OO-ABE. Their fans arrived on Sobelair DC-6s OO-CTL & OO-CTN, which both night-stopped. Manchester United were again victorious, winning 3-0 but the return two weeks later was a close run thing.

13th Cessna 172 N13727 f/t Blackpool (became OO-LCN), was the only light aircraft making its first visit this month.

14th The A538 Wilmslow-Altrincham 1,288ft road tunnel opened for business at a cost of £750,000. With a 12ft thick concrete roof, it could take the weight of Boeing 747s on the newly extended 9,000ft runway, which became operational in January 1969.

17th BEA introduced the Super 1-11 into service today on routes from Manchester. It now operated the type daily on its evening Heathrow service BE4108, with G-AVMM operating the inaugural flight, touching down on Runway 06 at 2022. The aircraft night-stops and returns to Heathrow the following morning as BE4065. Other aircraft used this month were G-AVML (f/v - 29th Nov) & G-AVMO (f/v - 28th Nov). Also from this date, BEA introduced the type on their German internal routes.

26th Sabena produced another Boeing 707 first visit, when OO-SJJ arrived on an additional freight service from Brussels (SN197A), departing later for Heathrow.

26th On an interesting day for variety, RAF Britannia XM518 made its first visit, arriving at 0856 as a Lyneham diversion (RR6641 from Nicosia). Also making its debut at Ringway was RAF Comet C.4 XR396 (EKX 49) at 1224 from RAF Lyneham, arriving to pick a senior RAF official off Britannia XM518.

27th Manchester United flew out this morning for their return match with Anderlecht, aboard British Air Services (an amalgamation of BKS and Cambrian) Viscount G-ATTA. British Midland Viscount G-AVJA provided a fans' charter. Regarding the match itself, United went one up within ten minutes to make it 4-0 on aggregate, which woke up the Belgians enough to make a spirited fight back. They pulled back three goals, but needed another two which proved a challenge too far!

27th Despite the weather towards the end of the month being in a changeable phase, today was foggy across Yorkshire, Lancashire and the Midlands. Twelve diversions descending on Ringway were mostly from Leeds and Blackpool. The only aircraft worthy of a mention was Jet Commander N111AC, arriving at 0048 from Keflavik, originally intended for Luton.

28th It was southern England's turn to be affected by fog, and although it was a very patchy affair, both Heathrow and Gatwick were affected at various times during the day. Another RAF Britannia, XN404, made its first visit at 1930 (RR6130 from Gibraltar), while Alitalia DC-9 I-DIKP (AZ284 from Milan) made its second visit, having only made its first the previous day operating the scheduled AZ296 flight.

3rd November 1968 – Dove G-ARDH, operated by engineering company David Brown Ltd, arrived at 1446 from Amsterdam, clearing customs en route for Crossland Moor. Converted to Riley standards during 1966 with uprated engines, it retained an original Dove tail. The remains of Yew Tree Lane seen at the top left of the photograph, gave excellent views across the apron at Fairey's, particularly during the 1950s when the Firefly conversions were in full swing. It was breached by the completion of the international pier and apron in the early 1960s. (Geoff Ball)

12th November 1968 - This month's West German Air Force training flight operated by Noratlas 52+79, is seen arriving at 1427 (DCN8223 from Neubiberg), departing for Erding the next morning. (Geoff Ball)

26th November 1968 - An interesting trio of Cessnas arrived today, to be placed on 'static display' for prospective buyers, before departing for Cranfield. They were Cessna 337 N2691S (from Luton - dep 2nd December), Cessna 401 N4065Q (from Glasgow - dep 9th December) and Cessna 411 N3256R (from Luton - dep 11th December). All were brand new 1968-built models, owned and operated by Cessna Aircraft Corp. If the Cessna 401 and Cessna 411 look similar, it's because they are! The 401 was basically a 411, but intended for different usage as medium to light executive transport, intended to be inexpensive to purchase and operate. These three Cessnas were all re-registered and placed on the UK register next month, when C.337 N2691S became G-AWVS, C.401 N4065Q became G-AWXM and C.411 N3256R became G-AWVT. (Both Geoff Ball)

28th Taking the airline industry completely by surprise, was today's announcement by Transglobe that they had ceased trading. This unexpected occurrence was brought about after two of their major shareholders introduced winding up proceedings. Seaboard World, who were leasing three CL-44s to the airline, were caught totally unaware, and said later that had they have known of Transglobe's problems, they would have given all possible assistance. However, nothing could have saved the collapse, and as a result Seaboard World restored their three aircraft to the US register and then leased them direct to Trans Mediterranean Airways. Subsequently, Seaboard assisted in the formation of a new British airline to operate the CL-44 fleet named Tradewinds. The last of Transglobe's Britannias to visit Ringway was G-ATGD (13th September - IK863 from Malaga) and the very final visit took place on 28th October, when CL-44 G-AWDK operated a freight flight to Beirut.

29th November 1968 – Europe Aero Service Viking F-BJES arrived from Le Bourget with the French Rugby League team for a match against St. Helens. Staying until the 1st December, it was the last visit of type. It was also the last serviceable Viking in Europe, operating until 1972, when it was withdrawn at Nice. It was later flown to Le Bourget and used for many years by the fire service for non-destructive practice. (Geoff Ball)

DECEMBER 1968
From April next year, BOAC will introduce non-stop direct SVC-10 flights to New York, three days a week (BA534/3) and via Prestwick (BA538/7) the other four days. Despite the introduction of direct flights, there will be no fare changes, typically £160 14s for an off-peak return and £196 7s in high season. Three-week excursion fares are available at £119 4s.

A ridge of high pressure extending westwards to Scandinavia from an anticyclone over central Europe maintained a southeasterly airstream over the UK during the first ten days. Frost was widespread at night, but the days were dull with drizzle and fog. By the 11th, pressure rose with winds leading to extensive all-day fog in places. On the 15th, a deepening depression brought in heavy rain across the UK. This was preceded by snow in northern areas and by the morning of the 16th, much of Lancashire was under 5-7cm of snow. Further disturbances moving eastwards brought heavy rain on the 17th and 20th. Another vigorous depression on the 22nd swept through with gales and heavy rain preceded by high pressure, which gave a dry day on the 23rd. Things got really interesting on Christmas Eve, when heavy rain turned to snow during the evening. On Christmas morning snow lay 10-15cm deep at many places in southern England. During the next three days under a northerly wind, snowfall was heavy in Norfolk, Lincolnshire and North Yorkshire, where the county suffered snowdrifts blocking many roads. Whitby was cut off for several days by 2m snowdrifts and even recorded a gust of 80kts during a blizzard. The year ended with freezing fog in the south with snow showers continuing in eastern districts. The month's temperature extremes saw 14°C at Bude (2nd) and a low of -11°C at Great Dun Fell (28th).

Scheduled first visits this month were BEA (BE4108): BAC 1-11s G-AVMN (24th) & G-AVMP (30th), KLM (KL153): DC-9 PH-DNS (27th), Sabena (SN623): B.727 OO-STC (9th) and Swissair (SR842): DC-9 HB-IFL (27th).

Very little GCA/ILS traffic was noted in December compared to previous months, Lan Chile HS.748 CC-CEI (12th), PA-30 Twin Comanche G-AVPF (19th) and RAF Britannias XM491 (17th) & XM498 (18th). Training flights were much more prominent with BEA Argosy G-ATTC (30th), 1-11s G-AVML & G-AVMM (both 5th) and BOAC Boeing 707s G-APFD (7th), G-APFM (12th) & G-ARWD (13th).

5th The first of three foreign light aircraft making their first visits was today's arrival of Beech 80 D-ILKE from/to Worms. The other two were PA-23 Aztec D-IBOV from Dusseldorf (13th) and Beagle Airedale EI-ATD from White Waltham. (24th)

6th Transair Sweden Douglas DC-7 SE-ERD made its second and final visit, which also marked the airline's final appearance at Ringway. Arriving at 1241 from Gatwick, it was operating a passenger charter to Malmo (TB206). In 1967 three Boeing 727-134s were acquired (SE-DDA/DDB & DDC) but they were sold to Scanair two years later. SAS would eventually take a majority holding in Transair Sweden, who continued to fly independently under its own colours taking tourists to Spain, the Canary Islands and other Mediterranean destinations. In 1981 SAS sold all the 727s and the employees were integrated into SAS.

6th Qantas B.707 VH-EAE (QF172) operated an outbound charter organised by the Overseas Friends and Families Association, for ninety parents paying from £290-£340 for the privilege of being reunited with their children in Australia. A similar charter was flown the following week (13th) operated by VH-EBV. The return flight arrived back into Manchester on the 20th January, operated by B.707 VH-EAC.

7th Australian Air Force HS.748 A10-604 arrived at 1849 today from Glasgow to operate a number of local crew training flights until the 9th, when it returned to Woodford.

12th The first major diversion day of the winter saw the arrival of nineteen aircraft, although it didn't start until mid-evening. Unfortunately over half were BEA aircraft and the only non-British aircraft was Qantas B.707 VH-EAE at 2350 (QF530 from New York).

12th Newly delivered to BAC as a corporate hack, was HS.125 G-AVPE, which made its first visit today. Operating from/to Bristol-Filton, it was on the ground for a mere ten minutes. Although it operated for BAC until 1989, it would not appear at Ringway again until the 16th August 1974.

13th Devon C.2 VP981 was the first of its type to be delivered to the Royal Air Force back in 1946. Today, it made its first visit to Ringway during the decade, arriving at 1039 (CUP 59) from St. Athan. In later years it was operated as transport for the Battle of Britain Memorial Flight, and is currently registered with Air Atlantique as G-DHDV.

13th The diversions continued into the early hours, again with the majority from BEA, but there were a couple of noteworthy arrivals. The last Breguet BR.760 to visit was F-BASU at 0633 (from Paris-Orly) and East African Comet 5X-AAO arrived at 0435 (from Benina). There was also two RAF diversions, with VC-10 XR807 at 1224 (RR2583 from Rome) and the first visit of their recently delivered C-130 Hercules, XV181, at 1404 (RR3370 from Gander). There were so many flights arriving at a time when staffing levels would have been low to say the least, so extra staff had to be called in at very short notice. Over one thousand passengers were eventually ferried back to London by coach and rail, or put up overnight.

13th Today's appearance of G-ANCE proved to be the final visit of a British United Britannia, operating from/to Hanover. All three remaining aircraft, G-ANCD & G-ANCE (both sold to Lloyd International) & G-APNB (sold to Donaldson International) had been sold by March 1969. This would leave the airline operating just three turboprops, Viscounts G-APTB/APTC/APTD, for the 1969 summer season. These Viscounts would also be disposed of by October 1969, leaving the airline operating an all-BAC fleet of VC-10s, BAC 1-11-500s and the smaller BAC 1-11-200s.

16th This month's West German Air Force training flight was operated by Noratlas 53+04, which arrived at 1327 today from Neubiberg, departing for Erding the following morning.

17th Wardair made an outbound Christmas charter to Vancouver (WD803) today, operated by Boeing 707 CF-FAN. A return flight for English families that had emigrated to Canada arrived the following morning (WD700 from Vancouver), again with B.707 CF-FAN.

27th December 1968 - While the eastern side of the UK was suffering real wintry weather, Ringway in contrast was basking in long periods of winter sunshine, although on the cold side. BEA were now settling into their Super 1-11 schedules, generally operating two a day, a night-stopping flight and one at lunchtime. G-AVMJ is seen here offloading its passengers from both forward and rear steps, having recently arrived as BE4080. (Geoff Ball)

FIRST/LAST ARRIVALS & DEPARTURES 1968

First arrival: Cambrian Viscount G-ALWF from Liverpool @ 0934
First departure: Aer Lingus Viscount EI-AJK (EI9215) to Dublin @ 0101
Last arrival: BEA Argosy G-ASXM from Glasgow @ 2209
Last departure: BEA Argosy G-ASXM to Heathrow @ 2318

Airport Stats 1968 (+/- % on Previous Year)		
Scheduled Passengers	1,058,000	-1.0%
Inclusive & Charter Passengers	407,000	+19.7%
Freight & Mail (Tonnes)	37,100	+11.0%
Movements	51,600	+1.3%

AIRPORT DIARY 1969

JANUARY 1969

BEA's Manchester-Heathrow flights, which were steadily losing passengers to British Rail, began to show signs of improvement with the introduction of the BAC 1-11 in November 1968. Both November and December showed healthy increases on the same months the year previously in 1967.

Swissair will upgrade its Zurich passenger service to daily from April, operating via Rotterdam, and night-stopping. The airline also planned to increase the frequency of its cargo flights up to four-weekly.

The UK was under the influence of an anti-cyclone to the southwest for the first three days, with cyclonic conditions for most of the month. Winds mainly from a southerly point brought lots of dull and mild weather. Heavy rain on some days caused local floods, with some very stormy periods. On the 17th, a gust of 79kts was recorded in the Scilly Isles, the same day the Lyme Regis inshore lifeboat capsized, drowning a member of the crew. However, cooler and brighter weather took over towards the end of the month. The month's temperature extremes saw 14°C at Prestatyn (20th) and a low of -11°C at Moor House (6th).

Scheduled first visits were Alitalia (AZ296): DC-9 I-DIKO (15th), BEA (BE4108): BAC 1-11s G-AVMS (13th) & Swissair (SR842): DC-9s HB-IFK (17th), HB-IFN (31st), HB-IFO (24th) & HB-IFS (10th). Equipment changes during January were confined to Sabena (SN623): B.727s OO-STD (7th/12th) & OO-STE (20th/27th) and DC-6 OO-CTL (13th).

GCA/ILS traffic noted during the month was RAF Britannia XL635 (8th), XL660 (14th), XN398 (21st), XM491 (30th) & Comet XR395 (22nd). HS.748s from Woodford were Australian Air Force A10-605 (9th/27th) and demonstrator G-AVRR (27th). Also Pelita Air Services HS.125 PK-PJR (13th), British Midland Viscount G-AVJA (13th) & Dove G-ANMJ (24th). Further training flights by BOAC were operated by B.707s G-APFD (9th) & G-APFL (13th/17th).

3rd   Fog at Ringway restricted movements today, with no arrivals prior to 1427. As so often was the case, fog in the north was followed by fog in the south and today was such an occasion!

4th January 1969 – In contrast to the cool, foggy conditions in the south, Manchester had a little rain during the morning, easing off by lunchtime. This early afternoon shot shows a busy apron. In the background, parked on the South Bay are Alitalia DC-8 I-DIWU & East African VC-10 5H-MMT. (Geoff Ball)

4th   Ringway saw the busiest day in a January since 1966! Twenty-two diversions arrived in less than five hours, all but one from Heathrow. Alitalia/Zambia DC-8 I-DIWU which made its first visit at 1115 (QZ800 from Pisa), was on lease to the Zambian President, attending a Commonwealth Conference in London.

Other first visits were East African Airways VC-10 5Y-ADA at 1126 (EC718 from Paris Orly), MEA VC-10 OD-AFA at 1256 (ME201 from Beirut), Qantas B.707 VH-EBN at 1200 (QF759 from Athens) and SAS DC-9s LN-RLK at 1215 (SK501 from Copenhagen) & SE-DBU at 1342 (SK513 from Stavanger). BOAC were represented by B.707s G-APFD (BA600 from Toronto) & G-APFI (BA921 from Rome) & VC-10s G-ARVB (BA799 from Tehran), G-ASGF (BA500 from New York), G-ASGI (BA568 from Montreal), G-ASGJ (BA506 from New York), G-ASGL (BA128 from Rome) & G-ASGN (BA130 from Zurich). Amongst some of the other foreign airlines diverting in were Sudan Airways Comet ST-AAW at 1005 (SD116 from Rome), Qantas B.707 VH-EBV at 1241 (QF739 from Rome) and Alitalia DC-9 I-DIKM (AZ284 from Milan). By 1500 Ringway was running short of space, but the remaining stubborn fog had started to clear. The final diversion of the day was British United VC-10 G-ASIW at 1807 (BR662 from Madrid).

6th   Falconair Viscount SE-CNL diverting in at 0337 (FZ1704 from Oslo) from Dublin, was the first visit to Ringway by this new Swedish airline. Formed in 1967 and based at Malmo, they operated two Vickers Viscounts (SE-CNK/CNL). They made three further visits during the year, all with their second Viscount, SE-CNK (29th June/27th July & 24th August). In August 1971 they were renamed Skyline Sweden, with SE-CNK continuing in service until August 1976 and SE-CNL only seeing service until October 1972.

6th   All-Air were due to take over the Lufthansa cargo flight from Aer Turas at the beginning of this month, but all flights were cancelled up until today, when Invicta C-54 G-ASEN took charge of LH934/5. Invicta operated all the flights, using C-54s G-ASEN & G-ASPN until the 22nd, when All-Air finally took over.

7th   Manchester Airport became truly international today! All aircraft movements were stopped for fifteen minutes as the Lord Mayor, Alderman Harold Stockdale, performed the opening ceremony and cut the ribbon. The extension of runway 06/24 from 7,900ft to 9,000ft was now complete and open for business. It was capable of allowing any plane to fly fully loaded, particularly transatlantic aircraft, without the need to stop at Shannon or Prestwick. The first aircraft to land on the newly extended strip was BOAC B.707 G-APFD (BA638 from Toronto/Montreal/Prestwick), which was also the first to depart on it when it left for Heathrow. However, the departure of Wardair B.707 CF-FAN (WD701) at 1135 was more significant. It was fully laden with fuel and passengers on the 4,800 mile direct flight to Vancouver.

7th   The first RAF visitor of 1969 was today's appearance of Rescue HAR.10 Whirlwind XP350 at 1225 from its base at RAF Valley, leaving an hour later for RAF Leconfield.

8th January 1969 - Brantly B2B G-AWIO would make numerous visits during 1969, calling in for fuel while operating pipeline patrol duties. A popular type during the early to mid 1960s, this UK-produced helicopter was quickly usurped by the likes of the Bell 47 and Jet Ranger. This particular example lasted longer than most, operating until 1995 when it was cancelled by the CAA. (Geoff Ball)

10th Emphasising the advantage the extended runway now gives Ringway, was Pan American B.707 N704PA operating direct from/to New York today with near full loads each way.

14th Hawker Siddeley demonstrator HS.125 G-AVXL was used by Granada today for two return trips to Heathrow, due to Granada's own HS.125 being serviced at Hawarden.

15th PA-23 Apache EI-ATI was this month's only light aircraft making its first visit to Manchester. It would make several more appearances until August 1970, when it crashed at Ballyfree. However, it was rebuilt by CSE at Oxford and re-registered as G-AYWY in April 1971.

16th Another foggy day at Ringway, with just five arrivals prior to 1708.

17th This month's West German Air Force training flight was operated by Noratlas 53+04 (DCN8485), which arrived at 1327 today from Upper Heyford, leaving later for Erding.

18th Cessna 421 G-AWRJ arriving at 0859 today (Flo Air 167 from Shannon), was the latest aircraft passing through on delivery for Rogers Aviation at Cranfield. In February 1969 it was sold to British Steel, who operated it until 1974, before passing it back to Rogers Aviation and later Bournemouth-based Shackleton Aviation. In August 1976 it was sold in the USA as N96192.

18th British United had lost BAC 1-11 G-ASJJ four days earlier, when it was damaged beyond repair in a landing accident at Milan-Linate. This resulted in a number of aircraft substitutions to cover the airline's trooping flights which began today with Caledonian Britannia G-ATMA (CA803 to Dusseldorf). The others were Autair BAC 1-11 G-AVOF (22nd/23rd), Caledonian Britannia G-ASTF (22nd - CA806 from Dusseldorf) and Viscount G-APTD (29th - BR564/3 f/t Hanover).

20th Canadian Air Force Douglas DC-3 KJ828 (CAF 460 from Zweibrucken) was the penultimate Canadian Dakota to visit Manchester. This aircraft formed part of the 1st Air Division, which was part of the Royal Canadian Air Force's contribution to NATO in Europe. The final one to visit, KG455 (26th April), would return to Canada during 1970 and be withdrawn from service in 1975. The RCAF operated 169 Dakotas from 1943 until 1989 when 402-Squadron based at Winnipeg retired the last of them.

22nd Transportflug finally recommenced cargo flights today on behalf of Lufthansa. Douglas DC-6F D-ABAZ made its first visit today, while another aircraft, C-54F D-ABOW, made its first visit on the 29th.

24th Amongst the cargo uploaded onto today's BOAC Cargo B.707F G-ASZF (BA067 to Montreal/New York), was a consignment of 3,762 record turntables bound for the USA.

29th Dan-Air Douglas DC-7 G-ATAB arriving at 1202 today to night-stop from Rome was also making its final visit, before departing for Budapest on a cargo charter. In June 1969, it was withdrawn from use at Lasham and sat around in relatively good condition until August 1973 when the scrapman finally got round to it!

FEBRUARY 1969

With the demise of British Eagle, Channel Airways had secured a contract for flights to Tunis on behalf of Wright's Holidays, which would have been operated by the airline's Tridents. However, the holiday company went into liquidation before any flights could take place.

By 1969 it was generally accepted that one of the most useful tools to any large industrial or business group was an aircraft. Not least amongst the motor manufacturing companies, whose aircraft were readily available to transport personnel between distant plants within the UK or Europe. Examples of these in the late-1960s were two executive Gulfstreams, G-ASXT & G-AWYF, owned by Ford and Cessna 411 G-ATEY owned by the Roote Group. With the increase in light aviation production, the cost of owning an aircraft was coming within reach of the retailers and garages unable to afford the more expensive executive types. One of the first garages in England to acquire their own aircraft was Renton's based in Hollinwood on the A62 Oldham Road. Mr. Ralph Renton, manager of the family business established since 1929, was keenly interested in aviation for business and pleasure. In June 1964, he bought his first aircraft, Cessna 172E G-ASSX and between 1964 and 1969 he owned several aircraft. Those connected with him during this time were Cessna 172G G-ATNH and Cessna 172Hs G-AVBZ, G-AVUF & G-AWGW. By February 1969 Renton's owned Cessna 172H G-AWMZ & Cessna 337 G-ATSM. As they were the main Ford agents in the Oldham area, these aircraft were used extensively, making frequent trips collecting urgently required spares from the Ford plant at Dagenham. On these occasions the flights operated to Stapleford, nine miles from Dagenham, or Southend which was eighteen miles. In some cases the Cessna 337, with its 1,390nm range, was also used to collect spares from Ford plants on the continent when unavailable in Britain. The cost of this type of operation was comparable with the rail fare, but a lot quicker! It paid dividends, as his customers were very appreciative of the service provided, as having one of their vehicles off the road could cost them hundred pounds a day. Mr. Renton also acted as an agent for Leeds-based Northair, selling Cessna 150 and Cessna 172 models to various customers over the past few years. He even placed a Cessna in his car showroom in November 1968. As Reims Aviation in France produced the Cessna 150 range under licence, an aircraft was flown to Yeadon, dismantled and brought by transporter to Hollinwood to be reassembled in the car showrooms by Northair staff. Sitting comfortably between a red Cortina and a red Escort, resplendent in a 1969 gold and white colour scheme, was Cessna F.150J G-AWTX. Complete with radio and priced at £6,466, its presence came as quite a surprise to those looking to purchase a new car!

Low pressure to the east and south and high pressure to the west and north of Britain led to NE winds, which were responsible for exceptionally cold weather. There were blizzards in many places, which severely curtailed any sporting activities. A record gust of 118kt at Kirkwall on the morning of the 7th was accompanied by a temperature of -4°C. It was the coldest February since 1963, with severe frost at night persisting all day in many places around mid-month. A thaw which began during the last week of the month was mainly in the south. The month's temperature extremes saw 13°C at Wisley (22nd) and a low of -21°C at Newton Rigg, Cumberland (16th).

Scheduled first visits were Alitalia (AZ296): DC-9 I-DIBD (12th), I-DIKC (5th), I-DIKY (19th) & I-DIKZ (14th), KLM (KL153): DC-9 PH-DNV (12th) and Swissair (SR842): DC-9s HB-IFT (28th) & HB-IFM (21st). Equipment changes were again confined to Sabena (SN623): B.727s OO-STA (17th) and DC-6s OO-CTK (3rd) & OO-CTL (10th/24th).

Due to the inclement weather mid-month, GCA/ILS traffic was much reduced. Noted was RAF Comet C.4 XR397 (12th), and three HS.748s from Woodford were Philippine Airlines PI-C1023 (5th) and Australian Air Force A10-605 (5th/22nd) & A10-606 (24th). Training flights were operated by BOAC B.707 G-APFO (3rd) & Laker Airways BAC 1-11 G-AVBY (25th).

1st US Army Sikorsky CH-34A 0-34506 was the fourth different Chocktaw to visit Manchester, arriving at 1125 from Manston en route for Burtonwood. Yet another CH-34A also making a first visit later in the year was 54-3006, calling in on consecutive days from the 9th to the 11th June.

4th BOAC had to cancel numerous transatlantic flights from Ringway during the first half of the month. 'Unprecedented' snowfalls meant that the 120ft wide strip cleared on the runway was not enough for their Boeing 707s. They needed the full 150ft to avoid the risk of the engines fouling up the snow banks. These cancellations affected the Montreal/Toronto and the New York/Caribbean flights, so British Midland operated numerous Viscount flights to/from Prestwick, collecting and dropping off passengers. Aircraft used were G-ASED/AVJA & AWGV.

5th British United continued sub-chartering aircraft to cover the airline's trooping flights. Used were Autair BAC 1-11s G-AVOF (5th/17th) & G-AWBL (12th/25th) to Hanover/Dusseldorf or Gutersloh. The RAF also operated two of these flights, with Britannia XM498 (15th-RR6425 to Gutersloh) & XL639 (19th -RR6427 to Hanover), which were both first visits. Relatively normal operations resumed on the 18th, when BAC 1-11 G-ASJC operated BR574/3 from/to Dusseldorf, with the occasional sub-charters continuing into March.

5th Aer Lingus Viscount EI-AOI (EI9212 from Dublin) came to grief this evening when one of its main wheels got embedded in soft ground on the fast turnoff. The first attempt to drag it clear with a ground tug and steel planks was abandoned, after the wheel's main strut threatened to buckle. It was then unloaded and its fuel tanks were drained to make it lighter for another attempt, which proved successful. It was inspected for undercarriage damage, and left several hours later with its full load of mail and cargo.

6th PA-23 Aztec F-BNFT from/to Le Bourget today, was part of this month's collection of foreign light aircraft first visits. Also during February were PA-30 Twin Comanche LN-BWS (20th) and Sabena Cessna 310 OO-SED (27th) operating a training flight from/to Brussels.

7th Snow badly affected operations today. There were no arrivals between 1027-1641 and no movements at all after 1751. BOAC VC-10 G-ARVG made three attempts to land, but as the conditions steadily worsened, the pilot gave up and diverted to Heathrow. These arctic conditions would hamper flights for the next two weeks. The airport came in for heavy criticism regarding their snow clearing and handling abilities in unusually bitter weather.

14th February 1969 – Seen here a day after its arrival during a particularly wintry spell of weather, is LOT Antonov AN-12 SP-LZB on its second visit from Poznan to collect engineering equipment. (Geoff Ball)

14th February 1969 - The airport was closed again for another seven hours today due to snow. An official representing all the airlines serving Manchester handed in a strongly worded letter to Manchester Corporation, expressing 'grave concern' over the inadequacy of Manchester's snow clearing equipment. In their defence, the newly appointed airport director, Jack Jackman, stated that two dozen men had been working almost nonstop for the last two weeks using all the equipment they had, including six snow ploughs and seven mechanical brushes. A snow-blowing machine was on order, but its delivery was delayed. During one night, a temperature of -14°C was recorded at the eastern end of the runway. Despite the difficult weather conditions illustrated in this photo, the crew and ground staff were readying Alitalia DC-9 I-DIKZ for departure as AZ297 to Milan/Rome. (Geoff Ball)

12th Transavia made its second visit to Ringway today with another Douglas DC-6, PH-TRC, arriving from/to Amsterdam. One of eight DC-6s operating for the Dutch charter airline from 1966 to 1969, PH-TRC was sold in May 1969 as TF-AAF, but donated the following year to the Peruvian Air Force.

17th The snow and freezing conditions gripping Ringway over the last few days were now affecting Liverpool, which was closed until early afternoon and again the following morning. Manchester saw four diversions today and six more on the 18th. However, the only two aircraft worth a mention were Dan-Air's Dakota G-AMPP & Ambassador G-AMAH, arriving at 0911 & 1038 respectively on the latter day.

19th It was southern England's turn to have its operations disrupted. Although Heathrow and Gatwick were closed late in the day, diversions away were not as numerous as they might have been. Of the nine diversions received, two were first visits from Alitalia DC-9 I-DIKU at 2121 (AZ290 from Milan) & Swissair DC-9 HB-IFY at 2318 (SR860 from Zurich). Four BEA Tridents arriving in quick succession were G-ARPA (from Belfast), G-ARPW (from Copenhagen), G-AVFF (from Paris) & G-AVFG (also from Paris), plus another Dan-Air Ambassador with G-ALZO at 2251 from Gothenburg.

23rd Qantas B.707 VH-EBW made its first visit today, arriving at 1018 (QF741 from Bahrain) operating the latest friends/families charter from Sydney.

24th This month's West German Air Force training flight was operated by Noratlas 52+28 (DCN8669), arriving at 1331 from Neubiberg. It stayed overnight and departed to Erding the following morning.

24th The second Martinair Douglas DC-9 to visit Manchester was PH-MAO on a return flight from Amsterdam today. The airline had ordered three Douglas DC-9s to eventually replace their ageing Douglas DC-6s. PH-MAR (f/v - 15th May) would be the third and final DC-9 to appear at Ringway.

25th Belgian International Douglas DC-6 OO-GER arrived at 1618 from Vienna via Rotterdam, with Rapid Vienna FC for their European Cup quarter-final first leg match with Manchester United at Old Trafford.

26th February 1969 – CSA introduced Manchester-Prague scheduled services in June 1992. In the interim the Czech national carrier made very few appearances at Ringway. OK-PAG seen above was the only one of the airline's Ilyushin IL-18s to visit, day-stopping on football charter with Rapid Vienna fans. (Geoff Ball)

28th Today saw the first visit of the military variant of the Beagle 206, when Bassett CC.1 XS766 (one of twenty that would eventually operate for the RAF) arrived at 1123 (EJZ15) from RAF Shawbury, staying for ten minutes before leaving for RAF Wyton. Two during 1969 were XS772 (7th Mar) & XS775 (15th Sept).

MARCH 1969

High pressure was concentrated to the northeast and low pressure to the southwest of the country, which brought dry weather, but resulted in east or southeast winds for most of the month. It was the coldest March since 1962, and from the 11th to the 19th snow or sleet was frequent. Snow fell for many hours in the north on the 12th and there were blizzards from north Wales to east Scotland over the next few days. There was some unusual weather phenomenon as well, with freezing rain and drizzle falling widely across the UK from the 16th to the 18th. There was extensive damage to trees, and telephone and power cables were brought down. On the 5th very dry air spread from the continent to southern England, and by the afternoon the relative humidity in parts of the Thames Valley was only 20-25%, although it fell as low as 11% at the London Weather Centre. Relative humidity of less than 20% is very rare in the British Isles. The month's temperature extremes saw 15°C at Shaftesbury, Dorset (14th) and a low of -8°C at Kew Gardens (8th).

Scheduled first visits this month were Alitalia (AZ296): DC-9 I-DIKS (21st) & I-DIKT (28th), BEA (BE4108): BAC 1-11 G-AVMU (22nd) & G-AVMT (29th). Equipment changes during March were BOAC (BA065/6/7/8): Caledonian B.707 G-AVTW (daily 19th-31st) was leased for a five-week period to provide additional cargo capacity and Sabena (SN623): B.727s OO-STE (10th).

Another thin month for GCA/ILS traffic. The only civil aircraft noted was Philippine Airlines HS.748 PI-C1023 (5th) on a test flight from Woodford. The only Royal Air Force flights during March were Britannias XM497 (6th), XL640 (11th) & XM490 (25th). Training flights were operated by BOAC Boeing 707s G-APFB (15th) & G-ASZG (3rd) and BEA Viscount G-AOHS (4th) & Argosy G-ASXO (11th).

1st   HS.748 G-AVRR arrived at 1733 from Woodford, prior to departing to Bucharest the following morning. It was on a week-long sales tour of Romania, demonstrating to a number of operators. It returned to the UK on the 6th March direct into Woodford.

4th   Britannia Airways Britannia G-ANBA took Manchester United to Vienna this morning for their return match with Rapid Vienna. Another two Britannias, G-ANBE & G-ANBL, and British Midland Viscount G-APND, were also used as fans' charters. All aircraft returned on the 6th, after United had secured a 0-0 draw. Having won 3-0 at home two weeks earlier, this meant that the Reds marched on towards the semi-finals in pursuit of the retention of the European Cup.

4th   Another Army Air Corps Scout making its first visit, was XV121 (Army 466), operating from/to Barnard Castle today. Other military visitors during a busy month were RAF Pembrokes WV736 (4th/7th) & XL929 (21st), Royal Navy Sea Herons XR441 (12th/13th) & XR445 (12th), RAF Devon VP963 (15th), VC-10 XV108 operating four trooping flights to Gutersloh (20th/21st), Queen's Flight HS.748 XS793 (26th) as 'Kitty 3' from Warton and finally a pair of Army Scouts with XV121 & XT617 (26th) from/to Barnard Castle.

7th   Qantas Boeing 707 VH-EAE arriving at 1111 today (QF171/2) from/to Tehran was operating a further friends and families flight from/to Australia.

8th   The husband of Princess Alexandra, Mr. Angus Ogilvy, was among hundreds of passengers that were diverted into Manchester due to fog at Heathrow. He was looked after in the VIP lounge until his BOAC B.707, G-ARWD (BA600 from Toronto), could continue onwards to Heathrow. Of the other diverted flights a further three from BOAC were VC-10 G-ARVF at 0650 (BA799 from Tehran), SVC10 G-ASGK at 0907 (BA508 from New York) & B.707 G-ARRB at 0914 (BA672 from Bermuda). Two from Pan American were B.707s N763PA at 0812 (PA102 from New York) & N881PA at 0828 (PA062 from Philadelphia).

9th   Five further weather diversions from Heathrow arrived during the morning. Of note were Qantas B.707 VH-EBD at 0755 (QF941 from Tehran) and the first visit of East African Airways VC-10 5H-MMT at 1012 (EC719 from Rome).

9th   The second Gulfstream 1 to visit Manchester was 1965-built N705G, operated by the IT & T Corporation. It arrived at 0808 this morning on a round-trip from Brussels.

10th   This month's West German Air Force training flight operated by Noratlas 52+86 (DCN8799), appeared at 1524 today from Erding, but went tech on arrival. Another Noratlas, 53+05, arrived at 1637 the following day from Hamburg (DCN8815), with spares for the aircraft. Noratlas 52+86 finally departed for Hamburg on the 13th.

12th   Snow during March is not unusual, but for the weather to be persistent or heavy enough to cause airport disruption is quite rare. However, Heathrow and Gatwick were closed for intermittent periods from late afternoon onwards, resulting in eleven more diversions. The only first visit was Alitalia DC-9 I-DIBC at

1621 (AZ280 from Rome), and the only other aircraft of interest was the final visit of a Sudan Airways Comet, with OT-AAX at 1949 (SD112 from Rome). Both aircraft operated by Sudan Airways, ST-AAW & ST-AAX, had visited before. They were withdrawn from service in late-1972 and offered for sale at £125,000 each. They were bought by 'the great Comet collector', Dan-Air, but with varying fortunes. ST-AAW became G-ASDZ and was flown to Teeside for storage on 14th November 1972. On 1st August 1975 it was flown to Lasham on its final flight, and was broken up for spares by October 1976. Having been stored at Khartoum since November 1972, ST-AAX was flown to Lasham on 2nd June 1975. After being in storage all that time, the ferry pilot was amazed to see a snake appearing over the glare shield during the flight. After scrambling clear, it disappeared, never to be seen again! It was re-registered as G-BDIF and flew with Dan-Air until the 5th November 1979, when it made its last revenue service.

13th First visits to Ringway were made by Cessna 421 HB-LDV today from/to Basle and Cessna 411 D-IFLA (18th) arriving from Amsterdam to clear customs, en route to Warton returning in the opposite direction the following day. Other first visits during the month were Cessna 210 N2245R (24th) from Brussels, Beech 55 N354RJ from Malmo (25th) and Jodel F-BOZM from Amsterdam (26th).

13th March 1969 - Besides RAF VC-10 XV108 making numerous trips f/t Gutersloh on behalf of BUA, Laker Airways also operated several trooping flights. Boeing 707 G-AWDG operated f/t Dusseldorf today (GK166/7) & G-AVZZ operated on the 20th (GK154/5) and the 27th (GK170/1). (Geoff Ball)

14th Cessna 310 N5745M arrived from Cranfield at 1529 for local demo flights, before returning there.
17th The Midlands was affected all day by fog and freezing drizzle. Amongst the diversions arriving at various times were British Midland Viscounts G-APNE, AVJA (twice) & AWGV; BEA Viscounts G-AOHH & G-AOYR; Aer Lingus flights EI-AMA (EI272), EI-AOI (EI2272) & EI-ANE (EI2274) and finally RAF Britannia XN398 at 2035 (RR6166 from Malta) which was also a first visit.
18th First visit RAF VC-10 XV106 arrived at 0504 today (RR2508 from Bahrain), on diversion from Brize Norton. This also led to the first visit of the RAF's latest transport aircraft, the Shorts Belfast C.1, XR365. Arriving at 1319 (callsign Ascot AW006), it was picking up the crew and equipment from the VC-10. Although the Shorts Belfast would be regularly seen on ILS training flights at Ringway, only two more would land, XR363 (1st June 1971) & XR371 (22nd September 1973). This aircraft had just one customer, the Royal Air Force, and only ten were ever built. All ten operated from 1967-1976, but when the new RAF Strike Command was totally reorganised; it would have repercussions on the Belfast fleet. Ushered into

retirement were a number of aircraft types, including the Bristol Britannia and the De Havilland Comet in 1975. By the end of 1976, the Belfast fleet had been retired and flown to RAF Kemble for storage.

19th Four diverted flights late the previous evening, and another nine in the early hours, meant that Manchester could not cope with any more and banned any further diversions. Apart from three aircraft, Qantas B.707 VH-EBQ at 0002 (QF530 from New York), Cambrian Viscount G-AMOH and RAF VC-10 XV107, the remainder were from BEA. Coaches were arranged to take the passengers to Crewe, for onward transportation to London by rail.

20th British Midland Viscount G-AVJA had diverted in the previous evening due to fog at East Midlands. It had lined up ready for departure back to East Midlands, but at 1658 shortly after leaving the ground, it banked steeply to the right, stalled, and fell to the ground almost completely inverted. Three crewmembers were killed and two stewardesses were seriously injured. In the absence of any obvious cause, the A.I.B. said severe pilot error must have been responsible.

20th G-AWYE was the latest HS.125 making its first visit. Operated by Rolls-Royce until its sale in 1986, it arrived at 0825 today from its base at Hucknall, returning from Luton the next day. Thereafter it became a rare visitor to Ringway.

23rd BOAC VC-10 G-ARVL arrived at 0855 (BA1171 from Heathrow) to operate the airline's inaugural flight to Tel Aviv, departing as BA312 at 1006. The flight operated via Heathrow on both the outward and return legs.

24th Although twenty-two years old, Dove G-AJOS was possibly making its first visit today, arriving from its base in Coventry. Registered in 1947, it was sold in the Sudan soon afterwards and only restored to the UK register again in 1967. It was on a short lease to the Nuclear Power Group, temporarily replacing Heron G-AWDT, which had left for Coventry for overhaul with Executive Air Engineering.

27th The third and final Kar-Air Douglas DC-6 to visit, OH-KDC, arrived at 1102 (BB7140 from Glasgow) under a Balair callsign, departing for Brussels the following day. It served Kar-Air until May 1972, when it was placed into storage at Antwerp. However, whilst it was there on the 2nd January 1974, it was burned out by activists protesting about future expansion at the airport.

29th Dan-Air began their summer programme today, when Comet G-APDL departed to Ibiza (DA0598). This year's inclusive tour flights saw a further increase on 1968, which was on top of operating extra flights due to the demise of British Eagle. Visits by the airline's dwindling fleet of Airspeed Ambassadors were few. Comets used this summer were G-APDJ/APDK/APDL/APDM/APDN & APDP. Another former BOAC Comet, G-APDD, would be added later in the year and made its first visit to Ringway as such on 21st December 1969. BAC 1-11s also operated for the first time with a twice-weekly flight to Munich, which provided first visits by G-AXCK (11th May) & G-AXCP (27th April).

29th Britannia Airways also started their summer IT programmes today. Boeing 737s operated to various destinations on certain days until May, when daily flights began with a based aircraft. Bristol Britannias would operate flights to Beauvais and Rotterdam until mid May. From the 17th, a Britannia was based from Friday to Monday and included a rotation to Munich formerly operated by Bavaria. Aircraft used were B.737s G-AVRL, AVRM, AVRN (f/v - 2nd May), AVRO (f/v - 26th May) & G-AWSY (f/v - 26th May) and Britannias G-ANBA/ANBE/ANBF/ANBI/ANBJ/ANBL & ANBO.

APRIL 1969

BEA began operations with their new Super 1-11s. A number of aircraft are now based to operate their European schedules, taking over from the Trident 1s, as well as introducing the type onto their Dublin flights. The Super 1-11 is currently operated on three of their seven Heathrow flights, but from July all but one will be flown by the type. A new destination was also added, with the launch of a weekday service to Berlin via Dusseldorf, ironically not with 1-11s but with Comets. Tridents will be used twice-weekly on their flights to Palma, which begin and terminate at Glasgow and on the three-times-weekly service to Malta.

A new £1.5 million Rhine army trooping contract was awarded to Britannia Airways. From 1st May 1969 they will replace British United, who had flown over 50,000 servicemen and their families from Manchester to Germany each year. Flights would now be transferred to Luton.

High pressure dominated the weather over the British Isles during the first week and on the 17th to the 19th. At other times low pressure over or near the country resulted in changeable, stormy, conditions. It was a sunny month, but rather cold, although Manchester had the sunniest Easter since 1902. The period from the 9th to the 16th was stormy with squally west or southwest winds. The month's temperature extremes saw 24°C at Southend (9th) and a low of -8°C at Alwen, Denbighshire (20th).

International flights were operated during the summer as follows:

AER LINGUS - Amsterdam (4 x weekly), Copenhagen (3 x weekly), Cork (up to 4 x weekly), Dusseldorf (3 x weekly), Frankfurt (3 x weekly), Shannon (2 x weekly) & Zurich (1 x weekly), all operated by BAC 1-11s, with the exception of Shannon and Cork, these routes still served by Viscounts.

AIR FRANCE - Three-weekly to Paris with SE.210s (AF960/1), increasing to daily from July to September.

ALITALIA - Twice-weekly to Milan & Rome (AZ296/7), aircraft type reverting back to SE.210 Caravelles.

BEA - Amsterdam/Barcelona/Brussels/Copenhagen/Dublin/Dusseldorf/Malta/Palma, all by Super 1-11s except for Malta (Trident 2). Inclusive tour flights operated to Barcelona & Palma with Tridents.

BOAC - Daily to New York via Prestwick with SVC-10s, extending to Antigua/Bridgetown/Port of Spain and Guyana on Fri/Sat/Sun. Also for the first time, two of these flights operate direct to New York. Boeing 707s operate daily to Montreal and Toronto (BA608/7). Cargo flights operate with B.707s to Montreal (4 x weekly) & New York (7 x weekly) while inbound flights operate from New York (4 x weekly). A fifth inbound flight (BA068) operates on Saturdays from New York and Philadelphia via Prestwick.

IBERIA - Twice-weekly to Madrid via Dublin with SE.210s (IB744/3). From 5th June-28th September, served Palma three-weekly with SE.210 Caravelles, one of these operated via Barcelona.

KLM - Passenger flights operated to Amsterdam on a weekday basis (KL153/4) and cargo operations continued from/to Amsterdam five-weekly via Glasgow (KL005). Both flights operated with Douglas DC-9s.

LUFTHANSA - Cargo flights five-weekly (LH934/5) to Frankfurt with All-Air Douglas C-54/DC-4/DC-6s.

SABENA - Night-stopping Brussels service continued four-times-weekly with SE.210 Caravelles (SN623/4). Cargo flights were four-weekly with B.727s f/t Brussels, the outbound via Heathrow (SN197/8).

SAS - Flights serving Copenhagen reduced to twice-weekly again for the summer, operating onto Dublin.

SWISSAIR – Zurich cargo flights increased to four-weekly, still operated by Douglas DC-4s (SR846/7). Daily night-stopping scheduled passenger service introduced to Zurich via Rotterdam with Douglas DC-9s (SR840/1) and a twice-weekly night tourist summer flight with SE.210 Caravelles (SR842/3).

Scheduled first visits this month were BEA: BAC 1-11 G-AVMV (22nd) & Trident 2s G-AVFC (21st), G-AVFI (6th), G-AVFJ (30th), G-AVFK (12th) and G-AVFL (5th); KLM (KL153): PH-DNW (23rd), and Swissair (SR840): DC-9s HB-IFP (9th), HB-IFR (3rd) & HB-IFU (3rd). Equipment changes were BOAC (BA065/6/7): Caledonian B.707 G-AVTW (11th/12th/14th/16th).

Yet another fairly thin month for GCA/ILS traffic, with just one civil movement, Transair HS.748 CF-TAZ (24th). Royal Air Force training flights were a little more plentiful with Britannias XL657 (1st), XN404 (9th), XL635 (21st), XL636 (22nd), XL635 (28th), XM519 (29th) and Argosy XN857 (10th).

1st BEA Super 1-11 G-AVMS arrived from Prestwick at 1043 today to operate the first based Super 1-11 flight from Manchester. It departed at 1217 as BE852 to Copenhagen.

1st Swissair were the first foreign airline to operate daily from Ringway, with their new night-stopping flight from/to Zurich routing via Rotterdam. Douglas DC-9 HB-IFU was in charge of today's inaugural flight.

3rd New UK-airline Donaldson International made its first visit to Ringway, with Bristol Britannia G-APNB at 1221, on a crew training flight from Gatwick to Prestwick. Formed in 1964, they purchased their first aircraft, Britannia G-APNA, in October 1967 which was immediately leased to Lloyd International until this month, when they operated their first commercial service. Several flights were operated through Ringway during 1969 with their three Britannias (G-AOVC/APNA & APNB). Some were transatlantic charters to/from Canada, but the bulk was from Glasgow and Gatwick. By the end of 1969, Donaldson had carried 40,598 passengers on its charter and inclusive tour services.

4th Channel Airways began a series of twice-weekly flights to Beauvais until the 7th May with Viscounts G-ATVR/AVHE/AVHK & AVIW. From the 10th May, a full summer IT programme began with all flights being operated by BAC 1-11 G-AWEJ, which made the first of its many visits to Manchester today.

6th Britain's largest independent airline, British United, began their first summer IT programme from Ringway with BAC 1-11 G-ASJH operating an outbound flight to Palma. Until the 26th October, the airline would operate BAC 1-11-200s & 500s to various holiday destinations, which provided a number of first visits by the larger 1-11-500s, with G-AWYR (23rd May), G-AWYS (9th May), G-AWYT (30th May), G-

AWYU (4th July) & G-AWYV (25th July). Also during the summer months, they would operate occasional VC-10 transatlantic charters to New York, Montreal and Toronto.

8th Cessna 310P YU-AFW arrived at 1442 from Reykjavik on its delivery flight. After clearing customs it continued onwards to Cranfield for avionics fitting with Rogers Aviation. Its callsign was 'Flo Air 238', the name of the aircraft ferrying company. Its arrival must have had local spotters on tenterhooks, not knowing what on earth would turn up!

8th French Air Force Noratlas No.97 (callsign F-RABN) was the first of two to visit during the year. This aircraft arrived from Pau to clear customs, before continuing onto Warton. It returned from Warton the following morning for customs clearance and departed again for Pau. The second French Air Force Noratlas, No.208, arrived on 9th December 1969 from/to Orleans under the callsign 'F-RABY'.

8th Operated by Gregory Air Services, HS.125 G-AWUF made its first visit today on a night-stopping flight from Luton. Operated by a variety of UK companies under a number of registrations, this aircraft remained on the UK register until 1995, when it was withdrawn from use.

10th This month's West German Air Force training flight was operated by Noratlas 53+20 (DCN8990). Arriving at 1311 today from Ahlhorn, it stayed overnight before departing the following morning for Erding.

10th G-AWRX made the first visit of the British-built Beagle Pup today, making a number of flights and a round-trip from Tollerton. The type made its first flight (G-AVDF) on 8th April 1967, just in time for the Paris Air Show. Another first visit of type took place on the 18th, when Maule M-4 LN-HHP diverted in at 2201 from Gatwick due to a shortage of fuel. Originally intended for Inverness, it left thirty minutes later for Edinburgh. The Maule M-4 Rocket was an American four-seat cabin monoplane, designed by Belford Maule and built by the Maule Aircraft Company that first flew in September 1960. The only other Maule to visit Ringway was ZK-DON on 27th December 1973.

10th Two RAF Argosies, XN819 (KLI 47 from Benson) & XP408 (KLI 37 from Benson), both performed touch-and-goes within twenty minutes of each other during the morning, en route to Gatwick.

14th From today, BEA were the latest airline to succumb to flight-number 'fever' for ATC purposes, no longer using the aircraft's registration. BOAC incidentally, had been using flight-numbers since the mid-1950s.

14th Another unusual arrival at 1251 was Andreasson BA-4B G-AWPZ from Goodwood. This single seat aerobatic bi-plane would eventually become a semi-resident, registered to Mr. J.R Crosby of Knutsford.

14th The Army Air Corps were out in force again this month, starting today with Scouts XT260 (also 16th/17th), XR601 (22nd) & Sioux XT559 (17th/18th).

16th Lego's PA-23 Aztec OY-BBL f/t Billund made the first of numerous visits today until its sale in 1975, when replaced by Cessna Citation 500 OY-DVL. Other first visits were Cessna 337 N85989 from Liverpool (22nd) which left after two days for Billund, and eventually became OY-EGU; Beech 55 F-BPIA from Shannon (25th) and PA-23 Aztec F-BIRT from Le Bourget (28th).

17th Still going strong twenty-four years later, but making its last visit to Ringway today arriving at 0857 from/to its base at Blackpool, was 1945-Percival Proctor G-AGTC. Unfortunately this Percival demonstrator at the 1949 Farnborough Air Show, crashed on the 2nd May 1969 at Malaga Airport after running out of fuel, and was completely written off.

18th Pan American N730PA operated the inaugural flight of the airline's extensive summer series of charter flights to New York, lasting until the 25th October. They used twenty-one different B.707s which produced first visits from N419PA (5th July), N492PA (19th July) & N722PA (20th August).

25th Australian Air Force HS.748 (VM-VJG) performed a touch-and-go from Woodford at 1138. Intended or not, it generated a landing fee!

26th Similar to Caledonian, Dan-Air also increased their presence at Ringway, by kicking off their summer programme today. Their first weekly flight with Boeing 707s from/to Palma (CA214/3) was operated by G-AVKA on this occasion. However, the remainder of their expanded flight schedule would be operated by their BAC 1-11-500s to various points in Italy, the Spanish mainland, the Balearic Islands and Tenerife, with the latter involving a refuelling stop at Lisbon. Prior to this the airline operated a couple of trooping flights on behalf of British United, with BAC 1-11s G-AWWX (2nd - CA852/3 f/t Hanover) & G-AWWY (16th - CA874/5 f/t Hanover) which was also a first visit.

29th BOAC SVC-10 G-ASGD operated the first scheduled non-stop transatlantic service from Ringway as BA533 to New York.

19th April 1969 - BOAC Cargo at Manchester continued growing during the first quarter, with a further 23% increase on 1968. They operated outbound to Montreal 4-weekly & New York 7-weekly and inbound from New York 5-weekly, with one also serving Philadelphia. Boeing 707-336F G-ASZG is seen during loading, having recently arrived from Heathrow, before its departure to Montreal & New York via Prestwick. (Geoff Ball)

20th April 1969 – RAF Britannia XL639 made its second visit today, arriving at 1447 (RR6449 from Lyneham), departing on another trooping flight to Dusseldorf. Britannia XL660 (28th) also made its debut operating to Dusseldorf (RR6463). These and numerous other trooping flights during April operated on behalf of British United, whose contract came to an end on the 30th April. From the following day, Britannia Airways took over these flights, with their Boeing 737s operating out of Luton. (Geoff Ball)

MAY 1969

For most of the month depressions were situated to the west of Britain, with troughs of low pressure crossing the country. It was changeable, alternating between thundery rain and brighter showery weather. Heavy rain was widespread, with flooding in many places including the Midlands. The 3rd was a day of contrasts with temperatures ranging from 4°C in Aberdeenshire to 21°C at Heathrow once the fog had cleared. A warm spell on the 13th was balanced out by Bidston, Cheshire, recording the wettest May since 1870 and Shrewsbury the wettest for 75 years. The month's temperature extremes saw 27°C at the London Weather Centre (13th) and a low of -5°C at Alwen, Denbighshire (20th).

Airlines operating ITs during the summer months to various destinations were Aviaco (Alicante/Gerona /Ibiza/Palma), Aviogenex (Dubrovnik/Ljubljana/Pula/Split), Balkan (Bourgas/Varna), Balair (Basle), Britannia Airways/ Alicante/Barcelona/Gerona/Ibiza/Munich/Palma/Rimini/Venice), British Midland (Barcelona/Gerona/Ostend/Luxembourg/Palma), British United (Alicante/Basle/Gerona/Ibiza/Palma/ Tunis/Venice), Caledonian (Alicante/Gerona/Ibiza/Malaga/Palma/Rimini/Tenerife/Venice), Channel Airways (Barcelona/Basle/Ibiza/Milan/Palma/Rimini/Valencia), Dan-Air (Alicante/Barcelona/Ibiza/ Malaga/Munich/Palma/Tenerife), Laker Airways (Barcelona/Ibiza/Malaga/Palma/Tenerife), Luxair (Luxembourg) and Spantax (Palma).

Despite the busy start to the summer, scheduled first visits were just Alitalia (AZ296): SE.210 I-DABE (21st) & BEA: Trident 2 G-AVFM (18th). The only equipment change was SAS (SK537): DC-9 SE-DBT on its first visit (27th).

GCA/ILS traffic was plentiful again this month, starting with numerous HS.748s out of Woodford, Ghana Airways 9G-ABV (7th), Avianca HK-1408 (8th), Australian Air Force HS.748 A10-607 (8th), COPA Panama HP-484 (9th) and Transair CF-TAZ (22nd). Training flights by the Royal Air Force were operated by Britannias XL657 (21st), XM490 (8th), XM491 (29th) & XM496 (6th/19th) and Comet XR395 (12th). Civilian training flights noted were BOAC SVC-10 G-ASGR (21st - overshot only) & B.707 G-APFC (27th) and BEA Comets G-APMD (20th) & G-ARJL (21st).

1st British United VC-10 G-ARTA, newly restored to the UK register after a period with MEA as OD-AFA, arrived from Gatwick at 0952 on its first visit, operating a transatlantic charter (BR2033 to Toronto).

2nd Brand-new BEA Super 1-11 G-AVMW made its first visit to Ringway today, being delivered direct from the BAC factory at Bournemouth for operations at Manchester.

3rd Morning fog was widespread in the Midlands, southern and eastern England, with visibility down to 30 yards in places. Heathrow and Gatwick were closed for several hours. Fifteen diversions arrived at Manchester within in a five hour spell during the morning. First visits were British Air Services/BKS Trident 1 G-AVYC at 0629 (from Ibiza), Seaboard World CL-44 N124SW in bare metal at 0545 (SB124 from New York), but perhaps the most significant arrival was TAP Boeing 727 CS-TBO at 0352 (TP046 from Lisbon), which quickly retreated to the South Bay.

4th Spantax began their summer programme today from Ringway. Until the 12th October, they would operate twice-weekly flights to Palma with CV-990s (Fri - BX157/6) & (Sun - BX061/0). There were two first visits during this period from EC-BQA (today) & EC-BQQ (25th May). Apart from these, the only other Spantax flight during the summer was operated by Douglas DC-7 EC-BBL (7th May), which was used on an outbound flight to San Sebastian.

4th The latest jet aircraft making its debut at Ringway today, was the Dutch-built Fokker F.28, with the arrival of LN-SUC. Delivered in March this year, this aircraft was operating an ad hoc flight from/to Oslo. Another, LN-SUN, also arriving from/to Oslo on a charter flight on the 13th December, became the second of its type to visit. Designed as a short range airliner, it was a collaboration between a number of European companies, namely Fokker, MBB of West Germany, Fokker-VFW and Short Brothers of Northern Ireland. There was also government money invested in the project, with the Dutch providing 50% of Fokker's stake and the West Germans having 60% of the 35% German stake. Norwegian airline Braathens would operate up to seven Fokker F.28s, intended as a part replacement for their Douglas DC-6s.

8th Qantas Boeing 707 VH-EBP was yet another first visit, arriving at 1111 today (QF171 from Tehran) on another friends and families charter.

3ʳᵈ May 1969 – Spantax Douglas DC-4 EC-AUY arriving at 0217 (BX025) on a cargo flight from Madrid, was plagued by technical problems and unable to leave until the 7ᵗʰ. Although the airline was moving headlong into the jet age by introducing more Convair CV-990s, they continued using piston aircraft well into the 1970s, mainly on domestic services. However, EC-AUY wasn't as fortunate as it had been withdrawn by 1971, and scrapped soon afterwards. (Geoff Ball)

4ᵗʰ May 1969 - Long before their problems with JAT last summer, Yugotours (a subsidiary of the General Export agency) had petitioned the government for permission to form their own 'in-house' airline. The tour company's plea coincided with Kremlin pressure on the Yugoslav regime to purchase Soviet-designed transport aircraft. JAT, operating an exclusively Western fleet, was unhappy with the prospect of operating such designs, so a compromise was reached. General Export would form its own airline, but would have to operate Tupolev TU-134s - not the most economic aircraft for IT operations. In exchange the Soviet Union would buy Yugoslavian goods from General Export. So on this date, the first TU-134, YU-AHH, arrived at Manchester. Along with their second aircraft, YU-AHI, both became frequent summer visitors, operating to the four Adriatic resorts of Dubrovnik, Pula, Split and Ljubljana. (Geoff Ball)

8th May - Vanguard G-APEP was involved in a bomb incident, and is seen here being fully searched. The plane was taxiing to the hold of runway 24, when it was notified by ATC that there may be a bomb onboard, but in the end it was proved to be a hoax. (Geoff Ball)

14th May 1969 – Ringway played host to many military flights, such as Dassault MD315 Flamant No.301, one of the more unusual types operated by the French Air Force and not common to Manchester. There were several visits by the Flamant during 1960, and one movement in 1967 until today, when No.301 operated a training flight en route from Arbroath - Paris-Le Bourget. (Geoff Ball)

8th Lear Jet 24 N321Q was the first of two new Lear Jets visiting Manchester this year. Arriving at 1651 today from Maastricht, and departing for Le Bourget the following morning, it was one of sixty-eight aircraft to take part in the first London-Victoria (British Columbia) race in July 1971. They would follow a regulated routing of Oxford-Quebec-Winnipeg-Regina-Calgary-Victoria, with a first prize of $50,000 plus a trophy. The second Lear Jet 24 to visit was HB-VAS, later in the year on the 5th August 1969.

10th Besides an extensive IT programme operating from Manchester with BAC 1-11s, Caledonian would also operate a weekly Boeing 707 flight from/to Palma (CA214/3). This would provide two first visits by G-AWWD (today) & G-AWTK (7th June). Caledonian B.707s could also be seen during the summer operating numerous transatlantic charters.

10th The first Royal Air Force flight of the month was another first visit, when VC-10 XV109 arrived at 1908 today from Brize Norton to operate a trooping flight to RAF Akrotiri (RR2750). Also during the month was a first visit by Varsity WJ913 (14th) operating as 'MPFFF' from/to Pershore. Other military visitors during May included Royal Navy Heron XR441 (15th), Britannia XM517 (18th/31st) & VC-10 XR810 (23rd - RR2755 from Akrotiri) which were both first visits and finally Army Air Corps Beaver XP807 (28th).

11th Aviaco commenced their summer IT programme with a flight from/to Alicante (AO1506/7) with SE.210 EC-AVZ. They would also operate flights to Gerona, Ibiza and Palma, mostly with SE.210 Caravelles, but from the 12th June they would use TAE BAC 1-11 EC-BQF on weekly flights to Gerona.

12th Just a week after beginning services, Aviogenex got one of their new TU-134s stuck in the mud, which closed the runway for an hour. YU-AHH touched down at 1822, only to leave the taxiway after landing. It was quickly dragged free, and departed back to Dubrovnik only two hours behind schedule.

13th AC Milan arrived onboard KLM DC-9 PH-DNB this afternoon, ahead of Thursday's vital European Cup semi-final second leg with Manchester United. Another KLM DC-9, PH-DND (16th), would arrive from Amsterdam to take the victorious Italian side back to Milan.

15th Around a thousand football fans flew into Manchester for the second leg of the European Cup semi-final, taking place at Old Trafford between Manchester United and AC Milan. The aircraft involved were all operated from/to Milan by Monarch Britannia G-AOVL (OM638/9), SAM SE.210 I-DABT (MQ408/9), Inex-Adria DC-9 YU-AHJ on its first visit, Caledonian Britannia G-AOVJ (CA396/401) and finally Itavia Herald I-TIVE (IH176/7), which made some return trips. Aer Lingus also produced three charters from Dublin with Viscounts EI-AMA (twice) & EI-AOI. The evenings match found United facing an uphill battle to turn round a 2-0 first leg defeat in Milan. The Italians did what they do best when defending a lead, which is to merely sit back and soak up the opposition's pressure, and tonight was no different. United had twenty corners that evening, compared to Milan's two. They also had 80% of the play, but only managed to pull one goal back. Things got ugly towards the end, when the Reds thought they had scored the equalizer, but the officials waved play on despite a Denis Law shot that was cleared off the line. United claimed it had crossed the line and the crowd registered their displeasure by throwing 'missiles' onto the pitch, one of which struck a Milan player, knocking him temporarily unconscious. In the end, Milan hung on until the final whistle to reach the final.

16th Balair began their summer programme with twice-weekly flights to Basle. Douglas DC-6 HB-IBU operated today's first (BB702/3), but DC-6 HB-IBZ was used exclusively for the remainder of the summer until the last flight on 30th September. The only time the airline deviated from this pattern ironically, was the on the last flight itself, when Fokker F.27 HB-AAU (BB700/1) was in charge.

17th Balkan begin their second summer season of flights from Ringway. Operating weekly until the 4th October to Bourgas and Varna, today's first flight was operated by Ilyushin IL-18 LZ-BET. Other aircraft used were LZ-BED (f/v - 14th June), LZ-BEK, LZ-BEL (f/v - 4th October), LZ-BEP (f/v - 28th June), LZ-BER (f/v - 31st May), LZ-BES & LZ-BET.

18th Another airline with an expanded summer programme from the previous year, was Laker Airways. As well as a based BAC 1-11 operating most days, a Boeing 707 was also operating three rotations on Sundays to Ibiza, Palma and Barcelona. Laker was also the first to offer direct flights to Minorca.

18th World Airways began another extensive series of transatlantic flights, with today's first being operated from Gatwick to Toronto by B.707 N375WA. Flights operated until the 20th October, and although the airline produced no first visits this year, the following B.707s were used, N368WA/N369WA/ N370WA/N371WA/N372WA/N373WA/N374WA/ N375WA & N376WA.

14th May 1969 – Southern Air L-100-200 N7951S, along with sister-ship N9232R, both arrived from Hucknall to pick up a consignment of RB-211 engines for transporting to the States. (Geoff Ball)

15th May 1969 – Another arrival bringing AC Milan fans into Manchester was Itavia Herald I-TIVE on its final visit. Having been a regular during the summer of 1966 on IT flights, this aircraft crashed at Rome in April 1971. (Geoff Ball)

15th May 1969 – SAM SE.210 Caravelle I-DABT is seen here resting on the South Bay, having brought in a load of AC Milan fans for their match with Manchester United. The Italian charter subsidiary of Alitalia returned to Manchester with a summer IT programme in 1971. (Geoff Ball)

19th May 1969 - Pacific Western operated the first of eleven transatlantic charters to/from Canada until the 21st September, all operated by Boeing 707 CF-PWV. The first of these arrived at 1339 from Keflavik (PW2782), before departing for Edmonton as (PW2882). (Geoff Ball)

27th May 1969 - Work on the MU-2, Mitsubishi's first post-war aircraft design, began in 1956. Designed as a light twin turboprop transport suitable for a variety of civil and military roles, it first flew on 14th September 1963. Today, not only was the type making its first visit to Ringway, but two arrived in close formation! SE-EDM at 1928 & HB-LEC at 1947, both from Gothenburg. The duo stayed until the 29th, when they left for Wick, ultimately bound for Reykjavik. (Geoff Ball)

29th May 1969 – HS.748 G-AVRR/CF-YQD arrived in the early hours from Reykjavik, returning off a short-term lease from Canadian-airline Transair. Seen later in the morning leaving for Woodford, this aircraft spent the first four years of its life as a demonstrator, or on short-term leases to various operators. In October 1971, it was purchased by Trans Gabon as TR-LQJ and sold to Eastern Provincial as C-GEPH in March 1976. (Geoff Ball)

20th The third airline in consecutive days to start flights to the USA/Canada was TWA, with B.707. N18709 (f/v) arriving at 1416 today from Heathrow (TW8987) to operate outbound to New York via Shannon. The other two aircraft used on their nine other flights this summer, which ended on 30th September, were both first visits by N18711 (f/v - 8th August) & N28727 (f/v - 4th June).

22nd Three foreign light aircraft first visits this month began today with Beech 55 SE-EUT from Glasgow. The other two were Beech 55 D-INOX from Cologne (22nd) and Cessna 310 N3804X from Reykjavik to Stansted (30th).

27th This month's West German Air Force training flight was operated by Noratlas 53+33 (DCN9308), which arrived at 1505 from Erding. It stayed overnight and returned the following morning back to Erding.

29th The Blue Eagles helicopter aerobatic team was formed in spring 1968, by instructors at the British Army Air Corps based at Middle Wallop, who practised in their spare time. A year later they were permanently established, with five Westland-Bell-47G-3B1 Sioux helicopters. Today all five plus a spare made their first visits to Ringway (XT193, XT206, XT498, XT509, XW191 & XW192) en route from Carlisle to Birmingham.

31st The latest Canadian Air Force CC-106 Yukon to visit Manchester was 15925, arriving at 1445 today on a training flight from Prestwick to RAF Valley.

JUNE 1969

The airport had drawn up plans to close the main runway overnight from 2300 to 0700 six nights a week from 1st November to 20th December, to undertake resurfacing work. However, a group of airlines complained it would seriously affect freight flights. After a meeting between the two parties, the closures were revised to 0030-0730 for six nights a week, but the overall programme would be extended to commence from the 13th October. Other work taking place during this time would be the laying of a 25ft-wide hard shoulder either side of the runway, and replacement of the runway's edge lights.

The airport introduced their new two channel customs system on the 10th June. Passengers with something to declare were required to pass through the red channel, and those with nothing to declare through the green channel.

The weather was unsettled at first but became fine and dry by the end of the first week. By mid-month, it was changeable again, with occasional heavy and thundery rain with exceptional falls in certain areas. On the 14th, 59mm of rain fell at Worsborough Dale, West Riding in just forty-five minutes, a statistical event only likely to happen once every 160 years. The following day another exceptional rainfall of 35mm in just eighteen minutes occurred at Dudley, Worcestershire. The opening day of Wimbledon (23rd) was cancelled due to the rain the first time since 1922. There was also a farming crisis due to the wet weather over the past few months, affecting an area of 80,000 acres in the east Midlands and East Anglia, where crops had still not been planted. However, dry weather had returned to much of country by the 26th. The month's temperature extremes saw 27°C at the Southampton (13th) and a low of -4°C at Moor House, Westmorland. (7th).

The only scheduled first visits this month were BEA (BE4090): BAC 1-11 G-AVMX (21st), BOAC (BA534): SVC-10 G-ASGR (4th) and Swissair (SR840): DC-9 HB-IFX (19th). The only equipment changes were Aer Lingus (EI630/650): B.737s EI-ASA (18th) & EI-ASB (10th) both first visits, and Swissair (SR846): All-Air C-54 D-ABOW (13th).

GCA/ILS traffic noted this month was Australian Air Force HS.748s A10-607 (4th/6th) & A10-608 (17th) and Transair CF-TAG (24th); RAF Britannias XL639 (24th), XL660 (16th) & XM490 (30th). BOAC were active again with numerous Boeing 707 training flights, G-APFG (23rd), G-APFH (5th), G-APFJ (4th), G-APFM (9th) & G-AVPB (16th).

1st June was incredible for foreign light visitors, with first visits by PA-23 Aztec SE-EIU (today) from Blackpool to Malmo, PA-28 Cherokee EI-ATN (2nd) which became a frequent visitor, Jodel DR.253 F-BOZM from Toussos to Liverpool (2nd) and also in the opposite direction (6th), Beech 55 SE-EWO clearing customs from Linkoping en route to Brough (4th), Beech 60 SE-EXT from/to Halmstad (5th), PA-23 Aztec D-IBHB from Luton (10th), Cessna 401 OY-AGP from/to Tirstrup (11th), Beech 55 SE-EKE from Gatwick (13th), Beech 90 HB-GDU from/to Basle (20th), Cessna 421 HB-LDV from Le Bourget (26th), Beech 55 HB-GDN Geneva/Aberdeen (28th) and finally Beech 35 D-EHMJ Cologne/Edinburgh (29th).

6th Boeing 707 CF-ZYP, the second aircraft for Wardair, made its first visit arriving at 1641 (WD501 from Gatwick). It departed for Vancouver later, operating the first of ten summer charters from/to Canada.

7th The first of two visits this year by a US Army Beech L-23D Seminole, was made by today's arrival of 68-9063 from/to Burtonwood. The second, 0-63696, was operated from Coleman Barracks to Burtonwood (26th August), and both were first time visitors to Manchester.

9th BUA/British Air Ferries Carvair G-AOFW arrived at 0805 from Southend to operate a cargo flight to Glasgow. This was one of only three Carvair visits to Manchester during 1969.

10th Aer Lingus substituted the usual BAC 1-11 for the first visit of one of their new Boeing 737s, EI-ASB, due to the rostered BAC 1-11 becoming unserviceable in Dublin.

11th Air Canada began the first of eight transatlantic flights today, with Douglas DC-8 CF-TJR making its first visit, positioning from Frankfurt (AC818) to operate as AC037 to Prestwick/Toronto. Apart from DC-8 CF-TJQ (24th August), all other flights during the summer were operated by CF-TJR.

12th June 1969 – As part of the celebrations marking the 50th anniversary of the first non-stop transatlantic flight by Mancunians, John Alcock and Arthur Whitten Brown, replica Vickers Vimy G-AWAU was built at BAC Weybridge. It was flown in yesterday to take part in an exhibition, officially opened by the Queen who arrived in HS.748 XS793 (Kitty 1 from Heathrow). (Geoff Ball)

14th American Flyers were yet another North American airline with a summer programme. They began today with Boeing 727 N12826, night-stopping from Gatwick prior to its lunchtime departure to New York via Keflavik. The airline operated ten flights with Boeing 727s N12826 & N12827 (f/v - 23rd July) and also DC-8 N793FT, which made its first visit to Ringway on 15th September 1969.

14th The Army Air Corps produced numerous Sioux visitors this month, including the first visits by XT552 (14th - Army 315 f/t Valley), XT814 (19th - Army 312 Liverpool/Valley), XW188 (20th - Army 349 Valley/Belle Vue), XT812 (23rd - Army Z40 f/t Warlock Range) & XT211 (30th - Army 349 f/t Belle Vue).

16th G-AMHJ was the final British United Douglas DC-3 to visit Ringway, operating an inbound freight flight from Billund. It would make further visits on the 14th July and the 18th August also from Billund. By 1970, it had been painted in the newly formed British Island Airways colours, carrying 'Air Cargo' titles.

17th PA-31 Navajo N6551L arrived at 1128 today from Dublin, on the last leg of its journey to commemorate Alcock and Brown's historical flight.

18th June 1969 – Sterling was one of two airlines still operating passenger flights with piston aircraft, with the other being Balair. Seen here overtaking the day-stopping C-54F D-ABOW, complete with tail-steady, is DC-6 OY-BAS on its way to the holding point for its departure to Copenhagen on the first of the airline's summer fortnightly flights. (Geoff Ball)

18th June 1969 - Operated by the Sherwood Flying Club, 1966-PA-28 Cherokee G-ATTV is seen here having recently arrived on a flight from Dublin, leaving later for its base at Tollerton, Nottinghamshire. One of an increasing amount of PA-28s that were now visiting Ringway, G-ATTV was used by the club until 1977 when it was sold to a new owner in Hertfordshire. As at June 2014, G-ATTV now based in Essex, was celebrating its 48th year of flying. (Geoff Ball)

18th Sterling operated an incredible seven Douglas DC-6s and two SE.210 Caravelles during the summer, which produced five first visits. The majority of these aircraft operated their weekly charter flight to Copenhagen, which also operated via Dublin. SE.210s OY-STC appeared on the 23rd July and OY-STF on the 9th July, with the latter only being delivered in February 1969. However, the first visiting DC-6s were of a different vintage altogether. OY-STP (f/v - 13th August) had been purchased from Australian National Airways in 1967, and OY-STR (f/v - 6th August) & OY-STS (f/v - 25th June) were both ex-Northwest. All three of these aircraft had been withdrawn and then sold by 1972.

19th Royal Aircraft Establishment Dove C.2 XA880 which was built in 1953, finally made its first visit to Ringway sixteen years later, arriving at 0951 today on a round-trip from Llanbedr. This aircraft had a very long military career until its sale in 1995 as G-BVXR.

21st TAE began a series of flights from/to Gerona on behalf of Aviaco (AO1322/3), using BAC 1-11 EC-BQF, operating until the 6th September. The story goes that the airline was so hard-pressed financially, that their sole 1-11 needed to be in the air 24 hours a day. Unsurprisingly, the airline suspended operations the following year, with BAC 1-11 EC-BQF being repossessed by the manufacturers.

22nd June 1969 – This picture emphasises the chaos on a busy summer Sunday! Hundreds of passengers spilling out of arrivals are seen trying to cross the busy terminal road, to catch a bus, taxi or get to their parked cars. In the space of seven years it was clear that the new terminal had already outgrown its usefulness. To tackle this, the airport produced a £5 million proposal later in the year, which would eventually sweep away these familiar scenes of the late-1960s. In 1972, work would begin on a brand-new terminal extension, a third pier and a multi-storey car park. (MA Archive via Ringway Publications)

25th June 1969 - RAF Wessex HC.2 XV726 arrived at 1633 as 'Rainbow' from Macclesfield with HRH Prince Philip for the opening of ARMEX (Army Exhibition) show at Belle Vue. He was then driven to Gorton Park, located opposite the exhibition itself. (Geoff Ball)

26th June 1969 – Army Air Corps Beaver XP822 arrived at 1038 today from Topcliffe (Army Air 439), and was based at Ringway until the 29th. In between it undertook regular parachute drops at the ARMEX (Army Exhibition) show, taking place at Belle Vue Zoological Gardens, Manchester. (Geoff Ball)

24th Aer Lingus operated eight transatlantic charters during the summer, starting with today's first visit of Boeing 707 EI-ASO at 1251, departing as IN911 for Shannon/New York. The flights were operated until the 28th September with three other B.707s, EI-AMW, APG & ASN (f/v - 26th September).

24th The West German Air Force operated two training flights this month. Nothing unusual in that, but both on the same day was a little different! Noratlas' 53+37 at 1258 (DCN 9514 from Erding) & 52+79 at 1315 (DCN9515 from Neubiberg) both departed to RAF Topcliffe. Noratlas 53+37 returned the following day from Topcliffe, before leaving again for Erding.

24th The Fairey Aviation hangar had an extremely rare aircraft movement today, with the arrival of Dakota G-ALWC at 2055 on a night-stopping flight from/to White Waltham.

30th Trans Union Douglas DC-6 F-BRID (also 28th July) arrived at 2346 and night-stopped. It departed to Prague at 0952 carrying a consignment of computer equipment.

30th The afternoon witnessed a 'Sioux' invasion, when six landed in just over an hour. Calling in for fuel was XT152 at 1330 (NFT85 Coventry/Liverpool), followed by XW188 at 1341 (NFT82 from Coventry), XT212 at 1358 (NFT91 from Birmingham), XT213 at 1401 (NFT89 from Birmingham), XT242 at 1430 (NFT86 from Birmingham) and XT243 at 1446 (NFT88 from Middle Wallop).

30th June 1969 – Overseas National DC-8-63 N793FT arrived at 1902 today from Le Bourget, on a much delayed departure to Toronto. The first of three summer charters, the other two were operated by DC-8s N865F (16th July - f/v) & N852F (7th September). (Geoff Ball)

JULY 1969

Business continues to boom at Manchester. During the first six months of the year there was an 8% increase in terminal passengers to 657,025 over the same period last year. Freight, including mail, showed an increase of 19% and freight carried by charter aircraft leapt by 164% to 373 tonnes over the same period.

Work was due to start in October, providing additional approach lights and centre-line lighting along the whole length of runway 24/06, at a cost of around £115,000. At the same time, the Board of Trade would upgrade the ILS, scheduled for completion by December 1969. When fully operational, it would enable aircraft to land with visibility as little as 1,300ft (400mtrs) and a cloud ceiling down to 150ft.

The outstanding feature of this month's weather was an exceptionally dry, and sometimes hot period from the 9th-27th. Preceding this was a day of heavy rain on the 6th, when Sittingbourne recorded 82mm and falls of over 60mm were recorded in many places. The dry spell ended on the 28th with exceptional rainfall in England and Wales. In the 24 hours ending at 0900 on the 29th, a number of falls classified as 'very rare' occurred. These included 145mm at Ellbridge, near Plymouth and 144mm at North Hessary Tor, on Dartmoor. Numerous daily falls in excess of 100mm were recorded in Somerset, Devon and Cornwall and thunderstorms were frequent and heavy. On the 16th, lightning damaged property in the Inverness region and according to the press, hailstones of 5cm across fell in Northamptonshire! The month's temperature extremes saw 32°C at Wittering (16th) and a low of 3°C at Warsop, Notts. (18th).

Scheduled first visits were BEA: BAC 1-11 G-AVMY (21st), Trident 2 G-AVFO (5th) and BOAC (BA533): SVC-10 G-ASGP (5th). The only equipment/sub-charter this month was Swissair (SR846): Martinair DC-6 PH-MAM (19th).

GCA/ILS traffic noted this month was dominated by the Royal Air Force providing Britannias XL639 (15th), XL657 (16th), XL658 (22nd), XM490 (30th), XM497 (2nd), XM520 (1st), XN392 (29th), XN398 (29th), XN404 (11th), VC-10s XR808 (10th/15th), Comet XR397 (18th) and a couple of increasingly rare types with RAE Varsity WJ491 (4th) & Hastings WD499 (17th). Rounding off a very much military-based month was Transair CF-MAK (16th). Surprisingly after the frenzied activity of the previous few months, there were no training flights during July.

1st BEA's Paris flight will be operated by a based Comet from today. G-APMG positioned in last night (BE303N from Glasgow) to operate during the week as BE794/5. It then operates an evening rotation to Glasgow, but this was short-lived as it had been replaced by Super 1-11s by the end of the month.

1st Electronics company Philips used two new aircraft this month. Today, Beech 90 PH-ILK operated from Maastricht, while Beech 65 PH-FSS arrived from Bristol (15th). Apart from these, the only other first visits were Cessna 337 OY-AGU (3rd) from Herning to Blackpool and PA-23 Aztec F-BOHV from Le Havre (17th).

4th Although not technically a visit, this afternoons overshoot by RAE Valetta WJ491 marked the last appearance of the type. Based at Boscombe Down with the A&AEE, it was in service until April 1972, when it was struck off charge. It was withdrawn at RAF Gatow, before eventually ending up on the fire dump until the late 1970s, when it was finally destroyed.

10th There were a couple of interesting light aircraft movements today. First was the first visit of Islander CF-YZT at 1021 on a round-trip from Bembridge, whilst being used as a company run-around/demonstrator. Second was another visit by the only Belgian-registered DH.Dove, OO-WIP, arriving at 1507 from Liverpool, leaving later for Southend.

14th Loganair Beech 18 G-ASUG made only its second visit to Ringway, arriving at 1445 today operating from/to Glasgow. Loganair were originally looking for three Beech 18s, which were duly purchased from the Royal Canadian Air Force, and planned to be the nucleus of the airline's scheduled network. However, these particular aircraft had not been assembled in the USA by Beech, but had arrived in Canada for assembly there. The result was their existence proved difficult to establish in the eyes of the British authorities, since their country of manufacture was the USA, but the aircraft had never been registered there. This anomaly presented a major obstacle in establishing the aircraft on the UK register. Finally one was sold, and the other two were used for spares. So, G-ASUG was purchased by the airline in 1968, having been used previously as a survey aircraft with BKS. It would continue to make occasional visits to Ringway, with the last being on 21st February 1975, just prior to its final retirement later in the year. It is now preserved with the Museum of Flight at East Fortune.

16th Another Army Air Corps Sioux making its first visit, was today's arrival of XT545 (Army 339) f/t Salisbury Plain. Also this month was Varsity WF379 (23rd) using the callsign 'MPFFR' from/to RAF Pershore and a number of trooping flights, with XL657 (16th - RR6475 to Gutersloh), XM490 (f/v 19th - RR6477 to Hanover) & (30th - RR6481 to Gutersloh) & XL637 (31st - RR6482 to Gutersloh).

18th The latest light aircraft to grace the south side with a demonstration was Beech 60 Duke N7204D. Arriving at 1712 from Oxford, it was present until the following morning, performing local flights before its departure to Liverpool. The first Beech 60 to be registered in the UK was G-AXEN in April 1969, with Eagle Aircraft Services of Leavesden. This aircraft made its only visit to Ringway on 24th August 1969 on a flight from Cologne, and was sold in Germany soon afterwards. Unfortunately, there were no takers from the companies based at Ringway for this sleek-looking aircraft.

19th Five flights were delayed when a rogue pelican, which had been circling the area, landed in the middle of the runway. It was reported in the local news later that the bird was coaxed away with fish fingers and a piece of haddock on a string, held by two airport policemen! The tug-of-war finally ended when the pelican gave up, and zoomed off into Styal woods.

8th July 1969 - HS.125 G-ATZN is seen in between flights, having just arrived from Blackpool, before its departure to East Midlands later. Delivered new to the Rank Organisation in 1966, it served with them until 1974, when it was sold in Zambia and re-registered as N93TC. (Geoff Ball)

14th July 1969 - Following a very successful month long exhibition marking the 50th Anniversary of the Alcock & Brown flight, disaster struck as the Vickers Vimy replica was being readied for departure to Hucknall. The sun's rays had ignited the canvas on the lower port wing, causing a fire. A quick reaction by the airport's fire service managed to contain the flames, and it is seen here shortly afterwards. Manchester Corporation opened an emergency repair fund office in Manchester whilst a detailed inspection got underway. The decision to repair the aircraft depended on how bad the damage was on the parts most subject to stress. More than £1,000 had been collected by October, and one local organisation even arranged for the Vimy to be transported back to Weybridge at their expense. Fortunately, it was eventually rebuilt and put on display at the RAF Museum at Hendon. (Geoff Ball)

22nd July 1969 – Having operated DC-8 flights into Ringway since 1965, including the first visit of a stretched DC-8, TIA used B.727-171C N1728T today on the first of two visits this year. These aircraft were clearly operating at the extreme limit of their range and performance, whilst carefully observing safety regulations regarding the operation of twin engined jet aircraft on Atlantic routes. During the summer, they would also operate two DC-8 flights, with N4863T (17th July - f/v) & N8961T (20th October). (Geoff Ball)

22nd July 1969 - Dan-Air Ambassador G-AMAH arrived at 1218 on a passenger charter from Brest. It would eventually leave for Glasgow, but at the time this shot was taken the crew and engineers were having difficulties starting the number one engine. It would make two more visits to Ringway, both in 1970, before its withdrawal in March 1971. (Graham Davies)

24th July 1969 – USAF Convair VT-29D Sabreliner made its second appearance today, having previously visited in December 1966. It arrived at 1537 from RAF Alconbury with a number of generals onboard for a base inspection of Burtonwood. They would normally be transferred by a CH-34A Chocktaw, but as none were available the VIPs had to 'slum' it, and make the short journey by surface transport. (Geoff Ball)

25th July 1969 – Universal Airlines made its debut last year, operating an ad hoc flight to New York. This year they were operating six transatlantic charters to New York and Toronto with DC-8-55 N805U, which made its first visit to Manchester today. (Geoff Ball)

22nd This month's West German Air Force training flight was operated by Noratlas 53+00 (DCN9853). Arriving at 1605 from Filton, it stayed overnight before departing the following morning to Cologne.

26th Trans Europa did not have a summer programme from Ringway this year, so any movement by this Spanish airline was worth a mention. DC-7 EC-BBH appeared at 1152 today (TR210 from Palma) operating an ad hoc flight, departing to Birmingham. Another DC-7, EC-BCH (6th August- TR212) also arrived from Palma, dropping off a number of passengers before continuing on to Birmingham.

26th Lloyd International operated the first of four inbound freight flights from Hong Kong, all via Istanbul. G-AOVS arrived at 1148 today (LW506), G-AOVP (28th - LW510 & 31st - LW516) and G-ANCD (30th - LW514).

27th Early morning fog sent in Gatwick diversion ex-Alitalia SE.210 I-DABR (MQ842 from Rimini), now operating for their charter subsidiary, SAM. Later RAF VC-10 XR808 arrived at 0936 (RR2169 from Akrotiri) on its first visit.

27th Dragon Rapide G-AKRS arrived at 1457 today from Halfpenny Green to operate a parachute drop in the Bolton area.

28th British Midland Viscount G-APPX was on a flight from East Midlands to Belfast, when it diverted into Manchester at 0923 having shut down one of its engines.

28th The first executive jet to make its first visit since May was Falcon 20 HB-VBL. It stayed overnight on a flight from Naples, before departing for Heathrow the following afternoon.

30th Jetstream D-INAH arrived at 1330 today on a test flight from/to Radlett. It was delivered to Bavaria in October 1969, but its existence was cut short, when on the 6th March 1970, it flew into power lines while on approach at Samedan, Switzerland.

30th Capitol produced two charters during 1969, both first visits by Douglas DC-8-31 aircraft. Today, N4902C arrived at 1512 from Frankfurt to operate a one-off passenger charter to Philadelphia. The return flight was operated by DC-8 N4901C on the 1st September.

AUGUST 1969

An ambitious £5 million blueprint was produced by the airport, by ex-airport director George Harvey and a work study group to take it into the 'Jumbo' era. The following recommendations have been set to meet a possible target date of 1973-74:

(1) A new long haul pier with associated aprons and taxiways on the west side of the current terminal building. This should be able to accommodate a mix of various numbers of VC-10/B.707 & B.747 aircraft, complete with nose-in parking with air bridges linked to the pier. (2) The building of a multi-storey car park for 2,500 vehicles. Part of the ground floor would serve as a baggage claim area, customs hall and a meet and greet area, with the remainder to be used as kerbside and short-term parking. (3) A new booking hall with sufficient space for 52 check-in desks at first floor level on the south of the multi-storey car park, connected by a bridge to the present concourse. (4) A new immigration hall on first-floor level. (5) A new baggage sorting area at ground-floor level. (6) Conversion of the present customs hall into an extension of the concourse and designed as an additional waiting area for international passengers. (7) An enlargement of the present international departure and transit lounge and the repositioning of the catering and duty-free concessions. (8) Extension at first and second-floor levels by about 30ft at the southern frontage of the current terminal. This would give increased area at the first-floor level for the international departure and transit lounge, restaurant, cocktail bar, concourse and domestic lounge, and at second-floor level for an extension of the private suite and other catering facilities. (9) Adaptation of the western half of the present booking hall as a domestic baggage claim area.

It was considered that the total estimated bill of £5,091,000 could be fully supported by the airport's finances. Projected terminal passengers were 1,650,000 by 1969, rising to 2,350,000 by 1973, 3,350,000 (1977) and 4,750,000 (1982). With hindsight the figures were very accurate up to 1973, but the 1974 fuel crisis and consequent economic depression resulted in slower overall growth up to 1977. The specification for these expanded facilities was accepted by the city council in 1970 and work proceeded in phases thereafter.

Plans to give Manchester its first scheduled service with Eastern Europe have been turned down by the Air Transport Licensing Board. They refused BUA's application to operate from Manchester and Gatwick to Sofia and Bucharest.

It was envisaged that ten Boeing 747s a week would be operating from Manchester by the mid-1970s. BOAC would operate ten flights per week with their yet-to-be-delivered 390-seater B.747s. The airline would also designate Manchester as a high-priority diversionary airport for the type by 1970.

The first three weeks of the month were very warm at times, but the last ten days were cooler with northwesterly winds. Thunderstorms occurred in most areas, with a number of exceptionally heavy rain falls, especially in the south. Holiday traffic was frequently disrupted by temporary flooding, following heavier outbreaks of rain. Two examples of the heavy rain begin on the 2nd at Hampton, southwest London, when over 96mm (nearly twice the monthly average) fell in ten hours. The example was on the 15th, when a 'remarkable' fall of 46mm in an hour was recorded at RAF Manston. The month's temperature extremes saw 31°C at North Heath, Sussex (11th) and a low of 2°C at Carlisle. (24th)

This month's scheduled first visits were BEA BAC 1-11 G-AVMZ (19th) and Trident 2 G-AVFN (10th). GCA/ILS traffic noted this month included Royal Air Force Britannias XL640 (12th), XL659 (5th), XM490 (25th), XM497 (27th) & Comet XR399 (18th/22nd), Dan-Air Ambassador G-AMAE (8th), Cessna 411 G-ATEY (19th) and CAA HS.748 G-AVXJ (15th). Just two BOAC training flights were B.707 G-APFF (19th) & G-ARRB (8th), plus Board of Trade Dove G-AJLV (14th).

1st Jetstream G-AXEK operated a couple of flights through Ringway today. Firstly, it arrived from Oxford at 0945 and departed to Dublin. Later in the day it appeared from Llanbedr and departed at 1745 back to Oxford. Until recently it had been on demonstration to Dan-Air, in Dan-Air Commuter titles, operating the airlines Bristol-Cardiff-Liverpool-Newcastle service on several occasions. During this period, they also trialled Twin Otter CF-WTE, but in the end both the Jetstream and the Twin Otter were found to be unsuitable.

1st Britannia XM520 (RR6413 from Hanover) operated a return trooping flight today. After numerous visits on training flights, it was the aircrafts first visit to Ringway. Further trooping flights during August were VC-10s XR807 (8th/14th), f/v XR806 (11th - RR2795 from Akrotiri), XV107 (13th/16th) & XV104 (16th - RR2798 from Prestwick).

1st Lloyd International continued to operate further inbound cargo flights from Hong Kong, via Istanbul, with G-AOVS arriving at 1342 today (LW518). The others used were G-ANCD (2nd - LW326) & G-AOVS (5th - LW340).

3rd Transmeridian had been registered as a company as far back as 1962, but their fleet was mainly leased out to other operators during the early to mid 1960s. In the summer of 1968, the airline transferred its operating base from Cambridge to Stansted. In December 1968 they took delivery of their first CL-44, G-AWWB. After conversion to the airline's requirements, it entered commercial service in February 1969. In the first three months of operation, G-AWWB was involved in the export of cattle to Ethiopia and manufactured tobacco goods to Sudan, with fruit and various other food stuffs making up the return loads to the United Kingdom. Today, G-AWWB was making its first visit on a night-stopping flight from Stansted, leaving the following afternoon to Budapest.

10th SAS Douglas DC-8 OY-KTC (SK095 from Bergen) arrived at 0703 today due to early morning fog at Prestwick. This was only the second SAS DC-8 to visit, after SE-DBA arrived on 22nd January 1966. KLM DC-8 PH-DCT (13th - KL070) which operated Amsterdam/New York was also a first visit to Manchester.

10th Beech 60 D-ILCA from/to Cologne (also 11th), began this month's crop of first time visiting light aircraft. Also during September was Beech 55 SE-EXG (14th), clearing customs before departing to Oulton Park and returning in the opposite direction four days later. The other arrivals were PA-31 Navajo Chieftain N9187Y f/t Fairoaks (14th), PA-32 Cherokee D-EMTK f/t Dusseldorf (18th), and finally Siai SM-208 OO-MAP Brussels-Edinburgh & Beech 55 D-IBIZ f/t Mannheim (both 24th).

17th The first of the four ex-KLM Douglas DC-7s purchased by Aer Turas to visit Ringway, was EI-ATU (ex PH-DSF), arriving at 1559 today on a return flight from Dublin. This aircraft would make several more visits during 1969 along with a second, EI-ATT (ex PH-DSE), which made its first appearance on the 13th September. The remaining two, EI-ATV (ex PH-DSI) and EI-ATW (ex PH-DSG), would not appear at Manchester, as they were sold to Affretair in May 1969.

26th Decca Navigator Ambassador G-ALZP, arriving at 1255 today from Bournemouth, was making its first visit since November 1966. It would make one final call at Manchester on 12th December 1969 (f/t Gatwick) before its sale to South Seas Airways as ZK-DFC in November 1971. However, the sale ultimately fell through and the aircraft was subsequently broken up.

17ᵗʰ August 1969 - Dan-Air began two-weekly Munich-based BAC 1-11 flights from Ringway in April 1969. BAC 1-11 G-AXCK is seen on a warm Sunday afternoon, awaiting its return load. The BAC 1-11 & DH.Comet, with the addition of Boeing 727s in the mid-1970s, would form the backbone of the airline's charter operations. Upon the impending retirement of the Comets, more BAC 1-11s were added, serving the airline until its collapse in 1992. (Geoff Ball)

18ᵗʰ August 1969 – Loganair Skyvan G-AWYG made its first visit today f/t Dublin. Delivered to the company on 3ʳᵈ March 1969, it was the first of its type to a British operator. It had a payload of up to 18 passengers or 4,000lbs of cargo. Much larger than any previous Loganair aircraft, it was chiefly used on services to Stornaway & Stavanger. Its unique box shape made it ideal for carrying bulky and heavy loads, putting it in a class of its own. However, abnormally large loads did not arise frequently enough for adequate utilisation of its unique carrying capability. It was expensive to operate, and fuel loadings for longer journeys often restricted the payload to between 12-15 passengers and their baggage. After five years service, it was phased out and in June 1974 it was sold in the USA as N28TC. (Geoff Ball)

24th August 1969 – Seen on a sunny Sunday afternoon, bringing out the spectators, is Falconair Vickers Viscount SE-CNK (FZ1718P from Malmo) making its third visit to Ringway. It was the longest serving aircraft with the airline, later renamed Skyline Sweden, continuing in service until August 1976. (Geoff Ball)

26th August 1969 – One of the most colourful airliners to Ringway during 1969 was Air Bahama Boeing 707 N525EJ (also 2nd September). Arriving at 1656 today (WO525 from Gatwick), it was operating a departure to New York on behalf of World Airways. In 1970, it was bought by British Caledonian and saw a further fifteen years service as G-AYEX. (Geoff Ball)

27th Tradewinds, which had risen from the ashes of Transglobe, were now operating as a pure cargo airline. G-AWGT, which had previously visited as a passenger aircraft but was now all-cargo, positioned in at 0943 from Stansted, departing for Abidjan the following morning.

27th Another batch of outbound trooping flights began today with two new RAF Britannias operating to Gutersloh. Arriving were XM497 (today - RR6415 & (29th - RR6417) plus XL637 (28th - RR6416).

29th This month's West German Air Force training flight was operated by Noratlas 52+91 (DCN0211). Arriving at 1114 today from Birmingham, it departed early evening for Erding.

31st Cessna 206 G-AXJY arriving at 1441 today from Keflavik, later departing for Rogers Aviation at Cranfield, was the latest delivery from the Cessna factory. It was sold to a private owner in Lincoln and remained on the UK register until 1997, when it was sold in the USA.

SEPTEMBER 1969

From April 1970, BOAC will begin a four-weekly service from Birmingham to New York. They will operate as an extension to the Manchester flights, but will be non-stop to/from New York.

The summer had been busy with charter flights to the USA & Canada. Taken as a whole, British airports had seen more than a 100% increase on last year. Between ten to twenty movements per week recorded at Ringway involved North American airlines such as Air Canada, CP Air, Wardair, Pacific Western, Capitol, TIA, Universal, American Flyers, World Airways & TWA and UK airlines Donaldson, British United, Laker Airways & Caledonian. For the first time in several years, BOAC had also been operating to various destinations including Toronto, New York & Philadelphia.

It was exceptionally dry month, with eastern England experiencing its driest September in ten years. Low rainfall in parts of west Scotland resulted in water rationing in the Glasgow area, but the month ended with strong winds and heavy rain. The month's temperature extremes saw 28°C at Dartmouth (12th) and a low of -6°C Santon Downham. (30th).

There were no scheduled first visits this month. Equipment changes were <u>Aer Lingus (EI602)</u>: B.737 EI-ASC (18th) which was a first visit & (<u>EI620/1</u>): B.707 EI-ASO (13th) and <u>Swissair (SR846)</u>: All-Air C-54 D-ABOW (2nd/3rd/19th) & Invicta C-54 G-ASPN (25th).

GCA/ILS traffic noted this month included numerous RAF training flights, with Britannias XL660 (3rd/13th/25th), XM490 (5th), XM496 (25th), XM497 (26th/29th), XM498 (29th/30th), XM518 (18th) and Comet XR396 (12th). Flight testing out of Woodford had been on the quiet side. The only HS.748 using the facilities was Fiji Airlines VQ-FBK (9th). For the first time in a while, two HS.125 test flights out of Hawarden were noted as Brazilian Air Force VC93-2125 (11th) & G-5-13 (30th). Training flights were plentiful again starting with BOAC who provided seven different Boeing 707s, with G-APFC (15th/27th), G-APFG (2nd), G-APFH (18th), G-APFJ (20th), G-APFM (13th), G-ARRA (22nd) & G-ASZG (22nd). Also during September were Cessna 411 G-ATEY (9th), BEA Argosy G-ASXN (15th), Dan-Air Ambassador G-AMAE (23rd) and CAA HS.748 G-AVXJ (30th).

3rd Another Belgian SIAI SM-208 visited during September, making it two in as many months. Today, OO-EMD arrived from Brussels for fuel en route for Glasgow. Other first visits were made by Commander 680 HB-GEK from Fairoaks (5th), Cessna 172 D-EFGC from Elstree (8th) and Cessna 337 OH-CBB from Heathrow (16th).

5th CP Air, formerly Canadian Pacific, made their first visit to Ringway since July 1965. DC-8-63 CF-CPQ (CP800 from Toronto), which arrived at 0723 today, was also making its first visit, later positioning to Gatwick. The return flight on the 28th was operated by DC-8 CF-CPQ again, departing to Toronto via Shannon (CP801). By the mid 1970s along with Wardair, CP Air would firmly establish themselves as a major player in the Canadian market out of Ringway.

8th Due to technical problems, Universal DC-8 N805U finally departed over 48 hours late to New York without four weary passengers, who had slept through several announcements for them to go the gate!

9th A BEA Viscount, operating BE5606 from Heathrow to Aberdeen, diverted into Manchester at 0857 having shut down one of its engines. A full emergency was declared and fire brigades from Cheadle and Wilmslow were called to supplement the airport's fire service, but in the end the Viscount with 62 passengers landed safely.

12th RAF C-130 XV216 made an emergency landing at 1900 (RR3213 from Belfast) with a faulty door, en route to Lyneham. The fault was serious enough to delay the aircraft's return to Lyneham until the 14th.

7th September 1969 - ONA Douglas DC-8 N852F (in the background) had suffered minor damage when landing at 0237 today on a flight from New York. The aircraft could not be moved, and delayed any arrivals for nearly three hours. PA-23 Aztec PH-EDG arrived from Amsterdam at 1712 bringing in spares for the 'sick' DC-8. In the foreground Alitalia DC-8 I-DIWI (AZ2660 from Belgrade) had arrived on a tech stop en route for Toronto. Sandwiched between the two was Aviogenex TU-134 YU-AHI, seen taxiing for departure bound for Ljubljana. (Geoff Ball)

12th Once a regular, American-airline Saturn made just one appearance during 1969, with today's arrival of DC-8 N8956U at 1818 from Le Bourget, to operate an ad hoc flight to Toronto via Keflavik.

13th RAF Britannia XL660 arrived at 1201 (Display 06 from Lyneham) with spares for the stricken C-130.

14th The weather affected operations at various airports during the month. The majority of the 38 diverted flights were British and not worth a mention, but there were a few exceptions. Today saw the most 'variety', with Austrian Airlines Viscount OE-LAH at 0206 (OB5081 from Salzburg), Wardair B.707 CF-FAN at 0657 (WD888 from Edmonton) and Iberia SE.210 EC-BIF (IB742 from Madrid). Finally, SAS DC-9 SE-DBW arrived at 1211 (28th - SK535A from Copenhagen) due to strong winds at Glasgow.

16th This month's West German Air Force training flight was again operated by Noratlas 52+91 (DCN0320). Arriving at 1204 from Neubiberg, it departed after a short stay for Birmingham.

17th Local aviation enthusiasts over the past few years had become used to the success of Manchester United, and the benefits to the hobby that it would bring. But that success had eluded them at the end of the previous season, which meant they had not qualified for any European competitions. The other Manchester side however, Manchester City, were very much on the up. Having only been promoted to the First Division in May 1967, they won the First Division championship the following season (1967/68) and had just completed the 1968/69 season by winning the FA Cup, although the championship went to Leeds United. The result of all this meant that Manchester City had qualified for the European Cup-Winners Cup, which began in earnest today with a trip to Spain to play Athletico Bilbao. The team left today aboard Britannia Airways Britannia G-ANBE, returning the following evening having achieved a credible 3-3 draw. The return leg took place two weeks later at Maine Road, where the Blues convincingly beat the Spaniards 3-0.

18th The final aircraft to operate from Manchester's third runway 02/20 took place today when Beech 23 G-ATBI arrived on runway 20 at 1450 operating a local fight. The very final departure was Eric Raffles'

Beech 55 G-ASZC, also off runway 20 at 1702 (23rd). It had been officially decommissioned by the end of 1969, and would find a new use as part taxiway and vital additional parking on diversion days.

26th The Blue Eagles helicopter display team (Siouxs XT134/XT192/XT193/XT206/ XT498) all arrived in formation at 1240 today from RAF Middle Wallop on a fuel stop. They left ninety minutes later bound for Carlisle.

26th The Gulfstream 2 would become the first of one of the most successful ranges of executive jets produced in the United States. The first to appear at Ringway was N902, arriving at 1929 today from Edinburgh, leaving later for Gatwick. It returned again the following day, also operating from/to Gatwick. It was operated by Owens Illinois, a major glass and bottle manufacturing company, serving with them until its sale in 1997.

27th BOAC Boeing 707 G-APFF (BA608 from Toronto/Montreal/Prestwick) landed safely after advising ATC of a hydraulic problem. However, it was unable to exit the runway and was towed by tug to its gate. Although the runway was closed for a short period until it was removed, no other flights were affected.

OCTOBER 1969

British United Airways made an application to take over BOAC's routes from London to various points in Africa, with Manchester being added to the route network at the same time. Cities to be linked included Johannesburg, Nairobi, Lagos, Accra and Cairo. VC-10 aircraft would be used, but the application would ultimately be opposed by BOAC, who had already announced their intention to inaugurate services between Manchester and Johannesburg next year. No dates were fixed for the introduction of services, which would operate via Heathrow initially. The licence would become effective from April 1970, but in the end it was just another route that did not operate.

The weather was exceptionally dry in the south and east of England. It was estimated that the general rainfall over England and Wales had not been lower in the month of October since 1784. Restrictions on the use of water were introduced in many urban areas, as reservoirs became depleted. Winds were often from a southerly direction, bringing warm, though sometimes foggy weather. It was the mildest October in Durham since 1847 and the mildest at Kew since 1868. The month's temperature extremes saw 26°C at East Dereham (9th) and a low of -4°C at Lacock, Wiltshire (30th).

There were no scheduled first visits during October. Equipment changes were (Aer Lingus): B.737s EI-ASA (26th - EI602/3) & EI-ASB (14th - EI630/1) and KLM (KL005): Martinair DC-9 PH-MAO (21st).

GCA/ILS traffic this month saw a marked improvement on HS.748s out of Woodford with BFS D-AFSD (3rd/10th/21st/27th), Fiji Airlines VQ-FBK (3rd), LIAT VP-LAA (7th), Philippine Airlines PI-C1025 (31st) & PI-C1026 (23rd). Royal Air Force aircraft noted were Britannias XL636 (16th/19th), XM490 (6th), XM491 (21st), XM518 (27th) & Comet XR399 (15th). Miscellaneous traffic included CAA HS.748 G-AVXJ (6th) and HS.125s G-AXDS & G-AXOB (both 22nd). Plenty of training flights again, starting with BOAC B.707s G-APFC (9th/24th), G-APFH (22nd), G-APFI (13th/15th), G-APFJ (6th), G-APFO (11th), G-AWHU (13th) and BEA Argosy G-ASXM (13th) & Vanguard G-APEF (18th).

1st Cessna 310 OE-FAW arrived at 1419 today from Stuttgart, clearing customs before leaving for Carlisle. It returned the following evening to night-stop and departed for Basle at 1234. Other first visits during October were Cessna 172 OO-SIV from Brussels (14th), PA-32 Cherokee EI-ASY from Shannon (15th), Cessna 402 OY-AGO from Aalborg (21st), Cessna 320 HB-LDB f/t Gatwick (23rd) & Cessna 421 OY-DNL from Billund (29th).

2nd A couple of interesting first time visitors today, started with French Air Force Caravelle '141' at 1018 (F-RAFG from Paris-Orly), en route to Stornaway. Until his death in 1970, this aircraft was primarily used as President De Gaulle's transport, and later as a communications aircraft until its withdrawal in March 1980. The second first visit was LOT Ilyushin IL-18 SP-LSB, operating a passenger charter from/to Warsaw.

3rd An extremely rare visit by Martin-Baker Douglas DC-3 G-APML took place today. Arriving at 0956 from Chalgrove, it departed to Jurby. This aircraft is normally employed on communication flights between Jurby and Langford Lodge, Northern Ireland, and is seldom seen elsewhere in the country.

3rd Royal Navy Wessex HU.5 XT764 (callsign Navy WL) arrived at 1406 on a local flight from St. Helens, departing for RAF Shawbury. The helicopter is used by the Royal Navy Presentation Team to visit UK schools and colleges.

5th October 1969 - Seen parked next to Autair BAC 1-11 G-AVGP, is Martinair Douglas DC-8 PH-DCD. It arrived at 0957 today from Amsterdam, to operate an outbound passenger charter to New York, via Keflavik. However, due to the number of diversions the airport had received during the morning, there were no stands available for the DC-8. This resulted in the passengers being taken by bus to the South Bay to join their flight. Hopefully they enjoyed their tour of the diverted aircraft on the way! (Geoff Ball)

19th October 1969 – Seen on a murky Sunday afternoon, is Iberia Douglas DC-9 EC-BIQ, employed by Aviaco on an extra charter flight from/to Ibiza (AO1228/9). In November, there would be a sudden explosion of Iberia DC-9 first visits, when the airline introduced the type on its twice-weekly schedule service to Madrid. Unfortunately, the service did not pay its way, and was axed in January 1970. (Geoff Ball)

4ᵗʰ Ferranti Jet Ranger G-AVSN and Army Air Corps Scout XP884 (Army 221) both arrived from Gatwick at 1721 in formation, before leaving twenty minutes later for Radbroke Hall, Knutsford. The Army Scout arrived back from Knutsford at 1905 to night-stop, returning to Gatwick the following morning.

5ᵗʰ The week saw a particularly foggy period across the country. Widespread fog was mostly confined to mornings and nights, but the thick fog persisted all day in certain areas. Today was the best in terms of numbers, with twenty diversions arriving from 0233 to 0829. Apart from TAE BAC 1-11 EC-BQF, they were all from British airlines.

6ᵗʰ Four diversions from Heathrow during the morning provided one first visit, with Qantas B.707 VH-EBR at 1044 (QF743 from Amsterdam). B.707 VH-EBR (QF757 from Rome) also diverted in on the 10ᵗʰ, and two days later another Qantas B.707 also making its first visit was VH-EAA (12ᵗʰ - QF173/4), operating from/to Tehran.

9ᵗʰ Two more French military visitors this month started today with Navy Flamant No.315 (callsign F-YCBH), at 1123 en route from Lorient to Ballykelly. On the 21ˢᵗ, French Air Force Nord 262 No.45 (callsign F-RAOB) arriving at 1303 from Tours was a first visit of type. It was carrying a stretcher case, and later left for Villacoublay.

9ᵗʰ Fairey's Dove G-AMKS based at White Waltham was an extremely rare visitor to Ringway, but it arrived at 1633 today for maintenance work. After leaving for White Waltham on the 13ᵗʰ, it returned again on the 31ˢᵗ and stayed for a further week.

10ᵗʰ In amongst another ten weather diversions from Heathrow was Pan American B.707 N402PA at 1233 (PA101 from Frankfurt) on its first visit.

12ᵗʰ Main runway closures for essential work on week nights during the winter commenced tonight.

13ᵗʰ This month's West German Air Force training flight was operated by Noratlas 53+12 (DCN7544). Arriving at 1623 today from Birmingham, it departed the following morning to Erding.

28ᵗʰ October 1969 – The month was an excellent one for visiting French military aircraft. As well as a SE.210 Caravelle, a Flamant and a Nord 262, today also saw the first visit of a French Air Force Falcon 20, with the arrival of No.93 (callsign F-RAFN) at 1456 from Stornaway. A second Falcon 20, No.167 (callsign F-RAFL), also arrived from Stornaway en route to Villacoublay on the 19ᵗʰ November. (Geoff Ball)

17th Six Heathrow diversions arrived this morning. Most passengers disembarked and cleared customs before resuming their final journey to Heathrow, once the fog and ATC delays had cleared. The only two of interest were Ghana Airways VC-10 9G-ABO at 0903 (GH706 from Accra/Rome) and Air Canada DC-8 CF-TIO at 1059 (AC856 from Montreal).

19th Visits by RAF Argosies to Ringway had been quite rare since their introduction into service, but XP441 arrived at 1325 (RR428 from Belfast), and stayed thirty minutes before leaving for its base at RAF Benson.

19th KLM Douglas DC-8 PH-DCU arrived at 2104 today from Amsterdam on its first visit, leaving at 2244 on a passenger charter to Berlin.

21st Weathermen were expecting a real 'pea-souper' to affect the southeast today. Fog did affect Heathrow during the morning, just like four days earlier, but the diverted aircraft provided little excitement with four from BOAC and three from BEA. It was Birmingham's turn for fog in the afternoon, but again all but two of the six diversions were from BEA.

23rd Wearing basic Transglobe/Tradewinds colours with TMA titles, was CL-44 N429SW arriving at 1652 today (TL429 from Benina) on its only visit. It was returned to Seaboard World in 1970, but was eventually re-purchased by Tradewinds and registered as G-AWOV.

NOVEMBER 1969

BEA would introduce their Merchantman aircraft onto services linking Heathrow, Glasgow, Manchester and Frankfurt during the month, which in turn replaced their Argosy aircraft. However, due to operating issues use of the Merchantman was limited and BEA was also forced to sub-charter Lloyd International Britannias during November and December. Aircraft used were G-ANCD/ANCE & AOVS.

BOAC will be doubling their flights to Canada next year from Manchester, with one of these daily flights also being extended to serve Chicago. Flight BA608/7 will operate to Toronto, while BA606/5 operates to Montreal and onto Chicago. Both flights will still operate via Prestwick.

Numerous depressions and troughs of low pressure over or near the British Isles during the month were accompanied by winds, frequently from the north and west. The result of this was a rather stormy and exceptionally fog free month. There were also frequent wintry showers, with some moderate to heavy snowfalls. In contrast to this, the month began with a number of places having the warmest November day since records began. However, it became cold after the 3rd, apart from a mild interlude around the 18th-23rd, with temperatures remaining below average for the rest of the month. Frost occurred frequently in the north and was widespread during the final week in the south. Most areas had above average rainfall, with the outstanding fall of the month going to parts of County Antrim, which saw 138mm during a 24 hour period on the 21st/22nd. Despite the seemingly gloomy weather during November, most areas were sunnier than normal, with Ringway recording nearly twice its average sunshine for the month. The month's temperature extremes saw 20°C at Totnes (3rd) and a low of -10°C at Lacock, Wiltshire (30th).

The following airlines could be seen during the winter months, operating ITs to various destinations, Britannia Airways (Munich/Palma), British United (Palma), Dan-Air (Alicante/Ibiza/Palma) and Laker Airways (Palma/Tenerife).

International flights were operated during the winter as follows:

AER LINGUS - Amsterdam (3 x weekly), Copenhagen (3 x weekly), Cork (1 x weekly), Dusseldorf (3 x weekly), Frankfurt (3 x weekly), Shannon (1 x weekly) & Zurich (1 x weekly), with the exception of Cork and Shannon, all other flights operated by BAC 1-11s/B.737s.

AIR FRANCE - Three-weekly to Paris with SE.210s (AF960/1).

ALITALIA - Operated twice-weekly to Milan, but Rome was dropped from the schedule. Flights operated by SE.210 Caravelles, which now night-stop.

BEA - Operated services to Amsterdam/Berlin/Brussels/Copenhagen/Dublin/Dusseldorf/ Malta & Paris. All flights now operated by Super 1-11s, except Malta which is a Trident 2 service.

BOAC - Daily to New York/Antigua/Barbados & Port of Spain via Prestwick (BA538/7) with VC-10s, extending to Georgetown on Mon/Wed/Fri/Sun. Boeing 707s now operate daily to Montreal & Toronto (BA608/7). Tel Aviv continued to be served once-weekly via Heathrow on Sundays by SVC-10s (BA312/3). Cargo flights operated outbound to Montreal (3 x weekly) & New York (5 x weekly) with the inbound flight from New York also operating 4 x weekly.

IBERIA - Twice-weekly to Madrid via Dublin now with Douglas DC-9s (IB744/3).

KLM - Passenger flights operated weekdays to Amsterdam (KL153/4) and cargo operations continued from/to Amsterdam five-weekly via Glasgow (KL005/7). Both were now operating with Douglas DC-9s.
LUFTHANSA - Operated their cargo flights five-weekly (LH934/5) to Frankfurt with All-Air Douglas C-54/DC-4/DC-6 aircraft.
SABENA - The night-stopping Brussels service continued four-times-weekly with SE.210 Caravelles. Cargo flights operated four-weekly with B.727s f/t Brussels, with the outbound via Heathrow (SN197/8).
SAS - Twice-weekly flights serving Copenhagen with SE.210s (SK537/8) extending onwards to Dublin.
SWISSAIR - Passenger flights continue daily to Zurich via Rotterdam with Douglas DC-9s (SR840/1). Cargo flights to Zurich operated four-weekly with Douglas DC-4s until the 7th November, when DC-9F HB-IFW took over all flights (SR846/7).

This month's scheduled first visits were (Aer Lingus): B.737 EI-ASD (2nd), Iberia (IB744): DC-9s EC-BIH (28th), EC-BIK (24th), EC-BIM (21st), EC-BIT (17th), EC-BPF (7th), EC-BPG (14th) & EC-BPH (10th), Swissair (SR840): DC-9s HB-IFV (5th) & HB-IFW (11th).

GCA/ILS traffic noted this month began with HS.748s BFS D-AFSD (3rd/7th), Philippine Airlines PI-C1025 (6th) & Air Malawi 7Q-YKA (19th). The Royal Air Force was out in force again with Britannias XL640 (10th), XL660 (27th), XM489 (7th), XM490 (17th); Nimrods XV229 (28th/30th), XV231 (6th); Comet XR399 (10th), VC-10 XV102 (22nd) and a pair of unidentified C-130s using callsigns RR735 & RR740 (both 26th). As the decade came to a close, BOAC were still active at Ringway using a variety of Boeing 707s, G-APFD (7th/14th), G-APFG (24th/26th), G-APFJ (28th), G-APFL (17th) & G-ARRC (21st).

2nd As tensions between the Catholic's and the Protestants began to increase, the relatively small number of army soldiers in Northern Ireland were increasingly becoming targets for the 'fanatics'. This meant a large expansion of the army's presence was required, and more troops began to arrive over the next few months. As part of this stepping up of the troop numbers, the Royal Air Force began a weekly Sunday RAF Argosy trooping flight, routing Benson-MAN-Belfast-MAN-Benson. Today's first was operated by XN848, which arrived at 0943 (RR4430). The remainder of flights during the month were operated by XR106 (9th), XR136 (16th), non-op (23rd) and finally XN819 (30th).

4th Sabena Boeing 707 OO-SJH arrived at 2011 for fuel en route from New York to Brussels. This aircraft became the ninth Sabena B.707 to visit Ringway since 1960.

7th Today's visit of Cessna 310 F-BHDV from Rennes was the only first time visiting foreign light aircraft.

7th The final Swissair freight service to be operated by a DC-4F took place this evening, when HB-ILD arrived as SR846 at 2142, making its final departure as SR847 at 0019. From Tuesday the 11th, the service was operated by Swissair's new DC-9F, HB-IFW. The other DC-4 used on these flights was HB-ILU, which had made its last visit on 29th October 1969.

7th Heavy snow showers affecting Teesside during the morning resulted in the diversion of two RAF Britannias, XL660 at 1110 (RR6428 at Wildenrath) & XM489 at 1307 (RR6429 from Wiesbaden), with the latter being another first visit.

11th Ex-Queen's Flight Heron XR391, which was on loan to the Royal Navy, arrived at 1838 today from Culdrose (Navy 821) with a number of Navy admirals. This was due to Heron XR441 being on maintenance at Hawarden.

13th Trans Union Douglas DC-6 F-BRID made a further visit, landing at 1045 today from Le Bourget, and departing to Brno on a freight flight. Another freight charter was operated by Aer Turas Douglas DC-7 EI-ATT (15th), which left for Benina.

14th This month's West German Air Force training flight was operated by Noratlas 53+12 (DCN0890). Arriving at 0927 today from Hatfield, it departed just over an hour later to Bristol-Filton.

14th Ex-Globe Air Herald HB-AAL, now operating with Europe Air Service as F-BOIZ, made its first visit operating a rugby charter. It arrived at 1323 from Le Bourget, and left the following afternoon for Leeds.

18th Eagle Aircraft Services Beech 90 G-AXFE arrived at 1548 on demonstration from Gatwick. It had just been purchased by Huddersfield-based engineering firm, David Brown Ltd, who had been operating Dove G-ARDH until recently. G-AXFE was sold in November 1971 to another industrial concern, GKN, who used it as one of their company hacks until 1984.

19th ITT-operated Gulfstream 1 N720G, which arrived at 1328 f/t Heathrow, became the fifth of its type to visit Ringway. The previous four were N1234X (October 1962), CF-MUR (September 1966), N360WT

(September 1967) & N705G (March 1969). In June 1992, now operating as I-MDDD, N720G was damaged beyond repair at Pantelleria Airport, Italy, when it yawed left during the takeoff roll in crosswind conditions. Takeoff was aborted, but the aircraft could not be stopped on the remaining runway length. It sustained substantial damage on the right side when the right main gear collapsed.

19th The first of several flights this month bringing in tomatoes, was operated by Tarom Ilyushin IL-18 YR-IMK (f/t Bucharest), with another being operated by YR-IML (25th). One more on the 19th December was IL-18 YR-IMD, and all were first visits. In order to operate these flights carrying 1,660 trays of tomatoes, the seats had to be removed from the aircraft. Flights also operated into Prestwick, Birmingham and Gatwick.

21st Intra Airways Jersey was formed earlier this year, after acquiring ex-BUA Dakota G-AKNB, which made its first visit today with its new owners. Arriving at 1404 from Guernsey with thirty-five Manchester United supporters to watch them the following afternoon beat Tottenham Hotspur 3-1, it returned to Guernsey on the 23rd.

21st Another batch of inbound VC-10 troop flights, this time from RAF Akrotiri, operated as follows, XV104 at 1321 (RR2765), XV102 (23rd - RR2766 & 24th - RR2768) and also XV109 (24th - RR2767).

25th British Air Ferries Carvairs G-APNH arriving at 1227 & G-AOFW at 1244, were operating trooping flights from Dusseldorf, along with Caledonian troop flights Britannias G-AOVJ at 0810 (CA750) & G-ATNZ at 1550 (CA758) and Boeing 707s G-AVKA at 0822 (CA746) & G-AWWD at 1713 (CA748).

26th Today's European match between Manchester City and Liersk provided a number of fans' charters. Sabena SE.210 OO-SRE at 1314 (SN1126), ex-Sabena and now operated by Inair NV Douglas DC-6 OO-CTK at 1351 (SN1126D) and Transavia Caravelles PH-TRO at 1225 (SN1126A - carrying the team), PH-TRM at 1320 (SN1126B) & PH-TRN at 1437 (SN1126C). All flights arrived from Ostend and interestingly all used Sabena flight numbers. The Transavia aircraft were all first visits, and had been recently purchased by the Dutch airline. PH-TRM was ex-LTU D-ABAF and had visited previously as such, PH-TRN was ex-SAS OY-KRG and PH-TRO was formerly with Swissair as HB-ICW.

26th November 1969 – Transavia SE.210 Caravelle PH-TRO (SN1126A from Ostend) arrived with Belgian side Lierse S.K for a European Cup-Winners cup match with Manchester City. This was the first of three Transavia Caravelles during the day. Having beaten Liersk 3-0 away two weeks ago, City completed the formality by putting another five past the Belgian side. (Geoff Ball)

DECEMBER 1969

The proposed completion of runway surfacing work this month was running late, due to several spells of cold weather, and was not finally completed until January 1970. Normal operations finally resumed on 24th January. The decade was drawing to a close and the jet age was looming large, but the month still provided a good selection of piston-engined airliners. Seven types were represented by Douglas DC-3/DC-4/DC-6/Bristol 170/Ambassador/Noratlas/L-1049 and Beech 18 aircraft, which were all in evidence.

There were reports that Aeroflot TU-104s were to supplement next year's Balkan flights to Varna and Bourgas. Flights would operate each Saturday from the 2nd May until the 17th October, but nothing ever came of this. There would be one new airline operating flights in 1970. BEA Airtours, recently formed with a number of ex-BEA Comets, would operate summer flights to Barcelona, Gerona, Ibiza and Palma. Prior to this, a weekly IT flight from/to Ibiza would operate from the end of March 1970.

Low pressure dominated the weather for most of December. North or east winds resulted in a cold and dull month, but there were changeable interludes especially in the south around the 9th and the 18th and in most areas during the final week. Fog occurred widely at times, persisting all day in places. During the month an influenza epidemic was reaching its peak, and the foggy spells caused major alarm. Fortunately, it did not persist long enough to aggravate the situation unduly. There were also a number of snowy periods, chiefly from the 17th-19th, but the snow did not lie on low ground for any length of time. The 14th was stormy in most areas, when trees were uprooted and power cables were brought down. On the same day, a freighter sank in heavy seas near the Pembrokeshire coast. The month's temperature extremes saw 14°C at Brize Norton (21st) and a low of -9°C at Sellafield, Cumberland (12th).

This month's scheduled first visits and rounding off the 1960s were (Aer Lingus): B.737 EI-ASE (2nd) and Iberia (IB744): DC-9s EC-BIL (22nd), EC-BIO (26th) & EC-BIU (1st). Equipment changes were Sabena (SN623): B.727s OO-STA (14th), OO-STB (1st), OO-STD (15th) & OO-STE (22nd/29th).

A fairly thin month for GCA/ILS traffic, possibly due to the gloomy weather, with BFS HS.748 D-AFSD (18th), Royal Air Force Britannias XL640 (5th), XM498 (2nd) & XN404 (15th); Comet XR398 (3rd) & Nimrod XV232 (10th). Training flights by BOAC continued even during the bad weather, with Boeing 707s G-APFN (1st/29th/30th), G-APFO (2nd), G-ASZF (30th) & G-ASZG (30th).

1st   Local businessman Mr. Eric Raffles had recently sold his Beech 95 Travelair G-ASZC, and replaced with a new Beech 55, SE-EXK, which made its first appearance today operating its usual f/t Heathrow rotation. This aircraft was only used short-term, because in June 1970 he purchased another, Baron G-AYID. Several other first visits during December were PA-23 Aztec D-IHGF f/t Hanover (1st), PA-31 Navajo N6605L (2nd) which left for Pisa returning on the 6th, and rounding off the year was Cessna 401 OO-GDA from Brussels (16th).

1st   Diversions during were plentiful, especially later in the month. This evening fog was the reason for six arrivals from Heathrow. There was nothing outstanding and the only foreign aircraft was Alitalia DC-9 I-DIKT at 2139 (AZ6290 from Milan).

3rd   Hawker Siddeley corporate HS.125 G-AVRG made its first visit today, night-stopping from Hatfield before departing for Bucharest early the following morning. In September 1971 it was purchased by Court Line, who repainted in full orange and yellow colours.

4th   Another two Qantas Boeing 707s made their first appearances at Ringway during December. The first, B.707 VH-EAB, arrived at 1152 (QF171/2) on an emigration charter. A further flight was operated by B.707 VH-EBP (11th - QF171 Tehran/Heathrow), but this aircraft had visited before.

4th   RAF Britannia XL640 arrived from Woodford at 2037 (RR6417). It departed for Gander the following morning as a support aircraft for Nimrod XV230, which was undertaking a sales tour of Canada. The Britannia, which was also a first visit, positioned over from Woodford due to a worsening weather situation with overnight snow forecast.

8th   Fog at Ringway prevented any arrivals all day and restricted departures to just seven.

9th   Despite today's gloomy conditions, it wasn't bad enough to prevent another batch of Heathrow diversions. Although there were fourteen, there could have been more if the fog had not been of a patchy nature. The diversions stretched throughout the day, starting with BOAC B.707 G-APFC at 0937 (BA672 from Bermuda) and finishing off with KLM DC-9 PH-DNV at 2152 (KL107 from Rotterdam). First visits were provided by MEA B.707 OD-AFE at 1533 (ME201 from Beirut) & I-DIBQ at 1215 (AZ282 from Rome).

BOAC aircraft during the day were SVC-10 G-ASGL (BA506 from New York) & B.707s G-APFH (BA508 from New York), G-APFK (BA913 from Tel Aviv), G-APFL (BA953 from Frankfurt) & G-ARRC (BA713 from Rome). Also of interest were two more Alitalia flights, with DC-9s I-DIKS at 1359 (AZ284 from Milan) & I-DIKT at 1619 (AZ280 from Rome).

9ᵗʰ December 1969 – Former Air France L-1049G F-BGNG, seen here still in basic colours on a gloomy Tuesday morning, was the final visit of its type to Ringway. It arrived empty from Paris-Orly and uploaded a load of cargo bound for Bratislava. It had been purchased by Catair in 1968, and operated with them until its withdrawal in 1976. (Bob Thorpe)

10ᵗʰ The Heathrow weather diversions continued again during the evening, which meant virtually all of the arrivals were European flights, with BEA providing the bulk. Fifteen arrived in 2½ hours, beginning with KLM DC-8 PH-DCC at 1943 (KL135 from Amsterdam). There was yet another Alitalia flight, DC-9 I-DIKU at 2111 (AZ6290 from Milan) and two BOAC VC-10 flights, with G-ARVL (BA775) & G-ASGA (BA698 from Antigua). Finally D-ABEQ arriving at 2148 (LH228R from Hamburg) made the first appearance at Manchester of a Lufthansa B.737, which from 1970 would become commonplace.

12ᵗʰ HS.125 G-AXPU arriving at 1151 from Gatwick, operating a flight to Lydd became the latest visit of this increasingly popular executive jet. Under a variety of various operators, but mainly operating for McAlpine Aviation, this aircraft would become a regular visitor to Manchester.

12ᵗʰ It was Ringway's turn again to be affected by the weather, with no arrivals from 1847 due to dense fog.

14ᵗʰ RAF Argosy flights continued during the month, starting with today's visit of XN856 (RR4456) and also XN850 (21ˢᵗ - RR4457). The following week transport was provided by C-130 XV219 (28ᵗʰ - RR3665), which originated from RAF Lyneham.

14ᵗʰ Germanair Douglas DC-6F D-ABAY made the first of several visits, operating LH934/5 f/t Frankfurt. However, Lufthansa were to sweep away the use of piston aircraft on their freight flights during January.

17ᵗʰ World Airways operated an outbound Christmas charter to New York with B.707 N369WA. Also today, Wardair B.707 CF-FAN (WD216) operated an inbound charter from Vancouver.

17ᵗʰ As well as weather problems, Heathrow also experienced a 24 hour fuel strike today. Although most flights fuelled up at Gatwick, a number heading north during the evening were East African Airways VC-10

5X-UVA at 2116 (EC709 to Rome), BEA Trident 1 G-ARPG at 2118 (BE5058 to Glasgow), BOAC SVC-10 G-ASGP at 2131 (BA025 to Frankfurt) and G-ASGM at 2238 (BA045 to Rome).

19th Mey-Air Douglas DC-3 LN-RTW, in an all metal colour/non-scheme, arrived at 1956 from Oslo on a freight charter, positioning later in the evening for Le Bourget. It was used by the airline until March 1971, when it was sold as OO-KVG.

20th The last few days in the region had seen a mix of heavy snow showers with occasional blizzards, then a quieter of spell, when lots of cloud and patchy fog took hold and a general thaw was well underway. Meanwhile in the south, freezing fog occurred in many areas, persisting all day in some places, including Heathrow and Gatwick. Twenty-seven diversions, primarily from the main two southern airports, but also from Birmingham and Castle Donington, provided much variety. First time visitors were three Alitalia DC-9s with I-DIBO at 1406 (AZ284 from Milan), I-DIKA at 1317 (AZ282 from Rome) & I-DIKE at 1647 (AZ280 from Rome); Qantas B.707 VH-EBT at 1402 (QF739 from Frankfurt), Capitol DC-8 N4907C at 1451 (CL907 from Niagara) and ALIA-Royal Jordanian SE.210 JY-ACT at 1948 (RJ102 from Rome). Some others of interest were Iberia SE.210 EC-BBR at 1341 (IB502 from Palma) from an airline that rarely diverted to Ringway; TIA DC-8 N8962T at 1410 (TV962 from Bangor), BUA VC-10s G-ARTA at 1945 (BR3006 from Nairobi) & G-ASIX at 2025 (BR662 from Madrid) and Caledonian B.707 G-AVTW at 1941 (CA1757 from Toronto).

20th Douglas DC-3 N3179Q operated by Welltrade, night-stopped on a late flight from Bremen, leaving the following morning. This was the first of several visits to Manchester. It was purchased by Dutch-operator Moormanair in late-1970. PH-WWW was reserved for the aircraft, but it was eventually registered as PH-MOA. On the 3rd June 1971 it was involved in a landing accident, after engine failure on a charter flight, carrying Ajax supporters inbound to Southend. The aircraft left the runway and the airfield, and ended up on a neighbouring golf course. Allegedly, the Dutch supporters onboard were still singing when the emergency services arrived! The aircraft was eventually scrapped the following year.

27th Today was the third in a row when fog affected the northwest. Ringway was affected all day and there were no aircraft movements.

28th Due to increased Christmas freight loads, KLM operated an extra flight, with DC-8 PH-DCT (KL007E/008E) operating from/to Amsterdam.

29th Beech 95 G-ASYJ crashed on landing at 1804 on a flight from Oxford, and managed to close the airport for two hours. It bounced off the runway and tore off the nosewheel, before coming to rest just off the active. The damage was considerable, but the aircraft was eventually repaired.

30th The penultimate day of the month, and also the decade, saw no less than three different BOAC B.707s operating training details. G-APFN and G-ASZG both appeared twice during the day, carrying out lengthy spells, and the third G-ASZF, landed and promptly taxied back to the holding point and left for Heathrow again.

FIRST/LAST ARRIVALS & DEPARTURES 1969

First arrival: Sabena B.727 OO-STD from Brussels @ 0026
First departure: Sabena B.727 OO-STD to Heathrow @ 0124
Last arrival: BEA Merchantman G-APEM from Heathrow @ 2331
Last departure: PA-23 Aztec G-AWIY to Heathrow @ 2312

Airport Stats 1969 (+/- % on Previous Year)		
Scheduled Passengers	1,079,000	+1.9%
Inclusive & Charter Passengers	473,000	+16.2%
Freight & Mail (Tonnes)	40,800	+9.9%
Movements	52,600	+1.9%

SOUTH SIDE AIRCRAFT & OPERATORS

AIRVIEWS

Airviews commenced operations in March 1949 with Autocrat G-AGXN, which flew in regularly from their base at Barton for pleasure flying. In May 1949, the pleasure flying season was well under way, and the choice of flights was between Airviews Autocrat G-AGXN (max 2 pax) and Sivewright Airways Rapides (max 8 pax) G-AJMY & G-AKMG and Aerovan (max 9 pax) G-AJOI. The cost of a pleasure flight at this time was ten shillings. In June 1949, they took delivery of Dragon Rapide G-AGDM, which later became the mainstay of their fleet until its sale in 1956. On 15th April 1950, they purchased Autocar G-AJYK, which crashed in an accident near Leicester in September that year, nearly costing the life of their managing director, Bruce Martin. Pleasure flying patrons of the early 1950s would remember their pilot hobbling to the aircraft on crutches, as he slowly recovered from his leg injuries. In 1953, they were awarded licences to operate summer only services to Southampton and Sandown. These flights proved so successful, they acquired more Rapides. This was followed in 1957 by the purchase of Dove G-AIWF, which opened up further scheduled routes to Newcastle and Newquay. By 1959, they had planned new routes to Teeside and Torquay (using the beach!), but before these could be introduced, their creditors pulled the financial plug and the company went into liquidation. Later that same year, Bruce Martin bought the name, goodwill and Auster G-AGXN to set up a new company, Airviews (Manchester) Ltd. The new operation now purely concentrated on aerial photography and pleasure flying. The founding aircraft, G-AGXN, was sold in 1966 and replaced by another Auster, G-AOBV, which had also been used by Airviews in the 1950s. They added Beagle Husky G-ASNC in 1970. The name Airviews eventually passed into history, when it became part of Hunting Surveys.

NORTHERN EXECUTIVE

July 1962 - Northern Executive Aviation's very first aircraft, PA-28 G-ARVS, is seen here about to set off on another pleasure flight. Sold in May 1966, it is still flying in 2014, now registered as G-JAKS and based at Stapleford Tawney. (MA Archive via Ringway Publications).

NEA was officially registered as a company on 24th December 1961. It was formed by local businessman Fred Dunkerley, who had also been active in the local aviation scene, participating in the King's Cup air races during the 1950s. He made the acquaintance of a young, recently qualified pilot called David

Antrobus, who would become company secretary and chief pilot, with Dunkerley as chairman. An order was placed with Vigors Aviation, who at the time were the main Piper dealers in the UK, for a brand new four-seater PA-28 Cherokee 160. G-ARVS was duly delivered to Barton in April 1962, and local companies were quick to appreciate its qualities over the more antiquated competition. It became extensively used during the week for air-taxi operations, and at weekends was used for joyrides, by the public and excited aviation enthusiasts. The company soon became dissatisfied with its Barton base. Although the landing fees and hangarage were relatively cheap, it lacked runway lighting and a customs facility, deemed essential for the business market. So on 2nd June 1962, G-ARVS positioned over from Barton to take up residence in hangar 522, with Ringway's various other light aircraft. The move was an instant success with business users, and at weekends supplemented Airviews Auster J1/N G-AGXN on the pleasure flight scene. These flights took place from the 'pleasure flight' apron, located immediately to the left of the entrance to the spectator terraces. Both aircraft were kept extremely busy for several years. Three years of solid trading convinced NEA for the need for further expansion. On 22nd October 1965, twin-engined PA-27 Aztec G-ATJR was delivered from CSE at Oxford (who were now the main UK Piper dealers). It performed its first revenue flight six days later, operating to Lydd on behalf of the Nuclear Power Group, carrying technicians from Knutsford to the Dungeness power station. Further expansion took place when another PA-28 Cherokee, G-ATRW, was added on 27th May 1966 and a second PA-27 Aztec, G-ATPR, was delivered to Ringway on 8th May 1967. Although G-ATPR operated with full NEA titling, it was actually registered to the Oldham Tyre Cord Company, operating on a 'leaseback' basis. Under this arrangement a company needing the use of an executive aircraft would purchase the machine outright, but then lease it to an air-taxi operator. This was considerably cheaper than 'going it alone', with the attendant liabilities for hangarage, maintenance, and aircrew salaries. NEA's third PA-27 Aztec, G-AWIY, delivered on 21st May 1969, was actually bought and owned by local businessman Tony Capper, operated under the 'leaseback' arrangement. The company's PA-28 Cherokees, G-ARVS & G-ATRW, had both left by the end of the decade in May 1966 and February 1969 respectively. This brought to an end their association with pleasure flying, but on 3rd November 1969, a fourth PA-27 Aztec, G-AXOW, was added. By the end of the 1960s, they had firmly established themselves as major players in the UK air-taxi market.

FAIREY AVIATION

The 1960s were a very quiet period as far as aircraft activity was concerned. Another part of the group, Fairey Engineering, had previously been active in the production of missiles in the post-war era, the most famous being the Fireflash air-to-air weapon. But in 1961 it was contracted to assemble and complete a batch of Jindivik 102 target-drones destined for the missile range at Cardigan Bay. The Jindiviks, which were a product of Australia's government aircraft factories, were dismantled and crated for container ship delivery to Manchester, and reassembled at Ringway. They were packed into larger crates and taken by road to Aberporth and Llanbedr, where they gave the RAF valuable target practice, but later models were used as tow targets. The first twenty of these machines were all Australian-manufactured, but the final twenty-nine arrived as bare airframes and received Bristol Siddeley Viper engines and complex avionics equipment from Fairey's. This work kept Fairey's busy during the 1960s, in the absence of any major aircraft work. They were responsible for the maintenance of two remarkable machines, Grumman Goose G-ASXG (1966-1969) and Grumman Mallard G-ASCS (1962-1968).

UNITED STEEL

This company also operated from Coal Aston, a private strip near Sheffield, but because there were no servicing facilities, their aircraft were based at Ringway. The group began in the late-1950s with PA-23 Apache G-APMY, and in March 1960 they added Piaggio P.166 G-APXK. In August 1965, another unusual type added to the fleet was Dornier Do.28 G-ATAL, one of only two ever to appear on the British register. Utilisation of these three aircraft was never high, and all three could usually be seen together on the south side. By early-1968, G-APXK had not flown for nearly two years and was ultimately sold to McAlpine Aviation of Luton. PA-23 Apache G-APMY was undergoing a C of A renewal, while G-ATAL departed to Germany for a major overhaul, but did not return. Since late-1967, United Steel had been 'trying out' Commander 680 HB-GBW, which they eventually purchased, becoming G-AWCU. However, in late-1968, the Labour government announced the nationalisation of the steel industry, and their remaining aircraft were sold. By this time they had relocated to the new headquarters at Coal Aston.

AIRLINES & ROUTES 1960-1969

Scheduled Passenger Routes

Amsterdam	Aer Lingus	1960-1969
"	BEA	1960-1969
"	KLM	1960-1969
Antigua	BOAC	November 1967-December 1969
Baltimore	BOAC	November 1961-June 1962
Barcelona	BEA	1962-1969 (Summer only)
"	Iberia	1964-1969 (Summer only)
Basle	BEA	1961 (Summer only)
"	Swissair	1960-1961, 1963-1968 (Summer only)
Belfast	BEA/British Airways	1960-1969
Bergen	British Eagle	1960-1962 (Summer only)
Berlin	BEA	April 1969-December 1969
Birmingham	BEA	1960-1969
Boston	BOAC	1960-March 1963
Bournemouth	British United	1960-October 1966
"	Mercury Airlines	1961-1962 (Summer only), November 1962-1964
"	Morton Air Services	November 1965-April 1969
Bridgetown	BOAC	November 1967-December 1969
Bristol	Cambrian Airways	1960-March 1969
Brussels	Aer Lingus	1960-March 1966
"	BEA	April 1966-1969
"	Sabena	1960-1969
Cardiff	Cambrian Airways	1960-March 1969
Copenhagen	Aer Lingus	1960-1969
"	BEA	April 1966-1969
"	British Eagle	1961 (Summer only)
"	SAS	April 1966-1969
Coventry	British United	1962-March 1965
Cork	Aer Lingus	1966 (Summer only), May 1967-1969
"	British Midland	1965 (Summer only)
"	Cambrian Airways	April 1967-December 1968, 1969 (Summer only)
Dublin	Aer Lingus	1960-1969
"	BEA	1960-1969
Dusseldorf	Aer Lingus	1960-1969
"	BEA	1960-1969

Dusseldorf	British United	November 1961-April 1969
Edinburgh	BEA	April 1968-1969
Exeter	British Midland	1965 (Summer only)
"	Mercury Airlines	1962-1964 (Summer only)
Frankfurt	Aer Lingus	1960-1969
"	British Eagle	June 1967-November 1968
Georgetown	BOAC	November 1968-December 1969
Glasgow	BEA	1960-1969
"	Cambrian Airways	1962-1967 (Summer only)
Guernsey	BEA	1960-1969 (Summer only)
"	Cambrian Airways	1960-March 1969
Gutersloh	British United	November 1961-April 1969
Hamburg	British Eagle	1961 (Summer only)
Hanover	British United	November 1961-April 1969
Jersey	BEA	1960-1969 (Summer only)
"	British United	1960-October 1963, 1964-1967 (Summer only)
"	Cambrian Airways	1960-March 1969
London-Heathrow	BEA/British Airways	1960-1969
Madrid	Iberia	November 1968-1969
Malta	BEA	1967-1968 (Summer only), April 1969 – December 196
Milan	Alitalia	July 1968-1969
"	BEA	1960-1964 (Summer only)
Montreal	BOAC	1960-1969
Newcastle	British Midland	November 1964-August 1965, April 1966-June 1966
"	Mercury Airlines	April 1963-October 1964
New York	BOAC	1960-1969
"	Sabena	1960-March 1964
Ostend	Sabena	1960-1965 (Summer only)
Oxford	British United	1960-October 1966
"	Mercury Airlines	1961-1962 (Summer only), Nov 1962-Oct 1964
"	Morton Air Services	November 1965-April 1969
Palma	BEA	1962-1969 (Summer only)
"	Iberia	1964-1969 (Summer only)
Paris	Air France	June 1961-1969
"	BEA	1960-1969
Perpignan	Air France	1966 (Summer only)
Port of Spain	BOAC	November 1968-December 1969
Rome	Alitalia	July 1968-1969

Ronaldsway	BEA	1960-March 1963
"	Cambrian Airways	April 1963-1969
Rotterdam	British Air Ferries	April 1966-February 1967
"	Swissair	April 1969-December 1969
Sandown	British Midland	1965-1967 (Summer only)
"	Mercury Airlines	1961-1964 (Summer only)
Shannon	Aer Lingus	1966-1968 (Summer only), April 1969 - Dec 1969
Southampton	British United	November 1965-March 1969
Teeside	British Midland	November 1964-August 1965
Tel Aviv	BOAC	March 1969-December 1969
Toronto	BOAC	1960-1969
Zurich	Aer Lingus	1960-1969
"	BEA	1960-1968

Scheduled Cargo Routes

Amsterdam	KLM	March 1962-1969
Belfast	BEA	1960-1969
"	Silver City	November 1962-March 1963
Basle	Swissair	November 1969-December 1969
Brussels	Sabena	1960-1969
Dublin	Aer Lingus	1960-1969
Dusseldorf	Lufthansa	November 1966-August 1968
Frankfurt	BEA	April 1967-1969
"	Lufthansa	November 1966-1969
Glasgow	BEA	1960-1969
London-Heathrow	BEA	1960-1962
Montreal	BOAC	November 1960-1969
New York	BOAC	November 1960-1969
"	Lufthansa	1960-1961
"	Swissair	1960
Paris	Air France	May 1962-March 1965
"	BEA	May 1965-March 1967
Philadelphia	BOAC	November 1962-March 1963 November 1968-December 1969
Ronaldsway	BKS	1960-May 1961
Zurich	Swissair	April 1967-1969